The Death of Privacy

The Battle for Personal Privacy in the Courts, the Media, and Society

Gini Graham Scott, Ph.D., J.D.

ISHI PRESS
INTERNATIONAL

The Death of Privacy
The Battle for Personal Privacy in the Courts, the Media, and Society

by Gini Graham Scott, Ph.D.

First published in 1995

This Printing in June, 2011
by Ishi Press in New York and Tokyo

ISBN 4-87187-412-5
978-4-87187-412-0

Ishi Press International
1664 Davidson Avenue, Suite 1B
Bronx NY 10453-7877

1-917-507-7226

Printed in the United States of America

Contents

Introduction

Today, an intense battle is going on over personal privacy, as recent social changes threaten to destroy this very basic right to personal liberty, autonomy, and one's personhood or personality. These changes include the new information-age technologies, threats of crime and unchecked immigration in a society experiencing an uncertain transforming economy, computerized marketing and sophisticated polling methods to a target market, concerns about threatening diseases, family members trying to evade responsibilities, an increasingly intrusive media racing to reveal secrets about celebrities and soon-to-be-created celebrities, and more. Society's response has been to try to crack down on personal privacy in various ways, while civil libertarians have been struggling to protect this privacy from unwarranted intrusions. But increasingly, bits and pieces of personal identity are being lost to the glare of these revelations as our society teeters uncertainly under both the opportunities and pressures of the nineties.

This battle for personal privacy has become a major defining battle, a kind of watershed in history, because the sense of personal privacy is so central to one's identity. It goes to the core of one's very persona, since it is central in defining the self and distinguishing the boundaries between self and society. This is because, as many social scientists and psychologists from Freud and Jung to Herbert Mead and Ervin Goffman have noted, we have both a private and a public self, much like actors on a stage, and we need a backstage area to prepare for and retreat from each public performance.

However, as more and more of the private self becomes open to public inspection, that boundary between public and private becomes swept away. As a result, we feel not only the fear of Big Brother watching—the Orwellian terror of the fifties and sixties, but of potentially everybody observing and knowing everything—employers, spouses, marketers, pollsters, and a gossip-hungry public eager to know more, as the latest personal saga is hung out for scrutiny on shows like *Oprah* and in magazines like *People.* The irony is that we both want public attention and adulation for recognition and success; yet we cringe in the destruction of the right to privacy too—a central paradox of our media- and information-driven age.

The Way Things Were

It wasn't always like this. At one time, before the industrial revolution, in a smaller, simpler America, we were a society in which the bonds of community were strong, and people knew, and expected to know, one another. There was relatively little privacy in the sense we think of it today, since people living in small towns and villages and on farms had tight bonds with one another. Also, everyone was interested in everyone else's business, which contributed to the sense of community. Those who felt this conformity and community oppressive could always strike out for the frontier, which many did, to remake themselves and live more private independent lives—although, in time, these tight-bonded communities spread to the frontier, too.

Then, as cities dotted the land, the notion of personal privacy gained new meaning, as people who wished could find anonymity in a new mix of strangers. Or people could choose who they wanted to be by joining in voluntary groups outside of the family. In fact, at this time, the concern of social scientists was with the threat of "anomie" or "alienation," the loss of connection and the isolation between people, as traditional communities lost power. Their fear was the danger of too much personal isolation, independence, and loneliness in the booming, heterogeneous cities that grew up in the late nineteenth and early twentieth centuries.

Yet, while the cities held this potential for anonymity and alienation, another powerful force was growing that threatened to derail privacy for many. This was the mass media which began to develop in the cities as industrialization spread in the 1870s and 1880s. Ironically, these early reporters and photographers were often as intrusive and obnoxious as many are in today's mass media circus, though they generally focused their attention on the already celebrated public figures and social elite. Still, their activities initiated the privacy battle that has gained center stage today.

While much of this initial impetus to protect privacy was a reaction to the intrusions of the media, in the 1950s and 1960s this struggle to define the boundaries between self and community and protect the self shifted to a new stage. Now the new concern was how to maintain one's independence from the growing tide of social conformity and the growing power of the government to check into what people were doing. This shift occurred because in the fifties, the big corporations rapidly gained power in a relatively peaceful postwar boom economy. As a result, social commentators now worried that people were turning into conformist sheep; we were becoming a nation of "organization men" ready to follow the lead of others—it was the heyday of the IBM look and ideology writ large. Meanwhile, the government hysteria over the Communist menace helped to foster this conformist mentality, since a growing public feared any taint or association with any "deviant" behavior that might be considered "un-American." And concurrently a reaction toward this trend grew, expressed as a fear of a "Big Brother" government that was intrusively snooping and scooping up the mostly innocent along with a few dangerous spies. In turn, the popular literature and films of the day reflected this growing concern about the power of big business and big government to engulf the individual. For example, this fear was nicely captured in one of the most popular 1950s horror movies—*The Invasion of the Body Snatchers.* Symbolically, it expressed the fear many people had that their very persona was in danger of being taken away by an alien force they had little power to control.

The reaction to this conformist trend was, of course, the social eruption of the late sixties. But this revolt was primarily expressed as an anti-Establishment cry for personal independence, freedom, and integrity, along with a growing movement for civil rights, rather than a struggle for personal privacy. In fact, many participants in the anti-Establishment movements were attracted by the new communal and collective groups which sprung up all over the country and reflected a desire to break down barriers between people. Then, as this collective impulse continued into the 1970s, the turn inward toward "finding oneself" led to an explosion of self-help groups, in which people were encouraged to share deeply with one another to relate on a more intimate personal level. So for many people, the boundaries between self and other were more open than ever. The issue of personal privacy was not of primary concern.

The Big Eighties Transformation

Then, in the 1980s, everything changed, opening the doors to today's battle for privacy. Basically, what transformed society was the explosion of the new technologies heralding the information age, accompanied by an emphasis on success and power and the breakdown of traditional institutions. Suddenly, we were hurled by the computer and the arrival of new devices like cellular phones, faxes, and digital data-gathering equipment into an age where all sorts of data could be easily gathered about anyone. As a result, personal information previously considered private was increasingly available for all to see. At the same time, the emphasis on success and power meant that there was a new concern with creating an idealized projected image and covering up the vulnerable public self. Thus, there were now good reasons for wanting to protect the self from these growing intrusions.

Conversely, other forces provided good reasons to support many of these intrusions—notably the growing perception of danger in an increasingly complex and out-of-control society. Life was getting more dangerous because of the breakdown in traditional institutions and because more and more people were throwing off traditional responsibilities from parenting to supporting kids. So as crime and other social problems grew like weeds, this contributed to a need to know to protect society. These dangers and fears are well known and are continuing to grow today—out-of-control crime in the streets, drive-by shootings, guns in schools, drug cases clogging the courts, "deadbeat" dads abandoning their kids, growing reports of child abuse and molestation, a fear of immigrants overwhelming a sputtering economy, devastating and often fatal diseases spreading through the population, and more.

These pressures have in turn led to a growing public cry for a crackdown, including using the growing power of technology to get more information about people to better keep track of and control them. Meanwhile, the expanding ability of the media to put anyone and everyone in the public eye has contributed to a growing cult of celebrity and public gossip that provides a sense of a national and international community to replace the traditional local community institutions that seem to have broken down.

On one level, we as a society want and need to know ever more to feel unified as a community and protect ourself from our fears. Yet, concurrently, as society seeks to know more about us, individually we feel more and more invaded personally. We feel our personal privacy being stripped away by the same forces that are pushing us as a society to want to know more about others.

The Privacy Battle of the Century

Thus, we are now witnessing an epic battle to define the rights and limits of privacy in a rapidly changing society. It is a battle to clarify the boundaries of what should be private and what should be public—like a civil war for the soul of the individual in society. On one side, the forces representing the establishment are trying to protect society against crime, irresponsible antisocial behavior, disease, and the use of technology to harm society. On the other side, the civil libertarians are fighting for personal liberty and freedom from the intrusion of government, the media, marketers, employers, and the public in general.

It is a battle that is occurring to a greater or lesser extent in different states and communities, depending on different local community values, customs, and interests. In some areas, such as California and Florida, the right to privacy has been enshrined in the state constitution and there is much more concern with individual privacy. By contrast, in other states, such as Texas and New York, which don't have such constitutional safeguards, the concern with community protection and the First Amendment free speech protections are more important. Thus, in varied ways, this struggle is going on in the communities, courts, and legislatures throughout the land, as individuals, groups, and public officials try to work out the balance between individual and community interests.

At this writing, this epic struggle of the 1990s is in its early stages and the boundaries are only gradually being clarified in different institutional areas of society. For instance, some heated battlegrounds include the rights of the media, the use of medical records, the efforts of employers to monitor and test employees for drugs, and the ability of marketers to buy and sell data on individuals. Often uncertainty reigns, but in general, the social institutions and groups seeking protection seem to be winning as we become a more fearful and complex society. More and more regulations are being used to shape us, control us, and further regulate what we must reveal about ourselves to others. For example, the trend is toward growing databases and the creation of a national ID card (that goes even further than the current use of our social security number or driver's license). Plus there's a trend toward laws that require us to reveal undesirable or embarrassing personal facts to others (such as telling insurance companies or intimate others if one has certain conditions or face penalties for the failure to disclose).

So Where's the Balance?

Somehow, we need to find a balance between two key needs: (1) the need of society to know certain facts to protect itself from individuals and groups that might otherwise harm us through crime, fraud, terrorism, and serious irresponsible behavior; and (2) the need of individuals to be protected from an overprotective, domineering, controlling, invasive society. Indeed, our society couldn't function if everyone sought total privacy, and it is virtually impossible for anyone to live as a completely private individual. Even if one opts to become a hermit and retreats into a cocoon of privacy there is virtually no place left to go. The frontier and the unregulated open spaces of the wild west and isolated rural America are gone. Even close-knit religious and communal groups can't find a little piece of America where they can drop out, because the surrounding neighbors or the government will soon intrude. Witness what happened in Waco, Texas, and in Montana and Oregon where different cult groups—the Branch Davidians, the Summit Lighthouse, and the followers of the guru Rajneesh—all soon came into conflict with the law.

Thus, complete privacy isn't possible for anyone, individual or group, and it can't be since society has genuine concerns about the potential dangers of an individual or group to the rest of society. But no one wants the opposite type of society either, an oppressive totalitarian environment where everyone knows everything about everyone, and every bit of private data is fair game for a public that wants to know.

So where is the balance point? What are the trade-offs in working out the boundaries between personal privacy and society's need to know? That is the struggle of the decade, which *Mind Your Own Business* explores. This investigation is designed to raise questions and make people aware of this issue, so they can better understand and deal with this struggle.

My own position is to want as much personal protection as possible, while recognizing the need for legitimate public knowledge and protection. But to apply that approach successfully, one must look at situations on a case by case basis, because in a highly complex, quickly changing society there are no easy answers.

This book thus focuses on current trends, drawing on the forces of public opinion, legislation, and legal battles that are helping to define the boundaries. After the first four chapters survey the fascinating history of this growing concern with privacy, the book focuses on the battle in 1992 and 1993, a time when this battle has become especially intense. Finally, it briefly notes some of the key late-breaking developments in 1994 and the first months of 1995 prior to going to press, and concludes with some reflections on where we are heading as this epic struggle continues, particularly on the information highway, already strewn with casualties of this battle along the way.

Chapter 1

The Importance of Personal Privacy

Why Is Privacy So Important?

Why has privacy become such an emotionally charged subject today? Why is its potential loss so important? Privacy is so basic to what makes us human. It is at the core of our sense of self, and it establishes the boundaries between the self and society. In fact, while the debate may focus on the laws concerning privacy today, for a long time, psychologists, philosophers, sociologists, and others have debated the concept of privacy, trying to explain it and show why it is so vitally important to humankind.

The Different Guises of Privacy

The very notion of privacy is sometimes confusing, because our ideas about what privacy is and how much "privacy" we should have in relation to society have changed. These confusions and changes have occurred, according to Julie Innes, author of *Privacy, Intimacy, and Isolation,* because there are three different aspects of "privacy"—and in different situations, people have different values about whether privacy is good or bad.[1]

One type of privacy involves a person's ability to regulate information about or access to him or herself—the kind of privacy usually associated with the invasion of privacy tort. This occurs where someone intrudes on another person's space or inappropriately reveals false or secret information about them. For example, say someone barges into your room without knocking and learns some secret information, or someone spreads false rumors about you. These invasions affect the information you want others to have about you.

This kind of privacy invasion is usually divided into four categories of legal harm: (1) the intrusion into a person's seclusion, solitude, or private affairs; (2) the public disclosure of embarrassing private facts about oneself which no one has a right to know; (3) the dissemination of publicity putting a person in a false light in public; and (4) the appropriation, to one's own advantage, of the person's name or likeness (i.e., commercializing the personality of someone else, such as putting a picture that looks like Barbra Streisand in an ad to suggest she likes your product).[2]

A second type of privacy involves the individual's freedom to make decisions about certain important personal actions, such as about sex, marriage, having children, abortion, using contraceptives, and child rearing. This kind of privacy is often the subject of fundamental or constitutional privacy debates on whether one has the right to make these very private decisions in the "private sphere" of life. Is the individual free or in control of these decisions or does society have a right to regulate them? Liberals tend to side with the individual and say yes; conservatives tend to side with society and say no.

Thirdly, there is the psychological notion of privacy as a form of personal control over intimacy, giving one the ability to decide how much love, caring, or affection to express or withhold in relating to others. For example, in many relations, women tend to want to be more open and share more with their partners. But men are generally raised to be more closed and reticent in relations; they experience the desire for openness as an invasion of their personal privacy, setting the stage for many family conflicts. She probes; he withdraws into his private shell. She feels left out; he withdraws some more; and they fight over her probing and his withdrawal. It's like the societal versus individual battle over personal privacy played out in personal relationships due to differing notions of what is appropriately shared with others and what is private.

In addition, many value privacy because they associate it with core

American democratic values such as individual freedom and liberty, free speech, and the "pursuit of happiness." Finally, some view privacy in spiritual or moral terms, claiming it expresses or shows respect for "man's spiritual nature," "individual dignity," or the "inviolate personality." Thus, privacy is a powerful core principle with many meanings, which is why any threat of losing privacy often triggers deep emotional reactions. It brings up feelings of "violation, harm, and loss of agency," as Inness points out in her privacy study.[3]

Privacy and Intimacy

A way to think about the importance of privacy for the individual is to recognize three key psychological benefits which it offers: (1) It's a way to *separate* a part of one's life from others. (2) It gives one *control* over a part of his or her life. (3) This separation or control gives one power over certain *"intimate" decisions, information, or access.*[4] Thus, through privacy, we can feel in charge of our ability to regulate the personal information we give out about ourselves and how accessible we are to others.

Thus, in recent years, a growing body of tort and constitutional fundamental privacy protections have grown up to respect this deep-seated human desire for autonomy and intimacy in certain areas of life, and the courts have acted to protect privacy in these areas.[5]

Yet at times this desire to protect privacy comes up against other very fundamental values, such as the desire to preserve life, which underlies the highly charged abortion issue. In turn, because these conflicting values are such deeply felt ideals, this makes for a very emotional and heated debate; fundamental beliefs and values are in conflict.

The Tension between Individual Privacy and the Community Desire to Know and Protect

Although the notion of privacy may trigger emotional desires for autonomy and intimacy, the irony is that for some people and in certain circumstances, privacy can trigger deep-seated negative associations, such as isolation, deprivation, and separation from others. This is because while privacy gives us control over personal information, access, and decisions, it also cuts us off from others. Often this separation or isolation is seen as a lonely or even dangerous thing, that can be harmful to the individual's psyche or for society as a whole. It might lead to harmful fantasies, to being out-of-touch with reality, or to negative emotional states.

As a result, there has always been a tension between the community's concern to know about its members in order to protect the community as a whole, and the individual's desire for personal privacy, freedom, and liberty. The essential tension is between the public's "right to know" and the individual's right to conceal information or withdraw from the community to prevent it from knowing.

Another irony is that as society gains certain advantages in knowing about the individual (such as protection against people who might threaten society and information to help order society so it can function), each person gains something by giving up a part of him- or herself to the community. These are powerful psychological benefits, such as a sense of recognition and pride for being known and respected by others, and a feeling of belonging to a larger group. A person may gain economically, too, in return for providing information about him- or herself.

The Loss of Community and Mutual Trust

At one time, the community's right to know reigned supreme, and little thought was given to individual privacy rights. Conformity and social control in a close-knit community were expected. That was so until new notions of individuality and individual rights developed in the eighteenth century in Western Europe and England. Philosophers, like Rousseau, began thinking of privacy as one of the individual's "natural" rights, necessary for growth and personal fulfillment. Later, beginning in the nineteenth century, as scholars from other disciplines—such as psychologists, sociologists, and legal scholars—paid growing attention to the nature, needs, and rights of the individual, they placed a growing value and importance on privacy, and some even viewed it as a "moral" or "natural" right, essential to what makes us human.[6]

These ideas developed because social changes were breaking down traditional community institutions as new urban centers and new ways of relating developed. As a result, the individual, as well as the theorists, came to see him- or herself more as a separate individual, and therefore, more entitled to have a private sphere of life. This development occurred because, as these urban centers expanded in the late 1800s, society increasingly lacked the old cohesive social bonds and informal social controls that were part of everyday custom in small town America and other preurbanized societies. People became increasingly, as Steven Nock describes it in *The Costs of Privacy,* a nation of strangers, where people didn't know each other, even when they lived side by side.[7]

This growing anonymity in turn contributed to a breakdown of trust, and society had to develop new methods of creating trust between people, since trust is the glue that keeps society together. Traditionally, trust develops because people are brought up with a sense of obligation toward one another. They expect to give and get mutual assistance and engage in reciprocal actions based on custom and moral codes.

But, when that sense of community breaks down, people may feel it doesn't matter so much what they do. They care less about what others think. They may not experience any immediate negative reaction from others when they don't act in a trustworthy way, because others may not know what has happened. Or if others do know and they wear out their good reputation, they can readily find new contacts in different local groups or in different communities. As a result, people feel less bound to conform or act in trustworthy ways, although this greater individuality can contribute to social progress, too.

Unfortunately, when people don't feel bound by convention, the community feels threatened, so society develops other more formal ways to promote good behavior, such as using various forms of surveillance to establish the person's reputation, so others know if he or she can be trusted. One method is using publicly available and formal credentials, such as credit cards, academic degrees, and driver's licenses. Another employs ordeals a person has to pass to show he or she is trustworthy, such as lie detector tests, drug tests, and integrity tests. But the downside of such methods is that they trigger the anger of the civil libertarians and others who feel that society is invading their privacy. Yet, paradoxically, society is using these tools because we have actually *gained* more privacy due to living in greater anonymity from one another in larger communities. That's because, as Nock explains:

> In an anonymous society of strangers . . . surveillance establishes reputations that permit us to trust strangers. Americans now enjoy vastly more privacy than in the past. But privacy makes it difficult to know much about other people; more privacy means more strangers . . .

> So . . . surveillance establishes and maintains reputations among strangers . . . The use of such credentials and ordeals, over time, is shown to be correlated with the number of strangers in our society.[8]

Changing Notions of Privacy

The Way It Was

As we'll see in the following chapters, before the modern Western way of thinking about privacy, freedom, liberty, and independence developed, people's "private" lives weren't very private at all. Not only did people commonly live at close quarters in small one-room dwellings or in larger extended family compounds, but even notions of privacy had a negative ring. For example, in ancient Greece, during the time of Aristotle, the word private was associated with being deprived of something. Withdrawing from public life was seen as something negative or unfortunate. As Aristotle observed, "an individual who lived only a private life could not be fully human."[9]

However, as a society of privilege emerged in the West, by about the fifteenth century privacy became associated with privilege and wealth, since the common people were still crowded together. For example, phrases like "private house, private education . . . private club . . . private property" conveyed a sense of privilege.[10]

Then, beginning in about the sixteenth century through the seventeenth and eighteenth centuries, privacy became associated even more with the advantages of having a "private life," including the idea of modern individualism. This notion emerged in the eighteenth century and was written about by the noted seventeenth and eighteenth century philosophers (Hobbes, Locke, and Rousseau) who spoke about individuality and self-interest.[11]

Meanwhile, these changing meanings of the word *privacy* reflected changes in society and the relationship of the individual to the community. At the time when *privacy* was associated with isolation, seclusion, and privation, the individual was more closely linked to a close-knit community. But as *privacy* became associated with the high value placed on individualism, traditional community bonds were becoming weaker, while people had a chance for more anonymity in the growing cities. This anonymity, in turn, helped to trigger the reaction to find other ways of checking up on people.[12]

The Need for "Surveillance" in a Privacy Society

So are we a "nation of strangers" or part of a "global village?" And do we need all this surveillance and monitoring in a world threatened by the loss of traditional community institutions and trust? In *The Costs of Privacy*, Steven Nock makes a strong case for the reason surveillance has developed as a societal protection in a nation increasingly made up of strangers. It's a way to keep people responsible and accountable, when we have no direct and personal way to know of their reputations; indeed, that's the reason many individuals use this approach to check on their dates and mates before making a date or a commitment, since they don't know whether to trust the person or not and can't find out from the usual community sources, because no one knows that person either.

A key reason for this turn of events, according to Nock, is the change in family living arrangements. At one time, people traditionally lived with their parents, or in extended families, until they got married and set up their own households. But an increasing number of single people have gone off on their own, so that today about a quarter of all males and females in their 20s do not live in a family setting, and these developments have broken up the traditional kin attachments that helped keep society together.[13]

The advantage to the individual has been more and more personal freedom and privacy. That's because we can increasingly live our lives in many different groups and places, and maintain separate reputations and personas in these different settings and with different people. Also, we can come home to our own place and do what we want, without answering to anyone.

But the downside is that all of these "emancipated" individuals can be a threat to the social order, according to Nock, because living free of family ties means that there's a lack of control or restraint over their behavior that has contributed to the breakdown of norms we know today.[14] And the paradox is that the growing freedom of this group is the key factor contributing to the growth of our surveillance society of today, since these freedoms and privacies due to emancipation result in ambiguous or unknown reputations. That's because people are living more independently, free of direct scrutiny and influence, so we don't know if we can trust them. And perhaps with good reason, because if no one is watching what they do, people feel freer not to conform, freer to express any deviant impulses to act in antisocial ways without feelings of guilt or shame.[15]

Thus, it is no wonder that it's hard to know people and consequently to trust them. We learn to relate to each other's separate selves and the external images we see. But beneath that image, we can all be quite different from how we seem outside. So increasing surveillance, through such methods as using credentials or ordeals, helps us gather information about others, so we can protect ourselves individually or as a society in dealing with one another. For we have become like strangers to each other.[16]

As much as we may personally object to such methods, Nock suggests these formal modes of checking up on people are used increasingly to enforce conformity in society, since other sources of social controls enforcing conformity have broken down—particularly the family, with the growing number of individuals living in independent, nonfamily living arrangements. It's a trend that has grown since the 1960s. And surveillance has become one of society's weapons to protect against such actions, which is why, as Nock points out, the growing emancipation of youth from the family has occurred at the same time that the number and types of surveillance methods used in society have grown exponentially.[17]

Thus, on one level we may be becoming a global village, but on another level, we are increasingly strangers to each other, too.

The Need for Privacy in a Surveillance Society

While an increase in surveillance may be society's response to growing individuality and autonomy, the individual response has been feeling an increasing need for privacy. We seek private zones of personal expression, intimacy, and control to feel fully human and to protect the self. Maybe at one time, before the search for individuality developed in the 1800s, this need for a private, separate self wasn't so important, because people were brought up to feel interconnected with others in a close community. But now that this need has developed, the increasing incursions of a surveillance society, however necessary to counter distrust, have led people to want and need privacy more, and to feel its loss even more intensely.

The Development of the Need for Privacy

Many psychologists, sociologists, and other scholars agree that privacy not only has psychological benefits, but we have a powerful psychological need for it. That's why we feel such intense emotional passion when we feel our privacy violated. For example, privacy scholars Edward J. Bloustein and Stanley Benn, writing in the mid-1960s and early 1970s respectively, have argued that privacy is an essential aspect of human dignity.[18] James Rachels, writing in the late 1960s, has claimed that privacy is essential for the individual to develop feelings of trust, love, and friendship, since it enables us to create personal boundaries and decide who we will let into or exclude from our life and to act accordingly.[19]

The noted sociologist, Erving Goffman, also writing during the 1960s, highlighted this distinction between the zones of public and private space in many of his books, pointing out how we act differently by putting on a public and a private persona. Among other things, he emphasized the dehumanizing qualities of limited privacy, such as his study of mental patients, prisoners, and others in "total" or closed institutions in *Asylums*. As he sees it, the lack of privacy in such places occurs because these institutions need to know about people in order to supervise and control them. But this surveillance strips the person psychologically, so he or she feels naked and experiences a loss of self. He or she feels the self "violated" because the boundary between the self and the environment is stripped away, so the self is "profaned." One way this occurs is by others being able to directly observe or learn discreditable facts about oneself that are ordinarily concealed.[20]

Using Privacy to Separate Our Back Stage from Our Public Persona

By contrast, with privacy, we can manage how we present ourselves to others in everyday life. We can use our private space as a sanctuary to retreat from the everyday world, and there craft an image of how we want to appear to others when we step out into the public arena. This way we can influence how others relate to us, since as Goffman observes, others use these presentational cues to decide who a person is and how to react to him. The implication is that one is thus stage-managing one's outer portrayal of self, while being presumably more authentic in the private arena.[21]

That's because in interacting with others, we try to shape the way we come across, and therefore how they will react to us, by appearing in the best possible light. We create a front or public persona as if we are performers on a stage when in public, often donning certain social roles or appearances so people will be favorably impressed and therefore react to us in a favorable way.[22]

But after we go off stage, in this backstage, private area, we can take off this public persona to be more who we are beneath the external persona we put on for others. Also, we can permit ourselves to express forbidden or taboo desires that aren't normally acceptable, for privacy gives us the freedom to indulge ourselves to satisfy certain inner needs and cravings, as well as to hide secret fears and weaknesses.

So no wonder privacy is so cherished. It is that backstage part of ourselves where we can express what we feel and desire very strongly, yet which may be publicly taboo, or may detract from the external impression of ourselves we want to project. Furthermore, in a complex society where we each belong to multiple communities with varying cultures and expectations of us, our privacy allows us to choose among the ways we might present ourselves to others. This way we can appear differently in different groups, while keeping our private self private.

Yet, as desirable as privacy is for us personally, it does open the door to a person creating a seriously false presentation of self that becomes misrepresentation or fraud. Within limits, we all engage in impression management, which is beneficial to the individual and society and we don't consider that "misrepresentation," as long as the image presented is within the accepted boundaries for creating a good impression. But the potential for becoming an imposter or fraud is always there, when the protections of privacy are used to harm others, not just to help ourselves.

Privacy and the Control of Personal Space

Privacy is also important in giving us a sense of the personal space around us and a feeling of control over it. So we resist undesired physical intrusions as invasions of this space.

In fact, we have become increasingly sensitive to such invasions today, resulting in more and more invasion of privacy claims in the courts. For example, victims not only charge someone who has threatened or attacked them with assault, battery or both, but with an "invasion of privacy" as a separate legal charge. Similarly, increasing numbers of women, and occasionally even men, who are charging sexual harassment, are claiming their privacy has been invaded as well. And those who win are getting additional "invasion of privacy" damages.

Why the greater modern sensitivity? Again, it seems related to the growing sense of individuality, personal integrity, self-identity, and separation from others since the 1960s, combined with living closer together as the population booms. For example, in *Relations in Public*, published in 1971, sociologist Erving Goffman points out that people have a sense of personal space in public. As a result, as the amount of space available increases, they want more space or separation from others to feel sufficiently apart from them, and they therefore feel "encroached upon" when others enter that space. An example is when people are riding on a crowded bus. As soon as there is more empty space, people tend to find seats further apart, or they move to another seat further away, to gain extra personal space.[23]

In turn, since we treat the space around us as a private possession over which we want control and ownership, and place boundaries around the self, we feel disturbed when our space is invaded without our permission or desire—a reaction that can range from just feeling annoyed to experiencing anger or fear. However, these responses vary greatly, since we differ greatly in the point at which we feel our own space invaded or how we respond, based on our personality, social background, culture, and other factors. For people differ greatly in how much they value personal privacy, how far they feel their personal space extends, what they consider an invasion, and how they react when this occurs.

Most of the time, we accept many everyday invasions, like being crowded on a bus, as one of the inconveniences of modern living in a crowded urban society. But some people are especially sensitive to these invasions, and in general, as a society, we seem to be more sensitive too, perhaps because we increasingly feel the pressure of others closing in on us, as well as being more aware of our own individuality and personal rights. Thus, we are more apt to consider an intrusion an "invasion of privacy."

Privacy and the Social Roles We Play

Finally, privacy is important in a society where we play multiple roles, because it enables us to prepare to assume these roles. Also, it gives us a place of refuge where we can put aside our public social roles to be ourselves. For example, in his 1963 book, *Behavior in Public Places,* Goffman notes that one can use the private backstage area as a place to regroup to restore one's sense of equilibrium, such as when things aren't going so well at work or in a relationship.[24] What gives us this psychological boost is that within this private personal space, one is free to take off any public role one is playing and the demands to perform a certain way to be more of oneself.

Summing Up

In sum, privacy has become so important today because we give much more recognition to the individual, and one's privacy is essential to maintaining that individuality. It is also vital for crafting the social roles we play in public and for providing a safe harbor where we can retreat from those social roles for a while. In addition, it gives us a sense of power through the feelings of autonomy and control we gain by creating physical or psychological boundaries that mark off our personal and private spaces from others.

These underlying social and psychological dynamics, in turn, give the issue of personal privacy rights and the invasion of privacy so much emotional power today. We experience our need for privacy intensely, and when we feel it is threatened or invaded, we react strongly, as is now the case when society is increasingly intruding on individual privacy in more areas of life. And that is why, in response, more and more individuals are fighting back.

Notes

1. Julie C. Inness, *Privacy, Intimacy and Isolation* (New York: Oxford University Press, 1992).
2. Ibid. 6, 16.
3. Ibid. 6–7, 16–18.
4. Ibid. 23.
5. Ibid. 124.
6. Heather MacNeil, *Without Concent: The Ethics of Disclosing Personal Information in Public Archives* (Methuchen, N.J.: The Scarecrow Press, 1992), 1.

7. Steven L. Nock, *The Costs of Privacy: Surveillance and Reputation in America* (New York: Aldine de Gruyter, 1993), vii–viii.
8. Ibid. viii.
9. MacNeil, 1.
10. Raymond Williams, *Keywords: A Vocabulary of Culture and Society* (Glasgow: Fantana, 1976), 203, cited in MacNeill, 1–2.
11. Richard F. Hixson, *Privacy in a Public Society: Human Rights in Conflict* (New York: Oxford University Press, 1987), 47.
12. Arthur Schafer, "Privacy: A Philosophical Overview," in *Aspects of Privacy Law: Essays in Honor of John M. Sharp*, ed. Dale Gibson (Toronto: Butterworths, 1980), 2.
13. Nock, 1.
14. Ibid. 5–6.
15. Ibid. 6.
16. Ibid. 2–3.
17. Ibid. 4–5.
18. Edward J. Bloustein, "Privacy as an Aspect of Human Dignity: An Answer to Dean Prosser," *New York University Law Review* 39 (December 1964): 962–1007; and Stanley Benn, "Privacy, Freedom and Respect for Persons," in *Nomos XIII: Privacy*, ed. J. R. Pennock and J. W. Chapman (New York: Atherton Press), 1971, 1–26.
19. James Rachels, "Why Privacy is Important," *Philosophy and Public Affairs* 4 (Summer 1975), 323–333.
20. Erving Goffman, *Asylums* (Garden City, New York: Anchor Books/Doubleday, 1961), 23–24.
21. Erving Goffman, *The Presentation of Self in Everyday Life* (Garden City, New York: Doubleday/Anchor Books, 1959), 13.
22. Ibid. 17–27.
23. Erving Goffman, *Relations in Public* (New York: Harper & Row, 1971), 29–31.
24. Erving Goffman, *Behavior in Public Places* (New York: The Free Press, 1963), 25–26.

Chapter 2

The Emerging Right of Privacy and the Growing Invasion of Privacy

In the Beginning

The heated battle over privacy today is of very recent origin. It is only since the 1950s and 1960s that there has been a growing reaction to the increasing power and control of big business and government to create a conformist society. The technological revolution, the social dislocations of modern society, and the pervasiveness—and invasiveness—of the media has escalated this concern since the 1970s, culminating in the privacy crisis of today. In fact, the concern has become so great that in November 1993, Senator Paul Simon of Illinois introduced legislation to create a privacy agency, the Privacy Protection Commission, to serve as a watchdog to protect personal privacy rights. This bill, the Privacy Protection Act of 1993 (S. 1735), was an attempt to bring some order to a growing battle that had been engaging the public, the media, and the courts with increased urgency for the past few decades. It has not yet passed, and today many other pieces of legislation are in the works, as the various institutions involved in the battle try to work out some general agreements and understandings to deal with privacy in a society undergoing extensive and often traumatic social change.

It wasn't always this way. For notions of personal privacy really emerged along with notions of individuality and personal liberty, freedom, and independence. In earlier times, individuals were not seen as separate from their families, small communities, or society as a whole. Rather, they were a part of their tribe or social group, and they lived in an environment where people spent much of their time living closely together or under the watchful eye of others in their family or community. Also, they spent little time alone or thinking private thoughts that might question the communal practices and pressure for conformity in the community. Each society had developed its own traditional ways, and all members were expected to be part of this tradition. They were expected to conform to the practices that had developed in that society over time.

For example, imagine a small community of hunter-gathers at the dawn of human society. People lived in small encampments for survival. Members of families commonly slept together in the same shelter—typically in a cave or a simple hut made from grasses, bark, or clay. They shared equally the food they gathered from hunting or gathering. Probably the most private act of someone in such societies was to individually carve or weave an object or to paint or carve a picture on the side of a rock or on a piece of bark. But even that act was done for the community as a whole, such as to contribute to the group effort to find or prepare food or for a group ritual. And it was done in the style common to the group. The individual didn't stand apart from the community.

Similarly, as the first farming communities emerged around 10,000 to 12,000 years ago, that connection between individual and community remained. People were still part of relatively small close-knit communities guided by traditions passed down from generation to generation. Typically, these communities were headed by a small group of elders, who passed on the group wisdom to the younger generation, and generally, everyone conformed to these group-supported practices without question. Those who deviated from accepted practices—such as the person who was lazy, the wife and husband who quarreled too loudly, the man who stole—were subjected to ridicule or even worse, exile from the group. For in those days, one conformed at the threat of group rejection. There was little other choice; nowhere else to go.

In turn, one gained a sense of self through one's relationship to others in the community. One was a member of a family and a tribe; a son or daughter of a man and woman. Likewise, when one married, it was into a whole family, not just an alliance between two individuals based on personal preference. In fact, such marriages might often be arranged, and to these societies, such an arrangement (which did not follow the ideal of romantic love we have today) was perfectly acceptable. That is because the community was more important than the individual, and marriage united families in the community, not just individuals. Thus, in these early societies, individuals were submerged in the larger group so a concern with personal privacy as we now conceive it was irrelevant.

One can still see the remnants of such group-oriented behavior in the isolated parts of the world where preliterate tribal communities have survived—the highlands of New Guinea, the Australian outback, the jungles of the Philippines, and the isolated river settlements on the Amazon in Brazil. At least until these people were confronted by the modernizing force of modern society, they still lived in their small communal groups, following traditional ways; and they had little concern for the personal privacy interests of individual members.

As the first civilizations emerged around five to six thousand years ago in the fertile river valleys, this same group-oriented focus remained. Societies became larger and more complex, so there were many more groups of different types. But people remained tightly embedded in these groups, except for perhaps a few powerful leaders who emerged at the top of the pyramid and whose names have come down to us in history. But otherwise, there was a lack of personal identity and individuality, and accordingly, a lack of concern with anyone's privacy needs. Indeed, one might question whether in such an environment if anyone felt the same kind of expectation of privacy one feels today.

This lack of individuality and personal privacy is reflected in numerous ways. The archaeological remains show large communal living areas. Art styles developed for the group as a whole; individual artists did not sign their work. Religious practices involved large communal ceremonies, participated in by the whole group, and they were led by priests or divine kings, who required adherence to the practices and beliefs of the group. Even the huge communal efforts needed to build the massive temples and palaces show this merger of the individual into the group.

For instance, in the Americas, archaeologists believe that many peoples, like the Mayans, voluntarily joined together to build the huge temples, because they saw themselves as the servants of their divine king or their gods. They were like ants working together in a communal society, where each was a part of the whole. In fact, some anthropologists believe this is why the Mayan and Aztec societies fell apart so quickly when a small number of Spanish arrived. Once the Spanish had captured or executed their king, people lost the central core of their society which had held it together, and they were unable to create an alternate structure or fight back. So they simply gave up.

Meanwhile, in other ancient societies, such as Egypt, this lack of concern with the individual made slavery an acceptable and common practice. And slaves, by definition, were not full participants in the community; their role was just to work and produce for their masters. They had no individual rights; and likewise no privacy right. In fact, many were housed together in barnlike accommodations like animals, and their masters traded or bred them like property—for they were regarded as possessions, not people. So privacy for them, like the masses of people who worked together voluntarily in service to their king, god, or larger community, was irrelevant, too.

Even the early law codes of the ancient civilizations showed little or no concern with individual or personal privacy rights. Just about every sort of behavior was considered subject to the law and open to state scrutiny. There was no concept, as today, that some things "are none of the government's business."[1] There was no zone set aside for personal privacy.

Such codes first were written down in the Middle East by the Babylonians in southern Mesopotamia and the Hittites in the area of modern Turkey. These codes formalized in writing behavior that had developed over the preceding centuries. And since these codes developed in warlike patriarchal empires, they were quite rigid and unforgiving. They laid out rules about how people should behave in various situations and the penalties for failing to conform. Nothing was said about individual rights, although some were implied in that people had a kind of property right to expect certain actions or obligations from others. For example, if a person did not receive a payment of a debt or suffered an injury from another, such as a theft of property, he was entitled to some retribution or recompense. But these early laws included none of the wrongs associated with an affront to one's personal identity which are central to privacy rights today, such as an attack on one's reputation or one's desire to be alone.

Thus, in ancient times, the individual was subservient to an all-powerful state, subjected to the rules of a harsh, unforgiving society, where little valuation was placed on individual human life. Individual rights were of little concern, and there was no conception of the right to personal privacy as we know it today.

The Early Emergence of the Individual in Ancient Times

But gradually, there was a growing recognition of the individual and the right to some autonomy from society and the state. This shift helped to provide the basis for the emergence of an individual privacy right.

This emerging awareness can perhaps be traced back to the beginnings of Judaism, as the early Jewish prophets and teachers struggled with trying to establish the relationship between the individual and the expectations of a single demanding God. Before then, the earlier cultures—from the beginnings of human society to the ancient civilizations, like the Babylonians, Persians, Greeks, and Romans—had believed in multiple gods controlling different aspects of life, and people worshiped and placated them through ritual, prayer, and other religious, and magical practices. So the individual was both subject to the demands of a religion run by priests and to a state controlled by a powerful king—a plight reflected in the literature and religious stories of these cultures. Common were heroic tales of great conquests by the kings and religious morality tales based on myths about gods or humans interacting with these gods, even bearing their children.

By contrast, in early Jewish culture, the struggles of everyday people became a part of the literature passed down in the community and eventually written in the Old Testament. These stories reflected a new awareness of the individual personality and the need of the individual for some degree of privacy, through having a private or secret part of the self, separated from others. For example, in *Privacy in a Public Society*, Richard Hixson notes glimmerings of this need for privacy in the Genesis story of Adam and Eve, where, as he points out, God's first gift to man besides life itself is "the right to be reticent before the eyes of each other."[2]

Also, he observes, privacy as a right against authority was "integral to early Hebrew culture." This came about because male scholars had a right to interpret and discuss the various points of doctrine that became part of the voluminous Hebrew writings about the individual's rights and responsibilities toward God. Yet, even so, this right was still limited, because, as in the earlier Middle Eastern societies, people were heavily bound by numerous laws that guided what they could do and when they could do it; such as what they could eat, who they could marry, and the penalties for doing anything wrong. They still lived in an authoritarian society, subject to the laws of the Jewish rabbis and leaders and to those of the various conquering societies, such as Egypt and Rome. And there was little distinction between public and private in everyday Hebrew life, although there was this slowly growing individual awareness.[3]

In classical Greek society, the notion of individuality and the right to personal autonomy took another step forward with the experiment with democracy in Athens. Though many people still had little power or autonomy—notably women and slaves—the ideal of democracy was vitally important to the development of ideas about privacy. That's because democracy meant that the individual was no longer subjected to the absolute power of the state to make the laws and guide his life by them. Instead, the individual who was considered a citizen of the community (in those days essentially the property-owning males) had a measure of freedom and autonomy to create those laws. If people objected to certain laws, they could discuss their objections and potentially change the laws. In turn, the individual's ability to debate and create these laws meant there was a basic respect for human dignity, which is essential for individual autonomy. And individual autonomy is necessary for the individual to seek seclusion or protection from society. In short, as Barrington Moore, Jr. observes in *Privacy: Studies in Social and Cultural History,* without democracy private rights are either stunted or absent.[4]

Yet, even so, the Athenian legal codes were not much different from those of the Hittites. All sorts of codes still governed personal activities, from rules on who could marry who, to lists of sexual offenses like seduction and rape, to property and commercial matters. The moral and legal codes of the state were still considered supreme, though some citizens might now have a hand in developing them.

The Early Battle between Private and Social Rights

After this brief experiment with democracy and increased individual rights in Greece, an authoritarian Roman state and centralized religious institutions soon took control. Again, the individual had little freedom and privacy for many centuries. This occurred in the fifth century B.C. as the Roman empire engulfed Greece and the rest of the Mediterranean world, bringing a hierarchical centralized state under the Roman emperor and his occupying armies and governors in the provinces. The rise of numerous new religious cults from about 100 B.C. to 100 A.D. might suggest that people were groping for an increase in personal autonomy and a private spiritual retreat to ease what was an otherwise very oppressive life for most people. But as these groups gained in numbers and power, Roman officials saw them as a possible threat to the state and quickly clamped down. For example, this is what happened when the small group of followers around Jesus became too visible. The local governor arrested Jesus, had him put to death on the cross, and his followers dispersed.

Then, as Christianity gained power after the fourth century A.D., the Roman Catholic Church became the dominant force in Europe through the Middle Ages, and increasingly intruded into the private life of the individual. More and more people's lives and morality were subjected to Church codes, which were developed through various Church Councils and Synods, as the Church became more and more hierarchical. Indeed, as Richard Hixson, author of *Privacy in Public Society* observes, the development of the confessional epitomized this notion of letting the church into the most private recesses of the individual's soul, for in confession, the individual is supposed to reveal any thoughts and actions that did not conform to the Church's principles of right thought and behavior.[5] In turn, the idea of sin helped to squelch individual autonomy, since some very basic individual desires and feelings were considered sins, especially anger, lust, gluttony, pride, envy, greed, and sloth or laziness, described as the seven deadly sins.

Meanwhile, corresponding to the Church's hierarchical controlling structure, medieval society itself was rigidly structured under the feudal system. In this system, each person had his place in the social hierarchy, from the high and mighty king and nobles on top to the lowly peasants and serfs on the bottom, and the individual was supposed to accept his place without question. The feudal law codes in turn supported these views with restrictions on everything from property ownership to rules about marriage, adultery, and providing service to one's higher-ups. The theology of the medieval Roman Catholic Church supposed this authoritarian social structure, too, and tolerated no dissent. As Darien McWhirter, a Texas attorney, and Jon Bible, an Associate Professor of Business Law at Southwest Texas State University, write: "Questions of life and death were to be decided by God, not man. . . . Religious dissent was not to be tolerated lest the whole system fall apart and bring about chaos. The task of both theology and philosophy was to justify the legitimacy of the social system and the one true faith."[6]

In short, under this authoritarian feudal system supported by an equally authoritarian Church, there was great pressure to control both individual actions and personal thoughts and desires to fit the social rules and theological beliefs of the times. So individuals had very little private life. Their whole being was subjected to a world ruled by princes and priests, and under the divine authority of God.

Should anyone too openly resist this divine order, the penalties were harsh. The danger was of being accused of witchcraft or heresy, charges which spread across continental Europe and Britain like wildfire during the eleventh through fifteenth centuries, the height of the Middle Ages. Such accusations were of engaging in the ultimate evil, personified by having links with the devil, thereby defiling the religious underpinnings of a theocratic state. And underlying these charges were a fear of the person carving out an area of private or secret personal life, viewed as extremely threatening by a society that wanted to keep everyone in thrall to the Church and the state.

A sampling of these charges shows this fear. They involve activities done in secret or evil or secret thoughts, such as women accused of going to secret black masses in the dark of night; casting secret spells to harm someone; having hidden markings on their bodies; or using secret potions to gain power. Certainly, many charges were motivated by a fear of sexuality in a rigid, puritanical society, where sex outside of marriage and for pleasure, not for reproduction, was regarded as a sin. Also, many charges were directed at women who got too uppity or at local misfits who angered or bothered someone, say a jealous neighbor who reacted with accusations of witchcraft. But another key reason for these charges, often overlooked, is that whatever the circumstances of each case, the people who were charged were trying to carve out an area of individuality or personal privacy for themselves. And that was what the Church and state found so threatening and intolerable in an authoritarian medieval society where both institutions ruled supreme and the individual was to bow to all higher authority, something these accused rebels failed to do.

The Rebirth of the Individual and the Right to Privacy

Though there was continued resistance here and there to Church and state control, overall, in this medieval world, Church and state ruled supreme and individual and privacy concerns were submerged.

But, in the late Middle Ages, things began to change for two key reasons. First, the mercantile towns began to develop, and in them a new bourgeois merchant class gained increasing influence. These merchants were imbued with a spirit of entrepreneurship that encouraged a new individuality, as people struggled to get ahead in a world where old notions of position and place were less and less relevant. Second, the Protestant Reformation swept from Germany across central Europe, emphasizing the value of the individual's personal faith, individual consciousness, and direct relationship with God. So, suddenly, around the middle of the sixteenth century, the individual gained a new sense of personal freedom and autonomy.[7]

In this new world of the Reformation followed by the Renaissance and the Age of Enlightenment, there were many ways in which people could now express themselves and acquire new private rights. For example, as the growing class of merchants did business together, they engaged in various private dealings and secret arrangements to get the best deal. Certain religious groups, like the Puritans, now demanded a right to their own private form of worship, and when they couldn't get their way, they set off for a new land that offered new opportunities for privacy. Of course, after they arrived, they, like other religious groups seeking freedom, soon created their own tight-knit communities based on their own beliefs and values. Thus, the members of these communities soon had little privacy themselves to do as they wished. Then, as more and more diverse settlers from other backgrounds poured into the United States this overarching control broke down,[8] although a few isolated groups, like the Amish and Mennonites, were able to cling to their old ways and clamp down on the individuality and privacy of group members.

Meanwhile, in America, the desire for privacy had even more chance to develop because of the less settled rural and frontier conditions. For example, there was more space between homes, particularly for those on farms, resulting in more everyday physical privacy and a greater expectation of this. As a result, the ordinary colonial family could enjoy more solitude than was common in the more communally oriented small towns and villages in Europe. Then, as new urban centers developed in the colonies, they provided a certain protective anonymity, even though people lived more closely together.

As people's lives improved economically, they created a greater sense of privacy in the home itself. Initially, most people lived cramped together in a few small rooms, without even corridors to separate individual rooms, so people had to pass through one room to get to another. But as homes became larger in the eighteenth century, they gained hallways, which increased individual privacy, because now one didn't need to go through other rooms when going from one place to another in the house.[9]

In fact, ideas about the sanctity of the home—the home as one's castle—began to emerge. For example, in colonial America, by the middle of the eighteenth century, the unwritten common or customary law recognized the citizen's right to privacy at home and his right to repel invaders who challenged that right, including tax collectors. Or as one pamphleteer observed in opposing the hated Massachusetts Excise Bill of 1754 which required each homeowner to report household consumption for the year: "It is essential to the English Constitution, that a Man should be safe in his own House; his House is commonly called his Castle, which the Law will not permit even a sheriff to enter into, but by his own Consent, unless in criminal cases."[10] Under the circumstances, some of the first invasion of privacy cases in the colonial courts involved violations of the home, such as by eavesdroppers and peeping toms.

Still, because people did live so close together in many communities, it was often hard to keep personal activities private within the home. For example, neighbors who lived close by, could easily see what was going on next door, and were often close enough to actually hear what others were saying.[11] Sometimes neighbors spread the news about what they heard if they perceived a disturbance, such as a husband and wife quarreling, that might threaten the general peace of the community. In fact, the local preachers of the day often encouraged neighbors to monitor their neighbors and report their misdeeds as a form of community control. Presumably, they had the duty, if not the right, to interfere with an individual's privacy in the interests of the higher moral code provided by their religion.[12]

Thus, as a growing sense of individual and personal privacy rights began to emerge in the sixteenth to eighteenth centuries, these helped to sow the seeds of a growing battle between the individual and community over these rights. On the one hand, the individual sought ways to gain more privacy—more personal spaces to call his own. But on the other hand, the community often invaded that space in the form of nosey neighbors, concerned preachers, and government agents, who wanted to preserve order and morality in the community or gain information (such as about earnings and taxes) the person might want to conceal.

But in contrast to today when so many disputes end up in court, in these early years, individuals usually resolved their battles more directly and quickly. For instance, if a man felt a neighbor was spying, he would say something—the colonial equivalent of "bug off." Then, if the neighbor persisted, he might retaliate with "fistcuffs and gunfire."[13] By today's standards, such measures might seem harsh, if not illegal. We honor the law, not taking justice into one's own hands. But back then, to quote Hixson: "Privacy was more a matter of honor than of law."[14] Not that there was much privacy, since people lived in much closer neighborly communities, and leisure time was commonly spent visiting and socializing with others—there weren't many solitary pleasures available. But as society grew larger and more complex, and the spirit of democracy and liberty spread through the colonies, people became increasingly determined to acquire more privacy for themselves.

The Growing Threat to Privacy in the Eighteenth and Nineteenth Century and the Fight for Individual Rights

Unfortunately, besides the potential intrusions of neighbors and the government, there was another looming threat, the spread of the new communications medium—newspapers. Through the eighteenth century, they became more and more pervasive. While they helped to make the information people got more reliable, since increasingly information came from public and other official sources, not just from friends and neighbors, the newspapers stimulated a desire for more and more information about others.[15]

Just think of the curiosity that is triggered today by the media's global reach. There are probing cameras, gossipy talk shows, exclusive tabloid interviews, and more. The same sort of process on a smaller scale began back in the middle of the eighteenth century as the print revolution gathered steam and printers like Benjamin Franklin and pamphleteers like Thomas Paine began spreading the news. And this news wasn't just political tracts and philosophical digressions about what the new, increasingly independent-minded society should be like. Instead, these early journalists increasingly reported the local news, which presented a threat to privacy to anyone who did anything that attracted attention.[16]

Meanwhile, in the early 1800s as the population expanded and city life increasingly closed in on the rural and small village communities, there were increased glimmerings of dissatisfaction. More and more voices were raised in opposition to intrusive laws and regulations. Instead, the values of "rugged individualism, personal freedom, and studied isolation"[17] were embraced that are echoed by many of the popular writers of the day. In the 1860s Ralph Waldo Emerson wrote his famous essay "Self-Reliance" praising the virtues of moral independence and the importance of nonconformity. Also, around this time, Henry David Thoreau made his famous retreat to Walden Pond, where he described in 1847 how he sought solitude in his cabin in the woods. Ironically, this pond was only five hundred yards from the railroad going to Boston, reflecting the new intrusive urban world that was rapidly encroaching. About two decades later, Walt Whitman issued his own cry celebrating individual freedom and the private self as an antidote to a world of innocence that was fast passing away.[18]

Yet, while there might be these growing intrusions—from neighbors, the government, press, and encroaching urban life—in the days of America's more simple life before about 1850, overall there was a balance between the individual's growing desire for privacy and the desire of the public to know. As Richard Hixson observes in *Privacy in a Public Society*, one's level of privacy was more a matter of personal circumstances, depending on where one lived, the space between neighbors, the strictness and moral concerns of one's local church, and the popularity and interests of the local newspaper. But privacy itself wasn't yet regarded as a legal, moral, or natural right. Rather, it was either not given much attention or it was taken for granted, because it was not seriously threatened. Instead, people worked out through everyday customs and occasional conflicts with one another the patterns of privacy of the day.

All this was possible, because America, like most of Europe, was still a largely rural and agrarian society before 1850, and people had a strong sense of bondedness with others in the community, as well as a desire to have a private space at home. Those who wanted even more privacy than was available to them in the more developed villages, towns, and emerging Eastern cities could always head out to the frontier, where there was a promise of being left alone. However, by the end of the 1800s, this promise would fade too. All of America was becoming a more interconnected urban world, where privacy everywhere was increasingly threatened. This led to new attempts in the late 1800s to formally define what privacy was and what the right to privacy should be.

Notes

1. Darien A. McWhirter and Jon D. Bible, *Privacy as a Constitutional Right* (New York: Quorum Books, 1992), 1.
2. Richard F. Hixson, *Privacy in a Public Society* (New York: Oxford University Press, 1987), 3.
3. Hixson, 5.
4. Barrington Moore, Jr., *Privacy: Studies in Social and Cultural History* (Armonk, New York: M.E. Sharpe, 1984), 267–277.
5. Hixson, 4.
6. McWhirter and Bible, 26–27.
7. Hixson, 6; Moore, 283.
8. David H. Flaherty, *Privacy in Colonial New England* (Charlottesville: University Press of Virginia, 1972), 26.
9. Flaherty, 30–39.
10. Massachusetts Excise Bill (1784), cited by Flaherty, 87.
11. Flaherty, 90–96.
12. Hixson, 14.
13. Flaherty, 96.
14. Hixson, 14.
15. Ibid., 15–16.
16. Flaherty, 106.
17. Hixson, 18.
18. Ibid., 19–20.

Chapter 3

The Beginnings of the Battle for Personal Privacy

From the 1850s through the 1950s

The Urbanization of America, the New Press, and the Growing Threat to Privacy

The big change that especially threatened privacy in the United States was the urbanization of America after the Civil War and the rise of the media. The burgeoning media were made possible by the development of new technologies (improvements in printing and the development of telegraphy and photography)[1]—just as today's technological explosion has created new privacy threats. Meanwhile, the new railroads crossing the country helped to create an interconnected country, hungry for new information.

Before the Civil War, newspapers had been small and expensive, and were generally published by local political parties to help gain voters. But after the war, a growing mass market developed in the cities, fueled in part by the rapid influx of immigrants.[2] The newspapers now targeted these masses, who for the most part had little education, and by the 1870s, all sorts of inexpensive new newspapers, gazettes, journals, pamphlets, and magazines appeared. Between 1850 and 1870, the number of newspapers in the larger cities shot up from about 100 newspapers circulating to 800,000 readers each day, to a couple of hundred with about 2½ million readers. And by 1890, there were about 900 urban papers with over 8 million readers—a circulation increase of over 1000 percent in forty years.[3] Thus, by the end of the century, just about everyone who could read or wanted to be read to had access to a daily newspaper.[4]

The result was a new popular journalism that, much like today, featured news presented in a sensational, colorful way. It soon came to be called "yellow journalism," after the color of the newspapers that blared out the headlines, and sometimes created the news as well. These publications tended to focus on news of the upper crust, along with accounts of the more colorful criminals and domestic battles. The main thrust of this new journalism promoted by the new media barons like Hearst and Pulitzer was to emphasize the curious, dramatic, and unusual, and to provide readers with an exciting mix of "sin, sex, and violence."[5] Until about 1890, the papers were largely restricted to print, because the cameras of the day were large and clunky and it was difficult to print photographs on newsprint. But the papers made up for this lack of photos with blaring headlines and stories about private as well as public figures.

In response, there was suddenly a growing concern about the threat to privacy. For example, in 1890, E.L. Godkin complained in *Scribner's Magazine,* a kind of *Harper's* or *Atlantic Monthly* of the day, that: "the advent of the newspaper . . . has converted . . . gossip into a marketable commodity."[6] He wasn't much concerned with oral gossip, since that was limited to a few people and could be ignored. But the real threat came from the new mass-circulation, sensation-seeking newspapers, which created a market for curiosity.

Toward the end of the century, the threat became even worse, because cameras became smaller and portable and newspapers began to print photographs. So now packs of journalists with cameras began snapping candid photos of unsuspecting victims to accompany their sensationalist copy.

Soon, too, advertisers uped the threat, since they sometimes used these candid shots to pump up their ads. Or worse, they even suggested that their subjects endorsed their products.[7]

In short, the period from the 1870s to the end of the century saw the birth of the tabloids, as the revolutionary new technology of the times created a mass media and mass audience. The trend was worldwide, though the problem was even greater in the United States, given its ideals of individualism, freedom, democracy, and go-go capitalism in a rapidly growing new nation. But in England, the writers and photographers of the Victorian tabloids of the 1890s stalked their subjects much like today's press hounds Princess Diana, the Duchess of York (Fergie), and Prince Charles, and other notables. In fact, according to one historian of the period: "By 1899 the public demand for candid pictures had grown so great that the Penny Pictorial Magazine began a regular page of photographs headed Taken Unawares: Snapshots of celebrated people."[8]

This feature was like the *Funniest Home Videos* of its day.

The Struggle to Preserve Privacy

Thus, between enterprising reporters, photographers, and advertisers in this new media circus, there was a real threat to one's personal privacy. The battle to preserve personal privacy began as a fight against this invading media army, and it took two forms. One was a growing number of court cases in the United States as well as in Britain, which was still very influential in shaping U.S. law. The other was the effort of some legal scholars to create guidelines for recognizing a right of privacy and defining when one's privacy was invaded.

For example, in one 1888 English case, *Pollard v. Photographic Company,* a woman became upset when she discovered a photo studio was selling Christmas cards using her picture. She hadn't given her permission and sued to stop them, which the English Court of Chancery did by issuing an injunction based on a breach of faith.[9] In New York there was the very highly publicized 1890 case of *Marion Manola v. Stevens & Myers.* A starlet who was appearing wearing tights in a Broadway play became angry when two photographers secretly photographed her during her performance, one with a flash. Afraid they would take her photo to the newspapers, she sued to prevent them, and the New York Supreme Court agreeably complied, by issuing an injunction.[10]

Such cases and the growing aggressiveness of the media in turn inspired two noted lawyers, Samuel Warren and Louis Brandeis, to write their famous, ground-breaking article on privacy for the *Harvard Law Review* in 1890. They had gone to Harvard Law School together between 1875 and 1877, and they were working together as partners in a small Boston law firm when they became concerned about the privacy problem. So they wrote their article, which shaped the history of privacy law, affecting the way privacy rights and the invasion of privacy "wrong" are viewed today.

In writing their article, they discovered there was no clear notion of privacy in American law, though they found occasional references to the idea that people had a "right to be let alone" or to the relationship between privacy and notions of independence and liberty. For example, one noted social philosopher of the day, John Stuart Mill, spoke in his famous treatise *On Liberty* about the need to protect liberty from the encroachment of the government.[11] Also, some notions about personal rights had long been part of the everyday common law, such as the view that people shouldn't trespass on other people's lands or assault others.* But there was no formal conception of privacy as a tort (personal injury) or as a constitutional notion anywhere in U.S. law.

Thus, Warren and Brandeis wrote their article for the *Harvard Law Review* on why there should be such laws,[12] using examples of cases primarily from Britain and Ireland and pointing to the havoc wrought by the media. As they argued, an invasion of privacy tort was needed in the legal system, so that people could seek justice and compensation when their own privacy was invaded. They particularly blamed the irresponsible press which had, as they saw it, gone wild. In fact, from their reaction to the media they might well have been writing about the prying, gossipy media of today. For example, as they wrote back in 1890: "The press is overstepping in every direction the obvious bounds of propriety and of decency. Gossip is no longer the resource of the idle and of the vicious, but has become a trade, which is pursued with industry as well as effrontery. To satisfy a prurient taste the details of sexual relations are spread broadcast in the columns of the daily papers."[13]

In their view, due to the growing complexity of modern life, people more than ever needed a "retreat from the world" through solitude and privacy. But they felt this was ever more in doubt because of the modern invasive press, subjecting the individual to deep mental pain and distress, far greater than could be inflicted by mere bodily injury.[14]

*Common laws are those laws which have come into general acceptance through everyday customs or from the rulings of the courts recognizing these customs, as opposed to laws created by the legislature.

In short, they felt the press was invading the individual's "inviolate personality," his private self, because they deeply believed the individual should have the right to determine the degree to which his own thoughts, feelings, and emotions should be communicated to others. This notion was already a generally accepted principle of everyday life, a common law notion, but Warren and Brandeis helped to formalize this principle through their article.[15]

Thereafter, in subsequent years, their original notion of privacy expanded into the five major areas where the battle for privacy is occurring today: the invasion of privacy as a personal tort or wrong against someone else; the protection of the individual from unjust searches and seizures by the government; the collision between one individual's right to free speech and another's right to privacy; one's right to make certain fundamental private decisions; and the special rights to privacy granted by certain states.[16]

The Early Battles to Protect Personal Privacy from the Media

At first, in the 1890s and early 1900s, the battle for privacy was primarily a battle against the media, reflected in a few cases from New York and Georgia. In the 1891 *MacKenzie v. Soden Mineral Springs Company* case, a New York doctor successfully sued a mineral springs company. He objected because the company used his name to advertise its "medicine" without his consent and the court ordered the company to stop.[17] In the 1893 *Marks v. Jaffa* case, also from New York, an actor discovered a newspaper was using his pictures to promote a newspaper popularity contest and he got the courts to order the paper to stop using it, since he had never consented.[18] And in the well-known 1905 case, *Pavesich v. New England Life Insurance Company,* a well-known artist objected to the insurance company publishing his picture in the *Atlanta Constitution* next to a picture of a man who looked sick and depressed. And worse, there was a statement attributed to him endorsing the insurance company. Eventually, the Georgia Supreme Court agreed that he not only had a claim for libel, but a claim that his privacy had been damaged, too.[19]

Meanwhile, as a few cases made it to court, some states began to pass the first privacy statutes. At the time they were primarily designed to stave off the offending newspapers and advertisers who published the names or pictures of people to promote one product or another without their consent. Today, about half the states have their own privacy laws or provisions in their constitutions which go much further. But initially only a handful of states passed such laws—California in 1899, New York and Pennsylvania in 1903, and Virginia and Utah in 1904 and 1909, respectively.[20]

Unfortunately, though, as is true today, the battle to protect one's privacy did not always lead to a favorable outcome. For example, a number of states decided that there was no right to privacy under the common or everyday law of the land. This is what happened in one famous and hotly disputed case, *Roberson v. Rochester Folding Box Company,* decided in 1902, shortly before New York adopted its own privacy law. In this case, the Franklin Mills Flour Company published the picture of Abigail Roberson on thousands of posters without her permission. And adding insult to the injury, the company published these words beneath her picture: "Flour of the Family." At the time, the New York Court of Appeals turned her down, saying there was no right of privacy under New York's unwritten everyday common law.[21] But the decision unleashed a storm of protest from members of the legal community, as well as the general public,[22] reflecting the growing sentiment for stronger privacy protection laws.

Meanwhile, though the outcomes varies, more and more privacy invasion cases were brought, mostly by people fighting back against the publication of their names and photos by pushy newspapers, photographers, and advertisers who hadn't gotten their permission to use their name or likeness.[23] Certainly, the energetic press of the early twentieth century did contribute some socially acclaimed benefits, such as when the activist journalists called "muckrakers," like Ida Tarbell, sought to right social wrongs (for example, breaking up the big business trusts like Standard Oil, leading to antitrust legislation). But when it came to the personal privacy arena, the popular sentiment was increasingly that the press went too far.

The Growing Concern about Snooping by the Government

While the growing war against the media was the first battlefield, beginning in the 1920s, as the U.S. government grew larger and became more intrusive into everyday life, government snooping became the next battle front. Eventually, this became the fight over Fourth Amendment privacy rights, based on the notion that the individual should be secure from unwarranted searches and seizures by the government.

Though this battle didn't formally begin until the 1920s, the underlying principles to this right go quite deep, back to the U.S. colonial period and English common law. In medieval England, people strongly believed in the principle that "a man's house is his castle," first cited in an English case from 1499, and they believed this principle should protect the individual, poor or rich, from any unjust criminal procedures against him, even an unjust investigation by the Crown.[24] As one English member of Parliament, William Pitt the Elder, put it in the mid-1700s in defending the privacy right in the face of a tax bill: "The poorest man may in his cottage bid defiance to all the force of the Crown. It may be frail—it's roof may shake—the wind may blow through it—the storm may enter, the rain may enter—but the King of England cannot enter—all his force dares not cross the threshold of the ruined tenement!"[25]

Much the same resentment exists in the U.S. today in the popular resistance to the Internal Revenue Service (IRS), Federal Bureau of Investigation (FBI), police, and other government investigators wanting to search the home.

In any case, this English ideal of the home as one's castle carried over to the colonies. For example, a Rhode Island Code of 1647 provided that "a man's house is to himselfe (sic), his family and goods as a castle."[26] And later, the founders of the United States enshrined this in the U.S. Constitution in the Third and Fourth Amendments. In the Third Amendment they prohibited the government from quartering troops in people's homes, and in the Fourth Amendment, which is even more important to the privacy battle, they required the government to obtain particularized warrants to guard against unreasonable searches and seizures. Initially, this amendment was drafted in reaction to the hated practice on the part of British customs officials and soldiers of sweeping into colonist's homes to search for contraband.[27] Subsequently, it became the basis for the battle against inappropriate government surveillance.

While the power of the government was still relatively weak, surveillance wasn't of as much concern as the media problem, so few cases involved search and seizure issues. But beginning in the 1920s, new technologies and an expanding government presence created a new arena for battle against government interference and snooping—an early echo of the current conflict over the government's desire to gain encryption keys so it can monitor cyberspace today.

What led up to this new arena for battle in the 1920s was the invention of an improved telephone technology that allowed the police and government officials to place wiretaps on telephone lines. Thus, instead of having to be present physically to eavesdrop, they could now listen in over the phone wires. But was tapping the phone lines an invasion of privacy? Many people felt it was, but initially, as is often the case with new technologies, the law and custom take awhile to catch up. In the first big wiretapping Supreme Court case, *Olmstead v. United States,* the courts said no. Some federal officers suspected that a group of men was violating the National Prohibition Act by importing, storing, and selling liquor—an early echo of the many drug cases today that likewise involve secret eavesdropping and surveillance. To get the evidence, the agents placed a wiretap on the lines of these suspects, and over the next five months, they collected about 775 pages of notes. The men objected, complaining this information was wrongly obtained, because the government agents shouldn't have been listening on the wires. The majority of the court, however, thinking of an official search and seizure in traditional terms, sided with the government. After all, Chief Justice Taft stated, speaking for the majority, the Fourth Amendment protections against warrantless searches and seizures didn't apply. That was because, he said, there had been no search, since the officers who picked up the voices of the men were not in the homes of anyone who was speaking. So there was no physical invasion of the house. Also, the agents hadn't seized anything, since the voices on the phone were not tangible material objects.[29] In short, the court concluded that there was no physical search and nothing physical to seize—so there was no invasion.

Still, one Supreme Court justice, Louis Brandeis, who had cowritten the earlier famous *Harvard Law* article on privacy, objected vigorously, and his ideas would later become incorporated into privacy law. He argued that the secret interception of any communication by wiretapping, even without a physical trespass or seizure of physical property, was in fact an illegal search and seizure. Thus, he claimed that still another type of privacy protection was needed, the protection from government invasions made possible by the development of new technologies. In fact, in an early draft of this opinion, he even warned of the potential dangers of television which had just been invented that same year, 1928.[30]

Initially, though, most of the early cases involving Fourth Amendment privacy rights went against those seeking protections against the intrusions from the new equipment. The usual conclusion was that no *physical* trespass or seizure had taken place, so there was no search or seizure as the Supreme Court had decided. In one case, *Goldman v. United States,* decided in 1942, some federal agents planted a dictaphone listening device in a partition wall separating two rooms so they could listen to conversations in the next room.[31] In *On Lee v. United States,* decided in 1952, an undercover agent wore a concealed microphone into a Chinese laundry to investigate narcotics violations, while another agent, stationed outside, listened in.[32] But since there had been no physical trespass in either case and nothing physical was taken, the court felt the government had done nothing wrong. The only time the court felt government agents went too far was in several later cases where government agents violated the individual's physical space, such as in the 1961 *Silverman v. United States* case. In this case, the agents put a spike mike in the wall of a row house so that it tapped into a heating duct; they could then listen to conversations throughout the house.[33]

Meanwhile, government snooping grew with the "red scare" of the 1950s, which led the government to look into private lives in the name of protecting the national security. In the process the government targeted many people who were suspected because they were simply different, such as homosexuals, or associated with other people or groups considered to be security threats. And if privacy rights got trampled in the process, well, that was the price for national security—an antiprivacy attitude that continued for much of the 1950s until the McCarthy witch-hunt was discredited. Meanwhile, as technology improved, so did the ability of government agents to snoop.

Only in the late 1960s did the tide begin to turn to benefit privacy advocates. One reason was the growing recognition that new technologies required new privacy protections. Also, the protest movement of the times became more vocal in criticizing the government. A sign of the times was the landmark *Katz v. United States* case in 1967. It began when Charles Katz was arrested in a Los Angeles telephone booth. He had thought he could use it to secretly engage in illegal bookmaking activities, but, unknown to him, federal agents had attached an electronic listening device outside the booth and recorded his conversations. Katz fought back and the Supreme Court agreed that even though the agents hadn't invaded his physical property, they had invaded his privacy, because he had a reasonable expectation of privacy in that space because the Fourth Amendment "protects people, not places."[34]

Though the debate has continued over what is a "reasonable"

expectation of privacy and what is a search or seizure, the Katz case helped to redefine the meaning of personal privacy in a high-tech age.

The Early Development of Other Types of Privacy Rights

Besides these first battles against the growing power of the media and the government, other sorts of privacy concerns began to surface by the middle of the twentieth century. One was the danger from the free speech of others in First Amendment cases—and not only involving the media, but private individuals and organizations. The other was in the controversy over fundamental rights in Fourteenth Amendment cases, which were over how much freedom of choice an individual really had without the government and society saying no, such as in cases of abortion, the right to die, and freedom to pursue an unconventional life-style or religion.

The Beginnings of the Privacy Right to Making Fundamental Decisions

The battle for letting the individual make fundamental personal decisions, not the government, began in the field of education. Parents, community groups, and private schools argued that individual parents should have a right to privacy in deciding how their children should be educated. Generally the higher courts agreed that they should, sometimes basing their decision on grounds of separation of church and state, when parochial schools or religious groups wanted to educate their children in their own way.

For example, in 1923, in *Meyer v. Nebraska,*[35] the Supreme Court threw out a state law prohibiting any school from teaching any modern language other than English. The furor began when Meyer, a teacher at the Zion Parochial School in Nebraska, was convicted of teaching German to a ten-year-old child.[36] When he protested, the court agreed he should be free to teach this. Though the state might be able to set up its own system and standards of education to improve the quality of its citizens "physically, mentally, and morally," the individual still had "certain fundamental rights" or "liberty" protections that must be respected, as provided by the Fourth Amendment, including: "the right . . . to contract, to engage in any of the common occupations of life, to acquire useful knowledge, to marry, establish a home and bring up children, to worship God according to the dictates of his own conscience. . . ."[37]

For similar reasons, in Oregon two years later, in *Pierce v. Society of the Sisters,* the Supreme Court threw out a state law that required children to attend public rather than parochial elementary schools. Both a Catholic school and a private military academy challenged this law, since it would prevent them from teaching children any longer, and once again the Supreme Court agreed that parents had a right to educational privacy—the right to direct the "destiny" of their own child.[38] Likewise, other education cases that followed soon after gave the Amish, Mennonites, and other religious groups the right to educate their children in their own way, while reaffirming the right to freedom of religion under the First Amendment.

Thus, these early cases established the principles of making personal decisions as a fundamental privacy right, though today these rights are being increasingly challenged again. This has occurred because new technological developments since the 1960s and 1970s like the birth control pill and IUD, accompanied by more liberal social attitudes, have made so many more personal decisions possible, in areas like contraception, abortion, and euthanasia. But now more conservative voices are questioning whether these technological breakthroughs should be used to satisfy personal desires, as will be discussed in Chapter 9.

The Beginnings of the Free Speech Privacy Right

As the free speech versus privacy right battle heated up in the 1920s, many cases involved the press, continuing the battle against the media that had begun in the late 1800s. However, while these early cases involved using outrageous and surreptitious means to get information or using pictures without consent for commercial purposes, starting around the mid-1960s cases involved the ability of the press to publish information, which revealed private and often embarrassing information, even if truthful or appropriately gathered. These battles will be discussed in the next chapter highlighting the battles from the 1960s to the present time.

The other kind of free speech/privacy battle that developed in the late 1930s and early 1940s occurred when individuals with something to say encountered those who didn't want to hear it. In a simpler America, people would work out such conflicts in the community. But in a more complex urban society, which threw people from different backgrounds together, at the same time that increasingly aggressive marketers, like door-to-door salesman, were seeking new customers, these rights came into sharper conflict. So without cohesive local communities in which to work out these problems, people increasingly went to court, and judges tried to develop guidelines for settling these conflicting rights.

For example, in 1939, the *Schneider v. State* door-to-door solicitation case ended up in the Supreme Court.[39] In this popularly known "Handbill Case," a group of Jehovah's Witnesses had been canvassing door-to-door with handbills about their group. When the city objected and passed an antileafleting ordinance to prevent them from doing this, the Witnesses went to court. And eventually, the court supported them, ruling that cities couldn't prevent groups from engaging in political or religious speech, which included door-to-door canvassing. Similarly, in the 1943 *Martin v. City of Struthers* case,[40] the court backed the Witnesses, too.

Thus, initially, the door-to-door solicitors' right to free speech overcame the homeowner's right to be left alone, even if an unwilling listener. The ideal of religious freedom helped sway the court to favor the solicitors. Yet, homeowners increasingly objected to such incursions, much like many people are protesting the telemarketers of today. So gradually, the tide turned, because as Justice Frankfurter commented in a dissent in the *Martin* case, there's a "lack of privacy and the hazards to peace of mind and body caused by people living not in individual houses but crowded together in large human beehives."[41]

Finally, in 1951, the growing pressure for more privacy scored a win for the homeowner in the case of *Breard v. City of Alexandria*. Breard had been convicted in Alexandria, Louisiana, for selling subscriptions door-to-door for some of the popular magazines of the day, such as the *Saturday Evening Post* and *Ladies' Home Journal*. Supposedly, "solicitors, peddlers, hawkers, itinerant merchants or transient vendors" weren't allowed to solicit at private homes unless invited in by the owner or occupant. But Breard appealed his conviction, arguing that the law wasn't constitutional. The Supreme Court decided for the first time that the homeowner's right to privacy did limit the salesperson's right to free speech, and it was the first time that the privacy right outweighed the First Amendment—a big win for the forces of privacy.[42]

Around this time, too, another privacy versus free speech right that was recognized was the right of a captive audience to be left alone and not have to hear or see something they didn't want to hear or see. It was an increasingly necessary right, since as cities grew there were more and more places where people gathered, like on streetcars or on the street, where they might encounter intrusions on their peace and quiet.

For example, in the 1930s *Packer Corporation v. Utah* case, the Packer Corporation objected to a Utah law which prohibited companies from advertising cigarettes and other tobacco products on billboards, street car signs, and placards. But the Supreme Court felt Utah was justified in passing this law, since these ads intruded on the privacy rights of the unwilling observer. As Justice Brandeis, who had coauthored the famous privacy article years before observed: "The radio can be turned off, but not so the billboard or street car placard."[43]

Likewise, in the 1949, *Kovacs v. Cooper* case, the Supreme Court agreed that Trenton, New Jersey could prevent unwilling listeners from being disturbed by "loud and raucus" music. These unwilling listeners were those who happened to be on the street when Kovacs drove by in a truck broadcasting music and his opinions on a local labor dispute. The city said he couldn't do this, because it had passed an ordinance prohibiting loud sound trucks and loudspeakers. And in the court's view, the city was quite justified in prohibiting them, since a passerby could turn down an offered pamphlet. By contrast, an unwilling listener was stuck and had to listen.[44]

But what about the free speech rights of the person with the message? Over the years, this question became subject to much dispute, and those with something to say, from politicians to homeless beggars, have used this free speech argument.

Thus, while there was a growing recognition that people had a privacy right to be let alone that might sometimes be stronger than free speech rights if people were annoyed by the message, this wasn't always the case. Instead, the battle see-sawed back and forth, and sometimes the public just had to tough it out. For example, in the 1950s *Public Utilities Commission v. Pollak* case from Washington, DC, the court decided that the passengers on a street railway had to listen to the music and radio programs broadcast on the railway, since they were on a public conveyance.[45] But in other cases, the people who wanted to be left alone won out—though in the tumultuous 1960s, the free speech position gained more support. And now it seems the pendulum is swinging the other way to support the demand for more privacy, given the climate of fear of crime and personal confrontation on city streets.

Summing Up—The State of Privacy from the 1850s to the 1950s

In sum, from the 1850s through the 1950s, a new concern with the right to privacy emerged, because in an increasingly complex, urbanized, multicultural society, there were more and more ways in which one's privacy might be invaded by others—from the government to the press and advertisers to other citizens. At the same time, there were fewer informal community ways to deal with these problems. Thus, in this context, various rights began to battle it out—privacy in the one corner versus free speech and freedom of religion in another. Soon claims to other rights, such as the right of free association and the right against unwarranted searches and seizures, joined the fray.

This 100-year period was thus a time when these privacy issues first surfaced, and in their classic article, Warren and Brandeis first tried to define this right and assess the state of privacy, or the lack of it, at the time, particularly in relationship to an increasingly prying press. When they first thought about it, they viewed the invasion of privacy in one way, as a tort or legal wrong which one party did to another. Then, over the following decades, the privacy issue began to grow like a branching tree or vine, as new categories of privacy developed in response to changing conditions, which resulted in new technologies, new social circumstances, and new political influences, leading to new types of invasions, resulting in new laws to regulate privacy and new battles to work out conflicting rights.

The new technologies and social turmoil of the 1960s to 1990s contributed to the growing intensity of this battle. Since then, this battle has become even more intense because of even more dramatic technological and social changes creating new battlegrounds and affecting the outcome of different battles.

Notes

1. Richard F. Hixson, *Privacy in a Public Society* (New York: Oxford University Press, 1987), 27.

2. Frank L. Mott, *American Journalism: A History 1690–1960*, 3rd ed (1962), cited in Ken Gormley, "100 Years of Privacy," *Wisconsin Law Review*, (1992): 1350–1351.
3. Hixson, 28.
4. Ibid., 27–28.
5. Mott, 440, cited in Gormley, 1351.
6. E.L. Godkin, "The Right of the Citizen, IV: To His Own Reputation," *Scribner's Magazine* (July 1890): 67, cited in Hixson, 29.
7. Gormley, 1353.
8. Nicholas Hiley, "The Candid Camera of the Edwardian Tabloids," *History Today*, 43 (August 1993): 16–23.
9. 40 Ch. D. 345 (Ch. 1888), cited in Gormley, 1347.
10. *New York Times*, 15, 18, 21 June 1890, cited in Gormley, 1346.
11. Mill, "Autobiography," in *The Essential Works of John Stuart Mill* (Bantam Matrix, 1961 ed.), 137, cited in Darien A. McWhirter and Jon D. Bible, *Privacy as a Constitutional Right* (New York: Quorum Books, 1992), 52.
12. Samuel D. Warren and Louis D. Brandeis, "The Right to Privacy," *Harvard Law Review*, (1890): 193.
13. Warren and Brandeis, 196, cited in Gormley, 1348.
14. Ibid., 196, cited in Gormley, 1348.
15. Ibid., 20, 198, 205, cited in Gormley, 1346.
16. Gormley, 1340.
17. *Mackenzie v. Soden Mineral Springs Co.* 18 N.Y.S 240 (N.Y. Sup. Ct. 1891), cited in Gormley, 1353, footnote.
18. *Marks v. Jaffa*, 26 N.Y. Sup. Ct. 908 (1893), cited by Gormley, 1353.
19. *Pavesich v. New England Life Insurance Company*, 50 S.E. 68 (Ga. 1905), cited in Gormley, 1353–54.
20. Gormley, 1355.
21. *Roberson v. Rochester Folding Box Company*, 64 N.E. 442 (N.Y. 1902), cited in Gormley, 1354–55.
22. Gormley, 1357.
23. Ibid., 1355.
24. Ibid., 1358.
25. *Frank v. Maryland*, 359 U.S. 360, 378–79 (1959), cited in Gormley, 1358.
26. R.I. Rec., I, 168–69 (1647), quoted in David H. Flaherty, *Privacy in Colonial New England* (Charlottesville: University of Virginia, 1972), 86.
27. Gormley, 1359.
28. *Olmstead v. United States*, 277 U.S. 438 (1928), cited in Gormley, 1360.
29. *Olmstead*, 466, cited in Gormley, 1360.
30. Gormley, 1361, quoting *Olmstead*, 478–79.
31. *Goldman v. United States*, 316 U.S. 129 (1942), 134–35, cited in Gormley, 1365.
32. *Lee v. United States*, 343 U.S. 747 (1952), cited in Gormley, 1365.
33. *Silverman v. United States*, 365 U.S. 505 (1961), cited in Gormley, 1365.

34. *Katz v. United States,* 389 U.S. 347 (1967), p. 351, cited in Gormley, 1366.
35. *Meyer v. Nebraska,* 262 U.S. 390 (1923), cited in Hixson, 72.
36. McWhirter and Bible, 94.
37. *Meyer v. Nebraska,* p. 399, cited in McWhirter and Bible, 95.
38. *Pierce v. Society of the Sisters,* 268 U.S. 510 (1925), cited in Hixson, 72.
39. *Schneider v. State,* 308 U.S. 147 (1939), cited in Gormley, 1377.
40. *Martin v. City of Struthers,* 319 U.S. 141 (1943), cited in Gormley, 1377.
41. *Martin,* 152–53, cited in Gormley, 1378.
42. *Breard v. City of Alexandria,* 341 U.S. 622 (1951), cited in Gormley, 1378–79.
43. *Packer Corporation v. Utah,* 285 U.S. 105 (1932), cited in Gormley, 1379.
44. *Kovacs v. Cooper,* 336 U.S. 77 (1949), pp. 82–83, 86–87, cited in Gormley, 1380.
45. *Public Utilities Commission v. Pollak,* 343 U.S. 45 (1952), 463–64, cited in Gormley, 1381–82.

Chapter 4

The Spreading Privacy Battle in a Postindustrial World

From the 1960s to the 1990s

In the 1960s the privacy battle became even more intense. As more people experienced their privacy being invaded, more fought back by taking their cases to court. There were many reasons for this trend. First, the mid-1960s were characterized by a growing antiestablishment political consciousness and a do-your-own-thing philosophy, reflected in the counterculture and protest movements that swept the country. Many people were more vocal in expressing their individuality. They wanted to be let alone by the establishment and do in private or otherwise what they wanted to do, which was often illegal or unacceptable to the establishment (most notably drugs and experiments with sex).

Second, there was an explosion in surveillance technology which brought more threats to privacy. This threat came not only from government and the media, but from an increasingly sophisticated marketing industry looking for more customers, from insurance companies seeking to detect fraud, from employers wanting to know more about their employees, and others.

Third, as traditional institutions—like the family, religion, and the educational system—increasingly came under attack and began breaking down, so the traditional social controls and relationships that keep people connected with and accountable to one another became weaker. Thus, there was an increasing sense of alienation, anonymity, and fear throughout the United States. The result was a growing public demand to keep records or find out about others, so society could monitor behavior which, increasingly, traditional community connections and personal relationships no longer did.

Thus, given all these social and technological changes from the 1960s to the 1990s, it's no wonder the battle for privacy heated up, and there was a growing struggle in more and more areas of life to define privacy rights—a legacy that has contributed to the battle today. These included incursions by the media and marketeers, government surveillance, and making private decisions in one's private life. In addition, many states now weighed in with their own versions of extra privacy protections.

The Battle over Making Fundamental Personal Decisions

Prior to the 1960s, little thought was given to one's privacy rights in making personal decisions. Perhaps this is because there were shared understandings about generally acceptable behavior, and people largely conformed with these ideals. There was still a sense of the United States being a unified, united society with shared ideals. For example, there was a sense of pulling together in the World War II years and its aftermath; and the 1950s were thought of as a decade of conformity. Family life was idealized in television programs like *Life with Father* and *Lassie*, although there was an undercurrent of fear that this ideal might be disturbed, reflected in the concern about Communism and the Red Scare launched by McCarthy in the 1950s. Also, there were the beginnings of rebellion against this veneer of conformity in movements like the Beatniks and the "rock" fans attracted to the increasingly popular rock and roll.

Then, in the mid-1960s, all this unity and conformity became open to question. Politically, it was challenged by a growing civil rights movement, and by a rising protest against the Vietnam War. Simultaneously, there were social challenges, such as when people began living together in new ways, taken for granted now, but generating a storm of controversy then.

For example, unmarried heterosexual couples started living together; gays in a few parts of the country started coming out of the closet and the gay liberation movement began; and small groups of middle-class people around the country opted to drop out of the mainstream, some moving to the country, others adopting a newly popular drugs, love, and peace life-style. In response, a rising tide of anger from the mainstream community greeted these new life-style decisions, while those making the choices wanted the freedom to decide freely and be left alone in choosing a "do your own thing" life-style. Or as popular 1960s guru Timothy Leary, the ex-Harvard professor who traded academia for drugs and divine inspiration, put it, "Tune in, turn on, drop out."

At the same time, new technologies made available many new choices about matters of life and death. As a result, the medical arena became a new battleground for debates about privacy as each new medical discovery opened up new areas of choice. But should people be able to choose, or was this human hubris, taking over decisions better left to God and natural processes? Such battles erupted as the pill preventing contraception was developed, as techniques of abortion became safer, and as new medical technologies enabled doctors to extend the life of severely injured and ill people. So now that people had new powers over beginning and extending life, should they choose to use them? When did people have the private right to choose life or death, and when not? When should the community have the right to prevail in making such choices?

Generally, in most of these cases as new areas of choice became possible and people started exercising these choices, the more conservative forces in the local community or in the states reacted in anger or fear. They sought to impose restrictions on these choices, such as a woman's right to choose an abortion, or a person's right to choose to terminate his or her own life. Then, in response, those whose rights were restricted fought back in the courts. While the courts often supported the right to choose, in other cases they did not—or they added many qualifications and exceptions. So this led to additional court battles further qualifying and defining these rights, as in the case of contraception, abortion, right to die, and privacy in the bedroom. Typically, these were extremely emotional and bruising battles, because what was at stake were fundamental questions about morality and values. The big question posed was what was an appropriate area for free private choice. The conservatives and fundamentalists lined up on one side of the battle, many claiming a God-given right to regulate; while civil libertarians grouped together on the other side, claiming the individual should be free to choose in this very personal area. It was like a classic struggle between good and evil. But what was good and what was evil? Each side had different ideas about what was right and what was wrong.

The First Battles for Fundamental Privacy— The Contraception and Abortion Struggles of the 1960s and Early 1970s

In the contraception area, the big battle was over giving out birth control information, once the pill came into popular use in the early 1960s. Eventually, the battle ended up in the Supreme Court, in the *Griswold v. Connecticut* case, decided in 1965. In this case, Connecticut had had an eighty-year-old law on the books that forbade the dissemination of birth control information, including the distribution of contraceptives.[1] But even so, the Planned Parenthood League of Connecticut made this information available, and in time, the organization's executive director and medical director were convicted for giving married couples information on preventing conception and prescribing a contraceptive for the wives to use. It was a test case, designed to challenge this usually unenforced state law still on the books, and it was triggered by the spirit of protest of the early 1960s.

The Court decision was an extremely important one in establishing a fundamental right to make these kinds of personal choices regarding private areas of one's life. As Justice William O. Douglas suggested, these rights were in fact implied by the Bill of Rights. Though they were not directly spelled out, they could be found in the "penumbra" or shadow of certain rights, such as those described in the First, Third, Fourth, Fifth, and Ninth Amendments.[2] So for the first time, the Court suggested there was an implied right to privacy in the Constitution.

This decision was a big turning point, since it provided the foundation for subsequent court decisions, which extended this privacy right to other areas of personal decision making, though conservatives and fundamentalist Christians strongly objected. The famous *Roe v. Wade* case of 1973[3] for the first time established a woman's right to abortion, and it used privacy grounds to do this. At the time, almost all states had restrictive abortion laws. Then, a woman, using the pseudonym Jane Roe, challenged the Texas law that made it a crime to abort a fetus or attempt an abortion unless it was necessary to save the mother's life. Roe claimed the Texas law was unfair on a number of grounds, including a mother's right to privacy under the First, Fourth, Fifth, Ninth, and Fourteenth Amendments, as noted in *Griswold.* And the court agreed that a woman did have this right, though it was not absolute. It could be subjected to the interest of the state in regulating such things as public health and medical standards, and protecting potential life.[4] Thus, in one decision, the Supreme Court ruled unconstitutional the laws of Texas and virtually every other state on privacy grounds based on the notion of due process and personal liberty found in the Fourteenth Amendment.

These two decisions opened up something of a Pandora's Box as more and more groups and individuals sought to apply these ideas about the fundamental right to privacy to other areas of personal choice. This occurred as these choices became possible due to new medical technologies and changing life-styles in the 1970s and 1980s.

Meanwhile, the contraception–abortion area itself became something of a political football, as more conservative and fundamentalist groups fought back in the late 1970s and 1980s. In turn, the contradictory court decisions reflected society's uncertainty about what to do. While some court decisions expanded a woman's privacy rights, others restricted it. For example, in a couple of cases, the Supreme Court struck down state laws requiring a woman to get permission from a husband, or parent if unmarried (such as in *Planned Parenthood v. Danforth* (1976), which struck down a Missouri law,[5] and *Bellotti v. Baird* in 443 U.S. 622 (1979), which struck down a Massachusetts law.[6] But in other cases, like *H.L. v. Matheson,* decided in 1981, the Court required notification under certain circumstances, for example, requiring doctors to notify the parents of dependent minors if possible.[7] Also, in a noted 1983 Ohio abortion clinic case and a 1986 Pennsylvania case over a law requiring a doctor to obtain a woman's informed consent, the Court threw out some regulations they considered unnecessary attempts to prevent abortions.[8] But then, in the famous 1989 *Webster* case[9] that started in Missouri, the Court agreed that the state had the right to forbid the use of public employees and facilities for nontherapeutic abortions and to restrict a physician from performing an abortion after twenty weeks. Subsequently, this ruling led many states to pass strict antiabortion laws, many of which are now being tested in the courts.

The Question of Life and Death? Is There a Private Right to Refuse Treatment or Die?

The questions about fundamental privacy rights raised by the contraception and abortion debates similarly began to be raised in other areas. Doctors could now prolong life for many types of patients who might have previously died—premature infants, patients severely crippled or brain damaged from accidents and illnesses, and patients in the last painful stages of terminal illnesses.

As a result, there was a new privacy issue to deal with. Did the patients or their parents or relatives, if the patients couldn't decide themselves, have a privacy right to choose to terminate treatment resulting in their death? Today, this question has become one of whether the individual has the right to actively choose suicide and gain the assistance of a physician in doing so. Dr. Jack Kevorkian is currently battling this issue in the media and the courts.

Initially, this issue became part of the battle for personal privacy in the 1980s, drawing on the ideas about privacy rights raised in the contraception and abortion cases. The first salvos were fired in California in 1984 and 1986, probably because California has among the strongest, if not the strongest, privacy protections in its state constitution, added in 1972.[10] One case involved an elderly man attached to a respirator who wanted to turn it off to end his suffering;[11] the other, the more well-known *Bouvia* case, which became a media cause célèbre, involved a woman suffering from cerebral palsy and quadriplegia, who wanted her feeding tubes removed.[12] She felt she had nothing more to live for and argued through her attorney and the press that she wanted to end it all. In both cases, the courts decided that yes, a person does have the right to refuse medical treatment, as part of a constitutionally guaranteed right of privacy. Though in an ironic footnote, after all the media publicity, Bouvia decided that she wanted to live.

But what if the individual was comatose or otherwise incompetent? Even in such cases, some courts began to recognize the right of an individual or a guardian acting on his or her behalf to terminate treatment. For example, this happened in the famous *Quinlan* case in New Jersey in the mid-1970s. After a car accident, Karen Quinlan was left brain dead and in a coma, from which doctors said she would never recover. But even so, the doctors didn't want to turn off the respirator and feeding tubes, afraid they might be accused of murder. However, recognizing the inevitable, Quinlan's parents fought for several years for the right to turn it off. Finally, in 1976, the New Jersey Supreme Court agreed, drawing on the decision handed down in the Roe abortion case. As the court explained, just as the right of privacy entitled a woman to make her own decision about abortion, it should be "broad enough to encompass a patient's decision to decline medical treatment under certain circumstances."[13]

Later, in the highly publicized *Cruzan* case, in which Nancy Cruzan was left in a persistent vegetative state due to an auto accident, the Supreme Court reaffirmed this "right to die," although since Cruzan was unconscious, the Court wouldn't let the doctors remove the respirator. There was, the Court said, no clear and convincing evidence of what Cruzan would have wanted.[14] Presumably, if she had been able to show she wanted this, she could have exercised this right. A few years later, when friends and relatives came forward with more convincing evidence showing her wishes, the Court finally agreed. Her parents could turn off the device without fear of legal consequences, and did so.

Privacy and Personal Choice in Sex and Porn

Still another area regarding fundamental personal privacy rights opened up in the 1960s; this had to do with sexual expression and the right to read and view pornographic books and movies.* This occurred because here too new life-styles were in conflict with the old, and the desire for more personal freedom in both areas came into conflict with traditional prohibitions and taboos. Back in the more repressive 1940s and 1950s, alternate life-styles and "vices" were commonly kept underground, so it is hard to imagine anyone trying to argue strongly for a right to practice taboo forms of sex or read forbidden literature in private. After all, these were the days of extensive censorship in Hollywood; there was

*Just what is pornography? The distinction between this and erotica is often unclear, as is the distinction between what is merely pornographic and what is obscene—sometimes a matter of long legal debate. Basically, the distinction is that pornography is material that shows sexually explicit activity and is designed to arouse sexual excitement, while erotica is such material which is considered to be literature or art. But, as many professionals in the sexology field say, what one person considers to be pornography (because he or she finds the material distasteful), another person would consider to be erotica.

no nudity in films; homosexuality was still very much in the closet; people didn't publicly acknowledge experiments with alternate forms of sexuality like S&M; and women were either good or bad, with the good ones carefully shielded from casual sex and the seamy side of life.

But in the 1960s, along with the free speech movement came the free love and sex movements, soon followed by the first wave of gays coming out of the closet, starting with the 1969 Stonewall march in New York City. Then, in response to establishment efforts to strike back with arrests or new restrictive laws, some individuals went to court, arguing for their freedom of choice, their privacy right, to engage in those activities. It was a scenario repeated again and again for various types of sexual conduct and choices in reading sexual literature to which the establishment objected. While in many cases the battle led to new privacy rights, in other cases, these rights were struck down.

For example, once easy-to-use contraceptives like the pill came into popular use and family planning clinics made these items more available, single people could live a much freer, more active sexual life-style. With greater access to protection, they had less fear of pregnancy, a fear that had kept sexual activity down. Then, as a natural outgrowth of this, many single couples started living together, whereas before, this wasn't commonly done. At the same time, others began experimenting with alternate forms of living together—communes, collectives, small groups of unrelated adults who decided that they were a "family."

In many communities, the more traditionally minded were appalled, and they tried to hold back the new ways, resulting in more court cases. But eventually two major Supreme Court decisions supported the individual's right to choice. For example, in the 1972 *Eisenstadt v. Baird* case, the Court decided that single people as well as married people had a right to obtain contraceptives,[15] and in the 1977 *Moore v. City of East Cleveland* case,[16] the Court agreed that people had a right to live with relatives who were not part of the nuclear family. Even though the majority of the population might still find such alternative life-style choices distasteful, a minority of people could now live in this way.

Meanwhile, in a number of states, people challenged and won various rights to sexual freedom. For example, in the 1970s, many states had fornication and sodomy or fellatio statutes on the books, which made sex outside of marriage or sex involving anal or oral intercourse illegal. But now, when these laws were challenged on privacy grounds, most of the sexual barriers came down. For instance, in one 1977 New Jersey case, two men were found guilty of fornication after they disputed rape charges by claiming that the two women had had sex with them in exchange for marijuana. After they challenged this law and their conviction based on it, the New Jersey Supreme Court agreed this fornication statute was unconstitutional, since it infringed on their right of privacy protected by the U.S. Constitution. After all, the Court reasoned, if people's right of privacy permitted them to obtain contraceptives, they should also have the right to have sex.[17]

But did this right to privacy also include homosexuals? A few states such as New York and Pennsylvania in 1980, seemed to think so, and threw out all sodomy laws applying to anyone.[18] But when a case from Georgia, *Bowers v. Hardwick,* dealing with sodomy between homosexuals made it to the Supreme Court in 1986, the Court didn't support this right for homosexuals. At the time, gays had not gained the visibility and political power they have today and the traditional hostility toward homosexuality was much more overt. Presumably, this prevailing social attitude helped to shape the court's decision. Though people could do in private what was becoming more acceptable throughout society, the Court wasn't ready to extend the right to engage in private activities to include activities found less acceptable. Or as the Court put it, those cases involving "family, marriage or procreation" could not be used to find a "fundamental right to engage in homosexual sodomy."[19]

But when it came to porn, the courts were more receptive to personal privacy, in part because pornography raised freedom of speech issues. The major decision here came in 1969 with the landmark *Stanley v. Georgia* case, in which the Supreme Court struck down a Georgia law that prohibited people from possessing pornography at home.[20] Though the state could still ban the sale of obscene material, it could not punish people for simply viewing it in their privacy of their home.

Thus, step-by-step, as the winds of change spread through the United States beginning in the 1960s, and attitudes became more tolerant to alternate life-styles and sexual expression, new privacy rights were recognized to permit people to be free in engaging in these activities. Yet, popular attitudes and court decisions still held back some groups, notably homosexuals, since heterosexuals and the courts were not quite ready to recognize their rights. It wasn't until the 1990s, with the election of Bill Clinton to the U.S. presidency in 1992, and the furor over gays in the military, that there was a new recognition of gay rights, including the right of privacy—at least officially. Still, conservatives appalled by homosexuals and by liberal attitudes toward sexuality have fought on, and the tide may be turning again.

The Battle over Privacy Protections from Government and Police Surveillance

Meanwhile, as one kind of battle occurred over personal privacy rights and decision making, another intensified over government and police surveillance, in response to the growing threat of more sophisticated snooping devices, which included such innovations as parabolic microphones, transmitters the size of cigarette packs, induction-coil devices, and miniature television transmitters. Though the Red Scare of the 1950s was over, the government and police had a dazzling array of equipment to use in monitoring, developed during the height of the Cold War in the forties and fifties. They now used this equipment to monitor what many ordinary citizens were doing since there was a growing fear of many of the new developments—most notably the growing antiwar, civil rights, and other protest movements of the 1960s and early 1970s; the spreading use of illegal drugs; and the rise in crime—capitalizing on the growing public fear of many of these new developments. In turn, new state laws helped to support these government and police crackdowns; for example, by creating broad exceptions for police eavesdropping, as well as for citizens who agreed to have their own phones tapped, say, to aid in a police investigation.[21] Meanwhile, in the private sector, a growing army of private eyes were being employed to gather information for companies and individuals who wished to check up on business partners, employees, errant spouses, and other family members.

Thus, in the 1960s, there was an explosion of national concern over gaining control over this growing ability of the government and private investigators to snoop, much like today's effort to protect privacy in the face of another explosion of new technologies. For example, in the early to mid-1960s, much like today's infohighway, Clipper Chip, and encryption debates, there were hearings over new legislation to ban private wiretaps and limit government taps to only those authorized by court orders. Reams of articles and editorials were written by noted scholars and journalists, including Harvard law professor Arthur Miller, whose *The Assault on Privacy: Computers, Data Banks, and Dossiers,* was published in 1971.[22] The title sounds like it could be written today.

One result of all this concern was that the courts and legislators did act to increase privacy protections in some areas. In other cases, though, particularly where individual drug use or sale was suspected, individual privacy rights were less respected. Then, in the late 1980s, as drugs and alcohol on the job became of increased concern, the government cracked down on government employees, too.

Fighting the Government and Police in the Courts

The first big breakthrough in gaining privacy protection in the courts was the famous *Katz v. United States* case, decided in 1967. In this case, as may be recalled from Chapter 3, Charles Katz, a California bookmaker, had been using a telephone booth in Los Angeles to run his bookmaking business, calling contacts in Boston and Miami. Tipped off to what he was doing, the federal authorities put an electronic listening device outside the booth, and listened in, recording hundreds of hours of conversation, and arrested him based on this information. But when Katz challenged the constitutionality of their listening in and took his case all the way to the Supreme Court, the court decided that the government couldn't listen. Even though the agents hadn't engaged in a physical search or seized any physical property, they still had violated his privacy under the Fourth Amendment, because he had a reasonable expectation of privacy in the phone booth.[23]

Once phone booths were declared off limits, the conflict turned to making other areas of life safe from government snooping with the new electronic devices, with most of these cases in the state and federal courts decided in the late 1960s and 1970s. For example, in a 1967 case from New York, which involved an investigation into a man believed to be accepting bribes for liquor licenses, *Berger v. New York,* the Court ruled against placing bugging devices in an office.[24]

Later, as the war against drugs heated up in the 1980s, the right of privacy got further battered, as the courts gave the government and police more leeway in searching for illegal substances, though they might not be so free in doing other kinds of searches. For example, in a 1983 airport search with a dog, *United States v. Place,* the Supreme Court found it was fine to use a dog to sniff a passenger's luggage for cocaine,[25] and in 1988, in the well-known *California v. Greenwood* case, the Court said it was fine to search someone's garbage—in this case for narcotics—

because a person no longer had a reasonable expectation of privacy in discarded garbage.[26]

At the same time, the police and federal agents gained additional powers to search in a number of cases in which they flew over private property or used high-powered photographic equipment to take pictures to show evidence of illegally grown marijuana and other drugs. For example, in one of the first of these cases in 1984, *Oliver v. United States*, the Supreme Court said it was fine that narcotics agents walked around a gate marked with "No Trespassing" signs and found a field of marijuana about a mile from the defendant's home. This was acceptable because the marijuana was growing outside the immediate vicinity of his home.[27]

In short, while the struggle in the courts for privacy from government intrusion resulted in some wins, making some places such as private phones, homes, and offices safe from unwarranted intrusion, in other areas, the government and police were increasingly free to search, such as in luggage in airports, automobiles, and open fields, particularly if they suspected illegal drugs. In the schools students were increasingly subject to searches.

The Move to Legislate New Privacy Rights

While all these skirmishes were going on in the courts, this growing concern with privacy also led to the first comprehensive efforts to create some federal legislation to protect privacy. Also, it led many states to pass laws or add privacy provisions to their constitutions, such as Hawaii in 1968; Illinois in 1970; Montana, Alaska, and California in 1972; South Carolina and Louisiana in 1974; and Florida in 1980.[28] And since then other states have followed suit, amending their constitutions or passing protective privacy laws, so that now, about half or more of the states have special privacy protections.

Meanwhile, the federal government took its own steps to protect personal privacy when government agencies and records were involved. This occurred when Congress passed the first national privacy protection statute—the Privacy Act of 1974. It was designed to protect privacy by regulating the government's use, exchange, and dissemination of records about the individual. In addition, the Act created a Privacy Protection Study Commission to monitor and report on the effectiveness of the Act.[29] In hindsight, this Commission had little effect, and in the 1990s, there have been efforts to strengthen it and turn it into a real advocate for privacy. Still, at the time, it was a bold first step by a government that had previously made no organized efforts to protect privacy.

In particular, the Act created a set of rules and regulations to govern the way information and the technology for managing information could be used by the federal government and its agencies. For example, the Act outlined specific procedures and guidelines agencies had to follow in keeping records, based generally on a "need to know" policy, in which the agencies were only supposed to keep "relevant and necessary" records to accomplish the tasks of that agency. Also, the Act required records to be kept with "the highest degree of practical accuracy, timeliness, and completeness possible," and the agencies had to establish internal procedures to keep their records confidential and secure. Then, too, there were detailed guidelines for how and when government agencies might exchange information with one another. There were rules about when an individual could look at records about him- or herself and correct them if wrong or incomplete, as well as civil remedies for violations. These latter ranged from getting a court to order the agency to correct its records or keep them closed to getting damages and legal costs.[30]

Yet, for all its good intentions, the act was quite limited, in that it just covered government records. It did not apply to any of the private collections of personal records that were similarly growing rapidly as the new technologies made data gathering easier and easier. That's why in one 1976 Supreme Court case, *U.S. v. Miller*, a man trying to keep his bank records out of court in a government prosecution, suffered a stinging rebuke. The bank produced his bank records in response to a government subpoena without telling him, and though Miller objected, the court refused to suppress his records. It reasoned that bank customers voluntarily disclose this information in order to use the bank's services. Thus, they don't have a reasonable expectation of privacy in their records, and they assume the risk the bank might release their records to the government.[31]

Needless to say, this decision appalled privacy advocates. They felt the Court simply didn't get it; it didn't understand that the individual should reasonably expect these records to be private. Thus, after protests by privacy advocates, including professional, business, and civil liberties groups, in 1978 Congress passed a follow-up act which added additional protections for personal financial records kept by private organizations not covered by the original act. Called the Right to Financial Privacy Act of 1978, this new act provided guidelines for the records kept by banks, insurance companies, and credit companies.[32]

In particular, it specified when these private organizations could release information to the government, and how the government should handle transferring financial information between agencies. For example, now the banks couldn't give out personal information to the government unless the customer agreed, the government had a valid subpoena or search record, or there were special circumstances, such as a legitimate law enforcement inquiry and the customer was notified. In addition, the act required the government to notify the customer that it was requesting bank records and why, so the individual might challenge the legitimacy of this request. The act also specified that financial records could only be transferred between agencies if the agency seeking the records had a legitimate law enforcement need for them and notified the individual. And should the government violate any of these provisions, the individual could seek civil penalties.[33]

Yet, while these laws were passed, in practice the protections were quite weak, and government agencies, particularly those in law enforcement, continued to make inroads against privacy in accessing records, especially in the war against drugs. In fact, these government efforts eventually led to the creation of an even more powerful database for gathering financial records in the Treasury Department—the Financial Crimes Enforcement Network (FinCEN), created in 1990.[34]

The Losing Privacy Fight against the Media and Free Speech

There were some significant gains in privacy rights in some areas, such as in making fundamental personal decisions and in establishing certain zones of limited protection from government snooping (like private phones and financial records). In the fight against privacy invasions by the media and individuals claiming free speech rights, however, the results were more uncertain. In general, whenever the conflicting right to privacy versus a free press was tested, as will be discussed in Chapter 8, much of the time the press, or the media in general, won, on the grounds that a free press was essential to a free society. But in the case of free speech, the courts were more likely to weigh each conflict on a case by case basis, deciding whether the one party should be free to express itself or the other had the right to be let alone.

Protecting the Press from Invasion of Privacy Claims

The individual also lost more privacy to the press and the radio and TV media after the 1960s as an increasingly aggressive media gained an even greater arsenal of sophisticated and intrusive news-gathering equipment—such as better long-range finder cameras; better tape recorders; and access to growing databases and other sources of public information.

In addition, now the media gained an even stronger weapon, the support of the Supreme Court in reaffirming the power of the First Amendment. Thus, in most situations, the press and the radio and TV media gained the upper hand against almost anyone claiming their privacy had been invaded. The battle for privacy against the press was essentially lost for most people back in 1964 when the Supreme Court handed down its famous *New York Times v. Sullivan* case.[35] In this case, a well-known public figure protested that the *New York Times* had printed some incorrect information about him that he felt was damaging to his reputation. But the Court came out four-square behind the press in handing down what has become known as the "New York Times" or "Sullivan" standard that has affected all media privacy cases even today. Basically, the court said that the press cannot be held liable for defamation or libel in the case of a public figure, even if it reports some wrong information, unless the person making this claim can show that the press (or the person reporting the information) is guilty of "actual malice"—in other words, having an evil intent to harm the person with this information.

Since then, in most public figure cases involving a false light invasion of privacy or the public disclosure of private information, the courts have continued to apply this same standard, and have generally tossed any invasion of privacy claim out of court on the grounds that the person was a public figure. Thus, if the person could show no malice, he or she didn't have a case. For example, General Westmoreland found this when he came up against *Time* magazine, which had published some disparaging information about his abilities, and so did many other well-known figures when they tried to fight the media in the 1960s, 1970s, and 1980s. Even when people claimed they weren't public figures, the courts generally found that the story about them was newsworthy enough to make them public figures or at least "quasi-public" figures, and the public had a right to know.

The first of these big cases eroding privacy rights by the media, was the *Time Inc. v. Hill* case in 1967.[36] The Hill family was held hostage by a group of escaped convicts, and thereafter their ordeal even inspired a play. But what especially angered the Hills is that *Life* magazine did a big story about them which created the impression that the fictionalized play actually presented the events they had experienced. But the play, they claimed, wasn't an accurate representation of the facts. Instead it cast them in a false light, as well as disrupting their lives by attracting public attention which invaded their private family life. Still, the Supreme Court supported the press. It concluded that although the Hills were private figures, they were a subject for public interest, so the story about them was newsworthy. Thus, they should be judged under the *New York Times*–Sullivan test. If there was no malice, which the court concluded there wasn't, they were out of luck. *Life* magazine had carte blanche to run the story.

In the 1970s and 1980s prospects became even worse for people who felt the media went too far. In case after case, the courts agreed that the media could print the information it obtained from public sources, as long as the information was essentially correct and lawfully obtained. Take the 1977 *Oklahoma Publishing Company v. District Court* case.[37] The parents of an eleven-year-old boy accused of murder protested that the paper published his name and picture: but why shouldn't it, the Supreme Court said. After all, the information was already "widely disseminated," and the newspaper obtained it at court proceedings open to the public. Thus, any privacy rights the juvenile might have were outweighed by the First Amendment freedom of the press.

In 1989, the outlook for privacy versus the media became even worse, when the Court decided the press could even print information that was improperly disclosed in public records. Thus, should public officials let the information slip, there was nothing to stop the press from publishing it. This occurred in the famous *Florida Star v. B.J.F.* case,[38] in which a cub reporter copied down the name of a rape victim that the local sheriff inadvertently included in his report. Yes, the law in Florida prohibited including the identity of a sexual battery victim in any public record, and yes, signs in the pressroom told reporters that the identity of these victims should not be in these records. The newspaper even had a policy of not printing these names. Yet, the woman's name was published. In fact, after publication, the woman's family even got calls from men threatening to rape her again, and soon after, she had to move and go to a mental health counselor to help her deal with the stress. But even so, the Supreme Court supported the right of the press. The newspaper reporter had lawfully obtained the information, even though it was mistakenly released in public records.

Thus, for the most part, the courts have given the press a green light to print just about anything about anybody, particularly when people are in the news or the story is newsworthy, if they obtain the information legally and it is largely correct and printed without malice. That policy has contributed to the gossipy, "open season on everyone" kind of media we have today, since radio and TV reporters have used these "free press" arguments to support their own ability to show and tell what they want.

Balancing the Right of Privacy against the Free Speech Right of Others

Yet, while the press and radio/TV media have had the upper hand in most cases on freedom of speech/free press grounds, when the privacy right of one person or group is pitted against the free speech rights of someone else, the results have been mixed. In some cases, one's right to be let alone has won out; in other cases, free speech rights have been victorious.

For example, in a few protest cases in the early 1970s, the free speech rights of the protestors on the public streets won out over the rights of passersby and observers who didn't want to hear the message. One was the much publicized *Cohen v. California* case in 1971 at the height of anti-Vietnam sentiment.[39] When Cohen walked up the steps of the Los Angeles County Courthouse wearing a jacket with the legend "Fuck the Draft," he was promptly arrested for doing so; however the Supreme Court ruled that he was free to express himself in this way. Similarly, in a 1991 Texas case, *Organization for a Better Austin v. Keefe,*[40] demonstrators were peacefully handing out leaflets supporting racial equality, when they were stopped from doing so, because they were disturbing others. But again, the Supreme Court supported their right to do this. Anyone who wasn't interested could pass up the flyers or look the other way.

At least privacy advocates had some small consolation, since the Court recognized that those passing by, viewing, or listening to what was happening did have a privacy right that was being affected by what was being done or said. But in these cases the court felt the free speech rights of those with something to say was more important. And in subsequent cases when the privacy/free speech encounter has been in public places, this has often been the result.

However, in other 1970s and 1980s cases when people's privacy in their homes has been disturbed, the courts have often supported their right to be let alone. Take the 1978 radio case, *FCC v. Pacifica Foundation,*[41] in which the comedian George Carlin offered a fairly racy monologue entitled "Filthy Words" on the air, which echoes the recent furor over Howard Stern. The FCC acted to ban Carlin, and the Court agreed it could, deciding that the individual's right to be let alone in the home "plainly outweighs the First Amendment rights of an intruder."

Soon after, in some residential picketing cases, the Court protected the right of homeowners to keep picketers from disturbing their peace and tranquility. In the 1980s *Carey v. Brown*[42] case, for example, the Supreme Court threw out an Illinois law which allowed labor picketing, but not other kinds of picketing, to support the ability of the state to protect "the wellbeing, tranquility and privacy of the home" in a "free and civilized society." And almost a decade later, in 1988 in *Frisby v. Schultz,*[43] the Supreme Court agreed that the Wisconsin town of Brookfield could pass a law which banned all residential picketing. The case ended up in court after some antiabortion picketers protested in front of the home of a doctor who performed abortions and the police arrested them. But the Court said they couldn't protest there, supporting the doctor's right to privacy at home. On the other hand, in other towns, peaceful picketing in front of private homes has been permitted.

In short, when the right of people to be let alone comes up against the right of others to express themselves—on the air, through protests, on city streets—it is not always clear who wins. It is a battle that continues today.

Notes

1. *Griswold v. Connecticut,* 381 U.S. 479 (1965), 485–86, cited in Ken Gormley, "100 Years of Privacy," *Wisconsin Law Review,* 1335 (1992): 1391, and in Richard F. Hixson, *Privacy in a Public Society* (New York: Oxford University Press, 1987), 75–80.
2. Hixson, 76; Gormley, 1391–92.
3. *Roe v. Wade,* 410 U.S. 113 (1973).
4. Hixson, 83–84, citing *Roe v. Wade.*
5. *Planned Parenthood v. Danforth,* 428 U.S. 52 (1976), cited in Darien A. McWhirter and Jon D. Bible, *Privacy as a Constitutional Right* (New York: Quorum Books, 1992), 128–29.

6. *Bellotti v. Baird,* 443 U.S. 622 (1979), cited in McWhirter and Bible, 129.
7. *H.L. v. Matheson,* 450 U.S. 398 (1981), cited in McWhirter & Bible, 129.
8. *City of Akron v. Akron Center for Reproductive Health,* 462 U.S. 416 (1983), cited in McWhirter & Bible, 129; *Thornburgh v. American College of Obstetricians and Gynecologists,* 476 U.S. 416 (1983), cited in McWhirter & Bible, 131.
9. *Webster v. Reproductive Health Services,* 109 S. Ct. 3040 (1989), cited in McWhirter and Bible, 131–32.
10. Gormley, 1423–24.
11. *Bartling v. Superior Court,* 209 Cal. Rptr. 220 (Cal. Ct. App. 1984), cited in Ken Gormley and Rhonda G. Hartmann, "Privacy and the States," *Temple Law Review,* 65 (1992): 1285.
12. *Bouvia v. Superior Court,* 225 Cal. Rptr. 297 (Cal. Ct. App. 1986), cited in Gormley and Hartmann, 1285.
13. *In re Quinlan,* 355 A.2d 647 (N.J.), cert denied, 429 U.S. 922 (1976), 663, cited in Gormley and Hartmann, 1287–88.
14. *Cruzan v. Director, Missouri Dept. of Health,* 110 S. Ct. 2841 (1990), cited in McWhirter and Bible, 132.
15. *Eisenstadt v. Baird,* 405 U.S. 438 (1972), cited in McWhirter and Bible, 116.
16. *Moore v. City of East Cleveland,* 431 U.S. 494 (1977), cited in McWhirter and Bible, 116.
17. *State v. Saunders,* 381 A.2d 333 (N.J. 1977), cited in McWhirter and Bible, 117.
18. *People v. Onofre,* 415 N.E.2d 936 (N.Y. 1980) cert. denied, 451 U.S. 987 (1981); *Commonwealth v. Bonadio,* 415 A.2d 47 (Penn. 1980), cited in McWhirter and Bible, 118–19.
19. *Bowers v. Hardwick,* 478 U.S. 186 (1986).
20. *Stanley v. Georgia,* 394 U.S. 557 (1969), cited in Matthew N. Kleiman, "The Right to Financial Privacy versus Computerized Law Enforcement: A New Fight in an Old Battle," *Northwestern University Law Review,* 86, (1992): 1169–1228; in McWhirter and Bible, 121.
21. Gormley, 1363.
22. Ibid., 1363–64; Arthur Miller, *The Assault on Privacy: Computers, Data Banks, and Dossiers* (1971).
23. *Katz v. United States,* 389 U.S. 347 (1967), 360–61.
24. *Berger v. New York,* 388 U.S. 41 (1967), cited in Gormley, 1369.
25. *United States v. Place,* 462 U.S. 696 (1983), cited in Gormley, 1370.
26. *California v. Greenwood,* 486 U.S. 35 (1988), cited in Gormley, 1370.
27. *Oliver v. United States,* 466 U.S. 170 (1984), cited in Gormley, 1370.
28. Gormley, 1423–24.
29. Matthew N. Kleiman, "The Right to Financial Privacy versus Computerized Law Enforcement: A New Fight in an Old Battle," 86, *Northwestern Law Review,* (1991–1992): 1169–1128, 1183.

30. Privacy Act of 1974, Pub. L. No. 94-579, $2(b), 88 Stat. 1896, 1905, cited in Kleiman, 1183–84.
31. *U.S. v. Miller,* 425 U.S. 435 (1976), cited in Kleiman, 1186–87.
32. Right to Financial Privacy Act (1978), cited in Kleiman, 1185–86.
33. Ibid., 1187–89.
34. Ibid., 1190.
35. *New York Times v. Sullivan,* 376 U.S. 254 (1964), cited in Gormley, 1387.
36. *Time Inc. v. Hill,* 385 U.S. 374 (1967), cited in Gormley, 1388.
37. *Oklahoma Publishing Company v. Distrist Court,* 430 U.S. 308 (1977), cited in Gormley, 1388–89.
38. *Florida Star v. B.J.F.,* 491 U.S. 524 (1989), cited in Gormley, 1389.
39. *Cohen v. California,* 403 U.S. 15 (1971), cited in Gormley, 1383.
40. *Organization for a Better Austin v. Keefe,* 402 U.S. 415 (1971), cited in Gormley, 1383.
41. *FCC v. Pacifica Foundation,* 438 U.S. 726 (1978), cited in Gormley, 1384.
42. *Carey v. Brown,* 447 U.S. 455 (1980), cited in Gormley, 1384.
43. *Frisby v. Schultz,* 487 U.S. 474 (1988), cited in Gormley, 1384.

Chapter 5

How Your Employer Is Watching You

The Ways in which Your Employer Is Watching You

Is your employer watching you? Today the question is not so much "is" but "how," since most large companies today use some form of monitoring and surveillance to promote safety, security, employee productivity, and quality control. Watchful supervisors and video monitors are the most obvious methods. Also, a growing number of companies, both big and small, are using security devices as monitoring systems, including company badges, smart cards, and door keys. Increasingly, these identifiers and keys are used not only to permit or refuse entrance to various company sites, but they track who is going where in the building. The employee leaves a trail of electronic fingerprints wherever he or she goes. Then, should the company subsequently have employee problems such as theft, employees taking unauthorized time off, or unauthorized accessing of computer files, the company can easily check its records to find out who was where and doing what when. The companies using these methods read like a roster of the Fortune 500 or the New York Stock Exchange.

Then, too, when employee theft, drug dealing, or sabotage become a problem, some companies bring in undercover investigators to pose as employees. The investigators actually do work at a regular job and get paid, just like other employees. But then they do a little bit extra for some extra pay as internal spies, reporting to the employer or investigative firm that hired them on what they have seen and heard.

But while employers consider such measures as good business to protect themselves against workplace problems, employees view these efforts as increasing invasions of their privacy. The conflict heated up in the late 1980s, as employers began a crackdown and used testing to create a drug and alcohol-free workplace. Soon, the battle spread to other frontiers, from the initial stages of hiring (with battles over what employers can rightfully find out), to checks on employees on and off the job, to what employers can say about a terminated employee without risking an invasion of privacy suit. At the same time, invasion of privacy claims have been added to many other employee claims against employers, most notably for sexual harassment. In effect, the invasion of privacy claim has become a kind of catch-all for anything anyone does to disturb or harm someone else.

Thus, employee privacy litigation has blossomed, and hundreds of cases have been working their way through the courts. Though they represent only a small fraction of the cases in the courts, the growing number of opinions from the higher state and federal courts are helping to create general guidelines on when employers can test and observe and what they can say about their employees, though there is still much variation from state to state and from industry to industry.

Getting Hired—What Employers Can Ask

One relatively uncontroversial area recently has been the personal and demographic characteristics employers can ask about, perhaps because many of these issues had already been settled earlier, such as in employer discrimination against many types of employees based on personal characteristics. The result has been that employers are prevented, at least officially by law, from asking questions about and from discriminating based on race, age, gender, religion, ethnicity, marital status, pregnancy, and other key personal and demographic factors, unless directly relevant to the job.

Checking into Credit and Criminal Convictions

Generally, employers are still able to get information on credit background and criminal convictions. But, since bad credit and criminal convictions are so damaging to employment chances, employees may at times be able to conceal this if the problem is not directly relevant to the job they are seeking (i.e., a bank manager might appropriately seek information about whether a prospective employee has a conviction for embezzlement. But if a former embezzler wants to work in a position where no money is handled, such as supervising production, then asking about embezzling might be taboo). But, conversely, many prospective employers may want to know about any convictions and sometimes, though they shouldn't, they find ways to get that information.

What are some of these "don't ask, shouldn't know" questions? Generally, most private employers are allowed to get credit and criminal background information, with the prospective employee's permission to get these records, but there are limits. For example, in California, most employers can't ask about any arrests if the person hasn't been convicted, if the record has been sealed, or if the conviction was for a misdemeanor and the prospective employee successfully completed probation. According to Peter Sechan, of the Alameda Legal Aid Society, who specializes in employee law, there are exceptions; for instance, in California, while most private employers can't access arrest data, banks and security firms can get data from the Federal Bureau of Investigation (FBI), which has arrest data from all over the country.[1]

Still another problem arises when employers do get this data, especially when they are not supposed to have access to it: some data is not fully accurate. This is because data collection standards vary from place to place, and in some areas, the data is often months behind. As a result, wrongly incriminating data can remain in the files, preventing a prospective employee from getting hired, such as when a charge has been dismissed or the person is not convicted. But the correct information may not show up for a year or two, instead of in a couple of months as it should. Thus, inaccurate information can easily compound the problem of what employers should or should not know.

Credit records are often a problem, too. Employers are generally not supposed to look at these records in making hiring decisions, and companies that maintain credit records are generally not supposed to give information to employers for employment credit checks, except under certain circumstances, such as when there is a signed consent form from a prospective employee where this is permitted. But some employers have found ways around the system, using methods which might be considered legal, illegal, or borderline legal.

For example, some larger companies have an employee on staff who goes to each court in the local area and checks the prospective employee's name to see if there are any convictions on file, which is possible where the records are available by the names of the defendant, as in California. These are public records, and it's perfectly legal for anyone to access them. But if an employer isn't given this information by a prospective employee and is seeking to obtain information that isn't supposed to be considered in hiring, should the employer be able to use this? Privacy advocates and prospective employees say no, but employers argue that they need this information to screen out bad risks. They say that if they don't check and they hire an employee who has a bad record (i.e., hire a man with a bad driving record to drive a bus), and someone later gets hurt when this employee is at fault, the employer could be sued for damages.

By the same token, though employers may not be able to gain credit information from the big credit companies due to restrictive laws, they can often get it through private investigative services that get their data from these companies or other sources, including on-line subscriber services where they just type in the prospective employee's name and a password. As with criminal records data, the information is often incomplete or inaccurate, compounding the problem of whether access should be authorized in the first place.

Some states, like California, have tried to deal with these problems by requiring the employee's agreement to permit checking. For instance, in California, if a prospective employer hires an outside company to do a background search, the employer is supposed to provide the prospective employee with a form indicating that such an investigation will be conducted and make a copy of the result of this search available to the prospect if requested.[2] But often employers are vague about what this background search will involve, so prospective employees aren't aware of how extensive this checking will be, or they are too concerned with wanting to get the job to find out or protest.

So should employers be able to check to protect themselves, particularly if they can be found liable for hiring someone with a criminal record? Or is checking an invasion of privacy? The outcome of the conflict is still unclear.

Checking into Personal Background Characteristics

By contrast, there are now some clear guidelines about what kind of personal background information employers can ask about, which has kept down the litigation in this area. For example, extensive federal legislation now prevents employers from asking questions that might enable them to discriminate, such as the Fair Employment, Housing, and Disabilities Act; Title VII of the Civil Rights Act; and the Immigration and Control Act. Additionally, some states have legislation that limits what employers can ask, too, such as California's privacy rights legislation and labor code. Some taboos include asking about age, national origin, and sexual orientation. Also, employers aren't supposed to ask about family status, including the number of children or plans to have any children. Often, too, there are restrictions on asking about citizenship, according to John True, of the San Francisco Legal Aid Society. Only certain employers, such as the government, can discriminate against noncitizens, while others are supposed to evaluate and hire them just like regular citizens as long as they are legally in the country.[3]

The basic guideline is that employers are limited to asking for personal information that is reasonably job related. But what is "reasonably job related"? Employers and employees and their attorneys may disagree on this point. Take the question of disabilities, for example. Today, an employer can't ask someone about any disabilities, including having acquired immunodeficiency syndrome (AIDS), if that disability doesn't limit the person's ability to do the job. But employers and employees may view the person's "disability" very differently, with employers thinking it will affect the person's ability, and employees feeling it will not and that the employer should not have a right to know.

Just how much can an employer legitimately ask? Some employers really seem to push the limit, and sometimes it seems they are testing as much for a job seeker's willingness to submit to a grueling interview or questionnaire process, a sign of a compliant worker, than to anything they might actually find out from the questions.

One chain store, for instance, according to John True, had a 30-page application for a clerk in one of its stores, which included questions like: "Do you smoke? Drink tea or coffee? Have you ever gone bankrupt?" The store even asked the prospect to submit a few bits of hair so they could test for illegal substances.[4] In this case, a lawyer for the Worker's Rights Center got the employer to back down, which often happens in such cases, which are settled as a result of quiet compromises, rather than ending up in court.

However, when employers do push too hard, employees and their lawyers may fight back, resulting in severe legal costs. For example, this happened to Delta Airlines, when it asked applicants for flight attendant and other positions about their marital status, sexual orientation, family life, and whether they had any abortions. About six hundred prospective employees took the matter to court, arguing in a class action suit that some of the questions violated New York State human rights laws. Eventually, Delta offered a monetary settlement, which resolved the case with most of the job seekers. But about 10 percent of the plaintiffs who felt they were subjected to the most abusive questioning dropped out of the class and hired their own attorney to decide whether to settle or pursue the matter to get more extensive damages.[5]

Using Testing

While most of these personal background issues seem to have been worked out through detailed legislation or local negotiations between employers, employees, employment lawyers, and worker rights organizations, one major hiring practice still under challenge in the courts is the use of different types of testing.

One major battleground has been drug and alcohol testing, whether used before the person gets the job or after he or she has begun work. In general, employers have somewhat more right to test before they hire than afterwards, particularly in safety sensitive industries. But since before and after hiring guidelines are so intermingled, both kinds of testing will be considered in the next section.

The other two major types of testing under fire by privacy advocates are the psychological and personality tests, such as the Minnesota Multiphasic Personality Inventory (MMPI) and lie detector and honesty tests.

Using Psychological and Personality Tests

Can an employer use psychological and personality tests? It depends on where that employer is located, what kinds of tests are used, and if any employees, lawyers, or organizations are disturbed enough to protest. Though the verdict is still unclear, psychological testing has increased since the early 1990s, partly because Congress banned polygraph tests in hiring about four years ago.[6]

But sometimes psychology tests go too far. For example, in California, which has some of the toughest privacy laws in the nation, privacy advocates scored a big victory against Target Stores, in the *Soroka v. Dayton Hudson*[7] case, which wound up in the State Supreme Court after several years of litigation. In a settlement, Target Stores agreed to pay over $2 million for forcing its job applicants to take the Psychscreen Test, a combination of the MMPI and the California Psychological Inventory (CPI), which asked deeply personal questions about their sexual interests, values, and religious beliefs.[8] Some of these MMPI questions were originally developed in order to identify mentally disturbed, even schizophrenic and psychotic individuals.

The case began back in 1989 when Sibi Soroka, a recent college graduate applied to be a $7 an hour security guard. His primary job was to stroll up and down the aisles in a T-shirt and jeans, looking like an ordinary shopper, and be on the lookout for shoplifters. But to get the job, he had to take the Psychscreen Test. He did take the test, but the questions bothered him as an invasion of privacy, so before turning it in, he made some copies at a nearby copy shop and showed them to lawyers and government regulators.

Here are some examples of the questions "I believe my sins are unpardonable." "I have never indulged in unusual sex practices." "I am very strongly attracted by members of my own sex." Although the test is still used by many law enforcement agencies and companies hiring employees in sensitive professions, the issue in the case against Target was that this test shouldn't be used for low-level jobs. Though Soroka lost at a trial, in 1991 the Court of Appeals agreed the test improperly asked questions about the religious beliefs and political and sexual activities of applicants, which didn't seem to bear on the ability to do the job. Then, after the State Supreme Court agreed to consider the case, it drew national attention and Target stopped using the tests in its 557 stores nationally. Finally, in 1993 Target agreed to a settlement.[9]

But while Target settled and other employers dropped psychological tests due to the settlement, the question remains over whether psychological testing is unconstitutional or not. The same confusion still surrounds interviewing. Though a company can't ask certain questions, if the person *volunteers* the information, it may be able to use that information against the person later on. For example, in one Massachusetts case decided in June 1993, *Lysak v. the Seiler Corporation,* the court ruled that an employer cannot ask an applicant if she is pregnant. But if she volunteers that she plans to have no more children whilst knowing she is pregnant, the company can fire her later when it discovers she is pregnant.[10]

Yet, whether the tests, interview questions, or polygraphs are legal or not, some companies still use them, and rather than fight in court, some applicants prefer to "psyche out" the tests and beat the testmakers at their own game.

Monitoring on the Job

Once an employee is on the job, monitoring becomes the big privacy issue. Beyond just supervision, employers use all sorts of increasingly sophisticated means to check up on their employees, including psychological tests for promotion and drug testing.

Employers claim they need monitoring for workplace safety, quality control, and to make sure workers are doing what they should, are being productive, and are not doing things they shouldn't, from cheating and stealing to taking and selling drugs. They claim the traditional methods of personal supervision are not enough in today's high-tech office. But in turn, employees and privacy advocates object to the resulting Big Brother office environments, in which observers and monitors are everywhere, invading the worker's privacy not only on the job, but often off the job, too.

New Modes of Monitoring

Monitoring is just about everywhere today, and going digital. Traditionally, before the high tech revolution, supervisors observed employees as they did their work and reviewed what they did. Sometimes they might eavesdrop at the door on conversations, maybe listen in on an extension, but that was about all, unless perhaps they suspected a theft or other wrongdoing. They might then hire an undercover investigator to observe the person further.

Then, starting in the 1970s, employers began using electronic devices to monitor their employees, starting with the phone companies which installed eavesdropping devices on the phones to check up on how their operators were doing.[11] Subsequently, monitoring expanded to other industries, particularly to occupations involving highly repetitive work, where monitoring is used to check on how fast and how well employees are working, say in the case of mail sorters, word processors, and data entry clerks.[12]

Now, high-tech surveillance and monitoring devices seem to be everywhere, linked to phones and computerized operating systems. Besides the routine checking for productivity and quality, a key reason for the big increase in monitoring today is there are so many more possibilities for fraud, crime, and employer liability that employers are running scared and feel compelled to check, because they don't trust their employees. Many of the traditional checks that in the past helped to keep employees loyal and responsible are gone (such as having more secure long-term employment in smaller, more personal workplaces). At the same time, there are more opportunities for employees to take advantage if so inclined, and many do.

For example, in California, about 10 to 20 percent of the claims for work-related accidents and injuries are deemed fraudulent. Meanwhile, employers report an increasing number of workers with drug or alcohol problems that interfere with job performance, and employee theft is up. And should an employee make a mistake, say due to drug or alcohol problems, the employer is generally liable.

Thus, employers are making increased use of monitoring as a form of protection in a workplace climate that seems increasingly adversarial, despite recent efforts to counter this, say through workshops on team-building. But then monitoring itself helps to increase this adversarial climate, as workers fight back against being watched.

This monitoring takes many forms. Among them are:

Computer Monitoring. Increasingly, computers are checking everything, and everything being done on the computer is being checked. For example, new software programs, such as PC-Sentry, Direct Access, and Peek and Spy monitor every word and keystroke command that crosses the computer screen, noting the time and date when different activities occur. They not only record how long a computer was used, what files were accessed, and typing speed, but even the length of the user's bathroom breaks.[13]

Ironically, according to research on monitoring effects by the Communications Workers of America and other organizations, monitored workers have more problems that can reduce the very productivity that their monitoring is designed to increase, such as higher levels of stress, depression, and fatigue, as well as more headaches, backaches, and wrist pain. But still computer monitoring has increased to about 20 million workers by 1993 according to a Macworld projection from a survey of 300 companies.[14] And about 30 percent of companies with 1,000 or more employees use monitoring to evaluate employee performance, while software sales indicate these numbers are likely to increase—they're up about 50 percent a year according to one study.[15]

Using Detailed Questionnaires about Personal Data. Employee questionnaires are becoming more and more common. These questionnaires go far beyond the kind of questioning used in prejob screening, and often employers use them as an investigative tool when they suspect something is wrong and want to find out who did it. But if these questions go too far, employers can find out more than they bargained for and end up in court or battling in the court of public opinion and backing off.

This is what happened to TWA when it suspected that many of its workers were abusing the company's sick leave policy to take off extra vacation days or even look for other jobs. While many companies routinely hire private investigators to check if their employees out sick are really sick (e.g., going by their house or calling to see if they are home), TWA secretly sent detailed questionnaires to several hundred managers. These asked them a number of highly personal questions about workers suspected of lying when they called in sick. Besides asking for extensive family information, including the names, ages, and employment of the worker's children, some of the more offensive questions asked were whether the employee had any identifying "scars and marks," smoked or drank alcohol, or had any physical restrictions. The questions even asked the managers to supply the names of the worker's physicians and therapists, appointment dates with them, the make and license plates of the worker's car, and the names and addresses of friends and relatives. Outraged, someone leaked the questionnaire anonymously to several news organizations, and soon after reporters began calling. TWA backed down, saying it would drop most of the form, although it still would pursue fraudulent sick leave requests in other ways.[16]

Using Badges, Smart Cards, Passwords, and Other Devices to Track Location. Employers also use various location tracking devices including badges, smart cards, and passwords to keep track of where their employees go in the company. Many of these devices are used primarily for security purposes, such as identifying cards or codes which employees use to gain access to different parts of the company, say by showing a badge, placing a card in a slot, entering a password or code in a computer terminal, or providing a handprint or palmprint to indicate they are who they claim to be and have the appropriate clearance to go where they want to go. In addition, such location data can contribute to office efficiency by making it easy to locate an employee to pass on an important message.[17]

But besides providing entry or quickly locating employees, such systems provide tracking capabilities, too, so employers can tell who has gone where and for how long. As a result, when employees are doing things they shouldn't, from engaging in secret trysts with coworkers to taking office property, employers can zero in on likely suspects.

Yet, while such uses may be legitimate employer efforts to protect against employee abuse and fraud, such information can be abused, and the act of collecting it contributes to the aura of suspicion and mistrust that increasingly pervades many workplaces. More and more employees feel as if their every move is observed, which it often is, contributing to worker alienation and stress.

To reduce such growing tensions, some employers are trying to balance their need to know with worker privacy concerns. For example, Olivetti Research created an Active Badge system that monitors the movements of everyone in the company, using an infrared transmitter which beeps out that person's location every fifteen seconds. But the system also provides users with some privacy protections. Employees can put a lens cap on the camera, put their Active Badge in a drawer, or look at a list of who has been monitoring them.[18]

Still, despite such well-intentioned efforts at finding a balance, many privacy advocates still worry about the potential for abusing information gained through high-tech monitoring, because not everyone using it may be so benign.

Video Surveillance. Video surveillance devices are becoming more common. These range from a single mounted camera in a room or hallway to moving cameras that sweep the room. Some larger companies mount dozens of cameras in different locations, and they have banks of monitors viewed by security personnel to check what is going on.

Such devices can have important protective uses, such as monitoring the perimeter of a building to prevent illegal entries, recording a crime in progress, and documenting meetings and events for a permanent company record. But great privacy abuses are possible, too. One such possible abuse is when a company uses a video camera in a private area where recording might be objectionable, such as videotaping in lockerrooms, dressing rooms, and bathrooms, which have all been the subject of lawsuits. Another abuse that has also ended up in court is when company officials, managers, or employees watch videos taken for security purposes for their own private enjoyment, as in some claims by female employees that male security guards have watched tapes of them in various stages of undress in a stag party setting.

Phone Call Tracking and Other Methods of Listening In. Phones have also become a common monitoring device. Many employers now track calls to record when and where an employee makes a call and for how long, which is a way to track improper calls to personal contacts or those out of a prescribed area. Sometimes, too, supervisors listen in on calls to determine if the worker is providing quality service. And sometimes, employers use some traditional methods to monitor, like bugging the rooms and phones, hiring private detectives to work undercover, and sending out investigators to check on workers' claims of illness and injury with stakeouts, videotaping, and by interviewing friends and neighbors.

In short, employers now use numerous monitoring techniques for various reasons to check up on employees, especially in occupations where tasks are highly repetitive, to measure productivity and quality, using increasingly sophisticated high-tech devices. Though the guidelines are still unclear, some general policies have emerged, as employers and employees have clashed over their rights in court, and as employee representatives and legislators have grappled with passing legislation.

The Employee Battle against Monitoring

Apart from going to court, employees and their advocates have tried various strategies to try to make monitoring less invasive when it crosses the line from monitoring the work to monitoring the worker. For example, one women's employee group—9-5: the National Association of Working Women—started a hotline for employees in 1989, and after receiving hundreds of complaints from employees stating that monitoring felt like spying and created an atmosphere of suspicion and distrust, it added its voice to the rising clamor for the federal government to take action to address the issue of privacy in the workplace.[19]

In the early 1990s, Congress responded. It began considering bills to limit the level of monitoring in the office, such as banning secret monitoring and regulating the use of information gained by monitoring. One such bill, Privacy for Consumers and Workers, introduced in 1991 by Representative Pat Williams of Montana, would require employers to notify workers with some kind of signal, such as a visual signal or beep tone, whenever they are using computer, video, or audio monitoring. In addition, the bill would limit monitoring to two hours a week, and employers would have to let employees know what information they had collected about them.[20] Senator Paul Simon of Illinois introduced a similar bill in the Senate. As of 1993, this bill was still working its way through Congress.[21]

Meanwhile, as this trend to establish national workplace policies continued, currently even if monitoring is carried out secretly, employers generally have been able to do it. For example, though the Electronics Communications Privacy Act of 1986 makes it normally illegal to intercept phone calls, eavesdropping "in the ordinary course of business" is acceptable, as shown by a rash of monitoring cases that hit the courts in the late 1970s through mid-1980.[22] However, if an employer discovers an employee is making a personal call, he or she is supposed to stop listening, though the employee might be penalized or terminated for making such calls, as a federal court decided in 1986, setting guidelines that are still influential today.[23]

The Response of Employers and Employees to Monitoring

Perhaps because employers do have the right by law to reasonably monitor their employees for work-related reasons, relatively little litigation has occurred in the courts over monitoring. While employees have protested in a few cases, employers have mostly prevailed. Thus, in this area, workers and privacy advocates have largely shifted to a strategy of trying to influence legislation to provide stricter monitoring guidelines or trying to persuade employers to ease off on the monitoring.

For example, one of the 1980s cases won by employers which set the tone for what is happening now, is the *O'Connor v. Ortega* case in 1987. A doctor at a California state hospital who was training young physicians in psychiatric medicine protested after his desk was searched during an investigation. It was searched because hospital administrators thought there were some improprieties in the way he was managing the program and were seeking evidence. After the doctor was fired, he sued the hospital. But eventually, the courts decided that though he had a reasonable expectation of privacy in his office, desk, and file cabinets, a supervisor was justified in searching an employee's office if he or she had reasonable grounds for suspecting the search would turn up evidence of employee misconduct or the search was necessary for a work-related purpose, such as retrieving a needed file.[24]

One Michigan court allowed employers to go even further in investigating their employees. This occurred in the 1989 *Saldana v. Kelsey-Hayes Company* case when an employee protested after his employer hired a private firm to check if he was really injured. The investigators spent several days tailing him, and they observed and photographed him through an open window in his home with a high-speed camera. Yet even if his employer might have used objectionable methods and intruded on his seclusion, the court felt he didn't show that he had a right to keep his activities private. After all, his employer had a legitimate interest in investigating its suspicions that he didn't have the work-related disability he claimed.[25]

Similarly, as the more recent electronic surveillance cases have hit the courts, the courts have been fairly sympathetic to the employer's need to monitor employee communications "in the ordinary course of business." For example, in one case the court decided it was fine for an employer to monitor a call in which a salesman discussed his employer's business with a former employee now working for a competitor.[26] In another case, the court agreed that an employer could use an extension phone to intercept the call of an employee who was being investigated for stealing the employer's merchandise.[27] In both cases, the court felt the employers were justified by the "business use" exemption in the Electronic Communications Privacy Act of 1986, which prevents most private wiretapping.

Continuing this trend, most of the 1992 and 1993 cases on monitoring have gone the employer's way, too. Typical was the result in *Jackson et al. v. Nationwide Credit,* decided in 1992. After Nationwide, a credit company, offered its employees $100 to sign an agreement not to compete, say, by working for a competitor, as a condition of employment, two employees refused to sign and one who signed the agreement was fired soon after when he missed work for two days. All of them soon ended up working for a competitor, and when Nationwide tried to prevent them from doing this, they filed a counterclaim. Among other things, they accused Nationwide of eavesdropping on their phone conversations while they worked there. But eventually the court turned down their claim, supporting Nationwide's right to monitor. After all, said the court: "All employees were advised that the telephones were for business only and that the telephones would be monitored." So Nationwide didn't unreasonably intrude into their private affairs.[28]

Just about the only time the courts found for the employee in these monitoring cases is when the employer went too far and used monitoring to not only check up on the worker's activities at work but listened in on personal communications, too. This is what happened in the 1992 case of *Deal v. Spears* when Newell and Junita Spears, who owned a retail store in Arkansas, taped the conversations of their employee, Sibbie Deal. They started taping since they suspected Sibbie was involved in an earlier burglary of the store, in which about $16,000 in merchandise was stolen. Believing the burglary to have been an inside job, and hoping to catch her in an unguarded admission, they purchased and installed a recording device on the extension phone in their mobile home near the store. Then they secretly taped about twenty-two hours of Sibbie's conversations between June and August 1990. They felt they had another good reason for taping, too, since Sibbie made or received numerous personal calls at work. They had previously asked her to cut down on these calls and had even told her they might monitor her calls or install a pay phone to curtail the abuse.

In any event, while trying to find out about the burglary, they found out many other things, including the fact that Sibbie was having an extramarital affair with one of her frequent callers and she had sold him a keg of beer at cost, a violation of store policy. The keg incident was the last straw. That night, when she came to work the evening shift, Newell played a few seconds of the incriminating tape and fired her on the spot. Sibbie and her lover, Calvin Lucas, shot back with an invasion of privacy suit, because the Spears taped her calls, and Sibbie and Lucas won.

The key difference here is that much of the Spears' taping had nothing to do with Sibbie's activities at work. Thus, not only did they not tell her they were actually monitoring the phone, but they monitored too much. Though they could have listened in long enough to determine that the calls were personal and in violation of store policy, they recorded twenty-two hours of calls, and as the court explained: "Newell Spears listened to all of them without regard to their relation to his business interests. Granted, Deal might have mentioned the burglary at any time during the conversation, but we do not believe that the Spearses' suspicions justified the extent of the intrusion." Yet, though the Spears lost, the court did show some sympathy for them in not ordering any punitive damages, since their motive for taping was due to their own business interests. Then, too, they didn't play the tape for anyone else except Sibbie Deal, and then only for a few seconds to let her know why they were firing her.[29]

How Employers Are Dealing with Monitoring Now

Though the courts are generally sympathetic toward reasonable business monitoring, the resistance of employees and the risk of lawsuits has led employers to feel some concern and confusion about what they can do to avoid problems and find a balance between their need to monitor to make sure employees are working as they should and their employees' privacy interests.

As a result, employers have been looking for guidelines they can safely follow and some guidelines have developed which some employers are using. For example, in an article in *Employee Relations*, attorneys Kenneth Jenero and Lynne D. Mapes-Riordon, provide some suggestions, noting that while employers have a "largely unrestricted" right to monitor for business reasons, they have to stay out of the workers' protected zone of privacy. For example, to avoid problems, they should avoid monitoring employees' personal calls (even if employees shouldn't be making them), shouldn't eavesdrop on their private communications, videotape them in highly private areas, or engage in any other monitoring that goes beyond "purely work-related matters or moves outside the workplace." Then, too, they should avoid any monitoring that seems unfair, even if it is legal, since this might motivate employee resistance, say by seeking unions to represent them, or this might stimulate legislators and courts to create new laws.[30]

Other guidelines they recommend, which are followed by many employers today, include:

1. Determining the applicable federal and state laws for the employer's industry and state;
2. Giving employees prior written notice of the kind of monitoring that will be used; perhaps even getting waivers in which employees acknowledge the employer's right to monitor;
3. Being prepared to justify why the monitoring is necessary;
4. Limiting the amount of monitoring in time and location to what is necessary for business purposes;
5. Keeping monitoring devices out of highly private areas, such as restrooms and lounges, and limiting any monitoring to the workplace, unless there is a strong work-related reason for doing more (such as investigating fraudulent or unlawful conduct at work);
6. Limiting any telephone monitoring to business purposes only, which means ending monitoring once a call is identified as a personal one;
7. Avoiding using bugs or other secret means to intercept conversations;
8. Giving employees an opportunity, when appropriate, to see what information has been gathered about them, and giving them a chance to explain and rebut any interpretation if this is used for any disciplinary action.[31]

Summing Up

In sum, the high-tech revolution, combined with social changes, has given employers new ways to watch what their employees are doing and new reasons to check up on them to make sure they are properly doing the work. For the most part they can check for legitimate business reasons. But they can only go so far, and when they cross those limits, that's when they run into problems of employee resistance and lose lawsuits. It isn't always clear where those limits are and when employers go too far, although gradually certain guidelines have emerged that govern the more routine forms of monitoring.

But in other areas the battle has been even more heated and the guidelines are even less certain—in the case of drug and alcohol testing, investigating sex harassment cases, and recently, tapping into employee E-mail. Still another area of bitter dispute is what happens when an employee leaves, particularly under a cloud, and wrongful termination lawsuits occur. What can an employer say or do? The next chapter explores these topics.

Notes

1. Talk by Peter Shechan to Experience Unlimited, 1993, Attorney specializing in employee law, with the Alameda Legal Aid Society, California.
2. Ibid.
3. Talk by John True, head of the Workers Rights Clinic at the Employee Law Center, San Francisco Legal Aid Society, to Experience Unlimited, 1993.
4. Ibid.
5. *Mehe v. Delta Air Lines,* 93-554-A (E.D. Virginia), cited in *Privacy Journal* 19 (June 1993): 6.
6. Dan Reed, "Target Stores to Pay $2 Million for Asking Intimate Questions," *San Francisco Chronicle,* 10 July 1993, A-19.
7. *Soroka v. Dayton Hudson,* H243579-3 (Cal. Super. Ct., September 23, 1993).
8. Betty Southard Murphy, Wayne E. Barlow, and D. Diane Hatch, "Manager's Newsfront: Pre-Employment Test Invades Privacy and Discriminates," *Personnel Journal* (February 1992): 23–24.
9. Dan Reed, "Target Stores to Pay $2 Million for Asking Intimate Questions," *San Francisco Chronicle,* 10 July 1993, A-1, A-19.
10. *Lysak v. The Seiler Corporation,* M-6095 (Mass. Sup. Jud. Ct, June 28, 1993), cited in *The Privacy Journal,* 20 (November 1993).
11. Laurie Flynn, "They're Watching You: Electronic Surveillance of Workers Raises Privacy Concerns," *San Jose Mercury News,* 13 June 1993, 1F.
12. Charles Piller, "Bosses with X-Ray Eyes," *MacWorld* (July 1993): 118–123.
13. Flynn, 1F, 5F.
14. Piller, 120.
15. Flynn, 1F, 5F.
16. Peter T. Kilborn, "Abuse of Sick Leave Rises and Companies Fight Back," *New York Times,* 29 November 1992.
17. Andy Hopper, "The Walk-and-Wear Office," *Computerworld* (20 April 1992): 99–101.
18. Lory Zottola, "Monitoring Raises Privacy Fears: Iterative Design May Help," *Computerworld* (20 April 1992): 101.
19. Julie Gannon Shoop, "Electronic Monitoring: Is Big Brother at the Office?" *Trial* (January 1992): 13–14.

20. Piller, 118–123.
21. J.W. Waks and C.R. Brewster, "Privacy Bill Targets Work Site Monitoring," *The National Law Journal* (18 January 1993): 20.
22. Among these were *Briggs v. American Air Filter Co., Inc.*, 455 F. Supp. 179 (N.D. Ga. 1978); aff'd, 630 F.2d 414 (5th Cir. 1980); *Epps v. St. Mary's Hospital of Athens, Inc.*, 802 F. 2d 412 (11th Cir. 1986).
23. *Watkins v. L.M. Berry & Co.*, 704 F.2d 577 (11th Cir. 1983).
24. *O'Conner v. Ortega*, 480 U.S. 709 (1987).
25. *Saldana V. Kelsey-Hayes Company*, 178 Mich. App. 230 (1989).
26. *Briggs v. American Air Filter Co., Inc.*, 630 F. 2d 414 (5th Cir. 1980).
27. *Burnett v. The State of Texas*, 789 S.W. 2d 376 (Tex. App. 1990).
28. *Jackson et al. v. Nationwide Credit, Inc.*, 426 S.E.2d 630 (Ga. App. 1992), 632.
29. *Deal v. Spears*, 980 F.2d 1153 (8th Cir. 1992), 1158–1159.
30. Kenneth A. Jenero and Lynne D. Mapes-Riordan, "Electronic Monitoring of Employees and the Elusive 'Right to Privacy'," *Employee Relations*, 18 (Summer 1992): 71–102.
31. Jenero and Mapes-Riordan, 97–100.

Chapter 6

The Nineties Work Blues

Drugs, Sex, the E-Mail Explosion, and Losing the Job

Besides the dispute over probing too deeply in interviews and tests, along with monitoring workers, the late eighties and nineties workplace privacy disputes have been in four main areas—drug and alcohol testing, sexual harassment, employers checking employee's E-mail and voice mail, and what employers say about terminated or soon-to-be-terminated employees. The controversy in these areas is still heated, while things seem to have settled down in areas discussed in the previous chapters. Perhaps this is because more private testing and personal matters are involved, and job loss for a terminated employee is a highly sensitive, emotional issue.

Drug and Alcohol Testing

The controversy over an employer's right to test for drugs or alcohol is truly a sign of the times, an outgrowth of the growing battle against drugs which went into full gear in the mid-1980s. Until then, drugs and alcohol in the workplace was not much of an issue, though from time to time, someone on drugs or suffering from alcoholism might be discovered and lose a job. But there was no big crackdown, as began in the 1980s and continues today.

For employers the big reason for drug or alcohol testing is to protect the productivity and safety of the workplace. The drug or alcohol impaired worker might be less efficient, interfere with production, cause damage, even provoke lawsuits from customers and outsiders injured due to worker impairment. Research results since the mid-1980s have supported these concerns, indicating that about 10 to 25 percent of all employees use drugs,[1] that employees who use drugs have three to four times as many accidents as other employees,[2] and that they have cost employers over $36 billion in lost productivity, medical expenses, and property loss. There were additional costs for either treating the worker with the problem, or if he or she was terminated, possibly rehiring or retraining a new employee.[3]

The drug wars began in response to this growing problem, and other drug problems throughout society. In 1986, Americans identified drug abuse as the nation's number one concern; Nancy Reagan launched her "Just Say No" to drugs campaign; and President Ronald Reagan issued an executive order to start drug testing federal employees. Soon testing spread to state employees and private employers, too.

Meanwhile, as testing started, so did vocal opposition, because the testing was very invasive. To test, employers had to obtain blood or urine samples; to avoid employees faking the tests, such as by secretly bringing a clean urine sample with them and substituting it for the true one, some employers used even more invasive methods to get an accurate sample. One especially disturbing method was having monitors watch the person give a urine sample to make sure there was no switching. Many employees also were disturbed by random spur-of-the moment testing and by employers using the tests to interfere with their lives off the job. For example, attending a weekend party might give them a positive on the job, even though they were, they felt, perfectly sober and performing up to top capacity.

The Heated Battle that Set the Stage for Today's Battle

Once Nancy Reagan urged everyone to "Say No" and federal testing and new state and national laws went into effect, the drug cases soon ended up in court. Many challenged the new regulations, and there were plenty of them. Among them were new regulations from the Federal Railroad and Federal Aviation Administrations, which decided to start testing rail and commercial airline employees, either after some accident or other incident led a supervisor to believe the employee was intoxicated, or to just test under random, scheduled, and suspicious circumstances.[4] And soon the Nuclear Regulatory Commission came out with regulations to make sure its employees in critical facilities were "fit for duty."[5]

Meanwhile, a growing number of states began passing drug testing laws—seven by 1989, while twenty-four more were considering such legislation. In general, these laws permitted employers to test, if they reasonably suspected or believed their employees were taking drugs or alcohol. Most laws permitted employers to test job applicants, too, as a condition of employment. Soon, many private employers began testing, although there was much confusion about what laws applied to them.[6]

In response to all these new laws, practices, and uncertainty about what employers could do, many employees and unions resisted this new privacy invasion. So starting in 1986, the first major cases ended up in court, and the courts began deciding them in 1988. Since most of the testing started in the public arena, the government employees and unions were the first to go to court, but gradually, more and more private employees began to challenge testing. Here's a quick overview of the background leading up to where we are now.

The Federal Government Gives Testing a Green Light

The first major breakthrough for drug testing occurred in 1989 when two Supreme Court cases gave a green light to much workplace testing—at least when employees worked for the government. This precedent contributed to the greater use of testing in the states and among private employees.

The two cases involved railway workers and treasury workers; one was the *Skinner v. Railway Labor Executives' Association* case;[7] the other the *National Treasury Employees Union v. Von Raab*.[8] Though the Fourth Amendment prohibited unreasonable searches and searches by anyone acting for the government, including government employers, these decisions gave employers much more freedom to search, since they approved carefully designed employee drug-screening programs. The

Court decided that a compelling social or government interest could "override the right to privacy" for reasons of health, safety, or law enforcement.[9]

In the *Skinner* case, the Supreme Court decided it was reasonable for the railroad to collect blood and urine tests when employees were involved in major train accidents or incidents or to give breath and urine tests to employees violating certain safety rules. The Court gave the green light because it felt the employees were performing safety-sensitive tasks making it especially crucial that they not use alcohol or drugs while on duty. The Court also felt the tests were minimally intrusive, since they involved giving samples in a medical environment without any direct observation.

As for the *National Treasury* case, the Court said it was fine for the U.S. Customs Service to set up a drug-screening program and require certain employees to take a urinalysis, specifically those who sought work in positions that involved seizing drugs, carrying firearms, or handling classified material. After all, the Court concluded, if these agents were going to check for drugs themselves and potentially use guns or deal with sensitive material, the government had a right to be sure they were physically fit and had unimpeachable integrity and judgment.

These two rulings significantly affected the future of drug and other testing because they sent a signal that employers could test for a good reason, since their own or society's interests would outweigh the individual's expectation of privacy. This meant that employers no longer had to suspect that a particular person was under the influence of drugs or alcohol. Also, these rulings set the stage for other government and private employers to claim they were justified in using randomized or broader drug testing programs. These were major changes, because as legal scholar Yale Kamisar of the University of Michigan Law School exclaimed dolefully: "[This ruling] cuts deeply into the core of the Fourth Amendment. The heart of the Fourth Amendment is individualized suspicion. If you haven't got that, you have ripped the heart out of the Fourth Amendment."[10]

The battle on testing soon ended up in the district, circuit, and state courts, and the outlook was not good for employees. Generally, the courts sided with the employers, placing the interests of the workplace and society over those of the individual.[11] Despite some exceptions, notably on the West Coast and especially in California, most of these court decisions gave employers the right to use random testing, particularly in industries where there were societal health and safety concerns.

The States Work It Out

The federal green light on testing led many state courts to similar conclusions, so employers were largely free to test. But in a few states, such as California, which added privacy rights to their constitutions, both government and private employers were more restricted. Most of these restrictions, though, kick in after the person gets hired.[12] Then, the employer has to show a compelling reason to invade the employee's privacy through testing, and also use reasonable testing methods.[13]

The *Wilkinson v. Times Mirror Corporation* case in California, decided in 1989, helped give employers a free hand to test prospective employees. It began in 1987 when the Matthew Bender Company, a Times Mirror Corporation subsidiary, adopted a policy of including a drug and alcohol test in a physical exam for job applicants. If an applicant passed a written test and interview and got a conditional job offer, he or she would then have to pass a medical exam, which included a drug and alcohol test.[14] But several applicants refused to take the test, claiming it was an invasion of privacy and an unfair business practice, and the case ended up in court.

But the California Appeals Court supported the employers, since these were only job applicants, not employees, and the drug screening program involved only a minimal intrusion on their privacy. Besides, said the court, the applicants could freely agree to this limited invasion of privacy or could decline both the test and the conditional job offer. The court felt a private employer should have "considerable discretion" to set job-related hiring standards, and had a legitimate interest in providing a "drug and alcohol-free work environment," and keeping out problem employees with a drug or alcohol problem that might hurt their job performance or themselves. Thus, with a reasonable testing approach, say one with advance notice, a minimally intrusive collection process, and confidential test results, it was fine to test job applicants, particularly since applicants have to disclose certain personal information to prospective employers, so these employers can decide if they are fit for the job.[15]

However, it is a little tougher to test when employees are already hired. For example, in California, employers have to show they have a "compelling interest" to test, as occurred in two 1990 cases. In one, *Semore v. Pool,* James Semore had been working at the Kerr-McGee Chemical Corporation since 1977, when the company asked all employees to take a pupillary reaction eye test to determine if they were under the influence of drugs. Semore refused, and after the company fired him for insubordination, he sued on the grounds that an employer has no right to conduct arbitrary drug tests. Eventually, the appeals court that heard the case agreed that an employer could perhaps require an employee to take a simple nonintrusive eye reaction test. But an employer had to show it had a compelling interest to do so in a particular situation (i.e., it couldn't be a general policy). So the case went back to the trial court to weigh the two interests of the employer's interest in the safe operation of its chemical plant versus the employee's expectation of privacy, to determine if Kerr-McGee could randomly test in this case.[16]

The situation might be different if an employer did safety-sensitive work and had a position where more extensive testing was already accepted, such as in the case of workers in nuclear power plants, customs officials trying to stop drug traffic, air traffic controllers, pilots, flight attendants, school bus drivers, railway and highway safety inspectors, police personnel, and employees with top security clearances. But for regular private employees, particularly in lower level positions such as a secretary, engineering technician, or research biologist, random testing was out, as the California Appeals Court decided in the *Luck v. Southern Pacific* case in 1990.[17] It began in 1985 when Barbara Luck, a computer programmer in the engineering department, was asked to give a urine sample and let the company test it for drugs, alcohol, and other medications. After she refused, the company fired her for insubordination, although there was no reason to think that anything was wrong with her job performance. After Luck sued for wrongful termination and won almost $500,000 from the jury, the appeals court sided with her, agreeing that an employer could not require employees to be tested for drugs without a compelling reason to test. Luck was not in such a position at Southern Pacific, so the court felt she should not have to take the test.*

*The general rule is that if an employee works for the federal government, he or she is subject to testing if in a safety-sensitive position or if the employer reasonably suspects drugs or alcohol. But if an employee works for a private employer or for the state in a state with greater privacy protections, then the employer must show a compelling interest to test, which means that the employee's work must be directly connected to workplace safety or pose a substantial risk of danger at work.

The Status of Drug and Alcohol Testing Today

The guidelines for testing have largely been settled as a result of several different cases, and for the most part, employers have won the latest challenges, as long as the worker is in an industry where safety is a special concern or there is reasonable suspicion that a problem may exist.

Tough Times for Workers in Safety-Sensitive Industries. Yes, it's tough for workers in a safety-sensitive industry or position to gain much privacy today. A Michigan union found this out quite clearly, when they fought a mandatory drug testing program up to federal court in the case of *Plane v. U.S.*, decided in 1992.[18] The union represented heavy equipment operators and environmental protection specialists handling hazardous materials, and they objected to the mandatory random urinalysis drug testing program set up by the Defense Logistics Agency to achieve a "Drug Free Workplace." The drug testing plan violated the workers' Fourth Amendment rights against search and seizure, the union complained, arguing that their workers were not affected by the Supreme Court's 1985 ruling in *Skinner* which permitted the testing of workers in safety-sensitive positions. The union claimed that *Skinner* referred only to transportation workers, and that the court was concerned specifically with "safe transportation."

However, the District Court quickly dismissed that fine distinction, pointing out that there were certainly major safety considerations here, even if the employees didn't carry any passengers. After all, the court noted, "the safety and health of people can be significantly endangered by employees operating equipment that do not carry passengers," and it gave some pointed examples: "If the fork-lift or crane operator improperly lifts a load and drops it onto other employees, the harm will be immediate. If a cutting torch operator improperly cuts into hazardous materials while other employees are nearby, the harm again could be immediate. If a tractor operator fails to navigate the trailers properly such that they tip over . . . the harm again could be immediate. . . . " In short, after listing numerous ways that a drug-impaired operator could hurt fellow employees or members of the general public who were on site, the court concluded that the government's interest in protecting people from the obvious dangers due to someone on drugs operating heavy machinery outweighed an employee's interests in privacy.[19]

Suspected of Using or Abusing? You Could Be Out of a Job. Even if workers are not in safety-sensitive positions, if employers can show they reasonably suspected a worker was under the influence of or was abusing drugs, they can fire him or her. That's what happened to Jim Ritchie and several other employees who failed a drug test in Nebraska and were fired. They sued the Walker Manufacturing Company in the case of *Ritchie v. Walker Manufacturing Company,* decided in 1992. The employees protested that their firing for failing the test was unfair, claiming this violated their employment contracts and the state and federal constitution and laws. After all, they claimed, they weren't working in a sensitive industry or in a sensitive position.

But the federal appeals court sided with Walker, concluding that an employer could fire such a worker if there was probable cause to believe he or she was using or under the influence of drugs on company property or on company time. Walker had hired an investigator to check if any employees were using or under the influence of drugs, and the investigator had pointed to Ritchie and the other dismissed workers. The company already suspected them of violating its drug policy before giving them the test, and thus had a good reason to test them.[20]

Submit or Be Fired. Still other recent cases have supported the employers' right to ask for information on drug use, give surprise drug tests, and fire employees who refuse to submit.

In Colorado, Carmela Mares refused to fill out a form asking about the prescription drugs she used or take a drug test, when the Conagra Poultry Company asked her to do this, so the company fired her. Though she claimed the company's request for medication information invaded her privacy, the federal court which decided her case—*Mares v. Conagra Poultry Company*—in 1992, sided with the company. Any invasion of her privacy was insignificant, said the court, particularly since the company was keeping the information confidential. The company had legitimate reasons for requiring employees to complete the form, such as protecting them from false positives in its drug test. Case dismissed.[21]

Likewise, a group of employees at a Michigan auto trim plant had much the same fate. After they refused to submit to a drug test or failed it, they were fired by the Eagle-Picher Industries Company's Trim Division Plant. Then, when they protested their firing in the *Baggs v. Eagle-Pitcher Industries* case, decided in 1992, the court gave Eagle-Pitcher its rousing support. Even though the court agreed that the company's mandatory workplace urine testing might be "an intrusion that a reasonable person would find objectionable," it felt under Michigan law that an employer had a right to "use intrusive and even objectionable means to obtain employment-related information about an employee." So if Eagle-Pitcher wanted to know if employees were reporting to work with drugs in their system, using a urine analysis test for drugs, that was fine.[22]

The Recent Backlash against Drug Testing. This overall victory on testing by employers has disturbed some privacy advocates and plaintiffs' attorneys. For example, attorney Judith S. Rosen expressed her dismay in an article in the *Golden Gate University Law Review* after the Department of Transportation registered a big win against the International Brotherhood of Teamsters in a West Coast case. As a result, the Federal Highway Administration could now freely require truck and bus drivers to submit to six forms of drug testing (including random, twice a year, before employment, and after an accident), and Rosen greeted the news as another defeat for the Fourth Amendment. As she concluded despondently: "This case appears to open the way for the future erosion of fourth amendment protection in other occupations and professions and in other aspects of individuals' lives."[23] Meanwhile, back at Temple University, another legal scholar decried the verdict, too, arguing that all of these different types of tests were just too much and only random testing made sense; by allowing all these tests, the court was permitting "an unnecessary intrusion" into the employees' "right to be free from unreasonable searches."[24]

Yet, while the higher courts have given their okay to most testing, some employees are still fighting and winning in the lower courts. Though they may not ultimately win as their victories are appealed up the court system, their wins in some trials are showing employers that drug testing can still be quite expensive, and may discourage some from doing it, though for now, increasingly more and more employers do.

Thus, the drug wars continue, though employers have won most of the battles. In 1993, the number of firms using drug testing reached an all-time high—85 percent, according to a yearly survey by the American Management Association reported in *Privacy Journal.* Yet, positive test results are down—down to 2.5 percent among current employees and 4.3 percent among applicants, perhaps because employees are aware employers are testing or because so many more workers are being tested.[25] Still, here and there, employees and privacy advocates fight on, trying to stop drug testing as an invasion of personal privacy.

Privacy and Sex Harassment. Another employment area recently affected by invasion of privacy claims is in connection with charges of sexual harassment. This connection started in the 1990s, with the sudden explosion of sexual harassment claims, particularly since the Clarence Thomas–Anita Hill hearings focused attention on this subject.

While these claims are commonly linked with assault, battery, wrongful discharge, emotional distress, and the like, the lawyers in these cases have recently thrown in invasion of privacy charges, too. They have done so because harassment victims claim their employer or coworker invaded their privacy by creating a hostile work environment or by wrongly touching or pressuring them. Then, too, invasion of privacy charges may come up in these cases, because in defending himself the employer or coworker has tried to investigate the employee pressing charges or has made derogatory comments about that employee, casting him or her in a false light. And even if only an employee is doing the actual harassing, the employer is commonly charged as being responsible, too. Yet, while these harassment/privacy claims have increased, employees have had somewhat mixed results.

One employee who lost was Ann Juarez, an administrative assistant at Ameritech Mobile Communications in Illinois. She sued her former employer in the case of *Juarez v. Ameritech Mobile Communications Incorporated,* decided in 1992, because a coworker, Peter Shkrutz, the company's assistant treasurer, had sexually harassed her back in 1986. At first, Juarez reported his increasingly offensive acts to another employee with whom she had become friendly. But after her friend told her supervisor, word of the harassment was passed on to the company's human resources department. They encouraged Juarez to file a formal complaint, and after she did, the company investigated, and suspended the offending coworker for a week without pay. Shkrutz stopped harassing Juarez after she filed her complaint, and left the company about six months after his suspension. But Juarez's work seemed to decline after this, and soon after Shkrutz left, the company terminated her too for poor work performance.

But was it just poor performance? Juarez suspected that the firing was due to her harassment claim. So in January 1989, she sued Ameritech, claiming the company was not only responsible for not preventing the harassment, but had terminated her in retaliation for her complaints. She charged invasion of privacy as well, on the grounds that Shkrutz's harassment had "violated her right to privacy . . . and invaded her seclusion, solitude, and private affairs." But regardless of what Shkrutz may have done, the court concluded that Ameritech did not know about his harassment before Juarez complained, and agreed that Ameritech fired her for poor performance, not for filing the complaint. So Juarez lost her case.[26]

By contrast, Michelle Ann Stockett from Florida struck pay dirt when she sued her former employer Frank Tolin and three Florida corporations she claimed he controlled, for sexual harassment and invasion of privacy. She sued because Tolin repeatedly touched the private parts of her body and several times entered the bathroom while she was there. The case, *Stockett v. Tolin,* decided in 1992, began when Stockett went to work for Tolin as a receptionist in 1985. Excited about the job being an entry into the film business, Stockett participated for a few months in 1986 in an on-the-job internship program to get training in the film business. Then, she continued working for Tolin until April 1987, when she finally quit, claiming she couldn't take the harassment anymore, having endured it quietly until then.

Just what did she put up with? According to Stockett, Tolin was after her from her first day on the job as a receptionist in December 1985. He sidled up to her at her desk and pressed his body against her, saying "I'd love to eat you all up." At once, she pushed him away, and soon after, another employee warned her to stay away from Tolin, because he "liked young girls." But avoidance didn't seem to work well, and soon there were numerous other incidents, many even more outrageous. For example, one time while Stockett was sitting in a chair typing, Tolin came up behind her, pressed down on her shoulders so she couldn't get up, and then reached over and squeezed her breasts. Another time, while she was at her desk, he came up from behind her, stuck his tongue in her ear, and crudely said he wanted to perform oral sex on her. Still another time, when Stockett was changing clothes in the ladies room after work, Tolin walked in, smiled, and said "hello." Though Stockett screamed at him to leave, he stood there staring at her for a few seconds before he left. Finally, a week before she left, she encountered him in a hallway, whereupon he asked how long she had been there. When she responded about one and a half years, Tolin said he was tired of waiting to "f . . . you," as it is euphemistically described in the court records. She always had an excuse, he griped, and after bragging about his sexual prowess, he demanded, "F . . . me or you're fired."

All of this lurid evidence was enough for the court, which agreed that Tolin's behavior not only created a "pervasively hostile work environment," but his "offensive sexual behavior was relentless, and can only be characterized as crossing all bounds of common decency." Thus, the court readily agreed that Tolin's actions had invaded her privacy, besides being wrong for other reasons, including battery, intentional infliction of emotional distress, and false imprisonment.[27]

In turn, Stockett's win was especially important, because this was the first time a plaintiff had successfully linked an invasion of privacy claim with a sexual harassment charge in a published court action. So more claims of this type are likely to follow, making sexual harassment still another way of invading someone else's privacy.

The Problem of Employer Investigations

Yet, even if an employer tries to stay out of employee affairs and maintain a harassment-free environment, he or she can run into problems in trying to support employees who do make a claim about someone else. This is because now the accused harasser may object to the employer checking into the accusation, claiming the investigation is an invasion of *his* privacy. Such challenges have recently come up in the context of investigating sexual harassment charges, but they can come up whenever an employer investigates an employee's charge about anything—whoever is being investigated may claim an invasion of privacy and sue. Although an employer is generally free to conduct a reasonable investigation, it can still cost a considerable amount to defend these cases, which have become increasingly common.

A typical case is what happened to one employer, John D. Powers, who owned a janitorial services company, Servicemaster by Rees in Arizona and won in the case of *Miller v. Servicemaster by Rees* decided in 1993. His wife worked alongside him in the company, and while she was working for one client, she claimed a man in the office suddenly touched her lower right leg as she walked toward a file drawer he had just opened. He claimed he had touched her to prevent her from tripping over the drawer. But she perceived his touch as harassment, and after her husband complained to the man's employer, the man sued for defamation and interference with his business relationship, among other things. Eventually, the county Superior Court and Appeals court judges agreed the man had no case, since she and her husband, who employed her, had a privilege to report a perceived act of sexual harassment, since the state's public policy is protecting employees from workplace harassment. It is therefore appropriate to report a charge, as long as this isn't a malicious false report or the charge isn't excessively published. Thus, Powers and his wife were absolved of any charges. Still, they had the considerable expense of defending themselves.[28] Thus, just reporting or investigating complaints to avoid harassment suits can lead to costly litigation.

How Far Can Investigations Go?—Using Private and Off the Job Investigations

Part of the problem is knowing just how far the employer can go to conduct a reasonable investigation. For while a *reasonable* investigation is fine, the question is what is "reasonable" and when do employers go too far, particularly when they bring in private investigators to help them investigate.

Here things get murky, although generally, as long as employers and their investigators restrict their observations to places where the employer is in charge or to public places, that's fine. But if the investigation becomes too intrusive and delves into the private areas of the employee, that's going too far. Unfortunately, one literally needs to be a lawyer today to figure out what is too private, intrusive, or unreasonable. The problem is made even more complicated because the laws and interpretations vary from state to state. Generally, though, when cases come to court, the employers prevail.

This is what occurred when Carl Munson, a former school principal, sued the Milwaukee Board of School Directors after he resigned, in the case, *Munson v. Milwaukee Board of School Directors,* decided in 1992. He left because of allegations that he didn't live in the district, although as a top school official, he was supposed to live there according to school policy. Munson's gripe, among other things, was that two school board safety aides invaded his privacy by following him on public streets and highways during his commute to determine if he lived in the district or not. The school board employed these aides to follow him since they suspected he lived outside the district, since one of his cars was registered to an address outside the city, and his credit report and real estate broker's license listed an outside address, too. The board wanted to get the evidence to prove this.

So did the aides go too far in investigating Munson? Eventually, the judge said no, finding all of his claims frivolous. In the judge's view, the aides' surveillance was fine, since they "never trespassed onto Munson's private property"; instead they only observed him from public streets or highways.[29]

Many worker's compensation and employee theft cases similarly involve special investigators, raising claims about how far employers can go in investigating. Can they hire undercover investigators, for example, to pretend to be other employees or assume other roles, such as that of market researchers, in order to ask questions? Can they employ investigators to stake out an employee's property and observe him or her? Generally, the laws and courts agree they can.

That's what happened in a Utah case, *Turner v. General Adjustment Bureau,* decided in 1992. Jackie Turner, the wife of a workers' compensation claimant, sued both the investigators from Inteltech, hired by the General Adjustment Bureau and her husband's original employer, Oak Norton, in 1984 for fraud and invasion of privacy. The investigators posed as market researchers, she griped, and as a result they gained access to the Turner home to gather information on her husband. They did this by asking the Turners to test various consumer products and invited Turner to participate in a shopping spree, which was subsequently canceled.

Eventually, though, the Court of Appeals supported the investigators, since despite their victory, their investigation was limited to gathering information on the worker's compensation claim, and they never entered the Turner's home without her permission and their visits were for a relatively short period.[30] If the Turners were fooled, that was their problem, and since they gave permission, though fooled, the investigators hadn't invaded their privacy.

Similarly, in Alabama, though an investigator got into a fight with an employee who discovered him staking out the house, the court favored the investigator. The case, *Johnson v. Corporate Special Services,* decided in 1992, began after Billy Johnson filed a claim against his employer for benefits after he was injured at work, claiming he was over 50 percent impaired in his ability to work. To find out whether his claim was true or false, his employer's insurance company hired Corporate Special Services, and they sent investigator Tim Jirgens to check him out. Jirgens first parked on the street outside Johnson's house. After the police asked him why he was prowling around the neighborhood, he explained and next pulled into a driveway across from Johnson's house. At this point, because of the commotion with the police, Johnson noticed Jirgens. He pulled his own car in front of the driveway, blocking Jirgen's car, and walked up to Jirgens to ask him what he was doing. Soon the two men began arguing. When Jirgens pulled out a gun, Johnson nervously backed down, and Jirgens maneuvered out of the driveway and drove away.

But this didn't end the incident. Instead, Johnson sued for invasion of privacy, as well as assault and battery because of the drawn gun. Though the jury decided the assault and battery charges in favor of Jirgens, Johnson pursued his privacy claim which had been dismissed by the trial judge, and the Alabama Supreme Court agreed he had no claim, concluding the investigation was perfectly legitimate. It felt this way because the investigation was designed to determine if the worker's compensation claim was valid, and Jirgens did nothing offensive or objectable in checking. He didn't intrude into Johnson's home and he was parked on a public street. Thus, he only observed Johnson while he was outside his home or in his front yard, where he was exposed to the public.[31] Johnson's activities could have been observed by any passerby, so an investigator could observe them, too.

The courts have also approved videotaping workers in the course of investigations, as occurred in the *Marrs v. Marriott Corporation* case, decided in December 1992. The Marriott Corporation fired Timothy Marrs, a security guard, after a hidden camera showed him breaking into the locked desk drawer of a security investigator. Marrs fought back, claiming wrongful termination and charging that the videotaping invaded his privacy, too. The court disagreed, since the company taped him in an open office area, to which all security guards had access. Besides, he was an employee at work, so using any surveillance, including videotaping, was fine, because, as the court put it: "there can be no liability for observing an employee at work since he is then not in seclusion."[32]

When an Investigation Goes Too Far

So when might a private investigation go too far? Generally, the answer seems to be when it invades an individual's private area, where he would expect to have personal privacy, even a refuge from others. Or if the investigation becomes too intrusive, obvious, and embarrassing, then that might overcome the right to conduct a legitimate investigation, too.

This is what happened in an Ohio case, *Sowards v. Norbar, Inc.*, decided in March 1992, when an employer tried to search an employee's private motel room. Even though Norbar had rented the room for its employees, it didn't have the right to search, too. The company had originally hired Charles Sowards in 1986 as an over-the-road truck driver to deliver mail from Columbus, Ohio to Washington, DC. After a twelve-hour layover in Washington, Sowards was supposed to return to Columbus with another mail shipment. The problem developed when Norbar wanted Sowards to make an extra stop on two days in August 1987, and his supervisor put a notice requesting this on his driver's clipboard. But Sowards claims he never got this message and that no one told him to make the stops. In any event, he missed them, and after Norbar fired him for this, Sowards sued for invasion of privacy, as well as wrongful termination, claiming that Norbar had violated his privacy when it sent an employee into his motel room where he was staying in Washington, DC to search for a missing permit book. Though Norbar claimed it had rented and paid for the room, and thus its employee could enter without Soward's consent, the appeals court agreed with the trial jury that an invasion of privacy had occurred. After all, the court observed, these single-occupancy hotel rooms "were meant as a private refuge for drivers laying over in Washington, DC."[33]

The Big E-Mail Battle

So if an employer can't check into an employee's private areas without invading his or her privacy, what about electronic mail (E-mail), which is delivered via modem from computer to computer? Is that private or not? This has become a new battlefield since the late 1980s, as more and more people are using E-mail at work, as well as for other communications. In 1980, there were only about 430,000 electronic mailboxes, addresses of individuals on computer; by 1992, the number was up to 19 million;[34] and there are even more today.

Yet, this area of controversy is so new that the cases are just starting to turn up in court. As a result, the laws and guidelines affecting E-mail haven't been fully tested. Still, the developing trend in these early decisions seems to be that the employee doesn't have an expectation of privacy in an E-mail system set up by an employer, so that employers have a right to monitor E-mail, much like they might monitor other business messages sent by letter or phone at work.

The battle over E-mail first exploded into public consciousness due to the struggle between two software giants in California, Borland International in Scotts Valley and Symantec in Cupertino. In October 1992, Eugene Wang, then a vice-president at Borland quit and joined rival Symantec. Soon after, Borland charged he left with some of the company's confidential documents, after discovering his alleged theft of trade secrets by reading his electronic mail to Gordon Eubanks, Symantec's CEO. Wang thought he had erased this information, but Borland one-upped him by asking its E-mail system provider, MCI, to undelete the messages in Wang's mailbox.[35] Then, with this information in hand, Borland filed a civil suit against Symantec and triggered a criminal investigation of Wang and Eubanks, which led to police searches of their homes.[36] The saga was turning into an E-mail thriller.

But could Borland legally intercept and use this intercepted E-mail information to show that Wang had stolen its secrets? A good question, because under the Electronic Communications Privacy Act of 1986, all E-mail systems are protected from unauthorized outside users. But who is "unauthorized?" The act primarily prohibits disclosing E-mail transmissions through public-service E-mail systems, but it does not protect the privacy rights of internal systems. Then, too, as of the end of 1993, no states had passed legislation restricting employers in looking at their employee's mail,[37] and when employer and employee rights collide, commonly employers' rights are given more priority.

Still, whatever the outcome in this Borland-Semantec face-off, there have been subsequent efforts to clarify the situation and provide more protection for employees. For example, in the spring of 1993, Illinois Senator Paul Simon introduced a bill entitled "Privacy for Consumers and Workers" to force companies to notify workers if they were monitoring electronic communications, including E-mail. Also, the bill required them to advise their employees if they were checking on their phone calls or data-entry keyboard activity. It is still working its way through Congress.[38]

Meanwhile, the privacy advocates and employers have been lining up their arguments in the battle for and against protecting E-mail. For example, on the one hand, the privacy advocates argue that E-mail does require a password, indicating that it should be considered private. But in rebuttal, employers claim the mailbox is more like a company property right. For example, in defending their search, Borland spokesman Steve Grady commented: "E-mail is like an in-box on someone's desk. When they leave it reverts to the corporation."[39]

Given this confusion, employers are being advised to establish clear E-mail policies, so employees understand their E-mail messages are not private, and are more like postcards than private letters. This is particularly so, since E-mail messages can be printed out, seen by anyone passing by an unattended screen, or monitored for legitimate reasons, such as auditing the communications system. Thus, many employers are taking the approach of trying to help everyone better understand the relative lack of privacy in E-mail technology and explaining their monitoring policies to keep everyone out of court and avoid employee discontent and distrust over unexpected snooping.[40]

What Happens When It's Over—What Employers Can and Can't Say

One final area of controversy relates to what the employer can or cannot say about an employee who was fired, left under a cloud, or a prospective employee who wasn't hired in the first place. This has developed into a privacy issue because many former or unhired prospective employees are charging that employer comments about them are damaging their reputations, presenting them in a false light, or both. Generally, as long as an employer states the truth and expresses an opinion to an interested party, such as another prospective employer, and is not publicizing the matter to make the employee look bad, or revealing truly private facts, like a medical condition, the employer can state what he or she really thinks. But even so, the increase in disgruntled former or never hired employees filing suit is causing many employers to be afraid to share an opinion at all, even if true. Instead, many will simply say a former employee worked there and left, but not why.

Some examples of the growing number of termination and talk cases include these, which largely support the employer's right to talk.

Sherwin J. Watkins griped about what his former employer said when he sued the General Refractories Company in Utah, where he had worked for almost twenty years in the case of *Watkins v. General Refractories Company,* decided in 1992. He had first worked as a cost supervisor and then as a glass marketing manager, but he was terminated in 1990, when the company was cutting back its workforce and decided his position was no longer necessary. Afterwards, when he tried to find another job at Geneva Steel, he was turned down, and he felt it was because a company official made defamatory statements about him, putting him in a false light, so his application was rejected. But the District Court in Utah supported the employer, stating that General Refractories had a "qualified privilege" to explain why it terminated Watkins with a prospective employer, which had a valid interest in knowing the reason Watkins was discharged. Then, too, the company only shared this information in a private conversation; it didn't publicize these statements, so Watkins couldn't claim any false light publicity.[41]

Even Edward Geick couldn't win what seemed like a stronger case, when he took on the President and Board of Trustees of the village of Lake Zurich in Illinois in the case of *Geick v. Kay*, decided in 1992. He claimed they all invaded his privacy and interfered with his economic prospects among other claims, after he resigned as a village administrator due to differences. It might have seemed he had a stronger case, since when he resigned, he and the city had signed a separation agreement that no one would make any statements to the public or the media about his resignation, his involvement in a federal court case, or previous employment as an administrator in another state. But then statements by the village board president James Kay turned up in the local *Daily Herald*, implying he was not trustworthy. In fact, the Lake Zurich village even sent out a press release implying he was a liar and referring to the settlement of a sexual harassment lawsuit Kay had been involved with. But despite the separation agreement, the Illinois Appellate Court decided he had no case. It ruled that because Geick was a public official he had to prove Kay and the Board acted with "absolute malice" in making any statements about him. Then, to make matters even more difficult, Kay and the Board had absolute immunity as town government officials, so they couldn't be held liable for any statements they made in performing their official duties, which they had done here.[42]

And in numerous other cases that arose following termination and resignation, invasion of privacy claims were similarly thrown out, brought by people in all sorts of fields: a former insurance agent in Maryland reported on in an insurer's letter to policy holders,[43] a former computer analyst in Kansas fired for dishonesty and filing false expense reimbursement requests reported to a national credit reporting agency;[44] a chief technician at a healthcare company in Washington, DC fired for neglect in maintaining equipment and ordering supplies, reported to an outside auditor and the Unemployment Compensation Board.[45] In all of these cases, the courts felt that the employers had a right to consult with or share truthful information with others who were legitimately interested in knowing about what happened. So they had no liability, had an absolute immunity, or had a qualified or conditional privilege to share this information. As a result, the former employees had no cause to object, even if what was said put them in an unfavorable light.

In short, employers are fairly free to talk about the reasons why a former employee was fired or resigned, if they tell the truth and share this information with others who have a reason to know this (such as prospective employers). They can even let the media know when a public official is involved.

Even so, increasingly disgruntled former employees are filing suit, even when they have left under a cloud, including criminal charges. For example, though he was convicted of contributing to the delinquency of a minor after he provided alcohol to one of his students and was sentenced to six months in jail, former teacher John McCartney sued the Oblates of St. Francis deSales High School in Ohio where he had worked for ten years until 1988 in the case of *McCartney v. Oblates of St. Francis deSales,* decided in May 1992. He complained that two St. Francis officials made statements that put him in a false light, because they told parents that he had been convicted of "corrupting a minor." This implied he was a homosexual, he said. But the appeals court thought these comments implied nothing of the sort. Rather, it agreed with the two fathers that they had made the statements in good faith, without actual malice, because they were concerned with furthering the education, development, and safety of the students in their care, and they believed that supplying alcohol to a student was "corrupting a minor." Thus, they were justified in making the remark.[46]

Still other cases have ended with similar results favoring employers when they have shared truthful information with interested parties about unsatisfactory employees without malice and with good intent.[47]

Summing Up

In sum, though employment invasion of privacy cases have mushroomed in the past few years, employers seem largely to have a free hand in what they do in the workplace. Generally, unless they step over the line by invading an employee's private space or by maliciously revealing information about an employee to the larger community, beyond the interested parties who have a reason to know this unfavorable information, such as prospective future employers who ask for recommendations, employers can pretty much make the rules. They still have to face the possibility of employee suits, which can be costly, but they are generally apt to win.

Notes

1. O'Donnell, "Employee Drug Testing—Balancing the Interests in the Workplace: A Reasonable Suspicion Standard," *Virginia Law Review*, 74 (1988): 969–1009.
2. Development in the Law, "Jar Wars: Drug Testing in the Workplace," *Williamette Law Review*, 23 (1987): 529–33.
3. O'Donnell, 971.
4. The Federal Railroad Administration regulation was 51 Fed. Reg. 44,431, 44,434 (1986); the Federal Aviation Administration regulation was 51 Fed. Reg. 27,921, 27,922 (1986).
5. McGovern, "Employee Drug-Testing Legislation: Redrawing the Battlelines in the War on Drugs," *Stanford Law Review*, 39 (1987): 1453–1517, 1454.
6. D.L. Rudley, "Invasion of Privacy and Drug Testing in the Private Workplace: A Case for the Application of Constitutional Concepts," *University of West Los Angeles Law Review*, 20 (1988): 43–85.
7. *Skinner v. Railway Labor Executives' Association*, 109 S. Ct. 1403 (1989).
8. *National Treasury Employees Union v. Von Raab*, 109 S. Ct. 1384 (1989).
9. Sand, "Drugs in the Workplace: The Supreme Court, Congress, and the Federal Agencies Declare War," *Employee Relations Law Journal*, 15 (1989): 125–34, 130.
10. Reuben, "Justices Uphold Some Worker Drug Testing," *Los Angeles Daily Journal*, March 22, 1989, 1.
11. Calbreath, "Ninth Circuit Courts Become Leader in Drug Testing Suits," *Los Angeles Daily Journal*, May 29, 1988, 1.
12. *Wilkinson v. Times Mirror Corporation*, 215 Cal. App. 3d 1034 (1989).
13. *Semore v. Pool*, 217 Cal. App. 3d 1087 (1990); *Luck v. Southern Pacific Transportation Company*, 119 Cal. App. Lexis 152 (1990).
14. *Wilkinson*, 1037–38.
15. *Wilkinson*, 1048–1051.
16. *Semore v. Pool*, 1092–93, 1097, 1105, 1100.

17. *Luck v. Southern Pacific Transportation Company,* 1990, Cal. App. Lexis 152.
18. *Plane v. U.S.,* 796 F. Supp. 1070 (W.D. Mich. 1992).
19. *Plane v. U.S.,* 1076–78.
20. *Ritchie v. Walker Manufacturing Company,* 963 F.2d 1119 (8th Circ. 1992), 1119–23.
21. *Mares v. Conagra Poultry Company, Inc.,* 971 F.2d 492 (10th Circ. 1992), 492–96.
22. *Baggs v. Eagle-Pitcher Industries, Inc.,* 957 F.2d 268 (6th Cir. 1992), 268–75.
23. Judith S. Rosen, "International Brotherhood of Teamsters v. Department of Transportation: The Fourth Amendment, Another Victim of the War on Drugs," *Golden Gate University Law Review,* 22, 127–141.
24. Vicki J. Moresi, "Drug Testing and the Fourth Amendment—An Excessive Intrusion Upon an Individual's Right to Privacy," *International Brotherhood of Teamsters v. Department of Transportation,* 932 F.2d 1292 (9th Cir. 1991), *Temple Law Review,* 65, 1039–1051.
25. "Drug Testing," *Privacy Journal,* 19 (May 1993): No. 7, p. 7.
26. *Juarez v. Ameritech Mobile Communications, Inc.,* 957 F.2d 317 (7th Cir. 1992), 318–22.
27. *Stockett v. Tolin,* 791 F. Supp. 1536 (S.D. Fla. 1992), 1542–55.
28. *Miller v. Servicemaster by Rees,* 851 P.2d (Ariz. App. Div. 1. 1992), 143–146.
29. *Munson v. Milwaukee Board of School Directors,* 969 F.2d 266 (7th Circ. 1992), 267–70.
30. *Turner v. General Adjustment Bureau,* 832 P. 2d 62 (Utah App. 1992), 64–67.
31. *Johnson v. Corporate Special Services,* 602 So. 2d 385 (Ala. 1992), 386–88.
32. *Marrs v. Marriott Corporation,* 62 FEP Cases 1221 (1992), 1227.
33. *Sowards v. Norbar, Inc.,* 605 N.E.2d 468 (Ohio App. 10 Dist. 1992), 470–75.
34. Ernest A. Kallman and Sanford Sherizen, "Private Matters," *Computerworld,* (23 November, 1992): 85.
35. Jonah McLeod, "E-Mail Remains Outside Current Privacy Protection Legislation," *Electronics* (14 December 1992): 12–13.
36. Mitchell Kapor, "Computer Spies," *Forbes,* 150 (9 November 1992): 288.
37. Anthony E. Schwartz, "E-Mail Privacy? Not on the Job!" *Computer Shopper,* 13 (August 1993): 23.
38. Richard A. Danca, "Privacy Act Would Force Firms to Inform Their Employees About E-Mail Monitoring," *PC Week,* 10 (28 June, 1993): 203–04.
39. Kapor, 288.

40. Bronwyn Fryer and Robert Furger, "Who's Reading Your E-Mail?" *PC World*, 11 (August 1993): 166–172.
41. *Watkins v. General Refractories Co.*, 805 F. Supp. 911 (D. Utah 1992).
42. *Geick v. Kay*, 603 N.E.2d 121 (Ill. App. 2 Dist. 1992).
43. *Veydt v. Lincoln National Life Insurance Company*, 614 A.2d 1318 (Md. App. 1992).
44. *Booth v. Electronic Data Systems Corporation*, 799 F. Supp. 1086 (D. Kan. 1992).
45. *Elliott v. Healthcare Corporation*, 629 A.2d 6 (D.C. App. 1993).
46. *McCartney v. Oblates of St. Francis deSales*, 609 N.E.2d 216 (Ohio App. 6 Dist. 1992).
47. *Smith v. Colorado Interstate Gas Company*, 794 F. Supp. 1035 (D. Colo. 1992); *Swanson v. Village of Lake in the Hills*, 962 F.2d 602 (7th Cir. 1992); and *Grossman v. Smart*, 807 F. Supp. 1404 (C.D. Ill. 1992).

Chapter 7

Cop Watch

The Growing Surveillance Society

The sanctity of one's home, car, or person is another arena where the privacy battle is playing itself out, as the cops, Federal Bureau of Investigation (FBI), and other law enforcement agencies struggle against crime in an increasingly lawless, violent time. On one side of the equation is the need to expand police powers to search and seize evidence and use undercover techniques to find criminals and combat criminal activity. Even neighborhood watch groups are joining forces with the police to help take back the streets from criminals.

But the downside of these efforts is the hapless individuals whose lives are disrupted by these searches and whose property may be seized because they fall under suspicion, although they may later be found innocent. One might question in some cases whether their private activities should even be considered a crime at all (such as smoking marijuana to relieve the pain of an illness). Increasingly privacy is losing out as we become more fearful of crime and the police increase surveillance. In response, many people are now fighting back to swing the balance to better preserve their privacy.

The Growth of Police Surveillance in the United States

The growing police presence through surveillance has been documented by sociologist Gary Marx in his book *Undercover: Police Surveil-*

lance in America. Initially, as he describes it, the first city police forces in the United States, in cities like New York and Philadelphia, were made up of nonuniformed and unarmed men, reflecting the antimilitary attitudes that characterized early U.S. policing.[1]

But then, beginning in the 1830s and starting a pattern that increased over the years, the police system became more formalized and the police were given more control. This occurred because crime and disorder increased as the United States became more urban and ethnically diverse. By the 1850s, many large cities like New York, Philadelphia, and Boston had uniformed municipal police departments which were under local, civilian control, and at first, they had only limited or no powers of crime detection. Their primary purpose was to provide a presence to deter criminals and the disorderly and to aid citizens who needed their help. They were not generally expected to take the initiative in looking for violations and wrongdoers. But as the nineteenth century wore on, and crime became more of a problem, most cities added small detective divisions, although initially these detectives were fairly passive in trying to detect crimes.

Then, in the beginning of the twentieth century, as city crime escalated, the police became more organized, gained more power, took more initiative, and new units were organized that began to make extensive use of covert techniques. These units were involved in checking into vice, alcohol, narcotics, gambling, and disruptive political groups, such as labor and radical organizations. Also, the police increasingly began to use paid informers or "stool pigeons" to gain evidence against other criminals.

Beginning in the 1920s, the police launched their first modern "war on crime" in their sweeps against prohibition and growing gang activity. Some even tried to infiltrate gangs of criminals through undercover work.[2]

Meanwhile, on the federal level, until the twentieth century, there was little organized police activity, since the federal government was much smaller than it is today. Private agencies, such as the Burns and Pinkerton Detective Agencies, were founded to help the growing industries, such as the railroads, banks, mines, and factories, combat crime. They commonly used undercover methods, too, in gathering evidence, and engaged in strike-breaking activities. Though the U.S. government made some preliminary efforts to create a national police force, such as the U.S. Post Office's Office of Inspection, established in 1836, and the

U.S. Treasury's Secret Service, created in 1865 to combat counterfeiting and filing false war bounty claims, often the U.S. turned to these private agents for detective work.[3]

Then, after the turn of the century, the federal government became more active in fighting crime after the FBI was founded in 1908 by Theodore Roosevelt. At first, it dealt primarily with auto thefts and bank robberies. But it became a major national police force in the 1930s, under J. Edgar Hoover, who became its director in 1924. In the mid-1930s, it became an increasingly high-profile organization, and developed a network of informants and used extensive surveillance and undercover techniques to obtain information, search for fugitives, and go after noted criminals like John Dillinger, as well as political groups perceived as a threat to the U.S., such as Communist and Fascist groups.

Later, in the 1960s and 1970s, the FBI further expanded its domestic intelligence activities in response to political unrest, social movements, and civil disorders, secretly monitoring many of these new left, black, and antiwar groups. Then, after these movements declined in the mid-seventies, and the FBI shifted its focus away from politics to using these techniques against conventional crime.[4]

The Growing Use of Undercover Techniques since the 1970s

Though the local and national police presence grew in the twentieth century due to increasing crime and social factors, the modern explosion of surveillance and undercover work really took off in the late 1960s and early 1970s, setting the stage for the surveillance society of today.

This occurred for several reasons. First, violence became a national issue, as people became shocked by a series of high-profile violent crimes, including the King and Kennedy political assassinations, growing civil disorders around the country, and an increase in crimes with weapons. Second, organized crime seemed to be expanding into new areas, and a concern with the spread of drugs grew, too. Meanwhile, new sophisticated white collar crimes emerged, as bureaucracies became more complex and new forms of financial property developed, making it easier to hide crimes in complex paper transactions.[5]

Thus, new, more complex and secret forms of policing were needed to deal with both local and nationwide crimes. At the same time, new technologies were developing that law enforcement personnel and private investigators could use to investigate through undercover and surveillance techniques.

The New Technologies

Among the first of these technologies was the use of bugs and wiretaps, beginning in the 1920s and 1930s. Their use spread in the fifties and sixties, fueled by fears of Communism and social disorders, and in the sixties and seventies, they became even more popular, as miniaturization and other technical developments reduced the size of equipment and made it more powerful, so it was easier to conceal, more portable, better able to pick up transmissions from greater distances. Also, there were now new remote-controlled and self-activated devices, radio transmitters, subminiature tape recorders, night-vision devices, and more powerful camera lenses, making secret surveillance easier. By the mid-1970s, video equipment was coming into common use, too, and soon there were all sorts of infrared, sensor, and tracking devices, as well as light amplifiers for viewing and taking photos at night.[6] In the 1980s, computer-aided videotape and the analysis of computer data trails were added to the mix.

New Organizations and Laws Supporting Undercover Work

Meanwhile, the need to combat crime and the grab bag of secret technologies to use against it was supported by the growth of supporting organizations, resources, laws, and court rulings expanding the power of the police.

For example, in the late 1960s, new national bureaucracies emerged, such as the Law Enforcement Assistance Administration (LEAA), created by the 1968 Omnibus Crime and Safe Streets Act, which existed until 1982. It was designed to provide funds and training to local agencies, including for setting up fencing, stings, and using decoy methods. Another new unit, the Federal Law Enforcement Training Center, established in 1970, provided courses for federal officers around the country, including techniques for surveillance, working undercover, and using informants.

In the mid-1980s, the 1984 Comprehensive Crime Control Act

allowed the government to keep or sell property seized in undercover operations and in conspiracy and drug busts. The Act allowed the U.S. Attorney General to turn over seized property to the states and local police agencies. In turn, the funds from selling seized properties (about $58 million between 1981 and 1982 for the Customs Service alone) financed further undercover efforts.[7] Many cities made several millions in sales, too.

Alongside these developments, starting in the 1970s, new organizations and data banks to investigate and keep track of all of this crime data were organized, some in cooperation with private industries, like the insurance industry, with a keen interest in protection against crime. Two examples were the Insurance Crime Prevention Institute (ICPI) and the National Auto Theft Bureau (NATB), set up to help law enforcement agencies arrest and prosecute those involved with insurance scams or auto theft and fraud.[8]

Meanwhile, as the police became more professionalized, with increased training and equipment, they took more initiative in fighting crime, which included advance planning and increasingly setting up sting and surveillance operations and using stop-and-search tactics. In turn, new laws and judicial decisions helped support the police in engaging in these surveillance operations, though these supporting laws subsequently triggered a countercrackdown on too enthusiastic police work led by more liberal legislators and civil rights organizations. As a result, increasingly rules have limited what the police can do, such as having to follow strict guidelines for questioning suspects and collecting evidence. Though now, the pendulum seems to be swinging back once again to give the police more leeway, reflected in the recent "three strikes and you're out" movement.

In any event, the irony of this crackdown on police behavior, as Marx observes, is an increase in using the very undercover work decried by civil libertarians to get around the restrictions in order to get the facts.[9] In turn, judicial decisions have generally supported these covert investigations, and the legislatures have generally left such practices to the police.

The Dangers of Growing Police Surveillance

Certainly, many of us would agree that covert techniques might sometimes be necessary to combat the increased spread of violent and more sophisticated crimes. But this spread of surveillance, search, and seizure methods can also seriously intrude on everyone's private lives, increasing the climate of fear and paranoia. Among the dangers:

1. Often, innocent people can be sucked into police stings and undercover operations, due to faulty tips, malicious informants, misinterpreted observations, and mistaken entries and searches.
2. Private behavior that would otherwise remain private and harm no one can be made public and be criminalized and prosecuted. There is wide disagreement over whether these are crimes or whether they are worth the time and expense of police investigation, arrest, and prosecution (such as the personal use of marijuana for a terminal illness).
3. The sense that law enforcement officials are watching and have vast data files on everyone can create a feeling of oppression, that one is increasingly living in a police state.

Today people indicate that one of their biggest fears is crime, resulting in a public call for increased police protection and crime fighting, while many people have retreated behind protected suburban enclaves or are less apt to go out at night. But many also decry the loss of personal privacy and freedom, as police and federal agents step up their efforts against crime, and use more and more search, surveillance, and undercover techniques in their fight. It's a Faustian bargain, and one that many people don't want to make as they fight back, claiming an invasion of privacy, as police efforts increasingly conflict with their own privacy rights.

Confronting the Police in the Courts

These battles against police surveillance have taken various forms in court, with challenges to car stop searches, unwarranted entries to the home and surrounding property, and stop and search efforts on the streets or in public buildings. Commonly these surveillances and searches have occurred during drug and pornography investigations, and the challengers are those arrested and sometimes convicted due to these searches.

Yet, the concern about such observing and searching extends beyond those who may be involved in illegal activity, since anyone potentially can be the subject of a surveillance or search. How much of our privacy do we want to sacrifice in the battle against crime? As the following examples illustrate, these privacy and policing interests are in a fine balance with each other which varies from situation to situation, community to community, state to state. The trend has been to weigh the balance in favor of the police in most of these battles, unless the police go too far in their investigations—though just what is "too far" is often unclear. The following cases illustrate these varying battlefronts.

On the Road

For many people, the car is much more than transportation, it is a symbol of success, power, a source of recreation, a kind of home away from home. But as many laws and court decisions make clear, it is not as protected as the home. That's because people have a "reduced expectation of privacy" in their cars.[10] So, the police have a greater right to check in a car, especially since cars are mobile and readily driven away. Thus, if a police officer suspects a problem, he often can immediately stop the car and search, whereas he might have to get a warrant to search a home. Routine stops at drunk driving checkpoints are likewise usually fine.

Martin Chaffee found this out in the case of *People v. Chaffee,* decided in November 1992, when he challenged a roadblock stop set up to detect and deter drunk driving. It was nearly 2 A.M. that night in August 1989, when Chaffee was driving alone a road in Allegheny, New York and observed the flares of a checkpoint ahead. It was not a stop he wanted to make and he quickly turned left into a parking lot to avoid the checkpoint. It was a legal turn, but a police trooper followed him, and after Chaffee circled the parking lot twice without parking, the trooper pulled Chaffee over. He quickly noticed several signs of intoxication—slurred speech, watery and bloodshot eyes, alcohol on Chaffee's breath, and so gave him a field sobriety test which he failed. Though Chaffee tried to fight the felony drunk driving charge, challenging the legality of the roadblock stop, he was soon out of luck. For as the New York Supreme Court decided, it was perfectly constitutional for the police to set up a roadblock to detect and deter drunk driving. Also, the police officer had a right to check out his car, thinking he was trying to avoid the checkpoint. None of this was sufficiently intrusive to interfere with Chaffee's privacy rights, for as the Court commented: "When the privacy interests of a motorist are balanced against the legitimate governmental interests in controlling drunk driving, the checkpoint procedure is a 'sufficiently productive mechanism to justify the minimal intrusion involved'."[11]

James Taylor was likewise out of luck in the case of *State v. Taylor*, decided in December 1992, when he claimed an officer didn't have a warrant to stop and search his car. The flap began when Taylor and a passenger were driving along a street in Yamhill, Oregon. After Taylor failed to signal for a turn, a police officer stopped him. Unfortunately Taylor was driving with a suspended license, and while he was stopped, the police officer noticed some two-way radio equipment on the backseat and a bulky pillowcase with many little jagged edges sticking out underneath the legs of Taylor's passenger in the front seat. At once the officer became suspicious, knowing that burglars frequently use pillowcases to collect stolen articles from a victim's house, and that similar radio equipment was used in a recent armed robbery and burglary in the area. So after asking Taylor a few more questions, he searched the pillowcase. When he found a money bag and jewelry, he arrested Taylor. To keep this incriminating evidence out of court, Taylor argued that the officer shouldn't have been allowed to search for it without a warrant. But the Oregon appeals court said no, since it felt that once the officer observed what he did and questioned Taylor's explanation, he had a reasonable suspicion that Taylor committed a crime. So he had a probable cause to search the pillowcase right away and didn't need a search warrant, since the car was mobile.[12]

Thus, at checkpoints and if they have a reasonable suspicion that something is wrong, the police can generally check further. But, if the police can't show they have a reasonable suspicion, personal privacy interests will prevail. Then, even if a person has committed a crime, the evidence against him cannot be used. It is the court's way of trying to protect everyone's privacy interests by keeping the police from going too far when they use surveillance and search methods.

This is what happened in the case of *People v. Woods*, decided in January 1993. A New York state trooper searched Darryl Woods' car after a traffic stop, because the small blue car had tinted windows, and a few days earlier, a small blue car with tinted windows was seen in the area where several hotel robberies and a larceny had occurred. So thinking maybe Woods was the hotel robber, the trooper made a quick U-turn to follow his car and pulled him over, though his only reason was that the tinted windows evoked the earlier blue car–hotel robbery association. But the trooper had no reason to believe that Woods or his passenger had just committed or were about to commit a crime. Still, the trooper asked to see Woods' license and registration, asked if Woods had any weapons in the car since he worked as a security guard. Then, he searched the entire car. Eventually he found what he thought was clear evidence that Woods was up to no good—a night stick, air rifle, mask, and army fatigues. Therefore, he arrested Woods for robbery, and in due course, Woods was convicted of both robbery and criminal possession of a weapon. But eventually, after Woods fought back, crying a privacy foul, the Supreme Court of New York threw the whole case out. This was because the trooper had no reason to question Woods about matters unrelated to the traffic violation (the tinted windows). Also, the officer couldn't simply search a motorist or vehicle unless he had reasonable grounds for believing the motorist guilty of a crime—not just a traffic offense. Though the trooper was justified in stopping Woods for the traffic violation, he went too far, so his actions were too intrusive for a normal traffic stop. So the evidence couldn't be used after all—case dismissed.[13]

Thus, unless the police have a good reason, they can't just start searching. Nor can they require individuals in stopped automobiles to submit to invasive tests.

Home, Sweet Home

Though people are supposed to have even more protection for privacy at home, since in theory, one's home is one's castle, increasingly, many protections have been chipped away. This has occurred primarily due to the search for drugs and pornography involving children or considered obscene. Also, in some states, if the police happen to observe people engaging in deviant sexual practices, even in the privacy of their own home, they can make an arrest.

Love It and Lose It

In some cases, the police and prosecutors have not only invaded people's homes in searching for illicit drugs and explicit materials, but they have confiscated their homes and other property as well, based on a suspicion alone that the property is involved in the use or sale of drugs. Recently, California changed its law to require a conviction before property can be seized, and by the time this book is published, this law may have been changed in other states too, because there has been a lot of public and political pressure over unfair confiscations. But in the meantime, the seizure laws are generally still in place, and as a result many people have lost their homes.

In *Presumed Guilty,* for example, Andrew Schneider and Mary Pat Flaherty, describe numerous cases in which people never charged with a crime have had cars, boats, money, and homes taken away due to federal forfeiture laws passed in 1984 which allow the police to seize the property of those even marginally involved with illegal drug activity. These laws were passed as a way to beef up the federal racketeering laws. But in about 80 percent of these confiscations, Schneider and Flaherty report, the people who lost property to the federal government were never charged with any crime. Rather, in many of these cases, which brought in about $2 billion dollars to the police departments involved between 1986 to 1991, the people lost their homes and other property simply because they looked like drug dealers (i.e., they were black, Hispanic, or flashily dressed), or because someone else, such as a relative or tenant, used their property for a crime, though they knew nothing about it.[14]

Through 1992 and 1993, these seizures were still going on, although people began fighting back against the more unfair seizures, stepping up the pressure to change the law.

An example of the kind of case mobilizing widespread opposition to these laws took place in 1993 in Placerville, California, where a well-loved elderly man, Byron Stamate, quietly raised some marijuana for his companion, who had cancer and other medical problems due to age. He couldn't bear to see her suffer, so in a small area in his house, he planted a little marijuana which he gave her to ease her pain. Unfortunately, when local law enforcement swept in, they not only took the plants, but they seized Stamate's house and other assets, including his bank accounts and stocks saved for his retirement, valued at over $400,000. After investigator and expert witness Ed Rosenthal, and defense attorney William Bonham got involved, they quickly alerted the community about what was going on, and the community rallied behind him. Besides the anger over the injustice of a man losing everything because of trying to help another person overcome suffering, people were also disturbed by the privacy invasion by the police, since the police had not observed anything suspicious at Stamate's house. Instead, they had based their suspicions that he was growing something by using heat detectors that sense how much heat is in different parts of the house. The additional heat suggests that something is growing. Thus, the local and electronic press began publicizing word of his plight, and the story went national.

But unfortunately, though the community and media support did result in Stamate getting back most of his property, the story did not have a happy ending. Stamate's companion killed herself with a bullet through her head, because she didn't want to testify against Stamate in the District Attorney's case and because she had worked all her life to put together a nest egg for her retirement and she was afraid if she didn't testify that the District Attorney would take her money as he threatened. In addition, Stamate was found guilty and lost about $26,000, $1,000 which he forfeited when the judge found him guilty, and about $25,000 which he had kept hidden away in his house. According to Stamate, the police took this money from his house when they raided it, but they did not report it as evidence, so he claims they stole his money, and that moreover the prosecutor who charged him was present when the money was found. So now Stamate has become an activist, joining the fight not only to help legalize marijuana for medical and recreational use, but to protect people's Fourth Amendment privacy rights from overzealous police intrusion.[15]

The Right to Search

These dramatic home confiscation cases reflect the extreme danger that can occur when concerns about crime and protecting society overwhelm personal privacy protections. Even many police feel we shouldn't wage the war against crime at the expense of personal rights. Sheriff Robert Ficano of Wayne County in Detroit, is quoted in *Presumed Guilty* by Andrew Schneider and Mary Pat Flaherty: "Seizure is an important tool," he stated. "But we'll lose it unless we keep a heavy emphasis on respecting individual rights."[16]

Perhaps the same might be said about the day-to-day police search and seizure practices for evidence of crimes. For here, too, there has been a continuing conflict over how far the police can go when they intrude upon personal privacy, particularly that of innocent people, in their efforts to combat crime.

A series of recent cases illustrate this struggle and the trend in court rulings on what the police can and cannot do. In general, the judges tend to give the police the benefit of the doubt, even when they make mistakes, unless they clearly go too far.

Minor Mistakes and Chance Encounters. What happens if the police enter your house by mistake or observe something illegal when they happen to be there for other reasons? Generally, judges have ruled they can do so, and this is not considered an invasion of privacy. In one Ohio case, *Linley v. DeMoss, City Commissioner,* decided in July 1992, Police Sergeant John Hammond had a search warrant for a house where a package of illegal methamphetamines was delivered in June 1990. But he mistakenly opened the door of the house next door and entered with his gun drawn. As he did, Geneva Linley, who lived there, fainted, and afterwards, still upset by the incident, she visited a psychologist who treated her for posttraumatic stress disorder, because the anxiety and depression she already suffered from worsened after the encounter with police. Fortunately, Hammond was able to hold back the rest of the strike team, so they correctly carried out the rest of the raid. But even though Hammond's entry was brief, it was disturbing enough that Linley sued for invasion of privacy and emotional damages. However, the Ohio Appeals Court concluded she had no case, since Hammond's entry was just a minor negligent mistake, not really a "wrongful premises" search.[17]

It is also generally not considered an invasion of privacy if a police officer happens to be in one's house for another reason and sees something illegal. Then he or she can seize and use it as evidence, according to what is known as the "plain view doctrine."

This is what happened in Oregon, in the case of *State v. Russell,* decided in March 1993. Police officer McDermott and an ambulance crew responded when Mrs. Russell went to her son's house to babysit for his sister's three young children after he left for work. She couldn't get in, because her daughter was lying on a couch, either asleep or unconscious, and after McDermott arrived, his loud knocks on the door still couldn't wake her. When he couldn't get in through the downstairs doors or windows, he tried to squeeze in through a basement window, and as he did, he observed potted marijuana plants beneath the window.

Though McDermott was successful in waking up the daughter, who was just a heavy sleeper, Russell was convicted for having the marijuana plants in his home. But could the police use the plants McDermott saw as evidence, or did the seizure invade his privacy rights in his home? That's what Russell tried to argue to suppress the evidence to reverse his conviction. But the Oregon Court of Appeals agreed that the officer could use the evidence, since he was just trying to be helpful in entering for what he reasonably believed was an emergency. Thus, he had a right to be at the window when he saw the marijuana plants and could therefore take them and use them as evidence against Russell.[18]

In other cases, if the police can claim they have probable cause to believe some kind of crime is going on inside, such as using or growing pot, they can get a warrant to look further. What reason do they need in order to be able to look? Basically, a tip from a reliable informant or observations from outside the house will do. Even a claimed smell emanating from the house may be enough, says Ed Rosenthal, the expert defense witness from Oakland who testifies in such cases.

This is what happened in the Washington case, *State v. Solberg,* decided in June 1992. The case began when a woman who said she was a real estate agent tipped off the police. She reported that while she was showing Solberg's residence to a prospective buyer, she was unable to show the basement because it was locked and she smelled a strong odor of marijuana at the house. As a result, the police checked the Seattle power and gas records and concluded that the extra power consumption records were consistent with Solberg using halide grow lamps for the plants. In addition, from outside, they saw blackened windows at Solberg's house. All this was enough, the judge agreed, to support the woman's tip, so they could get a warrant and search the house.[19]

In fact, the courts often support the police, even when officers have a technical slip-up in getting a search warrant or in conducting the search, such as not giving a person who won't consent, a full 24-hour notice before using a warrant to do the search,[20] or searching at 9:00 P.M. though the warrant says they can't search at night (here the court simply decided that night, for search warrant purposes, began at 10 P.M.).[21]

When the Police Go Too Far. But when police tactics go too far, the courts pull them back, so the police cannot use evidence illegally obtained at the expense of someone's privacy.

Say the police search warrant is too vague. The police can't go ahead and search everything and everyone, as occurred in an Oregon case, *State v. Ingram,* decided in April 1992. The Salem, Oregon police had gotten a warrant to search the home of Elaine Joyce Sink, several specified cars, and any individuals frequently at Sink's home, as well as all vehicles associated with the occupants. Yet, while the warrant was based on an extensive four-month investigation, which included several transactions in which an officer bought cocaine and marijuana from Sink, the court concluded the police went too far when they searched the pickup truck of a visitor. Though the truck was parked nearby and the police found methamphetamine in it, the court concluded the warrant was too vague to allow them to search all vehicles associated with the occupants. That is because it was so ambiguous and broad that the officers executing it could invade the privacy of people who shouldn't be searched, because the police didn't have any probable cause to search them. Thus, the Oregon Supreme Court threw out the evidence and Ingram's conviction.[22]

Then, too, judges have limited the police right to enter and search homes, when they have invaded the homes of tenants though their real suspect is the landlord; when an individual has not given consent; or when the police have broken in too quickly without giving anyone sufficient chance to consent. This is what happened in a series of cases coast to coast, in which judges dismissed or suppressed evidence when the police went too far.

For example, in a San Francisco Bay Area case, *Kreines v. U.S.* decided in March 1992, the police had gotten information that John Rupp, living in what appeared to be a one-family home, was involved in narcotics trafficking and money laundering for narcotics dealers. When they arrived with their warrant in hand in January 1986, Lorna Kreines, who lived in a lower level separate unit, showed them her six-month lease, explaining she was just a tenant. But the police barged into her house anyway and questioned her for almost an hour before they decided she was not involved in Rupp's activities and left.

But that wasn't the end of the matter for Kreines. A year later she sued various police and federal agents and the U.S. government for invasion of privacy, as well as trespass, assault, false imprisonment, and negligence for their invasive entry. And eventually, the U.S. Court of Appeals supported the jury's verdict on some of her claims. This was because the officers kept searching her apartment after they learned she had a separate residence at the address on the warrant and she showed them her lease, and that violated her constitutional rights, said the Court.[23]

Joseph Neftzer of Ohio found he had a right to refuse entry to an officer without a search warrant when that officer came to his house trying to arrest someone in the case of *State v. Neftzer,* decided in May

1992. The officer showed up at his home in December 1991 claiming he had an arrest warrant for Natalie Hardin, who he believed was there. When Neftzer asked to see the warrant, the officer declined, and when Hardin went to get her coat, Neftzer blocked the officer from entering and following her. By the time additional officers arrived and Neftzer agreed they could enter, Hardin had left by the backdoor, so the officer arrested Neftzer for interfering with the business of a law enforcement officer. But when Neftzer claimed he had a constitutional right to refuse the officer's entry, since he had no search warrant, the county court agreed, since there were no emergency circumstances permitting an entry without a warrant.[24]

The police also can't break down a door too quickly when they believe they have been refused entry, though they have a search warrant. A team of officers from Washington, DC, discovered this in the case of *Griffin v. U.S.*, decided in December 1992. They came looking for Bill Griffin, a high school student, at his mother's apartment; they believed Griffin had drugs there, because an undercover officer had bought drugs there a week before. Armed with a search warrant, they knocked loudly on the door at 1:40 A.M., and after about 30 seconds, when no one responded, they charged in, breaking open the door with a battering ram. Inside, they saw Griffin lying on a sofa in the living room, and on a nearby coffee table, they saw a package with a white rock of cocaine. As they searched, they found more packages of cocaine and money in the apartment, and arrested Griffin.

But when Griffin protested their overly eager, dramatic entry, the DC Court of Appeals agreed their forced entry was invalid, and therefore, they couldn't use any of the evidence from the bust. The Court felt they didn't wait long enough to give the people inside a chance to open the door willingly or to refuse, and they had no special emergency circumstances to justify their quick entry.

Moreover, their sudden intrusion not only affected Griffin, but his mother and three other presumably innocent overnight guests, who were not charged with anything. And breaking down the door was not only terrifying in itself, but undermined the security of the residents by leaving an open door that anyone could easily enter.[25]

Then, too, the courts have protected people's privacy when the police have brought along outsiders who weren't supposed to be involved in a search, such as occurred in one Michigan case *Bills v. Aseltine*, decided in 1992. A couple sued the police for allowing a private

GM security guard to help them look for property that might belong to the company. In the court's view, since the police shouldn't have allowed the guard to go in with them, the couple could pursue their case and collect damages.[26]

Thus, in preserving the sanctity and privacy of the home from overenergetic police intrusion, the courts and legislators have engaged in a kind of balancing act. They have given the police the benefit of the doubt in many cases when the police have made a good faith or minor error in intruding when they shouldn't. But at other times, the courts have supported the individual's privacy rights at home when the police have become too invasive, though the boundary lines are far from clear.

Outside These Walls. The lines are likewise muddy on what's private or not when the police investigate outside the house, or station themselves outside to look in. Generally, though, the police have more leeway in checking outside the house, whether in the hallways, driveways, surrounding property, or even in the garbage left in the yard or street to be taken away. That's what happened to Jose and Manuel Acosta and Martha Ovalle, in the Pennsylvania case of *U.S. v. Acosta,* decided in May 1992, when they were arrested for various cocaine and drug trafficking charges by a team of police, Drug Enforcement Agency personnel (DEA), and Alcohol, Firearms and Tobacco (AFT) agents. The law enforcement team arrived with an arrest warrant that listed the apartment building address but not the residence of the person they were seeking, Carlos Santiago. Though the agents weren't sure where Santiago lived, they began ringing doorbells downstairs. After no one answered and they discovered an unlocked outside door, they entered the hallway and knocked on the door of Acosta's first floor apartment; again, no one answered. But this time, after the officers heard scuffling sounds inside, followed by a toilet flushing, they broke down the door and charged in. Though they never did find Santiago, they found drugs, drug paraphernalia, cash, and weapons, and promptly arrested the three residents, Jose, Manuel, and Martha.

But the big privacy question was, did they have the right to be in the hallway where they heard the suspicious sounds leading to the bust. Acosta's attorney argued no, since the police weren't invited in. But the court said they could, since the hallway was easily accessible to the public, such as visitors, solicitors, and workmen, not only tenants. The residents had no expectation of privacy in these common areas, so the officers could go in, with a warrant or without.[27]

In the Fields and on the Streets. Likewise, in investigations, the police are usually free to use whatever they observe on private property if they are stationed on public property or far enough away from the house to be on what is considered "open fields" around a house. These rules also mean that the police can generally fly by in a helicopter, and if they see any indications of illegal activity, they can use this as evidence, as long as they don't get too close.

Commonly, the police use these practices to investigate drug, theft, and pornography cases, and private investigators have used them too, particularly in investigating insurance and worker's compensation cases and domestic spats. What these rules and practices mean is that outside the home, people generally have little privacy protection. If the public can see it, the police and investigators can generally use it, unless their actions are particularly invasive. That is why the Lamartinieres of Louisiana didn't have a very good holiday when they went on a hunting trip, as recounted in the case of *Lamartiniere v. Allstate Insurance Company,* decided in 1992. While they were away hunting back in November 1977, a fire broke out in their house, causing considerable damage. Was it a chance fire? Emerson Wilkerson, an investigator for the Allstate Insurance Company which covered the property, didn't think so. He had been in the house before as a prospective buyer, when the Lamartinieres were trying to sell their house through a local real estate agent. Wilkerson suspected that the Lamartinieres might have secretly hidden some of the furniture he had seen on the first floor, since it was gone when he came to investigate for Allstate, and he didn't think that the fire had burned down to this floor.

Thus, Wilkerson began checking storage warehouses in the area, thinking the furniture might have ended up there, and after he located a miniwarehouse storage facility rented by the Lamartinieres six weeks before the fire, he felt sure this was where the furniture was to be found. However, the miniwarehouse was locked, and only the Lamartinieres had the key. But the adjacent warehouse was vacant, the warehouse attendant told him. So using a stepladder the attendant provided, he climbed up and looked over the wall between the two warehouses. And, yes, there was some of the missing furniture.

After Wilkerson went to the local deputy sheriff with this information, the sheriff questioned Lamartiniere and subsequently arrested him for arson. Then, after searching the warehouse, the sheriff's office also turned up some tools that seemed to belong to the company where Lamartiniere worked. When the company found out it soon fired Lamartiniere, thinking he had taken the tools, though Lamartiniere pleaded innocent, claiming he had bought the tools at a junk sale.

No, the Lamartinieres did not have a very good holiday, and they ended the season feeling thoroughly embarrassed and humiliated by all these charges, as they claimed when they sued Allstate and the investigator for invasion of privacy because of the original peeking. But whether they were guilty or not, the appeals court finally concluded they had no case, since they couldn't show any damages from the peeking—at least from Allstate and the investigator. That's because Wilkerson turned his information over to the sheriff, who continued the investigation from there.[28]

James Mattingly of Georgia didn't fare very well either in the case of *Mattingly v. State* when he argued that a police officer had illegally intruded into the wooded area he owned around his house. He hoped the evidence against him, which included some marijuana found in his car, would be thrown out. But the appeals court turned him down, since the officer was in a wooded area beyond the part of his land that was maintained and cultivated. So the officer was in the "open fields" beyond the private area around Mattingly's house, and had a right to be there.[29]

However, putting up trespassing signs will sometimes work, as Guy Scott in rural New York discovered in the case of *People v. Scott,* decided in April 1992. Scott had posted "keep out" signs about every 20 to 30 feet around his property—about 165 acres of hilly, uncultivated fields and woodlands. Inside, he planted his small marijuana patch. Then, one day in the fall of 1987, a deer hunter shot a deer near his property, and followed the mortally wounded animal onto Scott's land. While there, he observed the remnants of a marijuana-growing operation, and the next summer, when he wandered onto Scott's property again, he saw about 50 plants and reported them to the police, bringing a leaf from one plant as proof. Soon after, a state investigator accompanied the hunter onto the property, passing Scott's "no trespassing" signs along the way.

Fortunately, the signs were what Scott needed. The New York Court of Appeals threw out his conviction, observing that he had an expectation of privacy in these areas, since he had put up the signs. So the police violated his property rights and trespassed on his land.

But while Scott's signs worked, in many areas they don't—witness the many raids, irrespective of signs, in Humbolt and Mendocino counties in California, by agents searching for illegal plants.[30]

Flying High. When planes fly by, so often do people's privacy rights, since then even signs don't matter. Generally, whatever law enforcement agents see is what they can use as evidence, as long as they fly high enough to be where planes ordinarily fly.

That's what Bernard Henderson in Colorado discovered in the case of *People v. Henderson*, decided in January 1993. When a police helicopter flew over his land, the officers noticed that part of a shed on his property was roofed with plastic sheeting, and beneath it, they could see a green leafy material. Probably marijuana, they thought, and so they took photos, while a news photographer videotaped the scene for a news broadcast. Then, using this information, plus some phone tips they received that Henderson was growing marijuana in the shed behind his house, the police got a search warrant and conducted a raid, which led to his conviction for cultivating marijuana.

Though Henderson's lawyer argued that the helicopter flyover revealing the suspicious shed violated Henderson's privacy rights because the police didn't have a search warrant, the court turned him down. There was no search and thus no need for a warrant, said the court, because the helicopter was flying in public airspace. It was up high enough, about 500 to 700 feet, that any aircraft could fly there. Thus, the officers were free to observe whatever they observed, including the contents of Henderson's shed.[31]

It's in the Can. Even garbage cans are subject to public scrutiny. The basic principle here seems to be "leave it and lose it." In other words, once you put any trash out for collection, it's readily accessible and up for grabs by the public, if the intended garbage collectors don't get it first.

The principle became the general rule nationally in 1988, when the U.S. Supreme Court made its widely noted decision in *California v. Greenwood* that garbage left at the curb is "readily accessible to members of the public and is placed on the curb for the express purpose of giving it away to a third party." Therefore, "there can be no reasonable expectation of privacy in that garbage."[32]

There is one exception in Washington, since in 1990, the Washington Supreme Court agreed with a trial court that a person does still have a privacy right in garbage, since he is putting it out for a *trash collector* to pick up, not just anybody.[33]

But generally, since the Greenwood case was decided, the trend has been to consider garbage abandoned and therefore not private. Alan Scott in Massachusetts discovered this when *U.S. v. Scott* was decided in 1992. He fought to keep the documents he had shredded and put out for collection away from Internal Revenue Service (IRS) agents and the grand jury. They wanted the records, since they believed Scott was involved in a tax evasion scheme by filing false income tax returns. However, Scott naturally didn't want them to see anything they might use to prove their case. And early on in his legal battles, a district court said, yes, he did expect his trash to be private, since he had shredded the documents, so the authorities needed a warrant, which they didn't have, to search his garbage. But unfortunately for Scott, after the government prosecutor appealed, the circuit court of appeals sided with the more general view that a person who places his trash at the curb abandons it.[34]

Thus, not only the cops can check through your garbage, but private investigators and others can look too, which they are increasingly doing, especially for insurance, worker's compensation fraud, and domestic cases.

Your Neighbor's Watching You

Not only are the cops better able to watch you by means of new technologies and favorable laws, but increasingly, neighbors are watching too. And often, they are doing this with the guidance or cooperation of the police to help combat neighborhood crime and graffiti. In many ways, this renewed neighborhood involvement is a good thing, such as when patrolling neighbors have taken back their communities from gangs, drug addicts, and graffiti painters. Also, neighbors watching neighbors can show an increased concern, care, and compassion for each other.

But the flip side is the increase in people prying into other people's private actions. Some people are reacting both to the threat of crime and the increase in snooping by moving into or creating personal forts that make the neighborhood look and feel like a walled encampment. This phenomenon contributes to a sense of separation between people that is contributing to the breakdown of many communities.

One example of this growing neighborhood watch is the creation of teams of neighborhood volunteers paired with police officers, such as in Los Angeles. The volunteers go to prime locations hit by graffiti vandals, such as walls, signs, and bridges, and they station themselves there in cars, on rooftops, and in private homes and businesses. Then, when they see something suspicious, they call the police, using small radios, and when they get the call, a nearby waiting patrol car sweeps in to arrest the vandals.[35]

Nearby, in the San Fernando Valley, an especially successful program led to over forty arrests of suspected burglars, drug dealers, car thieves, and vandals. Using camcorders, binoculars, radios, and notebooks, about fifty members of the Volunteer Surveillance Team went to assigned observation posts around the neighborhood to watch and report any suspicious incidents.[36] The success of such programs has led other police departments and neighborhood volunteers around the country to follow suit.

But while many people have eagerly joined forces with others to become volunteers using surveillance on others, some people have become fed up with all the surveillance by neighbors, cops, and intruders, and have tried to fortify their homes, creating a protected moat for themselves, sometimes to their neighbors' dismay. That is what occurred when Billy Davis, living in an unincorporated tract of modest homes called Whittier Downs near Los Angeles, tried to shut out his neighbors. He and his wife and mother just wanted to be left alone in their two-story home, so Davis proceeded to install barred windows, video monitors, and infrared alarms. He covered an outdoor patio with a metal case, put a Doberman in his yard, and hired an armed security guard to park in his driveway. And if this wasn't enough, he erected powerful security lighting which lit up his lot like a ballpark whenever a car drove past at night. He called the sheriff's department sixty times in one month to report suspected intruders.

Predictably, many neighbors were disturbed and formed a neighborhood association to take action against what Davis was doing. They sent dozens of complaints to the county agencies and eventually produced some changes, such as getting the county inspectors to cite Davis for a fence protruding onto land reserved for a public sidewalk.[37]

Yet, while Davis's actions may be extreme, they do raise questions about the individual's privacy rights. How far can one go, for example, in protecting his own privacy, and when does one person's quest for privacy and security impinge on the rights of neighbors. Such conflicts are hard to resolve, and they are a growing sign of the times, as people act in fear to protect their privacy from the violence and prying eyes of others, while others, also in fear, join together to watch their communities and their neighbors, for the signs that show they are involved in crime.

On the Go, in an Emergency, and More

This growing surveillance society, combined with an increasing awareness about privacy rights, has also meant a growing flurry of battles of where and when the police can search in other areas of life.

Traveling On. We now take the increased security barriers and checks at airports for granted, and as security checks go up at schools, offices, public events, and elsewhere, we accept these as an ordinary part of life, too. But what many people may not realize exists is the growing army of investigators observing people as they travel. Commonly, they are armed with a profile of what a typical drug courier, smuggler, or other miscreant looks like, so if they observe anyone looking like that or notice some suspicious behavior, they will stop and check out the suspect. Unfortunately, that can mean stopping and searching the innocent traveler who looks or acts the wrong way—such as someone who seems suspicious because he or she looks lost and confused or is traveling light. It could be you.

But whatever the pitfalls, the trend seems to be to give the police the benefit of the doubt in their ability to search. That's what Eddie Taylor discovered on his way through the Memphis International Airport in 1988, in the *U.S. v. Taylor* case, decided in February 1992. Taylor flew in from Miami, Florida, known as a major source of drug dealing, and he was the only African-American among the passengers leaving the plane. Several undercover officers thought he looked suspicious, because he had a new bag over his shoulder, though otherwise he was not well dressed, seemed a little nervous, and headed directly to the curb without claiming any luggage. After two officers met him there, they asked him about his trip plans, asked to search his bag, and found some cocaine. Though Taylor tried to suppress this evidence, which led to his conviction, he was out of luck. As the court decided, the officers had simply interviewed him at the curb, and he had apparently agreed to talk and let the officers check his bag. So there was no unwarranted surveillance, and no need to consider if it was motivated by Taylor's race, or whether including race in a drug courier's profile was unconstitutional.[38]

Med Alert. Medical emergencies can put one's privacy at risk, too. Though a police check at this time might be quite welcome when it turns up a dangerous criminal, it can also reveal embarrassing facts about an innocent person—or a person who otherwise might still be living a private life. Jerry Gilpin of Missouri, in the case of *State v. Gilpin*, decided in July 1992, had this experience after he was successfully revived from unconsciousness and given emergency treatment. He was subsequently charged with possessing cocaine, convicted, and sentenced to seven years in jail, plus a $5,000 fine. His troubles began when a police officer responding to a call for help at a trailer court arrived to find two men covered with blood and injured. Was it because of a fight involving a BB gun found nearby, the officer wondered? As the officer tried to determine what had happened, he heard Gilpin moaning, as he lay in a pool of blood, bleeding from his face. The officer called an ambulance at once, and after the ambulance attendants arrived, one slit Gilpin's trousers and removed them to look for any injuries to his legs.

Then, after the ambulance sped off with Gilpin, leaving his trousers behind, one of the detectives took them back to headquarters, and searched them for anything of value, to keep it secure for Gilpin. In the course of the search, she discovered a packet of cocaine powder. Tough luck for Gilpin. Though he tried to get the evidence thrown out on the grounds the officer did an unreasonable search, the Court of Appeals eventually affirmed his conviction, concluding that the police search was quite in order. After all, the ambulance attendants had acted reasonably in administering emergency treatment, and the detective did, too, in taking his bloody trousers back to the police department and checking them for anything of value. In fact, the trousers had been on a public street in plain view where they were found, so anyone had a right to be there. Thus, there was no invasion of privacy. Gilpin was simply the victim of the unfortunate circumstances, and the police had a perfect right to look. They may even have saved his life in the process.[39]

New Social Issues; New Questions of Privacy

Meanwhile, as new social issues become of concern, they raise questions about what the police can and cannot do. As a result, the right to privacy versus the needs of society and the need of the police to investigate and use the evidence they discover, keeps coming up. So this issue is reviewed again and again in different circumstances to decide who will prevail, the individual or the police in that situation.

For example, the growing homeless problem has raised questions about the privacy rights of homeless people. Can the police search a homeless person's belongings left unattended on public property (generally yes).[40] Likewise, as child abuse cases have skyrocketed, the question that keeps reoccurring is how far can the police investigate for signs of abuse. Can they inspect the child's body or search the parents' home before they come up against the parents' right to privacy? Again the answer is generally yes, if such actions are necessary to protect the child, though they need a warrant to search, whereas a social worker can check without this.[41]

Concurrently, as improved technology enables us to obtain more information from various parts of the body, the question increasingly comes up in criminal hearings and investigation as to what kind of evidence can be taken or requested—from hair, fingerprints, and blood samples for various purposes, including checking DNA. Moreover, complicating the matter is the fact that the courts have differing standards for different data. Some courts require a higher probable cause standard for obtaining hair and DNA samples, while requiring only individual suspicion to obtain the more usually collected fingerprints and palm prints.[42]

Listening In

Even the rules about listening in to phone conversations are becoming more complicated, as new technologies develop. While police wiretaps and bugs on the phone lines are generally accepted, particularly with a warrant, there are new questions about the rules for listening in with the new technologies, from mobile phones to fax and E-mail. These new laws and guidelines are just now being worked out by the legislatures and the courts.

Taps, Bugs, and Tracers

Generally, the police can use wiretaps, bugs, and phone line tracers, based on a series of laws and decisions dating back two or more decades. In the late 1960s, the U.S. Supreme Court decided that wiretapping authorized by warrant was fine under certain conditions, such as if the police specified that the particular person's phone be tapped and only listened in on conversations related to a particular crime if that person was a suspect.[43]

Though some recent challenges have occurred, for the most part, the police have prevailed. For example, after a California man was convicted of laundering money and evading currency reporting requirements when he tried to gain control of a gambling enterprise on the Rincon Indian Reservation in San Diego, he wasn't able to claim a wiretap on his phone, which provided evidence of his scheme, was illegal. He tried to argue in *U.S. v. Petti,* decided in August 1992, that a wiretap on his phone was illegal, stating that the warrant did not specifically describe the phone facilities from which the FBI planned to intercept his calls. But the U.S. Court of Appeals supported the FBI, concluding that it was too difficult for the FBI to be more specific, since it needed the taps to determine where the suspects' facilities were, and they kept changing the location.[44]

Law enforcement officers have also generally been able to overcome challenges that they listened in too long or didn't get the warrant for the tap or bug in time. This happened in the *U.S. v. Homick* case, decided in May 1992, after the Las Vegas police and FBI monitored calls to two residences for about 60 days to investigate a murder and robbery. One defendant, Delores Homick, tried to get the evidence thrown out by claiming that the FBI had listened in on numerous calls that were unrelated to the investigation. But the U.S. Court of Appeals felt the FBI's two-minute rule—of listening to conversations for two minutes to determine if relevant to the investigation and ceasing surveillance if not—was perfectly reasonable. So it could use the evidence it collected against her.[45]

Likewise, recent challenges to other methods used by law enforcement to listen in on phone calls have been turned down, among them using line tracers with the phone company's assistance, monitoring calls over pagers, and retrieving tapes from an answering machine.

For example, Joseph Riley, a computer hacker from Washington, couldn't get his computer trespass conviction reversed, after he used his home computer to obtain long distance telephone access codes from the phone company computer in the case of *State v. Riley* decided in March 1993. Though the Washington Supreme Court agreed the original warrant to search his home was too broad and threw out his conviction for having a stolen access device the police found when they searched his home, the court agreed the police could ask the phone company to use a line tracer to discover the number Riley was using to access the phone company's computers.[46]

Likewise, David Wojtyna of Washington had no luck appealing his conviction for attempting to purchase cocaine by claiming the police illegally picked up his number on a pager of a recently arrested local cocaine dealer, in the *State v. Wojtyna* case, decided in July 1993. Unfortunately, Wojtyna tried to call the dealer while the dealer's pager was in the hands of the police. But that was too bad, said the court, because one who sends a message to a pager runs the risk that the message will be received by whoever has the pager, so he or she can't expect any privacy when he calls the number. Anyone with the pager can call back—in this case, the police officer, who set up a meeting to deliver the cocaine to Wojtyna.[47]

Thomas Johnston of New Jersey had his brush with misfortune when he left an incriminating tape in an answering machine. A detective found it there when he was investigating the murder of Johnston's wife, in the *State v. Johnston* case, decided in May 1992. On the tape, Johnston's conversation with a third party helped to show he killed her. Though Johnston argued the tape shouldn't be used, because it recorded a private phone conversation, the New Jersey Supreme Court said no. Since the tape included conversations with third parties, it wasn't like finding private diaries or letters or a tape with only an individual's personal thoughts. Thus, it was fine to use the tape, and Johnston stayed in jail.[48]

Thus, when they investigate, law enforcement officers generally can listen in in a variety of ways, according to certain guidelines. And generally, they can use what they hear, as long as they obtain a warrant for bugs and taps, don't listen overly long to conversations that aren't relevant, and happen upon tapes or numbers on pagers in the course of their investigation.

Dealing with the New Communication Technologies

When it comes to the new communication technologies, faxes, E-mail, and digital or fiber optic transmissions, there are even more possibilities for secret surveillance and less clarity and agreement on what the police can do.

Privacy advocates fear the increased opportunities for snooping that open the innocent person up to even further invasions of privacy. Law enforcement agencies fear losing their traditional access to what used to be ordinary phone conversations, as the traditional wire and phone communication technologies become outdated, and they have to gain new rights to use the new technologies, as discussed in more detail in chapter 15 on high-tech privacy battles.

This basic law enforcement concern is expressed by Dorothy Denning, a professor of computer science and author of *Cryptography and Data Security,* in an article on the state of wiretapping. Under current U.S. law, with a court order, law enforcement officers can intercept or arrange for service providers to intercept wire, electronic, or oral communications. They just need to show a judge they have probable cause that the person being investigated committed a specific, serious felony, and they gain information about the offense through the intercepts, which is unavailable through other ordinary investigative methods. Then, if he or she agrees, the judge will issue an order for them to set up a tap or microphone device to listen in. About 7,500 such approved taps were done by state and federal agencies between 1982 and 1992, resulting in about 19,000 convictions to date.[49]

However, the new technologies are making many of the old methods used to intercept analogue voice communications over copper wires obsolete due to the new digital-based technologies, fiber optic transmissions, and mobile telecommunications. Thus, increasingly, law enforcement officers can't listen in any more due to technological problems, and they are trying to obtain new legislation to use surveillances with these new technologies, including having access to the Clipper Chip encryption keys, so they can break through the encryption codes of criminals, when they get a warrant to do so. But many individuals and privacy groups fear this access will threaten the ability of individuals and private industry to protect their personal confidences and trade secrets.

So the battle is on, with each side participating in government hearings and using media pressure to support or hold back the power of the police.

Finding the New Police Surveillance/Privacy Balance

Thus, between new social issues, new technologies, and increasing concerns about crime, leading the police to observe and investigate in more and more areas of life, there is increasing concern for privacy protections. At the same time, there is a growing confusion in many of these new areas of just what the rules are. What's private? What's not? When can the police look and search? When can't they? What must they do to get that right? And more generally, how do we balance society's need to know and protect itself and the individual's right to keep things private?

These are not easy questions, but more and more they are being raised, as a rapidly changing society seeks to work out new legal equations balancing the rights of the individual and of society. Certainly, we all want the protection that comes from law enforcement having the tools to investigate and convict the dangerous criminals who pose a serious threat. But at the same time, we want to protect our own privacy and avoid becoming a surveillance society where we all feel observed under law enforcement's microscope. Where do we draw the line; where do we find the balance? That is the challenge of our age.

Notes

1. Gary T. Marx, *Undercover: Police Surveillance in America* (Berkeley: University of California Press, 1988), 23.
2. Ibid., 23, 25–26.
3. Ibid., 27–29.
4. Ibid., 31–32.
5. Ibid., 37–38.
6. Ibid., 55–56.
7. Ibid., 43.
8. Ibid., 44–45.
9. Ibid., 45–47.
10. U.S.C.A. Const. Amend. 4.
11. *People v. Chaffee,* 590 N.Y.S. 2d 625 (A.D. 4 Dept. 1992), 627.
12. *State v. Taylor,* 842 P. 2d 460 (Or. App. 1992).
13. *People v. Woods,* 592 N.Y.S. 2d 748 (A.D. 2 Dept. 1993), 749–51.
14. Andrew Schneider and Mary Pat Flaherty, *Presumed Guilty* (Pittsburgh: Pittsburg Press, 1991).
15. Ed Rosenthal. Telephone interview with author, June, 1994.
16. Ibid.
17. *Linley v. DeMoss, City Commissioner,* 615 N.E.2d 631 (Ohio App. 10 Dist. 1992); 632–35.
18. *State v. Russell,* 848 P.2d 647 (Or. App. 1993), 658–59.
19. *State v. Solberg,* 831 P.2d 754 (Wash. App. Div. 1 1992), 755–61.

20. *People v. Lepeilbet,* 6 Ca. Rptr.2d 371 (Cal. App. 3 Dist. 1992).
21. *Commonwealth v. Grimshaw,* 595 N.E.2d 302 (Mass. 1992).
22. *State v. Ingram,* 831 P.2d 674 (Or. 1992); 675–77.
23. *Kreines v. U.S.,* 959 F.2d 834 (9th Cir. 1992), 835–39.
24. *State v. Neftzer,* 598 N.E.2d 938 (Ohio Mun. 1992), 939–40.
25. *Griffin v. U.S.,* 618 A.2d 114 (DC App. 1992), 118–25.
26. *Bills v. Aseltine,* 958 F.2d 697 (6th Cir. 1992).
27. *U.S. v. Acosta,* 965 F.2d 1248 (3rd Cr. 1992); 1250–52.
28. *Lamartiniere v. Allstate Insurance Company,* 597 So.2d 1158 (La.App. 1 Cir. 1992); 1158–62.
29. *Mattingley v. State,* 423 S.E.2d. 709 (Ga. App. 1992).
30. *People v. Scott,* 583 N.Y.S. 2d. 920 (Ct. App. 1992).
31. *People v. Henderson,* 847 P.2d 239 (Colo. App. 1993), 240–43.
32. *California v. Greenwood,* 486 U.S. 35, 39 (1988), 40–41.
33. William Jennison, "Privacy in the Can: *State v. Boland* and the Right to Privacy in Garbage," *Gonzaga Law Review,* 28 (1992/1993): 159–170, 164.
34. *U.S. v. Scott,* 975 F.2d 927 (1st Circ. 1992).
35. James Rainey, "Surveillance Teams to Help Fight Graffiti," *Los Angeles Times,* 2 June 1993. 1-A. Home Edition.
36. "More Eyes for the Police," *Los Angeles Times* 19 March 1993, 6-B., Col. 3. Home Edition, Metro.
37. Howard Blume, "Taking No Chances: Home Turned Into Fort, to Neighbors' Dismay," *Los Angeles Times,* 25 May 1992, 1-B, Home Edition, Metro.
38. *U.S. v. Taylor,* 956 F.2d 572 (6th Cir. 1992), 573–78.
39. *State v. Gilpin,* 836 S.W.2d 49 (Mo.App. W.D. 1992), 50–55.
40. *State v. Mooney,* 112 S. Ct. 330 (1991).
41. *Franz v. Lytle,* 997 F.2d 784 (10th Cir. 1993).
42. *In Re May 1991 Will County Grand Jury,* 604 N.E. 2d 929 (Ill. 1992).
43. The original 1967 cases that permitted wiretapping under certain conditions were *Berger v. New York,* 388 U.S. 41 (1967) and *Katz v. U.S.* 389 U.S. 347 (1967).
44. *U.S. v. Petti,* 973 F.2d 1441 (9th Cir. 1992), 1443–45.
45. *U.S. v. Homick,* 964 F.2d 899 (9th Cir. 1992), 901–903.
46. *State v. Riley,* 846 P.2d 1365 (Wash. 1993), 1367–72.
47. *State v. Wojtyna,* 855 P.2d 315 (Wash. App. Div. 1993), 315–316.
48. *State v. Johnson,* 608 A.2d 364 (N.J. Super. A.D. 1992).
49. Dorothy E. Denning, "To Tap or Not to Tap," *Communications of the ACM* 36, No. 3. (March 1993): 26–33.

Chapter 8

Copy Watch

All the News That Fits—and More!

From Free Press to the Freedom to Gossip

How did we get the media gossip tabloid circus we have today? Ironically, the situation wasn't much different when the first mass journalists began writing in the 1870s and 1880s, after the first portable cameras and mass-produced printed papers made popular journalism possible. It is just that the high-tech ability to snoop and broadcast the story is much greater now. But even back then the press did all it could to get the story, waving its First Amendment, freedom of the press shield. It was at this time that the first of the lawsuits against press intrusions were filed and the invasion of privacy tort was first formulated back in 1890 by Samuel D. Warren and Louis D. Brandeis, as described in chapter 1.[1]

Here and there, there were some privacy victories, such as in the 1905 Georgia case *Pavesich v. New England Life Insurance Company,* which occurred after a man objected because an insurance company used his picture on one of its ads without his permission, and the Supreme Court of Georgia agreed that his privacy had indeed been invaded.[2]

Yet, mostly, the fight for privacy against the press has been a losing battle, since the press has waved the Constitutional flag for the First Amendment freedom of the press, and usually the individual has lost out, as long as the information published is true, no matter how embarrassing or intimate it may be. That's because the press has usually been able to claim a story is newsworthy, so that by definition, just about everything that is published becomes news.

Thus, since the beginnings of mass journalism, the press has been free to pretty much publish anything, no matter how tasteless or salacious, which has contributed to the gossip-mongering tabloid media of today. This is reflected in the series of personal and private dramas that have become top mainstream press stories, no longer confined just to the tabloid racks. These include the sagas of the ice skaters Tonya Harding and Nancy Kerrigan; Amy Fisher and Joey Buttafuco; John and Lorena Bobbitt; and former football star O.J. Simpson. They reflect today's public fascination with sensational crime and scandal that goes beyond serious crime and news reporting. And celebrities seem to have lost all right to claim private lives. Even reclusive actress Greta Garbo couldn't keep her privacy, as secretly taken photos of a graying and haggard Garbo were featured in magazines that captured these pictures by using modern surveillance strategies, like a trophy for the press in the battle against an individual's desire for privacy.

How did we get to this point? A series of major press victories in the courts helped prepare the way for what is happening today.

Giving the Media the Go Ahead to Print Embarrassing Facts

One major victory occurred in 1940, when the *New Yorker* magazine won a big court case, *Sidis v. F-R Publishing Corporation,* after it published an exposé of a once famous child prodigy, William James Sidis. Sidis had been an eleven-year-old Harvard mathematics lecturer, and after graduating from Harvard College and Harvard Law School, he taught at the University of Texas. But then in a downward career move, Sidis decided to give it all up to become a semirecluse employed in relatively mindless jobs. However, he shot back into the news when the *New Yorker* featured him in a series of articles on formerly prominent individuals, describing his eccentric and dreary present, which included shunning publicity. Feeling the article exposed him to "unwanted and undesired publicity" and to "public scorn, ridicule, and contempt," Sidis sued. But the New York courts dismissed his case. The Circuit Court of Appeals even observed that the "prying of the press" deserves protection, concluding that only an outrage to the community's notion of decency would outweigh the public's interest in information.[3] But then, what is such an outrage? It's hard to find anything considered too outrageous for the media to print or broadcast. And so this key case helped to establish press guidelines that pretty much anything goes!

A Few Early Efforts to Restrain the Press

There were a few early exceptions. One was the 1931 *Melvin v. Reid*[4] case in California, in which a court felt a reformed prostitute's efforts to lead a new moral life were undermined by a movie depicting her as a prostitute involved in a murder trial, and decided her successful rehabilitation was more important than the public's right to know about her past activities. Another was the 1942 *Barber v. Time, Inc.* case, in which the court decided it was a bit much for the press to publish the intimate details and a photo of a hospitalized woman's exotic disease.[5] And in the 1960s, in *Daily Times Democrat v. Graham,*[6] a court agreed that publishing a photo of a woman with her dress blown above her waist by a fun house jet of air (shades of Marilyn Monroe) invaded her privacy.

But mostly, the press won these battles, as bodysurfer Mike Virgil found after his strange behavior was reported in *Sports Illustrated.* Among other things, the magazine noted that he ate spiders and insects, once bit off the cheek of a man in a six against thirty gang fight, and put out a lighted cigarette in his mouth. But when Virgil protested in *Virgil v. Time, Inc.*, decided in 1975, the district court agreed the article was fine because it wasn't offensive or sensational enough to support a privacy claim. Rather, it was just a legitimate journalistic attempt to explain Virgil's extremely "daring and dangerous style of bodysurfing."[7]

Some of the basic rules of today's press were established in the mid-1960s and early 1970s. One key case was the landmark *New York Times Co. v. Sullivan* case,[8] decided in 1964, when the Supreme Court ruled that a public figure suing for libel must prove that the press published the offending material knowing it was false or recklessly disregarding the truth. This established the actual malice standard for public or newsworthy figures that was later applied in defamation and privacy cases.[9]

The other big sixties case was *Time, Inc. v. Hill,* which began when the Hill family objected to a story that pried into their personal lives after a group of convicts took over their home for a couple of days before being captured by the police. But, it was fine to publish, said the Supreme Court, because the Hills had been thrust into the limelight by the incident, so anything true published about them was news.[10]

In fact, since 1967, when the Supreme Court decided this case, a plaintiff has never succeeded in recovering damages for a truthful disclosure by the press, according to author Theodore Glasser.[9] That's because the plaintiff must not only show that what the press printed was overly invasive, but that it was not newsworthy as well.[11]

The problem is that, almost by definition, whatever the media print or broadcast becomes newsworthy, by virtue of being published or broadcast around the world. So no wonder anyone battling the media is generally doomed to defeat, despite a few small victories.

At one time, the courts tried to distinguish between public and private figures in deciding on what the press could say in defamation, libel, slander, and invasion of privacy cases. The approach was designed to give private figures more protection, since public figures were already in the public eye or people became public figures when they voluntarily injected themselves or were drawn into a particular public controversy though they made no effort to do so.[12] Then, since they were already on the public stage, it seemed sensible that the press could say pretty much anything, even make negligent errors, without any penalty, as long as they showed no "actual malice." By contrast, this thinking went, a truly private person could hold the press liable for even negligent errors and invasions. But now it's hard to think of anyone as a private person anymore. Anyone can quickly become national or global news.

Once something appears in the public record, unless sealed by the courts, the media is generally free to print or broadcast it, even though it may be highly embarrassing or revealing. And again, this principle was established by another landmark Supreme Court decision—the *Cox Broadcasting v. Cohn* case, decided in 1975—in which a reporter broadcast the name of a deceased rape victim obtained from court records, though a Georgia law made it a misdemeanor to do so. After the victim's father sued, the court agreed the media could release the news, since this was accurate information already available in the public records.[13]

The rationale behind giving the media all these protections was to preserve their freedom to support spirited debate, the democratic process, and the ability of a free people to engage in self-government which depended on such controversy.[14] Now in the nineties, some recent cases seem to reflect the public's concern to impose new standards of restraint and decency on the media again. At the same time, many instant celebrities have decided they want their privacy back, or compensation from the media that took it away.

The Shifting Battlegrounds

Since it's fairly clear the media can print, broadcast, and televise just about anything true—or mostly or apparently true—about anyone because it's *news* and just about everyone can become (with a few seconds or minutes of fame) a *public figure,* the battle has turned in the nineties to other grounds for fighting the media. In television, the major thrust has been against the intrusiveness of the video cameras following along with the cops and turning criminal suspects into unwilling video stars. In the case of photojournalists, the big push has been to claim that photographers are taking pictures they shouldn't have taken because they have trespassed into a place they shouldn't be. In the realm of books, the major challenges have come in presenting information that's untrue, say by making up quotes, or in infringing on personal property rights in copyrighted material. Meanwhile, celebrities have been claiming financial rights in their persona—no pay, no play. In addition, certain groups of disadvantaged, stigmatized, or exploited people are claiming they should have special protections from the media's prying eyes. Among these groups are gays and individuals with AIDS, protesting against being outed, and victims of rape and child abuse, claiming their names and records shouldn't be revealed, because that interferes with their ability to heal. Thus, though the battle is still against the media, the nature of the battlefield has changed. Mostly the media is still winning, though some victories are helping to draw new lines for what the media can and cannot do.

It's on TV

Television reporters, talk show hosts, networks, and stations, for example, generally can reveal anything, no matter how unflattering or intimate, as long as they get that information legally and present it as news. This is what happened when Miriam (Mickey) Booher from Texas appeared on the Phil Donahue show in 1989 talking about how her husband had almost twenty years before raped her daughter Nancy, then eleven years old, who subsequently gave birth to a boy. The caption "Daughter Had Husband's Baby" occasionally flashed on the screen as she spoke. As she watched, daughter Nancy, now married to a loving husband, Michael Anonsen, was appalled to see her past dredged up, and afterwards, her now 16-year-old son William, Jr., was called a "bastard" at school by his classmates, and had to transfer to another school to escape the harassment. Thus, Nancy, husband, and son sued, in the case of *Anonsen v. Donahue,* decided in June 1993. But the Texas Court of Appeals supported the media's right to spread the news, saying the subject was a matter of public interest. Thus, Booher could tell her own story, protected by the First Amendment, and had the right to mention the names of others whose lives intersected her own, since they were part of her own story. To decide otherwise, the court felt, would mean "that one's autobiography must be written anonymously," which would "severely compromise" one's freedom of speech.[15]

School bus driver Melvina Lorraine Woodard had a similar "can't win" experience. When she sued a Florida TV station and reporter for reporting in 1990 that she had served four years in jail for murder back in 1972 under another name, her case—*Woodard v. Sunbeam Television Corporation,* decided in March 1993—was dismissed, too. The broadcast was part of an investigative series about the criminal records of many school bus drivers: *Your Kids on Board.* Though Woodward objected to drudging up this old charge, the court agreed with the station that the public had a right to know that many school bus drivers had these criminal records, and noted that as one of these drivers, she had served time in jail for murder. So since the story was essentially accurate and of public concern, she had no case.[16]

When TV Goes Too Far—False Images and Ridicule. On the other hand, when the media does present someone in a misleading or false light or unnecessarily makes fun of someone, then the victim may be able to win in court or at least get a quiet settlement, though lengthy appeals are par for the course.

One such case was *Rogers v. Buckel,* decided in November 1992. It began when Kim Rogers went to pick up her children at her babysitter's apartment in November 1989, just at the time when David Buckel, a reporter and anchor for TV-8 in Cleveland, Ohio was accompanying a group of Drug Enforcement Agency (DEA) agents on a drug raid. As the cameras whirred away, Rogers asked Buckel and his videographer, Herb Thomas, not to film her or her children, although Thomas disputes her doing this. Later, though the video of her wasn't used in Buckel's report, another TV-8 reporter, Mike Conway, used it for a special report on child victims of the drug epidemic. Even though Conway was aware from his research that Rogers was not charged, he used a dramatic clip of her, with her head down, huddled over her children during the drug raid. He also made this accusatory remark, though he didn't identify her by name, implying Rogers was that mother: "Last week, police raid a Warrensville Heights apartment. Four children are found. The mother is charged with allowing crack dealers to cook and sell in the apartment. The silent victims are everywhere, children caught in a parental crack trap."

Then, even worse, he implied that Rogers was a "strawberry mother," who prostituted herself for drugs, resulting in a terrible effect on her children. He never explained that Rogers was not charged with such a crime and had not done drugs, sold drugs, or ever traded sex for drugs, but was just in the apartment by chance.

Thus, the Ohio Court of Appeals agreed that Rogers might have an invasion of privacy case against the station, though a jury would still have to decide if she was sufficiently identified in the broadcast to make this claim. However, since Buckel had only taken the video footage and hadn't shown it, he was off the hook.[17]

The courts also came to the support of two musicians who claimed they were falsely ridiculed as inept comedians rather than presented as serious musicians in *Sharrif v. American Broadcasting Company,* decided in January 1993. Problems began when Umar Sharrif and fellow musician, Barry Martyn, performed at a concert in Germany on a Christmas tour in 1987. Suddenly, the stage collapsed, and as they fell off the stage, an eager video camera buff took an unauthorized video. It was subsequently shown on "America's Funniest Home Videos" and the German equivalent, "Germany's Funniest Home Videos." Not funny, said Sharrif and Martyn, and the Louisiana Court of Appeals agreed they might have a case for being portrayed in this objectionable false light. Now it was up to a jury to decide if they were.[18]

Smile: You're on Candid Camera. Television networks or stations usually lose these battles, however, when pushy camerapeople, who are following along when the cops are conducting an investigation or making an arrest, barge into people's homes without permission, casting them in an unflattering light. While they may be able to film freely if the subject is a public figure, they have problems when it is a private person. These TV camera crew cases first started appearing in the courts in the mid-1980s, and TV still keeps fighting and generally losing these battles.

One of the first of these cases was against NBC, *Miller v. National Broadcasting Company* decided in 1986. It began after a camera crew followed a team of paramedics into the home of a man who had suffered a heart attack and later died. The station used the film on its nightly news, and later in an ad about the paramedics' work. Upset, the man's wife and daughter sued for this intrusive privacy invasion, and also claimed trespass and emotional distress. The court agreed that the man's wife, who was there during the filming, had a claim, since the camera crew's actions went beyond the scope of ordinary newsgathering, protected by the First Amendment, to invade a person's privacy at home.[19]

Now in the 1990s, the courts have taken a similarly dim view of invading TV camera people, as they did in a case against CBS, *Baugh v. CBS, Inc.*, decided in June 1993. It began in January 1992, when a camera crew filming the weekly TV series *Street Stories*, followed Elaine Lopes in Oakland, California, as she helped to guide crime victims through the judicial process. One victim was Yolanda Baugh, who described graphically how her husband beat her up by kicking her, hitting her in the face, and kicking her on the floor. Unfortunately, when they first arrived, the camera crew had told Yolanda they were filming for the District Attorney's office, and she agreed to be filmed, but only if the footage was not on anyone's television program. But the crew never mentioned CBS, the local station, or *Street Stories,* and when Baugh learned the show was going to air and tried to stop it, even threatening legal action, CBS and the *Street Stories* producer aired it anyway that April. A rude, arrogant CBS lawyer told her she had no case, and there was nothing she could do. But she could. The U.S. District Court judge felt she couldn't claim trespass, since she had consented, although the crew members had tricked her into doing so. But it thought she might be able to claim fraud and the intentional infliction of emotional distress. That was because the crew misrepresented their identity to gain her consent and then took advantage of her in revealing offensive private information. Here, too, it would be up to a jury to decide.[20]

It's the News

While TV has been fairly battered in its battles, the more traditional media, newspapers, magazines, and radio, have generally fared better.

As long as the story is in the public interest and essentially true, generally they can print or report it, even if it is embarrassing and humiliating. It's the news!

That's what Earl Carey found after the *St. Louis Post-Dispatch* published six articles about him when he unsuccessfully ran for a U.S. Senate seat in Missouri, in 1992. When he sued, in the case of *Carey v. Pulitzer Publishing Company,* decided in July 1993, he claimed some of the statements were libelous and invaded his privacy. Among other things, he felt the paper falsely stated that he was running because he had a dispute with IBM over his firing as a computer salesman in 1988 and that he had filed misconduct complaints against some federal judges for dismissing his claim that IBM had no good cause to fire him. But the court of appeals dismissed his claim, since much of what was printed was essentially true. Also, observed the court, even if Carey decided to run for the Senate due to his dispute with IBM, this fact alone didn't reflect on his integrity, character, or good name, or expose him to public hatred, contempt, or disgrace. So he had no case.[21]

A few individuals who didn't want their identities used in stores also didn't fare very well.

Jill Ruzicka had this experience after a reporter promised she wouldn't be identifiable as a source in a magazine article. Ruzicka claimed she was identifiable in her case, *Ruzicka v. Conde Nast Publications, Inc.,* decided in May 1992. The conflict began when she was interviewed by Claudia Dreifus for an article about sexual abuse by therapists for a 1988 issue of *Glamour* magazine. Ruzicka agreed to talk about her own abuse if she wouldn't be identifiable, since she was starting a new job and didn't want her colleagues to recognize her. The reporter promised and tried to disguise her identity by leaving out information about a previous job and by using a phony surname. But, Ruzicka complained, the reporter used her real first name, and included enough details to make her identifiable, such as that she had filed a complaint with the state board of medical examiners, sued the offending psychiatrist, and attended law school after the suit settled. But the U.S. District Court decided she had no case, since it felt the reporter's promise was too vague, and that the reporter had no way to know what information would threaten Ruzicka's anonymity, since that would depend on what her friends and acquaintances already knew, and since Ruzicka didn't tell her what not to publish. Also, the court felt if reporters and editors had to figure out what not to say to avoid identifying someone they had promised not to identify, that would be an impossible task of trying to guess what not to say.[22]

Calling a Foul a Foul

However, when the media does intentionally humiliate or make a fool of someone, it has gone too far, such as when a radio D.J. goes overboard in kidding someone or pulling a prank. Then, that's no longer news—and the media can be liable for revealing embarrassing facts.

This is what happened when Anthony Kolegas sued an Illinois radio station, WLUP-AM, and two of its D.J.'s, Tim and Beth Disa, in the case of *Kolegas v. Heftel Broadcasting Corporation,* decided in 1992. The problem began in 1988, when Kolegas called the station to say he was promoting a classic cartoon festival as a benefit to encourage public awareness of neurofibromatosis, commonly known as Elephant Man disease. When D.J. Beth Disa asked him how he was involved, he mentioned that his wife and son had the disease.

At once, both D.J.'s dissed him. "You're gone," Tim Disa stated on the air, hanging up on him. Afterwards, Disa commented that Kolegas was "not for real," and Beth Disa suggested that he was "scamming" them, that there was no festival. Then they joked about the disease, making fun of Kolegas and his wife, making comments like: "Why would someone marry a woman if she had Elephant Man disease? It's not like he couldn't tell—unless it was a shotgun wedding."

Eventually, the Illinois Supreme Court agreed that the D.J.s' remarks were outrageous enough for Kolegas and his family to claim they had invaded their privacy by placing them in a false light, as well as causing them emotional distress. The D.J.'s had gone beyond making jokes or "mere insults," and because the media had so much power to harm, they should be held liable for their "extreme and outrageous" remarks.[23]

Taking Pictures

Photographers, photojournalists, and TV camerapeople similarly have to watch the boundaries between legitimate news they can photograph and print, and taking pictures when they shouldn't. Generally, the rule seems to be if it's news, you can use the photo if you are permitted to take it, and you can take it if you are on public property at the time (though you can't use news photos for advertising and commercial purposes).

Where is the line? In today's world of super high-powered zoom cameras, photographers are fairly free to get those long-distance shots like Fergie sucking the toes of her Texas lover while married to Prince Andrew, and Princess Diana frolicking in the surf in a bikini. But they can't physically get too close.

One famous case from the early 1970s, in which photographer Ron Galella was enjoined from following his favorite subject Jackie Onassis too closely, helped establish this basic principle. Galella argued free press, but the New York federal district court found his obnoxious persistent pursuit of Jackie, like a quarry, a bit too much. For example, once he hid behind a coat rack in a restaurant as he photographed her; another time he jumped out from behind the bushes in front of Jackie's children as she walked with them on the street.

Such actions, the judge felt, went beyond the bounds of decency, and among other things, he ordered damages and issued a restraining order for Galella to stay at least 200 feet away from Onassis, since he felt Galella had gone too far in physically invading Jackie's private space, in effect stalking her to get the picture, which was beyond the acceptable limit.

Conversely, when photographers are someplace they are allowed to be, such as on public property or invited into a private place, they can take the picture. Even minor inoffensive trespassing may be acceptable, as Pamela Howell, a patient at a private psychiatric facility in Westchester County, New York, discovered. She objected to a photographer taking her picture which was published in the *New York Post* in 1988, in the case of *Howell v. New York Post Company,* decided in April 1993. Ironically, the photographer was not specifically trying to take her picture. Rather, he was trying to photograph Hedda Nussbaum, another patient who had become widely known as the former live-in lover of the accused (and subsequently convicted) child-killer Joel Steinberg.

After Nussbaum was acquitted, she went to the Four Winds Hospital in Westchester to heal both physically and emotionally, and the photographer tried to photograph her there, sneaking onto the grounds to do so. But while taking this photo, he snapped her walking beside Pamela Howell, who was also a patient. Though Howell objected, claiming an invasion of privacy and emotional distress, the court turned her down, concluding the photo was news in the public interest, because of general concern about the Hedda Nussbaum story. In fact, the court felt including Howell in the picture contributed to the story, since it showed that Nussbaum was healing from her experience with Steinberg, since her facial wounds were visibly healed and she was smartly dressed, as she walked alongside Howell, who was smiling in tennis attire and sneakers. Also, the court felt the photographer had a right to take the photo, because his trespass was only a minor one, since he took the pictures outdoors and from a distance. So given the photo's news value, public interest in the Nussbaum case, and the photographer's minimal intrusion, though trespassing, by taking the photo from a distance, it was fine for the newspaper to publish the photo.[24]

It's All in Fun. But what if a story really isn't news, but more in the nature of making fun? If it's a clear parody in good taste (whatever that is), it is generally acceptable to use someone's photo. But if the photo is misleading and seems outrageous, then it is not acceptable. The lawyers in these cases have plenty of work arguing about what is parody, what is in good taste, misleading, and outrageous, and what's just good clean fun.

One such debate occurred when Sylvia Salek, a private schoolteacher at the Passaic Collegiate School in New Jersey, saw the 1988 yearbook; she did not think the section called "The Funny Pages" was very funny. It presented pictures of students and faculty with humorous captions, and two captioned photos suggested that she proposed to engage in a sexual relationship with another faculty member, John DeVita. One photo featured her sitting next to and facing DeVita, who had his right hand raised to his forehead. Underneath, the caption read: "Not tonight Ms. Salek. I have a headache." The other photo, showing DeVita eating, had the provocative caption: "What are you really thinking about, Mr. DeVita." When she sued in the case of *Salek v. Passaic Collegiate School* decided in April 1992, she argued that these photos presented her in a false light, as well as libeled and defamed her. But the Superior Court judge quickly dismissed her case, observing that the publication of the photos and captions was clearly "parody, satire, humor, or fantasy," so no one could reasonably take the implied sexual relationship seriously.[25]

Perhaps since these photos appeared in a respectable student publication that helped the school's case. In contrast, the *Sun*, a wild tabloid, did not fare well when it printed a photo with a false caption in the case of *People Bank and Trust v. Globe International Publishing, Inc.*, decided in November 1992. "Pregnancy Forces Granny to Quit Work at Age 101," the paper's headline screamed, and it used a photo of a 95-year-old newspaper carrier in Arkansas, Nellie Mitchell, to illustrate the article. Then, its fabricated story described how this randy 101-year-old Australian woman had gotten pregnant after having an extramarital fling with a millionaire client on her route. It used an old picture from an earlier story about Nellie operating a newsstand and delivering papers in her hometown for almost fifty years, assuming that Nellie had died, without bothering to check. But Nellie was very much alive and upset, since people in her community quickly spread the word about her picture and teased her about "being pregnant."

So she sued, eventually collecting $850,000 in punitive damages, because the U.S. Court of Appeals agreed the *Sun* had recklessly published a false story, and it felt Mitchell's privacy had been invaded by this outrageous, humiliating story, since people could identify her though the photo and enough true information. And contributing to this decision was the juxtaposition of her picture with what the court called the "slime" of other outrageous stories, with headlines like "Road Kill Cannibal" and "Farmer Becomes a Millionaire Making Whips for Wifebeaters."[26]

No Permission. It can also be an invasion of privacy if photographers try to take a photo in a place where they need permission and don't have it. That's what happened when a photographer for the *Marin Independent Journal* in Marin County, California, tried to snap a picture of a suspect in a criminal proceeding, in the case of the *Marin Independent Journal v. Municipal Court,* decided in February 1993. This occurred after a young boy, Maurice H, was arrested as a suspect in the shooting death of another young boy at a Marin City rap festival in August 1992. Before his first court appearance, the prosecutor and defense attorney agreed they didn't want any photography in court, so the judge refused a petition by the *Journal* to take pictures. But even so, a photographer, who was told she couldn't take photos by the bailiff, was allowed to sit in the jury box.

Then, when the boy was arraigned, she took several photos of him, later claiming that the bailiff gave her a "wink and a nod," which she took as a go-ahead to take the picture. But as soon as she took the photos, the prosecutor and defense attorney objected and the judge ordered the bailiff to seize her film. Though she and the paper tried to get it back, the

Court of Appeals refused, though the paper argued freedom of the press, claiming the film's confiscation was an unconstitutional prior restraint of speech. But no, said the court, because the trial court had the power to limit or prevent courtroom media coverage, as it did here to protect the identity of a juvenile suspect before he appeared in a lineup, since the publication of a photo might taint the identification process. Thus, the photographer couldn't take the photos and the paper couldn't use them or get them back.[27]

Celebrity Tracks. The media is still relatively free to publish just about anything about public figures, as long as it's true, without malice even if not true, or obtained legally—or mostly legally. But there is a new invasion of privacy catch based on dollar signs. That is because the celebrity reputation has become worth something, so increasingly celebrities are fighting back, not because their private lives and reputations have been revealed, but because they haven't been paid for the revelation. And they are winning if they can show the piece about them wasn't strictly news, as in the case of a docudrama or the use of a look-alike, stand-in, or sound-alike voice in an ad. They are claiming the media inappropriately used their personality or persona, and sometimes they are claiming infringement of copyright, too, if the media quotes something they have written down or recorded.

So enter the era of checkbook, tabloid journalism, where the media pays the people who make the news to get the behind-the-scenes details, and to avoid the potential lawsuits that might arise if they got these details in the more traditional newsgathering way. How did we get to this state of affairs, with celebrities wanting to control and get paid for their story? A little history is in order.

The Historical Roots of the Celebrity-Media Pay-to-Play Fight

The roots of the current pay-to-use-the-story-or-picture fight go back to the 1950s, when the new mass media dawned after World War II. Now, as even more powerful stars emerged, fueled by a growing publicity engine, so did the idea that there were new privacy rights to protect—the right of the celebrity to control his or her image in order to make money. In other words, the celebrity now had a "right of publicity," which allowed one to either preserve or reveal one's private self as a commodity.

The Fight to Turn Celebrity into Money Begins. The right to cash in on celebrity was first formally recognized in 1953 when one bubble gum company sued another over who could use the picture of a famous ballplayer, in the *Haelen Laboratories v. Topps Chewing Gum* case. A ballplayer had signed an agreement giving Haelen the sole right to use his photograph to sell gum. But then Topps Chewing Gum persuaded him to let them use his photo to sell *their* gum. The case ended in something of a muddle, which the appeals court sent back to the trial court to sort out. The appeals court said that Topps was not liable for breaching Haelen's contract, though Haelen might have a claim against Topps if Topps used the photo knowing of Haelen's contract. But the court for the first time proclaimed that a player had a right of publicity in the "publicity value" of his photograph. So only he had the privilege of authorizing publication of his picture.[28]

Thus, the right of celebrities to control their images and stories for money was born, and through the sixties, seventies, and eighties, celebrities increasingly fought to get compensated, get damages if they weren't, or block use of their photo or story if it was used for anything other than a news story. And they won, since according to legal scholar L. Lee Byrd, writing in the *Entertainment and Sports Law Journal,* "celebrities have a monetary value associated with their name, image, or likeness. Their 'personality' may be worth a large sum of money."[29]

One celebrity who proved this point in the late 1970s was Muhammad Ali, who had recently been proclaimed the heavyweight boxing champion of the world. He sued *Playgirl* magazine, in the case of *Ali v. Playgirl* decided in 1978, because it ran a portrait of him without permission. Even though *Playgirl* didn't identify him by name, the portrait of a nude black man seated in the corner of a boxing ring with an accompanying verse that called him "The Greatest," was enough to make the association, since Ali frequently claimed this name for himself. Thus, the court eventually granted Ali an injunction, agreeing the magazine was not only unlawfully appropriating this valuable commodity (his likeness and reputation), but was inflicting damage to his marketable reputation.[30]

Numerous other celebrity cases involving the use of their name or image without consent or beyond the consent given, have similarly ended up with celebrity wins. For example, in 1973, Cary Grant prevailed when he sued *Esquire* magazine because the magazine, without his consent, superimposed a picture of his head on a picture of a model's body in a clothing advertisement. The court said he could win if a jury agreed that *Esquire* used his picture for commercial purposes.[31] And Woody Allen won a case in 1985 when the National Video Company used an actor who looked like him in a commercial.[32]

The upshot of all these cases is that a celebrity can win an invasion of privacy-publicity case if he or she can show his or her name or likeness has publicity value, that the person has "exploited" this name or likeness to make money, and that the party sued has used this name or likeness for advertising or trade purposes without the celebrity's consent.[33]

Even look-alikes and sound-alikes count for this, at least in the case of a very much alive celebrity, though apparently the impersonators of Elvis and other dead celebrities, like Marilyn Monroe and W.C. Fields, are fine. For example, one advertiser found this out when it tried to use Bette Midler's voice in a commercial, and when she wouldn't agree, used someone who sounded like her. Since he shouldn't have done so, he had to pay.

But No Money if It's News—Or Fiction. But if it's news, or an account of a celebrity's life story, then the media can use the material, even when the celebrity doesn't approve, as long as the story is essentially true and the information is obtained without otherwise invading the person's privacy, because then the freedom of the press principal prevails. This is what happened in the late 1940s in one of the earliest of these cases, when Serge Koussevitzsky, a world-famous symphony conductor with the Boston Symphony, sued a publisher to prevent the publication of an unauthorized biography about his musical career. Despite some incorrect statements, the court, in the *Koussevitzsky v. Allen, Towne and Heath* case, decided in 1947, agreed this was a "legitimate dissemination on a subject of general interest." So as a public figure, Koussevitzsky couldn't prevent its publication. His story was news.[34]

Subsequently, in the high-profile Howard Hughes case in the late 1960s, the courts reaffirmed this right of the media to publish true (or mostly true) but unauthorized biographies of famous people. In this case, *Rosemont Enterprises v. Random House,* the secretive and increasingly eccentric Hughes tried to prevent Random House from publishing the story of his life. He said he had not consented and he claimed the publisher was trying to commercially exploit his "name, likeness, and personality." But again the court supported the media, observing that when the right of publicity conflicted with the "free dissemination of thoughts, ideas, newsworthy events, and matters of public interest," then the public interest should prevail, and the right of publicity must "give way to public interest."[35]

Even actress Ann-Margret lost when she sued *High Society* magazine in 1980, after it reproduced a seminude movie still of her. Though she claimed no consent, the court said the magazine had a right to publish her photo, since it depicted a public performance by a public figure. So here, too, First Amendment considerations were more important than her commercial privacy rights to her image.[36]

If the story is so totally fictionalized that it becomes literature—such as when writers include public figures in novels, plays, and films—then the media can prevail again. This principle was established in two big cases. One was a 1965 case involving the film and novel *John Goldfarb, Please Come Home,*[37] in which the filmmakers featured Notre Dame and its president in a wild farce. It was a story about the King of an Arab country who creates his own team and beats Notre Dame, because the school won't let his own son on the team. The other case from 1978 involved a fictionalized account in the film *Casablanca,* about what happened when Agatha Christie disappeared for 11 days. Although she had really been reported missing, the film added its own fantasy story of what had occurred. In both cases, the court concluded the accounts were clearly fictionalized so no one was "deceived" or "confused," so such literary fictional uses of public figures were fine.[38]

Getting Away with Parody and Satire. The media can usually get away with saying pretty much anything, too, if it's clearly wild and crazy parody or satire. A series of angry cases against *Hustler* magazine in the late 1980s helped to establish that point, after *Hustler,* known primarily for its irreverence, raunchy sex, and sleaze appeal, took on some antiporn feminists and a fundamentalist religious leader. It presented them in a demeaning, degrading way, and included some false, reputation-tarnishing information in its stories.

In one notable case, *Dworkin v. Hustler* magazine, decided in 1989, outspoken feminist author and activist, Andrea Dworkin, well known for her attacks on pornography, was livid when *Hustler* featured several cartoons, photographs, and statements presenting her as involved in various types of sexual activity—just the sort of porn images she railed against. One such cartoon showed two women engaged in lesbian oral sex, and underneath, the caption: "You remind me so much of Andrea Dworkin, Edna. It's a dog-eat-dog world." Another featured a man performing oral sex on an obese woman while masturbating, and underneath the caption included this statement: "We don't believe it for a minute, but one of our editors swears that this woman in the throes of ecstasy is the mother of radical feminist Andrea Dworkin."

But the Wyoming district court supported *Hustler*'s right to publish, since it felt the material, though objectionable, was clearly protected opinion. Also, *Hustler* hadn't appropriated her image in a commercial sense because it used it in expressing an opinion about something newsworthy, and therefore protected by the First Amendment—ironically, the ongoing political debate to outlaw the industry of which *Hustler* was a part.[39]

Hustler got away with wild insulting parody, too, when it published a parody ad of Jerry Falwell, the preacher and Moral Majority leader, which portrayed him as having a "drunken incestuous rendezvous" with his mother in an outhouse. The ad featured a mock Campari Liquor ad with a photo of Falwell and the caption "Jerry Falwell talks about his first time"—a mockery of the regular Campari ads that featured interviews with celebrities about their "first time" trying Campari. But as outrageous as the ad might be, the Supreme Court in 1989 ruled in *Hustler*'s favor, emphasizing the importance of protecting free expression through opinion or parody.[40]

Winning the Media-Celebrity Free-For-All

More recently, the media has also been getting the benefit of the doubt where the lines are unclear between what's entertainment and what's news. Take what happened to James Brown in *Brown v. Twentieth Century Fox Film Corporation,* decided in July 1992. He objected when a film production company used a brief 27-second clip from a 1965 TV show performance in the 1991 film *The Commitments,* about a group of young Irishmen and women who form a soul music band. Brown had signed an agreement giving the TV show producers the right to use his appearance in a variety of ways, though Brown contended it didn't include use of films, film promotions, and videocassettes. But a district court concluded that the company not only could use his performance, but it could mention his name in the film, without violating his "right of publicity." After all, it was just a single mention, along with the names of several other entertainers, as soul performers whom the band members should study as models. So this limited use was not the "wholesale appropriation" needed for a celebrity to make a right of publicity claim.[41]

Similarly, Joplin Enterprises, which represented the persona of Janis Joplin, the 1960s pop/rock icon who died in 1970, failed when it tried to prevent her name from being used in a two-act play that fictionally portrayed her experiences over a day before an evening concert. They couldn't stop her name from being used, the district court concluded in the *Joplin Enterprises v. Allen* case, decided in June 1992, because they could only restrict the commercial use of a deceased personality's persona in merchandise, advertising, or endorsements. But this was just a play, and so like a book, the right to free expression should prevail. In fact, the court noted, even the law of California where the play occurred excepted plays, like books, from such restrictions.[42]

Moreover, once someone becomes part of history, they may be out of luck in preventing the free use of their image or story, as the famous surfer Mickey Dora discovered when he protested that film footage of him surfing and a background interview with him appeared without his consent in a 1987 video documentary about "The Legends of Malibu." He sued in the *Dora v. Frontline Video, Inc.* case, decided in April 1993. But again the court of appeal decided in favor of the media, because the documentary featured "matters of public interest." As the court observed nostalgically, the documentary was about "a certain time and place in California history and, indeed, in American legend" in which the people there contributed to creating a lifestyle which became "world-famous and celebrated in popular culture." Thus, Dora's story belonged to the world.[43]

News or Ad? The New Debate

However, if a person's name, story, photo, or endorsement is used in an ad or commercial product, normally, the celebrity or anyone else featured must give permission, which today, generally means getting paid. Yet, it can sometimes be difficult to tell the difference between advertising and news. Then, too, given the growth of infomercials, where advertising is garbed as a news story, and the way big companies try to create news stories to sell their products, the big question is, when does a story become a commercial? When does the media have to get consent and/or pay? A few recent cases hint at the possible struggle to come.

Consider what happened to the well-known chef Paul Prudhomme, when he saw an actor who looked like him describe how much he liked Folger's coffee in some commercials. He sued in the *Prudhomme v. Procter & Gamble Company* case, decided in September 1992, claiming the P&G had invaded his privacy with their ads, since his likeness had become a protectible image, like a trademark, and they were trying to imply he endorsed their coffee, when he had not given his consent. In turn, the Louisiana district court agreed, noting that Prudhomme had become famous for popularizing cajun-style cooking and for his restaurants, cookbooks, and food-related products and services. So he might have a claim that P&G had misappropriated his image.[44]

Even noncelebrities whose images are used in ads posing as news stories may have a claim, as was the case for Angie Geary, who appeared in a commercial for Wasa Crispbread, a Swedish bread product, in the case of *Geary v. Al Goldstein,* decided in August 1993. Geary was not well known nor was Wasa Crispbread, but Al Goldstein, executive producer of the sexually explicit late-night cable TV program *Midnight Blue,* asked his staff to create an adaptation satirizing this commercial. In the original commercial, Geary, wrapped around with a towel, emerges from a morning shower and enters a kitchen where a male companion in a bathrobe is washing his breakfast dishes. Then, the commercial cuts to pictures of bread, as a voiceover praises Wasa Crispbread. But in the *Midnight Blue* version, the camera cuts instead to videotapes of scantily clad couples, engaging in various types of sex, while the original voiceover now suggests that millions of people "eat" in a sexual sense.

Mortified to be associated with all this, Geary sued to stop the revamped commercials and gain money damages. But though Goldstein argued freedom of the press, claiming this was simply a humorous adaptation and editorial comment on the "sexual and seductive nature of the original commercial," the New York district court turned him down. One reason was that since neither Geary nor Wasa Crispbread were well known, viewers might not be aware that this was a parody, and they could readily think Geary was associated with it. Also, the court didn't consider this adaptation a form of editorial comment, and it questioned whether it was really in the public interest. Thus, to use Geary's image commercially, the producer of *Midnight Blue* had to get her consent and/or pay.[45]

Protecting the Victim

In this age of the "victim," another privacy issue concerns what the media can say about victims and other groups deemed worthy of special protections—such as gays trying to keep their secret and juveniles accused of committing crimes. While many victims have become celebrities, talking about their experiences on *Oprah, Inside Edition,* and other talk and news shows, other victims really do want to keep their privacy to avoid being stigmatized or harassed if people learn what happened to them.

The result has been a growing number of cases involving victims versus the media, particularly in three main areas: rape or child abuse victims; gays and HIV victims; and juveniles accused of crimes.

Sex and the Media

In the case of sex cases, the basic rule seems to be that if the media can legally find out the name of the victim or the perpetrator or any information about that person, they can publish or broadcast it. In response, the courts, police, and social agencies dealing with victims often try to mask that person's identity or seal records, and sometimes the media have agreed voluntarily to go along with requests to keep that identity concealed.

Rape. Commonly, the names of rape victims are withheld, because rape is considered more personal, traumatic, and stigmatizing than other crimes. There is fear that the rapist or his friends might retaliate against the victim, and the state wants to encourage the victim to come forward to report the crime without fearing exposure. Rape is underreported because many victims fear the resulting loss of privacy.[46]

This key principle of protecting the rape victim developed in the late 1970s in a series of cases in which the Supreme Court sided with the media,[47] and in the 1989 landmark case, *The Florida Star v. B.J.F.* The case began when an enterprising young trainee reporter picked up a police report about a robbery and rape in the pressroom which included BJF's full name. Then, using this report, a *Florida Star* reporter wrote up a short story describing the woman's brutal rape near a bus stop. Yet, while BJF was very upset by the story, received several threatening phone calls from a man who stated he would rape her again, and eventually changed her phone number, moved, sought police protection, and went for mental health counseling, that wasn't enough to sway the court. Nor was the *Florida Star*'s admission that it had inadvertently violated its own rule against publishing the names of sexual offense victims. Instead, the Supreme Court firmly supported the newspaper's right to publish, establishing the guidelines still with us today. The newspaper could publish, said the court, because the reporter got her name from courthouse records open to the public; this was a truthful report of a matter of public significance; and it was up to the government, which had control over these records, to conceal the sensitive information in them if it wished. Then, too, the court feared the "timidity and self-censorship" of the media that might result if the media could "be punished for publishing certain truthful information.[48]

No Privacy Promised for Rape Victims Today. The most recent battles have reinforced this principle. But if the media doesn't get the information lawfully, isn't truthful, or tries to discredit the rape victim's story, that's when the media run into trouble. For example, Nancy Tomlinson Tatum had no success keeping her name out of the news in the case of *Macon Telegraph Publishing Company v. Tatum,* decided in December 1993. She was asleep in her bedroom when Shedrick Hill Jr. broke into her home at 4:00 A.M. on a Saturday morning with a knife in his hand and his pants unzipped. Fortunately, Tatum escaped rape, injury, or death, since she zipped out a gun and killed Hill, which the Macon police concluded was self-defense, and so justifiable homicide. But Tatum, unfortunately, couldn't keep her name out of the news. Her name was published after the investigating officers gave her name to two *Macon Telegraph* reporters. Though the police asked the reporters not to publish her name, they did so anyway, and indicated the street where she lived in an article about the incident and in a follow-up article about Hill's life. Despite a sympathetic jury which awarded Tatum $100,000, the Georgia Supreme Court quickly shot down her brief victory, deciding that the newspaper wasn't liable, since as in the *Florida Star* case, it had legally obtained truthful information about a matter of public significance. Furthermore, the matter was of public concern, since the articles showed she defended herself against a sexual attack by shooting and killing the intruder; and the crime, investigation, and police decision that she acted in self-defense were all matters of public interest.[49]

But if the media gets the information illegally, they may lose their right to publish the news, as happened to reporter Betsy Tong and the *Fort Worth Star-Telegram* in the case of *Doe v. The Star-Telegram, Inc.*, decided in November 1993. Tong wrote two articles about Doe's rape, published in September 1989, describing how Doe was "repeatedly raped . . . terrorized with a butcher knife . . . and tied up with bed sheets." She also revealed in her first article details about Doe's distinctive imported luxury car, her age, medication she was taking, and approximate location of her residence where she lived alone. Although Doe called to complain about the distress the article was causing her, the paper published the second one anyway, with further details, including that Doe owned a travel agency.

Unfortunately, there was a question of whether the paper got all of this identifying information legally from the police, since the sergeant who gave Tong a police report claimed he did not provide any identifying information about Doe and told Tong it was against department policy to release such information. So, the paper might be liable for printing information illegally obtained and the matter was sent back to trial court for trial.[50]

False or discrediting information about the victim can also spell trouble for the media. One newspaper, newspaper owner, and author found this out in the case of *Thrasher v. Cox Enterprises,* decided in June 1993, after they published an article falsely implying that a woman had chlamydia, an infectious disease transmitted by sexual intercourse, as a result of promiscuous conduct. Corlis Thrasher sued, claiming, among other things, that she had been tricked into doing an interview on what she thought was a story on infertility, in which she and her husband would be portrayed as a wholesome couple successful in their quest for a baby. But instead the focus of the article was on sexually transmitted diseases and infertility due to chlamydia. Eventually, the Georgia Appeals Court agreed there was a question about the truthfulness of the article and that the paper might have been reckless in disregarding the truth in portraying Thrasher as it did. So the case went back to trial.[51]

Even expressing unwarranted skepticism can lead to liability, as occurred when the courts found that Sarah Weinstein might have a case against CBS and Police Officer Richard Bullick, head of the Philadelphia Police Sex Crimes Unit, when he made several remarks on the local WCAU-TV evening news showing he was skeptical of Weinstein's claim of being sexually assaulted. In the case, *Weinstein v. Bullick,* decided in June 1993, Sarah Weinstein, a student at Bryn Mawr, complained to the

Philadelphia Police in November 1991 that she had just been abducted from a Philadelphia street by a man who sexually assaulted her before releasing her. However, Bullick, in charge of the investigation, wondered if the assault could have really happened as she claimed. As he remarked:

> She's saying a lot of things that went on in the car—she's driving—she's driving 80 miles an hour having sex with the guy—in a little Nissan. I couldn't do it, maybe she could. I don't know. And even if there was sex, that doesn't mean it was forcible sex. So it's all of these things we have to look into before we come to a conclusion. But, you know I'm skeptical at the beginning of the investigation.

Though he didn't mention her by name, his remarks could have placed her in a false light, and what he said might have been enough to let others at her school know who it was.[52]

Publicizing the Child Molester

As child sex abuse cases have increased, so has the battle over revealing the identity of the accused child molester. Normally, the child's identity is kept confidential, and everyone, the general public, courts, the media, agree about that. But a growing number of accused abusers are fighting back, claiming their reputations have been damaged before they have been proved guilty of anything, leading them to be vilified, tried, and convicted in the press, even if they are ultimately found not guilty or it turns out a bitter ex-wife is using the accusation as a ploy in a custody case.

But so far the accused don't seem to have much hope in battling the media. Generally, the public interest in these cases is considered so important, that the media is free to publish any charges, as long as it provides an accurate report. Take the case of Eric A. Foretich, who had a highly publicized battle with ex-wife Elizabeth Morgan over the custody of his daughter Hilary. At one point, Morgan gained worldwide sympathy by going to jail, where she spent two years, rather than reveal where she had hidden her child, later discovered with her parents in New Zealand. Her claim, publicized worldwide, was that Foretich had sexually abused their daughter Hilary and another daughter, Heather, by his former wife. Meanwhile, as this custody dispute dragged on, Morgan and Foretich's former wife appeared on the 1989 CBS program, *People Magazine on TV*, in which they described his alleged sexual abuse of his daughters. But claiming he never abused them, Foretich sued in the case of *Foretich v. CBS, Inc.*, decided in January 1993. Among other things, he claimed that CBS, his ex-wives, and others named in the suit maliciously defamed him and intentionally caused him emotional distress in making these false accusations, without any concern for his version of the facts, and presented them "in a sensationalist style that contributed to the ratings." But since Foretich declined to disprove these allegations, the Court of Appeals in Washington, DC agreed the TV show could run the program. Though the court recognized it might be hard for Foretich to disprove these charges, since this meant proving a negative, if he couldn't show the charges were false, he couldn't show he had been defamed and his reputation and character wrongfully damaged.[53]

Being Gay

Still another privacy battlefront exists over revealing whether someone is gay when he (usually a he) hasn't revealed it himself. Although the outing of closeted gays has occurred to some extent for centuries, there was no active gay movement until the 1960s, and gays first fought back in the mid-1970s against being outed by reporters and columnists in the course of ordinary news gathering.

An early salvo was the high-profile *Sipple v. Chronicle Publishing Co.* case, decided in 1984, which dragged through the courts for a decade. It began in 1975 when ex-Marine Oliver Sipple foiled an attempt on President Gerald Ford's life by striking the arm of the assailant Sara Jane Moore as she was about to fire her gun. At once, the media became interested in this hero who possibly saved Ford's life, and during the ensuing media frenzy, the *San Francisco Chronicle* published a column revealing Sipple's prominence in the local gay community, which thereafter was broadcast nationally. However, Sipple found this national attention unwelcome, and sued for this public disclosure, claiming it had exposed his homosexuality to his relatives, and as a result his family had abandoned him, causing him much grief and humiliation. But the courts turned down his claims, since his homosexuality was already widely known in the gay community, and the *Chronicle*'s articles just further publicized this information already in the public arena. Besides, the court felt the stories were newsworthy, prompted by "legitimate political considerations," including combatting the stereotype of gays as "timid, weak, and unheroic."[54]

Then, in the mid-1980s, the idea of "outing" gays became a social movement and media phenomenon within the gay community itself, as many gay activists began using "outing" as a political strategy to expose prominent closeted gays living double lives, particularly those in political power who took positions opposing gay rights and AIDS legislation. Some groups used this approach to reveal prominent and high-status gay individuals as role models for other gays, including gay children and teens.[55] Initially, most outing reports were confined to the gay press and tabloids, but in the 1990s some mainstream publications reported specific allegations and named names, including *USA Today, The Philadelphia Inquirer, Oakland Tribune,* and *Miami Herald.*[56]

The gay movement itself has been very split on the ethics of outing. At one time, the general consensus in the gay community was to honor an individual's desire for privacy and reveal only what he or she wished to outsiders. But as many activists became supporters of using outing as a political statement, they argued that outing was in the best interests of the gay community in making the public aware of the contributions of homosexuals to society and thereby promoting tolerance by heterosexuals. Conversely, opponents saw outing as not only a violation of individual privacy, but a strategy that could damage the gay movement itself by destroying the informal networks of relationships around a person when he or she was exposed, or by undermining privacy claims in other areas where gays want privacy, such as in AIDS testing and reporting.[57]

Meanwhile, caught in the middle of this struggle, the media has had to decide for itself whether to report these revelations or not. Though the results of gay exposure cases in the courts, like Sipple's, along with the long-established freedom of the media to print and broadcast true and newsworthy facts, has meant that the media can generally publish and broadcast these revelations, the media has undergone its own soul-searching to decide what to do. And so, since the early 1990s, the gay outing issue seems to have died down, with the media largely deciding only to bring up the issue of sexuality when someone has become a public figure in the news and his or her sexuality seems relevant to the particular news story—or if a person hiding his or her own homosexuality is viewed as bashing the gay community.

Then, normally, the media can freely publish that news, even if it inadvertently identifies someone as being gay who isn't, as happened to special agent Larry Buendorf, then in charge of the secret service detail protecting former President Ford. National Public Radio mistakenly identified Buendorf as a homosexual in a 1992 broadcast of *Weekend Edition* in a report by Daniel Schorr, when in fact he was a married heterosexual with one daughter. But when he sued for this mistake in the case of *Buendorf v. National Public Radio,* decided in May 1993, the U.S. District Court in Washington, DC quickly threw out the case. Yes, reporter Daniel Schorr had been negligent, because he mixed up Buendorf's role in grabbing a gun from Lynnette "Squeaky" Fromme to protect Ford from an assassination attempt with Sipple's action, when he had similarly protected Ford by grabbing a gun from Sarah Jane Moore. But since Buendorf was a public figure, the court decided just negligence wasn't enough. He had to show that Schorr and the radio network had demonstrated "actual malice" or "reckless disregard" for the truth in the broadcast. But since Schorr had just made an unknowing mistake, Buendorf had no case.[58]

In short, the media is generally free to identify someone as a homosexual, or even make an innocent negligent error in making an identification, if it's news. However, as the issue of gay outing has become interlinked with the subject of AIDS and the privacy rights of AIDS victims since the late eighties, the media has not been generally free to identify someone as being HIV positive or having AIDS, because this is so stigmatizing. Identification would be appropriate if there was some public interest reason to do so, such as when a gay person or intravenous drug user with HIV or AIDS has been convicted of a crime involving risky behavior that could infect others with AIDS. The recent trend has been to reveal the status of the convicted rapist (and even of the accused and charged rapist), so the victim knows, though there is still much uncertainty in this area. Then, too, these restrictions on identifying someone with AIDS, like making revelations about other diseases, brings up the whole issue of protecting very personal medical records, while balancing this with public health concerns. This is an issue made even more complicated by recent efforts to reform the health care system and possibly create universal health care protection and a national health care database.

Book Beat

Book publishers and authors have sometimes been drawn into the privacy battle, too, when they write about someone who doesn't want to be written about or thinks they have been put in a false light by a book or article. But as with the media in general, book publishers and authors mostly win, since they too have free press/First Amendment protections. For example, authors can usually write freely about public figures and even make good faith, or maybe not so good faith mistakes: witness the Kitty Kelley books about Frank Sinatra and Nancy Reagan, and the Joe MacGinniss clunker about Ted Kennedy. So though unauthorized biographers may find that many in the know won't speak to them, if they get any information, unless perhaps they obtain it illegally, they can largely print what they want about newsworthy people. And if they can create a fictionalized fantasy that becomes a novel, it's literature, and thus usually they can invent stories about public figures, too.

It's the Truth—Or Appears to Be

As Brian Freeman found out, authors are generally protected when they write the truth or close to it when he sued Moira Johnson, who had written about him in her book about the struggle to control TWA in her book: *Takeover: The New Wall Street Warriors—The Men, The Money, The Impact.* Freeman, a lawyer, had been a financial advisor for the International Association of Machinists (IAM), one of two labor unions negotiating over who would own TWA in the future, and he was at a key TWA board meeting in 1985 when control was determined. But Freeman objected to one statement which Johnson attributed to him in which he warned that "being sold into bondage to [Frank] Lorenzo would provoke night time trashing of airplanes and other sabotage." He claimed in his suit, *Freeman v. Johnson,* decided in August 1993, that the false statement suggested that he "threatened, condoned, and encouraged his clients to commit acts of physical sabotage and other illegal conduct." But New York Supreme Court quickly disposed of his claim, since New York state not only did not recognize a "false light" invasion of privacy claim, but at most Johnston made a mistaken inference about Freeman's role at the meeting, since the statement attributed to him simply described the attitudes of the union membership he represented. It wasn't an "endorsement of illegal activity by a lawyer." So no harm; no case.[59]

Likewise, Donald Bailey failed when he sued Dell Publishing for libel in the *Bailey v. Dell Publishing Company* case, decided in April 1992. He claimed he was libeled in a book about the unsuccessful effort to free the

American POWs from Laos in 1982, *The Heroes Who Fell from Grace* by Lee Tippin, first published in 1985, since a single mention of him suggested he had engaged in criminal embezzlement. The offending remark was made by Gordon Wilson, who was helping with fund raising for the rescue team, when he commented to another organizer, Bo Gritz, that "over $27,000 had been collected in the fund raising" but that "there was nothing left because Jack Bailey and retired Congressman Donald Bailey (no relation) had taken off with the money to Geneva." But since Bailey was a public figure (a Congressman from 1979 to 1982 and the Auditor General of Pennsylvania from 1985 to 1989) he had to show the quote was made with "actual malice," or that Dell had been knowingly untruthful or reckless. But he couldn't, because the author, Tippin, and the source of the offending remark, Gordon Wilson, were considered reliable sources with credible reputations. Thus, Dell had no reason to know the statement was untrue. So again, no "malice," no case.[60]

And Now You're History

Once you're part of history, it becomes even more difficult to preserve your privacy. It's like signing on "for better or worse," so that authors can write about the "worse" too. One woman who found this out was Adjua Abi Naantaanbuu who had dinner at the home of Dr. Martin Luther King, Jr. the night before he was assassinated. Among the guests was the Reverend Ralph Abernathy, who subsequently recounted the evening in his 1989 book *And the Walls Came Tumbling Down,* in which he suggested that Naantaanbuu had an extramarital affair with Dr. King. Though in the book he stated that King's woman friend had gone into the bedroom with him after dinner and though he didn't mention Adjua by name, she was upset by the reference, since a number of people believed her to be the "friend" to whom Abernathy referred. As a result, she sued, in the case of *Naantaanbuu v. Abernathy,* decided in March 1993. But though she claimed that she and King had never been alone in the bedroom, the U.S. District Court in New York felt that even if all she said was true and even if she could be identified by this indirect reference to her, the book was about a matter of legitimate public concern. The author or publisher had no reason to doubt Abernathy's veracity in telling the story or think him grossly irresponsible in reporting what he recalled, even if he recalled it incorrectly or misinterpreted what he saw. So once again, case dismissed.[61]

But You Can't Make It Up!

The plaintiff has the best chance when the published information is clearly untrue and the writer has actively made up some information, such as "quotes" for a true report—not fictionalized literature. But even then, if the author hasn't recklessly made up this information, or if the plaintiff can't prove this, the press can still prevail.

That's what happened when Janet Malcolm wrote about Jeffrey Masson in *The New Yorker,* and subsequently turned her account into a book. While *The New Yorker* escaped the consequences on the grounds that Malcolm was an independent contractor and it could reasonably rely on her knowledge and credibility to believe her report was true, in her first jury trial Malcolm was initially held responsible for her fudging, since she manufactured several quotes. But since the jury couldn't agree on the damages, in September 1993, the U.S. District Court in Northern California sent the case, *Masson v. The New Yorker Magazine and Malcolm,* back for a retrial. The case was finally decided in Malcolm's favor in November 1994, since the new jury didn't feel she deliberately or recklessly falsified any statements or that Masson proved that what she said was false.

In particular, the first jury found that Malcolm had used five false quotations, which presented Masson, a psychologist well known for taking on the Freudian establishment after working in the Freud archives, in a false light. These quotes made Masson seem like a less than serious, somewhat disreputable scholar, such as one quote in which Masson referred to himself as "an intellectual gigolo" and another in which he spoke of turning the Freudian archives into a place of "sex, women, and fun."

In the first trial, *The New Yorker* was able to get out of the charges on the grounds that it wasn't reckless or irresponsible in trusting Malcolm, which is a kind of victory for the press—at least when it uses independent or freelance writers and reasonably reliable sources.[62] Eventually, as noted above, Malcolm was absolved too. Yet still Masson is appealing, on the grounds the judge gave the jury faulty and incomplete instructions which confused them, and so the struggle goes on.[63]

The Pitfalls of Being a Writer

However, while these generally strong legal supports for freedom of the press may help the media, these freedoms may not be enough to help the writer keep his or her own job, when what the writer wants to say conflicts with the desire of someone he works with (or for) to keep that information from becoming public. That is what happened to aspiring State Attorney Stephen Eberhardt in the *Eberhardt v. O'Malley* case, decided in May 1993. Besides his legal career, Eberhardt had literary aspirations, and in 1990, eight years after being hired as an Assistant State Attorney in Cook County, Illinois, he began working on a fictional novel involving fictitious prosecutors and others in the criminal justice system. Unfortunately, Eberhardt made the mistake of asking fellow Assistant State Attorney, Judy Mondello to review a draft of his manuscript and make comments. And she did have plenty to say—to others in the State Attorney's office.

In reading the manuscript, she found that one of the homes described in it appeared to be that of her parents, and she imagined that Eberhardt must have obtained this information by following and spying on her. Whether he did or not, she quickly wrote up her suspicions and sent them off to the Chief Deputy State's Attorney in the criminal division, Patrick O'Brien, complaining about the manuscript, and soon after O'Brien asked Eberhardt into his office to discuss her charges. Plus O'Brien had his own concerns, as well, about "office confidences" appearing in the manuscript.

Though Eberhardt argued he had just created a composite of persons and places he had become familiar with as a police officer and prosecutor, O'Brien feared that anything Eberhardt learned in preparing his cases for a trial might turn up in a book someday. So he transferred Eberhardt from the Felony Trial Division to the Special Remedies Unit, which was like being assigned to an office Siberia, since for 14 months, Eberhardt received only about five hours of work a week.

Finally, in January 1992, Eberhardt was fired, too, ostensibly for "being gone quite a bit" because of vacation and sick time, although Eberhardt was convinced he was demoted and eventually fired because of the manuscript. But while he claimed in his suit that his "First Amendment rights were violated," and that he suffered from others in the office spreading false and stigmatizing charges about his termination without letting him clear his name, the District Court of Illinois didn't buy his arguments. It dismissed his novel as just fiction, that at most might provide some "interesting insights into the criminal justice system," but it didn't seriously address any matters of public import, such as potential wrongdoing in the State Attorney's Office, for which "free and open debate is vital to informed decision-making by the electorate." So Eberhardt couldn't claim any First Amendment rights violations when his superiors possibly tried to "silence" the manuscript by shunting him off to an obscure office position. And he couldn't even claim a violation of privacy against these superiors for circulating the charges against him around the office, because they hadn't disclosed these charges beyond the office. So Eberhardt was out of court, having, if anything, done too much revealing himself by writing his manuscript and showing it to the wrong person.[64]

Summing Up

In sum, the press is generally free to publish, broadcast, televise, and publicize most anything—since doing so makes it news—and once something is newsworthy, a person generally can't stop the spread of information about him- or herself. And once one becomes a public figure—potentially almost anyone in today's age of instant celebrity—one's bio essentially belongs to history.

The main pitfall for the media is getting the information illegally or too aggressively invading someone's privacy to get that information. However, unpublished writers appear to have fewer protections, because if something's unpublished and unpublicized, it's not clearly a matter of public concern and not yet news.

What this means is the media have gained incredible power to define and disseminate what it considers news, and the average individual can do little to prevent something from being publicized. The upside is the free press tradition, allowing the media to be society's watchdog, uncovering wrongs in government and other powerful social institutions. But the downside is the trivialization of this free speech tradition into the gossipy, prying, and scandal-driven journalism of today.

So what's right and wrong, good and bad for oneself or society? These are not easy issues, and few would want to put formal controls on the press and First Amendment. But the risk to privacy and the loss of selfhood is great, given the power and pervasiveness of the media. There are signs the media is aware of these risks and is making some effort to curb its ability to expose all. For example, most media organizations have made a voluntary decision to withhold the identities of rape victims, juveniles charged with crimes, and HIV/AIDS sufferers, though legally they might be able to publish their names or photos. Still, there are many other areas where additional voluntary restraints might be used to protect the privacy of unwilling "newsmakers" thrust into the news. In this day when tabloid and checkbook journalism has gone mainstream and the pressure to get the story is more and more intense (witness the media frenzy over the O.J. Simpson story) there is an increasing incentive to thrust privacy concerns aside, because along with the media frenzy to get the story, there is the public's rising demand for information.

At one time, many people fled small towns, complaining of the watchful gaze of others as a problem of small town living. But now, in our global society, the media is helping to bring back that small town sense of everyone watching everyone else. And we need to ask ourselves, is this what we want? Or do we need to balance this growing media watchfulness with some more considerations for the right of privacy, and the right of self, too?

Notes

1. Samuel D. Warren and Louis D. Brandeis, "The Right to Privacy," *Harvard Law Review*, 4 (1890): 193.
2. *Pavesich v. New England Life Insurance Company*, 50 S.E. 68 (Georgia 1905), 68–69.
3. *Sidis v. F-R Publishing Corporation*, 113 F.2d 806 (2d Cir. 1940), 807–808.
4. *Melvin v. Reid*, 112 Cal. Appl. 285, 297 P. 91 (1931).
5. *Barber v. Time*, 348 Mo. 1199, 159 s.w. 2d 291 12 (1942).
6. *Daily Times Democrat v. Graham*, 276 Ala. 380, 162 So. 2d 474 (1964).
7. *Virgil v. Time, Inc.*, 527 F.2d 1122 (9th Cir. 1975).
8. *New York Times v. Sullivan*, 376 U.S. 254 (1964).
9. Jeanne Ellen Courtney, "Fellows v. National Enquirer: Limiting the False Light Invasion of Privacy Tort," *Pacific Law Journal*, 8 (1988): 355.
10. *Time, Inc., v. Hill*, 385 U.S. 374 (1967).
11. Theodore L. Glasser, "Resolving the Press–Privacy Conflict: Approaches to the Newsworthiness Defense," *Privacy and Publicity*, Westport, CT: Meckler, 1990, 15–34, pp. 19–20.
12. *Gertz v. Robert Welch, Inc.*, 418 U.S. 323 (1974), 345–46, 252–52.
13. *Cox Broadcasting Corp. v. Cohn*, 420 U.S. 469 (1975), 472–73, 495–96.
14. *Ibid.*
15. *Anonsen v. Donahue*, 857 S.W.2d 700 (Tex. App.—Houston [1st Div.] 1993), 701–706.

16. *Woodward v. Sunbeam Television Corporation*, 616 So.2d 501 (Fla. App. 3 Dist. 1993), 502–503.
17. *Rogers v. Buckel*, 615 N.E.2d 669 (Ohio App. 8 Dist. 1992), pp. 670–73.
18. *Sharrif v. American Broadcasting Company*, 613 So.2d 768 (La. App. 4th Cir. 1993).
19. *Miller v. National Broadcasting Co.*, 187 Cal. App. 3d 1463 (Second Dist. 1986), 1492.
20. *Baugh v. CBS*, 93 Daily Journal D.A.R. (August 13, 1993), 10373–79.
21. *Carey v. Pulitzer Publishing Company*, 859 S.W.2d 851 (Mo. App. E.D. 1993), 853–856.
22. *Ruzicka v. Conde Nast Publications, Inc.*, 794 F. Supp. 303 (D. Minn. 1992).
23. *Kolegas v. Heftel Broadcasting Corporation*, 607 N.E.2d 201 (Ill. 1992).
24. *Howell v. New York Post Company, Inc.*, 612 N.E.2d 699 (N.Y. 1993), 680–704.
25. *Salek v. Passaic Collegiate School*, 605 A.2d 276 (N.J. Super. A.D. 1992), 277–78.
26. *Peoples Bank and Trust v. Globe International Publishing, Inc.*, 786 F. Supp. 791 (W.D. A.N. 1992); 978 F.2d 1065 (8th Cir. 1992).
27. *Marin Independent Journal v. Municipal Court*, 16 Cal. Rptr.2d 550 (Cal. App. 1 Dist. 1993), 551–55.
28. *Haelen Laboratories v. Topps Chewing Gum*, 202 F.2d 866 (2nd Cir. 1953), 868–69.
29. L. Lee Byrd, "Privacy Rights of Entertainers and Other Celebrities: A Need for Change," *Entertainment and Sports Law Journal*, 5 (Fall 1988): 95–116.
30. *Ali v. Playgirl*, 447 F. Supp. 723 (S.D. N.Y. 1978).
31. *Grant v. Esquire, Inc.*, 367 F. Supp. 876, 881 (S.D. N.Y. 1993).
32. *Allen v. National Video*, 610 F. Supp. 612 (S.D. N.Y. 1985).
33. Deborah Manson, "The Television Docudrama and the Right of Publicity," *Privacy and Publicity* (1990): 44–46.
34. *Koussevitzsky v. Allen, Towne and Heath*, 188 Mis. 479, 68 N.Y.S.2d 779 (1947), 783–784.
35. *Rosemont Enterprises v. Random House*, 58 Misc.2d 1, 294 N.Y.S.2d 122 (1968), 123–29.
36. *Ann-Margret v. High Society Magazine, Inc.*, 498 F. Supp. 401 (S.D.N.Y. 1980), 404, 406.
37. *University of Notre Dame v. Twentieth Century Fox*, 22 A.D. 2d 452, 256 N.Y. 5 2d. 301 (1965).
38. *Hicks v. Casablanca*, 464 F. Supp. 426 (S.D. N.Y. 1978).
39. *Dworkin v. Hustler Magazine, Inc.*, 867 F.2d 1188 (Wyoming 9th Circ. 1989), 1190–99.
40. *Hustler Magazine v. Falwell*, 108 S. Ct. 876 (1988), 877–79.

41. *Brown v. Twentieth Century Fox Film Corporation*, 799 F. Supp. 166 (D. D.C. 1992), 168–72.
42. *Joplin Enterprises v. Allen*, 795 F. Supp. 349 (W.D. Wash. 1992), 349–52.
43. *Dora v. Frontline Video, Inc.*, 18 Cal. Rptr. 2d 790 (Cal. App. 2. Dist. 1993).
44. *Prudhomme v. Procter & Gamble Co.*, 800 F. Supp. 390 (E.D.La 1992), 393–96.
45. *Geary v. Goldstein*, 831 F. Supp. 269, U.S. Dist. (1993), cited in Lexis 11994, 21 Media L. Rep. 1906, 1–24.
46. Suzanne M. Leone, "Protecting Rape Victims' Identities: Balance between the Right of Privacy and the First Amendment," *New England Law Review*, 27 (Spring 1993): 883–913.
47. These cases were the frequently cited *Cox Broadcasting Corporation v. Cohn*, 420 U.S. 469 (1975); *Oklahoma Publishing Company v. District Court*, 430 U.S. 308 (1977); and *Smith v. Daily Mail Publishing Co.*, 443 U.S. 97 (1979).
48. *The Florida Star v. B.J.F.*, 491 U.S. 524 (1989).
49. *Macon Telegraph Publishing Company v. Tatum*, 436 S.E.2d 655 (1993), cited in Ga. Lexis 825, 93 Fulton County Dr, 4–6.
50. *Doe v. The Star Telegram, Inc.*, 864 S.W. 2d. 790 (Tex. App. 1993), cited in Lexis.
51. *Thrasher v. Cox Enterprises, Inc.*, 434 S.E.2d 497 (Ga. Appl. 1993), 498.
52. *Weinstein v. Bullick*, 827 F. Supp. 1193 (E.D. Ca. 1993).
53. *Foretich v. CBS, Inc.*, 619 A.2d 48 (D.C. App. 1993), 52–63.
54. *Sipple v. Chronicle Publishing Company*, 201 Cal. Rptr. 665 (Ct. App. 1984), 666–70.
55. David H. Pollack, "Forced Out of the Closet: Sexual Orientation and the Legal Dilemma of 'Outing'," *University of Miami Law Review*, 46 (1992): 711–50; 715–16.
56. John P. Elwood, "Outing, Privacy, and the First Amendment," *The Yale Law Journal*, 102 (1992): 747–76; 748.
57. Elwood, 766–68.
58. *Buendorf v. National Public Radio*, 822 F. Supp. 6 (D.D.C. 1993), 7–12.
59. *Freeman v. Johnston*, 601 N.Y.S.2d 606 (A.D. 1 Dept. 1993), 606–607.
60. *Bailey v. Dell Publishing Company*, 790 F. Supp. 101 (W.D. Pa. 1992), 102–106.
61. *Naantaanbuu v. Abernathy*, 816 F. Supp. 218 (S.D.N.Y. 1993), 220–30.
62. *Masson v. The New Yorker Magazine*, 832 F. Supp. 1350 (U.S. Dist. 1993), cited in Lexis 12767, 2–25.
63. Ken Kelly, "Leggo My Ego!" *East Bay Monthly*, February, 1995, 15.
64. *Eberhardt v. O'Malley*, 820 F. Supp. 1090 (N.D. Ill. 1993), 1091–94.

Chapter 9

Med Alert and Other Fundamental Rights

The Growing Information Explosion and the Concern about Medical and Health Privacy

Today, the concern with medical and health care privacy has become especially intense because of the possibility of creating a national health care program, which will mean gathering even more centralized records and possibly creating a national ID number to access health care records. But the question is, who will have control of records, who will be permitted access to them, and how can we protect that information? Generally, we agree in principle that most health and medical information should be shared confidentially between the patient and doctor. But as the ability to access and distribute information grows, along with societal pressures to release certain information for the good of society (such as for protection from AIDS or to perform sophisticated medical tests to establish paternity or criminal guilt), the fear grows that this very private information will be released inappropriately to the public.

It's a fear well documented in recent surveys. For example, in 1993, Louis Harris & Associates conducted a comprehensive *Health Information Privacy Survey* for Equifax which reflected this growing concern. After calling 1000 individuals throughout the United States and interviewing 650 leaders in the medical field, including hospital and health maintenance organization (HMO) CEOs, insurance executives, doctors, nurses, medical society directors, and legislators and aides dealing with health care, Harris found these key concerns:

- About 60 percent of all those surveyed were concerned about confidentiality or how their personal medical information was being used.
- About half of the American public was concerned about the use of computers by health care providers to keep medical records, and about 60 percent felt that computerized records contained mistakes in patient medical records and that access was given to people not supposed to see the supposedly confidential information.
- About 40 percent were concerned their job opportunities or position might be adversely affected if their medical claims information was seen by employers.
- And slightly over half (56%) favored new comprehensive federal legislation to protect the privacy of medical records.

Thus, although a big majority of Americans felt a single health care identity card would be acceptable (84%) or felt it acceptable for insurance companies to access detailed health information about people applying for insurance (62–81%, depending on the type of information sought), they expressed serious concerns about how this information might be used or misused.

The survey also found that the concern about threats to personal privacy was higher than ever—up from 64 percent in 1978 when Harris started conducting its surveys to 80 percent in 1993. In fact, about a quarter of the respondents had already experienced having medical information about them improperly disclosed by individuals or organizations—most commonly by health insurance companies, clinics or hospitals, public health agencies, employers, and doctors.

The survey further found that people had certain special objections, such as the use of medical information without permission for direct mail marketing by drug companies or hospital fund raising using patient records to ask for donations (about 60–66% opposed, respectively).

With the increasing computerization of health records and the growing movement toward health care reform, other privacy concerns mentioned by about half or more of those surveyed included:

- The ability of outsiders to tap into computers to obtain medical information for improper purposes;
- The use of the computerized health care information system for many nonhealth care purposes;
- The improper disclosure of private medical records by persons using the computers inside the health care system.[1]

In short, there are some very real fears about the use and misuse of private medical and health records, and a growing conflict over when these records and other information about a person's medical or health status are improperly revealed.

The Problem with Medical Records

The basic problem with medical records in the United States is the general lack of privacy protections for these records. Sheri Alpert, an Information Policy Analyst for the Internal Revenue Service (IRS) made this point at a big 1993 conference on privacy, The Third Conference on Computers, Freedom, and Privacy, held in Burlingame, California. As she observed:

> With the exception of records relating to mental health and drug and alcohol abuse or records in the custody of the federal government, there are no federal laws to protect the confidentiality of medical records. Only a handful of states have adopted any laws to protect these records, but they vary in scope and applicability, and often contain provisions more favorable to information exchange than to patient privacy. In fact, video rental records are afforded more federal protection than are medical records. As current federal law stands, while the unauthorized disclosure of medical records may be ethically reprehensible, in the majority of states in this country, it is not illegal.[2]

This concern is echoed by Janlori Goldman, when she was the Director of the American Civil Liberties Union's (ACLU) Privacy and Technology Project. The project was started in 1984 to evaluate the impact of new technology on individual privacy, and recently it has been focusing on privacy and health care. One strategy has been to get these concerns translated into legislation by presenting them to policy-making groups in Washington, such as the American Health Information Management Association (AHIMA). In this way they hope medical professionals will not only use the new information technologies for better health care (say by a doctor using a cellular phone, fax, or computer to transmit relevant patient information, even X rays, to leading experts in the field for other opinions),[3] but will recognize the dangers to personal privacy, such as the problem of keeping the information recorded or transmitted confidential.

Among some of the dangers she noted: Marketers might use these data bases to make pitches to individuals with certain medical conditions. Or medical personnel, insurers, and others with improper access might make unauthorized disclosures of damaging information, such as in hot political races.

This had already happened. In a recent political race, a New York Congresswoman, Nydia Velasquez found that her medical records, including details of a bout with depression and a suicide attempt, were faxed to a New York newspaper and television station during the campaign, and she had to overcome this embarrassing information to win her seat. Though she managed to win anyway with much cost and effort, others have lost due to such disclosures, such as Tommy Robinson, a Republican member of Congress, who ran for governor against Bill Clinton in the 1990 campaign. An insurer leaked an incorrect diagnosis from his files that Robinson had a problem with alcohol. The doctor had made a mistake, but due to the improper leak Robinson lost the race,[4] perhaps even indirectly affecting the future presidency of the United States today (had there been no leak and had he become Arkansas governor instead of Bill Clinton).

But while such privacy invasions are more high profile and potentially influence national and global events, the more common, ongoing dangers are the everyday breaches of confidentiality resulting in discrimination against ordinary individuals. Such discrimination may occur because when damaging information gets out, say to insurers and employers, the individual can be denied insurance and employment, because of this adverse information from their records—such as information showing they are genetically predisposed to a disease, in a high-risk group, or infected with a life-threatening illness.

In turn, if people fear their medical information isn't secure, they may fail to give important personal information to their doctors or to national health surveys that can help them or society. For example, as Goldman notes, many patients "routinely ask doctors to write down a different diagnosis from the real one because they fear their employer may see the file." Many patients seeing psychiatrists ask them not to take any notes, because they fear the notes "could be leaked or even obtained legally with a subpoena."

This resistance contributes to difficulties in taking the census, too, since many individuals don't want to complete the long, detailed census forms because of prying questions like: "Have you ever been pregnant?" or "Have you been treated for mental illness?" Thus, though it is against the law not to complete these forms, this resistance may be a reason the 1990 census had the lowest return rate ever, as Goldman speculates.[5]

Meanwhile, the health reform proposals to insure everyone has created other potential privacy problems, such as the creation of a health care security card, with a unique identifier, like one's social security number or another newly created number. There is a fear that this will add to a growing comprehensive database, with the potential for misuse and abuse, without sufficient privacy protections.

Potentially, according to Goldman, an organized but regulated and protected national medical care record-keeping system could provide better protections than the current piecemeal state-by-state system, since individuals are subject to varying degrees of privacy protection depending upon where they receive their health care. Then, too, if a patient has to go from one county or state to another to receive the necessary medical treatment, he or she may lose the ability to control how health care information is used, since some counties and states have looser privacy protections than others.

That is why Goldman and the ACLU's Privacy and Technology Project are urging the creation of "a uniform federal law that will protect individuals' health care information and provide guidance to the states and localities engaged in health care reform." At a minimum, they want to see a system in which any personally identifiable health records are in the control of the individual and only disclosed with that person's meaningful consent. Also, they believe there should be built-in security measures to protect personal information against unauthorized access and disclosure from those in the organization. In addition, individuals should have a right to see, copy, and correct all information in their records, and be notified about how personal information will be used and by whom. And further, any identification card should be used only for identification purposes and limited to the health care system.[6]

Such views, in turn, are widely shared among others interested in medical record information, as illustrated by other presenters in their remarks on medical issues at the 1993 Computers, Freedom, and Privacy Conference.

Sheri Alpert, IRS Information Policy Analyst, said: "Because there are so few federal legal protections and inconsistent state protections for medical records, federal protections should be placed on the collection, use, storage, disclosure of and access to all medical records prior to or as a concurrent effort with health care reform."[7]

Dr. Daniel Z. Sands, of the Center for Clinical Computing at the Harvard Medical School and the Beth Israel Hospital, Boston, described how the hospital introduced a computerized patient information system, with multitiered security access and an audit system to identify all those accessing the system in order to protect privacy. Then he expressed the opinion that: "Patients should expect that only authorized personnel will view their medical records, which may contain sensitive demographic, financial, personal, and medical information. . . . The future will bring issues of inter-institution transfer of medical records in which data encryption and error-free transmissions will be important."[8]

In short, there is growing agreement about the need to protect medical records, although there is still much dispute over just what can and cannot be revealed and by whom, and what recourse people have when their records are inappropriately revealed, resulting in adverse effects.

The Right over Who Can See and Disclose the Records

Some disclosures of medical records are clearly illegal, such as when an employee in a hospital or doctor's office leaks them to the press, or when a private investigator gains access to records and discloses them to the media. Though the media may be off the hook for its exposé, due to freedom of the press considerations, the person actually taking the records, if discovered, could be subjected to criminal and civil proceedings.

But at other times, the question of whether records should be released gets very murky, such as when one organization or agency wants to get the records for some official or business purpose, and the doctor, hospital, or patient doesn't want to release them. Generally, the rule is that if the records are needed for an official investigation, say by the government, police, or medical board, then the concern with averting wrongdoing will be considered more important than the patient's right to privacy. But if the records are needed for a private business purpose or civil matter, the individual will have more protection.

One patient who learned she couldn't keep her records out of an official investigation of a doctor was patient A. The medical board wanted to get the mental health records of Dr. K, who treated her, to learn if Dr. K had an improper romantic relationship with her in the Maryland case of *Dr. K. et al. v. State Board of Physician Quality Assurance,* decided in November 1993. Dr. K tried to argue that the records shouldn't be disclosed, since patient A wasn't complaining. But that didn't matter, argued the board, because a doctor might be able to persuade a patient not to complain.[9] So ultimately, the battle for the records came down to weighing the patient's privacy right to withhold those records from the state's "compelling" interest in getting those records. Finally, the court decided to favor the state, citing some previous cases—*Whalen v. Roe*[10] and *In Re Search Warrant*[11]—in which doctors had to turn over their records to hospital personnel, insurance companies, public health agencies, or law enforcement agencies, as part of medical practice. As much as the court recognized patient A's privacy right in her medical records, because they were very personal and psychiatric records were especially sensitive, it concluded her right wasn't absolute and the legitimate right of the state here was stronger, so she had to turn them over.[12] It felt the Board needed the records to investigate a case of physician wrongdoing, and it had to be able to conduct meaningful investigations as part of its mission of regulating the use of physician licenses in the state.

Likewise, a doctor in Minnesota, James Robinson Poole, couldn't beat the board when he was charged and later convicted of various acts of criminal sexual conduct against eleven female patients in the case of *State v. Poole,* decided in April 1993. Poole had a family practice which included obstetrical and gynecological care, and some of his patients complained he did a bit more, too. The case began when one of his patients complained to the Minnesota Board of Medical Examiners about a pelvic exam he conducted, and eventually, the Board's investigation uncovered eleven female victims. Typically, the young women received several gynecological exams, in which Poole entered the examination room with them, locked the door behind him, and instructed the patient to undress. Then, as the patient lay naked on the examining table, he would conduct a breast exam and move his fingers in and out of the patient's vagina for about ten to twenty minutes in an examination that normally takes two to three minutes. In some cases, he even used his thumb to stimulate the patient's clitoris, and three of the patients even experienced an orgasm during the examination.

Obviously, this was not a standard medical examination, if the accusations were true. But could the prosecutors use the doctor's patient's records to show this? After the Minnesota Bureau of Criminal Apprehension, investigating the case for the Board, got a search warrant and seized the records of fifty-eight patients, the doctor's lawyers tried to suppress them. But, the Supreme Court of Minnesota concluded that the prosecutors could use the records, since the doctor had no standing to benefit from any decision that the rights of his patients had been invaded, since he was being investigated for abusing some of these patients himself. Also, the court felt there were various safeguards to protect the privacy rights of innocent third parties in the investigation, such as sealing the records and having them reviewed by the judge who issued the warrant to be sure the patient's privacy rights were protected before turning them over to law enforcement.[13]

Thus, generally, investigators can get access to patient records in criminal and medical licensing board investigations.

It seems pharmaceutical records can be readily opened up to in official investigations, too, as illustrated by one battle over them in Ohio, in *Stone v. City of Stow*, decided in July 1992. The controversy began after Stow and several nearby villages and towns set up a program in 1988 with their local police departments to collect and analyze data (without a warrant) on the diversion of controlled substances from legitimate to illegitimate channels of distribution. They did so, suspecting that some patients might be getting multiple prescriptions or that multiple physicians or pharmacies were supplying the same prescription.

But after the police began collecting and analyzing the data, several physicians, patients, and pharmacists protested, and sued to keep the government from getting these records, including a woman whose child was using Ritalin and a man who was taking Percodan for chronic pain. They argued that this collection and analysis infringed on their right of privacy. But eventually the trial court and Ohio Supreme Court sided with the officials, since they concluded the pharmaceutical industry was already a "pervasively regulated industry," so the pharmacist has a "reduced expectation of privacy in the prescription records he or she keeps." At the same time, they felt the state had a strong interest in regulating prescription drugs. As for the patients and physicians, they just had a privacy right not to have this information disclosed to the general public.

But here the information was only being disclosed to police officers or State Pharmacy Board officials. Thus, an administrative search such as this without a warrant to regulate these drugs was fine.[14]

When Disclosure Is Wrong: A Leak for Business and Insurance Purposes

So when can't someone see your records? A good rule of thumb is when someone releases confidential information for an unauthorized purpose, such as leaking the contents of a private file to an insurance company. That is what happened when Doris Heller, a left-handed bookkeeper, went in for treatment in June 1987 at the Sierra Hospital in Fresno, California, and had a bone spur removed from her left hand, in the case of *Heller v. Norcal Mutual Insurance Company,* decided in July 1993. Unfortunately, soon after it was removed, she developed an infection, which led to her whole third finger being amputated and continued pain in the nerves leading to this digit. Eventually, she sued the doctors involved in the amputation, Dr. Kent Yamaguchi and Dr. Geis, for malpractice, and during the litigation that followed, her attorney discovered that the Norcal Insurance Company, representing Dr. Geis, secretly interviewed Dr. Yamaguchi and obtained private records about Heller without her consent or knowledge. In addition, she and her attorney came to believe that Norcal asked Dr. Yamaguchi to testify falsely that Dr. Geis's treatment was "within the standard of care" so that she could no longer claim damages.

These were serious charges: that Yamaguchi agreed to testify falsely against her to benefit Dr. Geis and Norcal and secretly disclosed confidential and private information to Norcal and its agents. And adding insult to injury, after obtaining this information from her treating physician, Norcal retained him to testify as an expert against her claim, among the twelve causes of action listed in her suit. However, while Heller couldn't recover on all of her claims, the Fresno Superior Court agreed her privacy had been violated. In particular, Norcal and Yamaguchi had violated the Confidentiality of Medical Information Act, by which medical information can only be disclosed to authorized organizations and individuals, including insurers. But this disclosure about Heller wasn't authorized, since as Heller pointed out, she had submitted to Yamaguchi's treatment and shared confidential information with him on the basis that he was to be her treating physician. But when Yamaguchi passed on her confidences to Norcal, this was for an unauthorized purpose to unauthorized persons, so both of them violated her state and federal constitutional right to privacy.[15]

In short, unauthorized release of medical information violates constitutional rights, which could result in civil, even criminal penalties, depending on the state.

Talking about AIDS and Other Diseases

But what happens when someone has HIV or AIDS or some other dread disease? Though the press can generally say just about anything if they find out legally, the trend is to prevent medical professionals, employers, and others from revealing this information, unless they are legally required to do so, such as when a judge issues a subpoena in a criminal or civil suit. It seems as if each case is decided on a case by case basis, in which the judge weighs the privacy interests of the individual who doesn't want this stigmatizing revelation against the interests of the private party or government to know. Examples of this would be when a woman sues a former lover who may have knowingly exposed her to AIDS, when an employee claims discrimination because an employer fires him after discovering he is HIV positive and fears he can't do a particular job, or when the state claims an HIV positive rapist is guilty of not just rape but attempted murder, since he knows he can give his victim this fatal disease. (In fact, in California, Governor Wilson signed a new law on 1 July 1994, which allows a sex crime victim to learn if the attacker tested positive for HIV.)[16] These have become difficult questions for our times, because they starkly contrast the right of the individual to preserve the sanctity of the self from others, versus the public's right to know when there are public health and economic issues at stake for those exposed to the disease.

Increasingly, we have been grappling with these issues—in the press, personally, and in the courts—and gradually some general policies have been emerging. Here are some of the basic trends today.

Spreading Medical Secrets in the News: The Story of Arthur Ashe and the Media

The media's ability to print or broadcast the story if it wants is reflected in what happened in April 1992, when Arthur Ashe, the famous former tennis star who has since died, gave a press conference to announce that he had AIDS. He made the announcement, since he knew *USA Today* was considering running the story after a sports reporter received a tip that Ashe had AIDS—a fact he had tried to conceal for about six years, telling only a few confidants. But now, since the story had leaked to the press, Ashe wanted to maintain control over how it was handled. So Ashe made his own announcement, and also raised the ethical question about the propriety of publicizing private health information. Though he triggered a debate over what a news organization could and should reveal with his comments, such as in an interview about a month after his conference that, "We need to draw the line someplace, with a big red pencil," not much changed for the media and privacy. Even the rising cry of public outrage which urged press restraint made no difference. For example, about 95 percent of the over 700 readers who called or wrote *USA Today* in the weeks after Ashe's announcement thought the story should not have been reported.[17]

Thus, in keeping with the general tell-all trend, the media have continued to spread the news about noted people with HIV, AIDS, and other health problems. Meanwhile, those who want to keep their medical problems out of the news have generally sought to keep such information as confidential as possible by telling few others, pledging them to silence, and avoiding leaks.

Who Can't Tell

Ironically, though the press can generally publish what it discovers legally, there are many restrictions on who can tell, making anyone from individuals to hospitals, doctors, and towns liable if they pass on confidential medical information, although under certain circumstances, the person with the condition may be required to provide this information himself. That could occur if this condition is later revealed and he or she has put someone at risk, such as a person who is HIV positive or has AIDS and infects a lover, or a doctor with AIDS who doesn't tell a surgical patient who later tests HIV positive.

But then, what about the individual who knows someone is infected, such as a health worker or counselor in a community health organization? Even though the infected person is legally supposed to tell in certain circumstances (such as the individual who is supposed to inform a partner), but doesn't reveal this information, the third party cannot tell. It seems that the best they can do is try to persuade that person to inform others. But they cannot announce the individual's condition or they will be penalized for invading the privacy of the infected person.

An example of this paradox occurred soon after it was revealed in 1991 that a now deceased Florida dentist, David Acer, might have infected three patients—it is now believed to be six or seven. At once, hospital boards, professional associations, federal agencies, and state legislators began debating whether to place restrictions on HIV positive medical personnel. And soon a 1991 New Jersey case decision established the first of these "inform the patient" guidelines, setting forth the requirement that a patient should be told that a doctor or dentist is HIV positive, and must agree to be operated on by such a doctor for them to give a legally valid informed consent. The New Jersey court established this guideline when it ruled that the Medical Center at Princeton had the right to require an infected ear, nose, and throat specialist, Dr. William Behringer, to get written consent from his patients before operating on them. Yet, ironically, the court found that the hospital was itself liable for invading Behringer's own privacy rights, because it didn't keep his own test results private, so eventually it had to pay damages to Behringer's estate after he died.[18]

Since then, as more medical exposure cases, particularly of AIDS, have hit the courts, the trend has been to impose damages on anyone revealing confidential medical information. This is what Dr. "Jane Roe" found in a worker's compensation case after she told a patient's employer's attorney that the patient had tested HIV positive. The case, entitled *Doe v. Roe,* decided in May 1993, began when John Doe, a flight attendant with a commercial airline based in Pittsburgh, Pennsylvania, appeared at Roe's office to obtain medical treatment for ear and sinus problems. While receiving treatment, he informed Roe he had tested HIV positive, and he asked Roe to keep this confidential, because he was afraid that if released the information could jeopardize his employment. Doe claimed the doctor agreed verbally to keep his confidence.

But a few months later in April 1990, after Doe filed a worker's compensation claim, noting that he had been treated by Roe for his ear and sinus problems as a work related injury, Roe was subpoenaed to appear at a worker's compensation hearing at the offices of Doe's employer's lawyer. The attorney advised her she could skip the hearing if she simply sent the requested medical records about Doe's treatment, which she did. Unfortunately, one chart she sent referred to Doe's HIV-positive status, which Roe claimed, breached her promised confidentiality. The New York Supreme Court agreed that it did, particularly because the New York Legislature had recently passed a public health law to protect the confidentiality of those who were already or might be infected with HIV or were suffering from AIDS, to encourage people to participate in voluntary testing, obtain treatment, and change their behavior to reduce the risk of infection of themselves and others.

Under this law, a doctor or any other person with HIV-related information could only tell those authorized to receive it, such as a health provider or insurance company, if the patient consented. But here, the patient hadn't given any authorization, and the subpoena didn't authorize the doctor to release the information either. Rather, the patient had only told the doctor to help the doctor more safely test his ear and sinus condition, and he agreed to treatment in return for the doctor's promise to keep his condition confidential. So the doctor violated both the public health law and her agreement with her patient, and Doe could collect punitive and other damages accordingly.[19]

Even a comment intended as a helpful warning to another person can open someone to liability for saying too much, as one police officer in Massachusetts found out when a woman with HIV successfully sued for revealing her condition, in the case of *Doe v. Town of Plymouth,* decided in July 1993. The story began in 1988, when Jane Doe was in her apartment with her sister. Suddenly, her upstairs neighbor, Anna Magnifico, burst in, proclaiming that her own daughter was "chanting about evil things," and dumped the contents of her pocketbook on the coffee table, where Doe had a bottle of AZT medication. After Doe called the police and they took Magnifico to the police station and local hospital, leaving Magnifico's daughter at Doe's house, Officer Tibbetts found the AZT bottle with Doe's name on it in Magnifico's purse at the hospital. A doctor explained the medicine was used for AIDS, and Tibbetts called Doe, asking about the medicine. Though she acknowledged she was HIV positive, she asked him to keep the information confidential and Tibbetts assured her that no one would ever know and returned her medication and picked up Magnifico's daughter.

But people soon did know, because about two-and-a-half months later, Magnifico had a fight with a neighbor, Bosari. After Tibbetts arrived, in response to a call to the police, he advised Bosari to "insulate herself and her children" from Magnifico and her daughter, adding that Doe was a "sad case" because of her AIDS. Bosari told another neighbor, and the word spread around that Doe had AIDS. As a result, Doe soon found that none of the neighborhood children would play with her daughter, and shortly after she moved, because of the stress of people knowing she had AIDS.

Though Tibbetts later claimed he didn't recall telling anything to Bosari, the U.S. District Court agreed he could be liable if he had, since he had revealed Doe's medical condition without her consent, thereby violating her right to privacy. Also, he was wrong to have discussed her AZT medication with various nurses and doctors. So now it was up to a trial court or jury to determine if he actually said these things, as Doe claimed.[20]

When Telling Is Okay

Yet, while keeping confidences about HIV and AIDS is usually the rule, sometimes special circumstances make telling acceptable if not required. For example, in a court case where someone's HIV/AIDS status is an issue (such as a blood supply/blood donor case), knowledge of AIDS/HIV status is critical to the outcome of the case. Or if someone with HIV/AIDS or a sexually transmitted disease is in an intimate relationship, the trend is to say that he or she has a duty to inform the partner, so that person can take precautions, knowingly take the risk, or end the relationship. Alternatively, if the person with the disease doesn't tell, he or she could be liable should the partner contract it and sue.

It's in the Blood. The blood cases have ended up in the courts, because many people who died of AIDS received blood transfusions and sued the centers where they got the blood either in the course of surgery or because they suffered from hemophilia. Then, to show their transfusion resulted in their getting AIDS, they or their estates have sought to discover the normally confidential identity of the blood donor. When the blood bank wouldn't tell them voluntarily during the discovery phase of a lawsuit, a time when the lawyers from both sides question witnesses and parties from each side, they filed motions with the court asking for this information. The outcome of these cases has been that generally blood banks and donors have to reveal this information.

For example, in one Ohio case, *Long v. American Red Cross,* decided in February 1993, the estate of AIDS victim Judy Long, who died in 1992, sued the American Red Cross, which had given her a blood transfusion back in 1984. During litigation, the estate wanted to know the name of the donor, so it could find out more about him or her. Even though the Red Cross agreed that Long contracted AIDS from its transfusion, the estate still wanted to show, by knowing about the donor, that the Red Cross had been negligent, since it didn't use surrogate blood testing* or use adequate screening procedures. And eventually, the U.S. District Court agreed that Long's estate's need for information was strong enough to overcome the privacy interests of the donor, particularly since he was already dead. Then, too, the court felt that allowing disclosure would contribute to promoting the safety of the blood supply and encourage blood banks to act responsibly in screening donors.[21]

Cynthia Watson, likewise, was able to obtain information on a Red Cross donor, after she gave birth to premature twins in Charleston, South Carolina, in 1985, in the case of *Watson v. Lowcountry Red Cross,* decided in November 1992. One of her sons had a short and painful life. He received a number of blood transfusions to keep him alive for about two months after he was born, and the following year he tested positive for HIV and soon developed AIDS. After he died in 1988, Watson sued the Red Cross, which supplied the blood, and the hospital where he received the transfusions for wrongful death. Here, too, the Red Cross didn't want to reveal the identity of the one of six donors whose blood might have been HIV positive, or let her question him through a court-appointed intermediary. Though it supplied many nonidentifying pieces of information about him, as well as a screening questionnaire with identifying data crossed out, Watson still wanted to know more. And here, too, the U.S. Court of Appeals agreed she should, particularly since the donor's privacy would be protected through a variety of procedures used in the discovery process, such as only revealing his identity to the court and the court-appointed lawyer. In this way, while the donor could keep his privacy, Watson would get the information she needed to help her win her case—a result which the judge felt was in the public interest of compensating injuries.[22]

In short, in these blood donor cases, the courts have favored the victim's need to win the case and get compensated, and part of the

*A test which does not test directly for the presence of HIV, but produces a positive response in 80 percent of the cases where the blood comes from an HIV-positive donor.

rationale for doing so is to help keep the national blood supply safe. So on balance, the public's right to know becomes more important than individual privacy rights to confidentiality.

Friends and Lovers. The same concern with protecting the public also has contributed to the "if you have it, you have to tell" attitude in intimate relationships when HIV, AIDS, or other transmittable diseases are involved. This approach was first reflected in a late-1980s herpes case, when a woman sued her secretive boyfriend for infecting her and he was found liable. At the time, the case was treated as something of a joke, in that herpes is an irritating but not life-threatening disease, and the idea of one lover taking another to court over a private matter in the bedroom seemed amusing and titillating. But now as the cases largely involve HIV and AIDS, no one is laughing. Instead, these cases have become a sad reminder that the individual sometimes has a duty to reveal damaging personal information to protect both intimate others and society from a spreading deadly plague.

A powerful example of this classic battle occurred when a woman sued the popular basketball player Magic Johnson in the *Doe v. Johnson* case, decided in February 1993. Johnson had become an HIV positive role model to many, because of his work to promote AIDS awareness, which included serving on President Bush's AIDS commission for a while. However, before he acknowledged his HIV status and reaffirmed his commitment to his wife Cookie, he was something of a man about town. As such, he enjoyed plenty of women as one of the perks of superstar sports status, and sometime around the evening of 22 June 1990, he had sex with Jane Doe, who subsequently found she was HIV positive, too.

So "Jane Doe" sued, claiming that Johnson "knew or should have known" he had a high risk of becoming infected because of his 'sexually active, promiscuous lifestyle'." Therefore, he should have warned her about his past lifestyle, informed her he may have HIV, not have sex with her, or used a condom or other method to protect her. Johnson and his lawyer claimed he had no such duty.

Significantly, both sides agreed that an individual could be liable for negligence or fraud in transmitting the HIV virus, if that person knew he or she was infected, suffered from symptoms associated with the virus, or knew a prior sex partner was HIV positive. This is because the general legal consensus seems to be that such a person has a legal duty to reveal this information to a partner, given the severity of the risk and the interests of society in combatting this problem.

But the big if was what did Johnson know? If an individual simply lived a high risk life-style in which he might be exposed to AIDS, the U.S. District Court judge in Michigan thought it might be going too far to make him responsible, since anyone in a matrimonial case alleging adultery could add in a claim for damages due to the fear of AIDS. But if a person engaged in "high-risk" activity and had any suspicious HIV symptoms, then he might have a duty to check out his own status or warn his sex partners of the possible risk of AIDS. So a high-risk life-style might be relevant in an AIDS suit.[23]

Johnson never waited for the final verdict and quietly arranged for an out-of-court settlement, as many high-profile celebrities do. The message of the ruling in the case, however, is that anyone who has a serious disease or suspects this has a responsibility to warn his or her partner, take precautions, or both. This way the partner at risk can knowingly decide whether to have sex, and if so, whether it should be protected or unprotected. But while that's the theory, in reality, many people use the "don't tell/don't ask/don't tell the truth" approach, when it comes to HIV and AIDS. But should the matter come to court because the uninformed partner gets HIV or AIDS, he or she will generally prevail, because of the growing agreement that the person who has it or suspects has to tell.

AIDS and Other Illnesses at Work, and a Philadelphia Story

The battle for privacy concerning AIDS and other illnesses has also swept through the workplace. The film *Philadelphia* with Tom Hanks as the embattled AIDS-infected lawyer brought this struggle home dramatically to the American public when it was released in December 1993. In the film, he tries to keep his condition secret for several years and continues to do good work. But once his condition is discovered, the partners of his law firm oust him.

Ironically, in a case that mirrors the film mirroring life, a real Philadelphia lawyer with AIDS sued his former law firm, Kohn, Nast, and Graft, claiming he was similarly fired when one partner, Steven A. Asher, discovered he had AIDS and spread the word through the firm. And as in the film, when John Doe sued, he claimed "his work was very good, but when the firm discovered his illness, it criticized his work and fired him."

Initially, Kohn recruited Doe by persuading him to leave a large Philadelphia law firm, and in July 1991 he started working there, almost exclusively with Steven Asher, one of the partners. At first, Asher highly praised his work, even telling him he had "the potential to make it as a shareholder" in the firm, because of his "A-quality work," and for about a year, things were fine. But in September 1992, Doe came down with a sudden illness and went to an infectious disease specialist who conducted blood tests. Over the next few months, things at the law firm began to change. For example, as he lost weight, people at the firm began to gossip about him, including one secretary who remarked that he "looked like he had AIDS," and in December 1992, Asher told him he would not be assigning him any more work, stopped speaking with him, and "avoided physical contact with him." Doe believed this is because Asher might have seen some confidential medical and health information on or inside his own desk.

Then, in January 1993, the day Doe's doctor told him he had tested positive for AIDS, Asher urged him to find another job as soon as possible, saying that Doe did not meet his expectations and that the firm would not be renewing his contract for the following year. Even worse, according to Doe, after that termination, Asher spread a memo around the firm saying his work was substantially below par. Soon, too, he claimed the firm began a surreptitious harassment campaign to get him to leave earlier, which included giving his computer to another attorney and falsely accusing him of "rifling" through files and "stealing" computer discs.

Finally, on 19 March, Doe was fired, and these charges, which he claimed were trumped up, were circulated to the firm's employees, stating that confidential documents have been found in his office. Then the firm told the state unemployment office that he had been fired for spreading confidential matters to outsiders. On top of all this, claimed Doe, the firm interfered with a job interview he had with a Washington, DC firm, Steptoe and Johnson, by telling them he was HIV positive and was claiming that Kohn discriminated against him. He was disturbed, too, because, subsequently, Kohn hired Steptoe to help Kohn in its own dispute with Doe, so of course, Steptoe couldn't extend an offer to hire Doe, as Steptoe told Doe in April.[24]

So now the case is working its way through the system, and Doe included the invasion of privacy charges because of the way Asher may have obtained the information about Doe having AIDS.

General Policies on AIDS, Other Diseases, and Privacy in the Workplace

While this and other cases are percolating through the system, commonly taking years to resolve, certain policies have been developing to protect the privacy of and avoid discrimination against those with AIDS and other diseases and disabilities if they can do the work. These policies represent a mix of federal and state laws and guidelines developed by employers and employment lawyers.

For example, under the Americans with Disabilities Act, a federal law, employers have to provide the same health insurance benefits to workers with disabilities, and cannot discriminate in hiring, promoting, or firing an individual based on a disability.[25] Also, many state laws, such as those in California, Florida, Michigan, and Missouri to name a few of the larger states, protect the privacy of individuals with illnesses and disabilities, to help them avoid discrimination in hiring, promotion, or firing or getting insurance. Among other things, these state laws "generally prohibit discrimination against individuals with HIV or AIDS, allow no testing without consent, and require confidentiality of test results," according to a workplace privacy article in the *American Business Law Journal*. In addition, some state laws, such as Maryland's, prohibit questions about physical, psychological, or psychiatric illnesses, disability or treatment without a direct relationship to the individual's ability to do the job.[26]

Moreover, an employer can't spread private information about an employee's condition to others—whether in- or outside the company. The general rule is that employers cannot discriminate against employees with diseases or disabilities that don't put other employees at risk or prevent the employee from doing a job, and they also should not invade an employee's privacy to find out or spread information about an employee with such a condition.

Unfortunately, some employers do seek out and use this negative confidential information to discriminate or try to conceal what they know and how they found out. And the problem seems likely to grow as the AIDS crisis spreads, along with other modern environmental and chronic diseases that are increasingly hitting younger workers. On the other hand, for the employee whose condition is revealed, the need for protection is a matter of survival. So the battle is joined, with the government generally trying to protect the employee, while many employers resist.

Mental Illness and Therapy

The treatment for mental illness and therapy generally is shrouded with privacy protections, too. In general, psychological treatments are treated like medical records, so that anyone else working with a client or patient or their records is not supposed to reveal any information without that person's permission.[27] Even in court hearings, the records of a therapist may remain confidential. A key reason for these protections is so the patient or client expects any communications, even the fact of being treated, to be in confidence. Then, presumably the patient will feel free to talk openly and honestly about whatever is bothering him, which is considered essential for effective treatment and healing. This approach is similar to the bond of confidentiality protecting medical doctor and patient, priest and parishioner, and other special relationships. In effect, therapy providers are held to the same rules as M.D.'s, as well as other key professionals considered to have a "special" confidential relationship with the individual.

Yet one big exception, affecting all therapists, medical professionals, and many others in confidential relationships, is that if a client or patient indicates that he or she intends to harm a potential victim and the admission is reasonably believable, then the professional must report this admission to the appropriate authorities (commonly the police). That is because the potential harm to the victim is considered to outweigh the privacy rights of the client or patient.

A landmark case establishing this principle is the widely known *Tarasoff* case in California in 1976. It began when a client told his therapist he intended to kill a woman who had ended their relationship, and eventually he did kill her, setting off a battle over whether the therapist was responsible, since he didn't warn the intended victim directly, though he told the police, who didn't take any action. Eventually, the decision in the case was that a therapist must warn a potential victim of a dangerous act if he or she reasonably believes the client intends to carry it out against that person, even though the admission is private and confidential.[28] Now, besides similar decisions in other states,[29] numerous laws require therapists, doctors, nurses, social workers, and other helping professionals to warn of potential dangers or certain types of abuses, such as when they hear a threat against a victim or suspect child abuse. As an example, this is one reason the Michael Jackson case burst into the news, when a thirteen-year-old boy reported sexual abuse to a therapist, who then reported this, as required, to the police.

The danger of requiring these revelations is that it has the potential of exposing an innocent or troubled but harmless person to the glare of exposure. But alternatively, not telling risks concealing a crime if the potential or actual perpetrator is not exposed. Generally our choice as a society today is to expose the potential harm or alleged crime, even at the expense of revealing a private confidence, exposing a patient's problems, or ruining the reputation of a wrongly charged innocent person.

Should we make that trade-off of free speech and openness over privacy and concealment in this case? It's a battle that is still being fought, such as in a growing number of false memory cases just now turning up in the courts, pitting former patients and relatives of patients, who feel they have been harmed by the treatment, against therapists who feel what they did was not only correct but a privileged, confidential matter between themselves and their patient.

Exposing the Fraudulent Medical Practitioner

This spirit of openness likewise goes to revealing the medical or therapeutic practitioner who has lost a license or has been found guilty of malpractice. Even the names of practitioners who have only been charged may be known. For example, in California, the Board of Behavioral Examiners, part of the State Consumer Affairs Department, publishes a list of current disciplinary actions, listing the charges and dispositions against marriage, family, and child counselors; clinical social workers; educational psychologists; and other practitioners licensed by its agency. Any member of the public can get this list, as well as a full record of the disposition hearing, just by writing to the agency. Similarly, the Medical Board of California, also a part of the Consumer Affairs Department, publishes a monthly disciplinary summary, "The Hot Street," available to members of the public, listing the health care practitioners—including physicians, surgeons, physical therapists, and psychologists—against whom there have been accusations or decisions.

DNA, Genes, and You

Another recent battlefield has been over what the new knowledge about genes (or, more specifically, DNA) reveals about the individual. The earlier battles over fingerprinting and taking blood tests for identification purposes were over privacy issues, though certain widely accepted guidelines have developed, such as providing fingerprints for a driver's license in those states where that is demanded, and giving blood samples in a paternity suit.

There are still occasional battles, such as in 1993 and 1994 in San Francisco, when the city wanted to crack down on welfare fraud by asking applicants to provide fingerprints. Some city supervisors triggered a dispute that rocked the city and city hall over the invasion of privacy issue involved in making this request, since this would stigmatize the recipients, some claimed, while others argued that fingerprinting is used as a matter of course in getting a professional license and other services. The issue was finally put on the ballot and passed, so now fingerprinting is required for general assistance.

This recent battle has involved DNA and genetic information due to new developments in biogenetics that permit us to gain even more information about individuals on the genetic level. The implications of what we can know are vast, and the privacy protections are just being worked out through battles in the legislatures and the courts. Currently, about two dozen states accept some form of DNA testing in court, while the status is uncertain elsewhere.[30] Meanwhile, legal scholars and researchers are weighing in with their own views on how to deal with this new technology.

There are three key areas where this battle has developed. The first area involves the use of DNA testing as evidence in police investigations and court cases. The second area involves the use of genetic data in family conflicts, such as in adoption and paternity cases. Third, is the use of genetic information in getting health insurance and medical treatment. It seems the more we know, through improved technology, the more questions arise about what we *can* know and who should know it.

Using DNA for Crime Fighting and in the Courts

Deoxyribonucleic acid testing is being used more frequently and has been gaining increasing acceptance by the police and in the courts as evidence has accumulated regarding its accuracy. Indeed, this has been one of the big battles in the O.J. Simpson case: Can the DNA evidence be used to show if he committed the two murders? The trend here, as in other cases nationally, has been to let the evidence in, and eventually Simpson's lawyer's gave up their challenge, recognizing that Judge Ito was likely to allow the evidence. Yet, while DNA comparisons may help in identifying who did what, or who didn't do it, such as when the police find evidence at a crime scene that can be tested, many experts still raise concerns about the reliability of testing and its accuracy. For example, a *Newsweek* article on the O.J. Simpson case cites geneticist Victor McKusick of John Hopkins University who suggests the chance of a false match may range from 1 in 100,000 to 1 in a billion, depending on which expert one asks.[31]

Privacy advocates have also raised concerns about how this testing could be misused. For example, the results could be inappropriately passed on to employers, insurers, or other private parties, who might use any negative results to deny the individual a job or insurance. There are also fears that tests might be used to create a national DNA database, with DNA results being like a national identifier, that could subject each person to oppressive government control and scrutiny.[32] Or perhaps marketers might target consumers with certain genetic profiles, making them likely candidates for a product (such as health products). Then, too, people with a profile associated with negative traits could be subject to discrimination, treatment, or social engineering.

Still, much of this scare may be overblown, since there is widespread misunderstanding about how genetic material is used for DNA testing. People often think that a DNA identification test can reveal everything, since an individual's DNA provides a complete genetic "blueprint" for all of their physical traits. But as Dan L. Burk points out in an article on DNA testing, the DNA ID test used by law enforcement and in the courts only uses a small part of the DNA. This just gives a banding pattern for certain chemical combinations which are highly specific to a particular individual. But the information used in the test is limited to the makeup of this particular molecule.[33]

Thus, as Burk emphasizes, the possibility of discovering additional private genetic or personal data is remote, although if preserved, a DNA sample could be used to extract additional information—say by another agency, a researcher, or the Human Genome Project which is trying to create a map of all human genes. So precautions should be taken on how the information on DNA testing is used to protect the privacy of everyone tested. But on the positive side, DNA testing might be used for other useful identifying purposes, such as identifying missing children or identifying battlefield or accidental casualties for the military.[34]

Thus, while there are real privacy concerns in protecting the use of DNA material, many of these privacy protections are already in place (such as limiting the genetic material sampled for ID purposes only), and some of the worst *1984*-type fears of a DNA-national identity card are overdrawn.

DNA and Family Conflicts

What should family members be able to know about each other's genes, as genetic information becomes increasingly available? Say a person has been tested to learn if he or she is likely to have a heritable disease so he or she can take precautions against its symptoms early or decide whether to have children. The person may not want anyone else to know the results, if positive, because of the stigma. But now that the technology exists that makes testing possible, it raises questions about whether close relatives or spouses should know, since they might be affected by this condition and might want to be protected against harm to themselves or their children.

Meanwhile, as we can know more, there may be growing pressure on the state and federal government to pass legislation to compel genetic testing and to advise those affected by the results if that information will protect them against harm.

In turn, while medical practitioners have a duty to preserve patient confidentiality, at times they may be compelled to disclose what they know in order to warn others, such as when a mentally disturbed patient has threatened to harm someone, as noted earlier. Some believe there are similarly compelling reasons to disclose genetic information to others, now that we have gained this knowledge, so they can make certain informed decisions, such as deciding whether to risk having a child that might have this gene, or getting tested themselves to determine if a fetus has the gene, and decide accordingly whether to have that child or choose an abortion.[35] Also, society as a whole may want to know about genetic information to protect the public from genetic disease or gather information about it to develop ways to protect future generations.

Many public health measures already do intrude upon personal liberty, such as mandatory vaccinations, quarantine, and blood testing. But should we know the results of genetic testing since it impacts on the individual's fundamental privacy right? As one legal scholar raising these questions about genetic testing observes, genetic testing is even more personal than these other methods since it reveals very basic information about the individual's own genetic makeup. It does so because "the knowledge that one carries a disease gene may influence one's self-perception and definition of 'one's own concept of existence' in a way most infectious diseases do not."[36] Thus, forced testing may confront the individual with information he or she wants to avoid knowing personally—as well as not wanting others to know.

Genetic Information and Health

The arena of health is another big battlefield in the gene wars. This is particularly so because of efforts to establish a comprehensive health care plan, coupled with research on the Human Genome Project to map the genetic makeup of the human race. The health care plan, though scaled down and still being reworked in Congress, has the potential for creating a national health care data base, including DNA identifiers and other genetic information.

On the plus side, the genetic map can help people better know what to expect and help prevent or treat inherited diseases. This is because, as legal scholar Carol Lee observes, new diagnostic tests of DNA sequences can predict illnesses long before they are clinically manifested and can indicate an inherited predisposition not only to physical and mental illness, but to physical and personality traits, such as the recently discovered "obesity gene."

But on the minus side, this information could potentially be used by insurers, employers, and others to create a two or more tiered society, in which those with better genes are given more opportunities while others are discriminated against as being poorer risks. For example, Lee notes that in the field of health insurance, genetic testing can "be used to separate individuals into 'insurable' and 'uninsurable' groups," and then insurers can use genetic markers as "a basis for denying coverage or determining rates and eligibility unfairly."[37]

But even if certain genes may be associated with the probabilities of having a certain condition, the problem of discrimination remains. So far, laws and court cases have protected the rights of the disabled, including their right not to reveal certain stigmatizing information. Now the genetically disfavored may need similar legal protections, and a battle is shaping up between those wanting to know—primarily insurers, employers, and the government—and those wanting to limit knowledge, especially doctors, genetic counselors, and patients.

How do we make choices as a society? On the one hand, knowing may bring some economic and social benefits—for example, insurers can use genetic information to set insurance rates more fairly for people with different risks, and employers can avoid hiring high-risk employees in positions that would increase their danger of getting an illness, such as putting a cancer-prone individual in an environment with high cancer risk factors like higher than average radiation. But on the other hand, revealing genetic information without sufficient personal privacy protections threatens to create a eugenics-based society by giving those with "better" genes more opportunities and discriminating against those with identified genetic weaknesses and disorders. In the 1920s and 1930s, a eugenics movement in the United States and Western Europe contributed to the rise of Nazism, and certainly, the mainstream of society does not want that today. But the use of genetic mapping, testing, and a data pool, without sufficient protections, does risk that kind of discrimination, particularly if a national health care plan and data base is developed that covers everyone.

That is why, because a few cases of genetic discrimination have ended up in court, there have been recent efforts to pass legislation that provides guidelines for genetic testing and disclosure. For example, there is now a growing movement to prevent health insurance discrimination. Employees with genetic diseases may already be protected from discrimination in the workplace by the Americans with Disabilities Act of 1990, but this legislation doesn't prohibit *insurance* bias.

Additionally, since the early 1990s, state and federal legislators have started introducing legislation to prevent genetic discrimination, such as the Genetic Privacy Bill introduced in 1991, which prohibits federal agencies from disclosing an individual's genetic record without written consent. Another bill prohibits law enforcement agencies from releasing DNA information to the private sector. Meanwhile, several states, including California, Iowa, Rhode Island, Wisconsin, and Wyoming have been considering or have passed genetic privacy legislation. Even the American Society of Human Genetics has taken an active role in seeking protection, including testifying before the U.S. Congress to guard against the unauthorized disclosure of genetic data to third parties.[38]

The Coming Health Care Data Bank

Meanwhile, as all these conflicts over protecting health privacy from encroaching technologies and new disease conditions continue, another threat is the creation of a national health care data bank as part of the Clinton health care plan. At this point, its not certain whether this data bank or the health care plan will be passed, at least in a comprehensive form. But the notion of a national health care data bank is gathering steam, along with the push to merge this computerized data with other records in some sort of national data base, in light of concerns about immigration, welfare fraud, and growing crime problems.

Unfortunately, this compilation of data further magnifies the concern about the release of stigmatizing medical data of any sort. The general agreement seems to be that medical data shouldn't be released to third parties without permission. But the creation of any huge data base and the pooling of records from numerous sources, ups the risk that confidential data may be released inappropriately to the wrong parties, and to the detriment of the person in question.

That is why there is a growing cry from privacy advocates, such as the American Civil Liberties Union (ACLU), to tighten laws protecting the confidentiality of medical records as data is further computerized and pooled. As Janlori Goldman, then director of the ACLU's Project on Privacy and Technology, commented in an article on Clinton's plans for a national medical data bank, the big threat is that the explosion of computer technology may make it impossible for Americans to shield the intimate details of their medical histories from prying fingers on a keyboard once their records are in the data base. As she observed to San Francisco *Chronicle* reporter Sam Fulwood: "While a hospital storage room full of paper files may raise some very serious worries, the threat to privacy is at least limited to those who are physically there and can get into the room. With remote access from around the country and around the world, electronic data interchange might make possible multiple invasions at the same time by people scattered across the globe."[39]

Thus, between new medical technologies providing new sources of personal information and new computer technologies providing new ways to spread that information, the threat to revealing private medical information is very real. The unauthorized and undesired release of this information is especially disturbing, because it is so intimate and personal, striking at the essence of the individual's inner self, in physical, emotional, and mental terms.

The Battle over Other Fundamental Rights

This discussion of medical and health issues has illustrated how intense and emotional this battle can be when fundamental rights are involved. The same kind of emotional intensity has fueled several other battles that deal with personal choices about life-styles, ethics, and morality, with privacy advocates arguing for freedom of choice and others asking for government intervention on behalf of their vision of society. The five main areas of fundamental privacy rights today include abortion and contraception, gay rights, pornography and unacceptable sexual activity, gun ownership, and drugs.

Abortion and Contraception. While fundamentalists and many abortion opponents see this as a morality or crime issue, the legal trend, furthered by the Clinton administration's prochoice stance, has been to view abortion as a privacy right. The basis for this approach is two key cases from the 1960s and 1970s. One was the landmark case of *Griswold v. Connecticut* in 1965, in which the Supreme Court ruled that a state law which prohibited using contraceptives or providing advice on their use to others invaded the individual's privacy and was therefore unconstitutional. In coming to this conclusion, Justice William O. Douglas observed that the "right to privacy is older than the Bill of Rights," and thus he suggested that this right existed in the "penumbra" or shadow of other constitutional guarantees. Then, in 1973, in the landmark *Roe v. Wade* and *Doe v. Bolton* cases, the Court expanded this privacy right to include abortion when it struck down two state laws prohibiting abortion, asserting that the right to privacy was "broad enough to encompass a woman's decision whether or not to terminate her pregnancy," although it could be subject to certain governmental limitations.[40]

The big questions have been what governmental limitations should there be, and should women even have this privacy right? The Reagan and Bush years marked a gradual erosion of abortion rights, but during the Clinton administration, the trend has been reversed, reaffirming women's right to privacy. Moreover, the popular sentiment is clearly in favor of the more legalistic privacy approach, since according to surveys reported in the media, about 70 percent of the American public supports the view that abortion should be a matter of personal choice. In fact, the conviction and death penalty sentence of self-styled abortionist executioner Paul Hill, who killed an abortion doctor in Virginia, serves to support this message by affirming that the women who make this choice and the doctors who aid them should be protected. Yet, given the fervor of the antiabortionists and the fears of physical harm by those seeking to exercise this privacy right, this is an issue that is not likely to go away.

Homosexuality and Gay Rights

Legally, the trend is likewise to support gay privacy rights. The highly controversial "don't ask, don't tell" ruling, sparked by Clinton's support of gays in the military, is an example of this. Also, several court decisions in 1993 have supported the individual's right to be gay as a fundamental right, including *Dahl v. Secretary of the U.S. Navy,*[41] decided in August 1993, and *Steffan v. U.S. Court of Appeals,*[42] decided in November 1993. In both cases, the Navy tried to discharge a person because he admitted he was gay. In Dahl's case, he was already in the Navy, having enlisted in 1980, and had an excellent service record. But in an official interview in March 1981, he disclosed during questioning that he was a homosexual, and the Navy honorably discharged him as a result in 1982. But after he appealed, eventually, the U.S. District court ordered the U.S. Navy to reinstate him, concluding among other things that any order requiring his separation from the service because of his homosexual status was unconstitutional.[43] In Steffan's case, he had a highly praised record at the U.S. Naval Academy, he was even selected in his senior year to be the Battalion Commander. But as he prepared to graduate with honors in 1987, a superior officer asked him, "Are you a homosexual?" and when he answered truthfully the Academy forced him to resign, denying him a degree and a Navy commission. But here, too, the U.S. Appeals Court found the Navy's rule, excluding him solely because he truthfully admitted his sexual orientation, to be unconstitutional, and ordered the Navy to grant him his diploma, reinstate him, and commission him as an officer.[44]

In turn, these gay military cases are a sign of the growing legal recognition of homosexual rights in society, although as in the abortion cases, the battle is far from over because of the strong fundamentalist sentiment against homosexuality, particularly in the South. As a result, in many areas, gay relationships are still being exposed and attacked, such as in a case in Ovett, Mississippi, in which two gay women, Brenda Henson and Wanda Henson, who set up a gay and lesbian center, Camp Sister Spirit, have been, since late 1993, under increasing pressure from locals to leave. They have received death threats and even found their dog hanging on a fence post.[45]

Thus, like the battle over abortion, the gay rights conflict is spilling out into vocal protests and criminal attacks by fundamentalists who see this not as a privacy issue but as a direct affront to their notions of sin and morality.

Sex, Drugs, and Guns

The irony is that we are a society awash in sex, drugs, and guns, yet we have all sorts of laws restricting them. For civil libertarians and privacy advocates, these are three more arenas where society has been interfering with personal privacy rights instead of letting the individual make his or her own choices about sexual practices and literature, using drugs, or owning guns.

Sex: The Battle over Pornography and Prostitution. In the case of sex, the two major areas where privacy issues have been fought over involve pornography and prostitution. In the area of pornography, the recent trend seems to be to let people read pretty much what they want, as long as it is basic adult porn, particularly since the line between "porn" and mainstream sexual material has become very fuzzy, with the release of very explicit books like Madonna's *Sex,* graphic videos on MTV, and racy interviews on talk shows. Shock jock Howard Stern has become a nationally syndicated radio and TV star with the first or second most popular radio show, despite million-dollar Federal Communications Commission (FCC) fines for indecency, and his book *Private Parts* has sold millions. Even once taboo S & M, B & D, and erotic dominance and submission have, to a great extent, joined the acceptable mainstream, leaving people free to read and see this in private, or even openly when it is presented as literature, art, or popular entertainment, such as in the book and movie versions of *Exit to Eden*.

But there is a backlash against both porn and prostitution by some groups. Some feminists view most porn and prostitution, and particularly S&M as putting women in the submissive role, as violence against women. The religious fundamentalists want to get rid of all porn, as well as erotic material in general. The other major type of backlash is the growing concern about child porn, because it is considered extremely perverse and damaging to the child, and this has been developing in tandem with a growing movement to stamp out child abuse and sexual molestation. In these cases, the anti-porn view is that the privacy right of anyone to read, see, or sell this material should give way to the welfare of society, since these materials downgrade and exploit women and/or children.

For the most part, though, the women and fundamentalists fighting porn generally have been fighting a losing cause, since the interest of society and the constitutional protections of free speech and the courts are largely against them. But in contrast, the move against child pornography (along with the crackdown on child molesters and kidnappers) has been gathering force, perhaps because of the growing concern today about parenting and restoring family values. There is also a strong emphasis in the courts now on doing what is in the best interest of the child.

The high profile Michael Jackson case illustrates this trend. Once the accusation that he might be involved sexually with children surfaced, this was no longer a case where an eccentric Michael Jackson could pursue his private fantasies to do what he wanted with his child friends at his Neverland fantasy ranch or on jaunts around the world with them. Now his behavior was of concern to everyone, and the possibility that the accusations might be true, despite his multimillion dollar settlement, was enough to puncture his rising celebrity balloon and severely damage his career (though his subsequent marriage to Lisa Marie Presley and efforts to distance himself from friendships with children have contributed to the repair of his image).

Drugs. Though most people and the criminal justice system generally lump illegal drugs together in the same category as crime (think inner city, drug wars, crack babies, cocaine, though drug use is pervasive throughout society), there is a growing movement that views the use of certain drugs, most notably marijuana for medical purposes, as a privacy issue. In this view, individuals should have the right to use drugs if they want, particularly for medical purposes, and drug use problems should be treated as medical, not criminal problems. Among these groups are several organizations favoring the medical use of marijuana, and NORML, which supports the total legalization of marijuana. Libertarians generally favor the legalization of all drugs.

In part, this legalization effort is due to the view that the efforts to criminalize drug use have proved to be uneconomical and unworkable, due to a number of factors including the high cost of arresting, prosecuting, and imprisoning drug offenders who constitute about 70 percent of all criminal cases and prisoners. In addition, these cases have ended up crowding jails with nonviolent drug offenders, often pushing out truly violent and dangerous offenders. Also, the legalization movement has been fueled in reaction to the drug busts which have affected otherwise law-abiding, respected citizens, invading their privacy and costing them money and property.

Thus, there has been increasing pressure by some groups to look on drug use as more of a privacy and medical issue and less of a criminal one. For example, the California legislature passed a resolution in 1993 urging that doctors be allowed to prescribe marijuana for patients with chronic, terminal, or incurable diseases. But despite this sympathetic sentiment, no legislation was passed making this a law, nor has any other state or the federal government passed such a law. In fact, the coordinator of California NORML, Dale Gierenger, reports that since 1987 when he became active in the legalization movement, there has not been a single law passed by any state or federal government to expand the right of privacy in drug use and little legislation has been proposed. Instead, most recently, the pressure has been for tightening drug laws. For example, since 1992, California, New York, Texas, and about a dozen other states have passed what are popularly known as "smoke a joint, lose your license" laws. The person just needs to be in violation of any drug law, including possessing marijuana in his or her own home, and he or she can lose her license to drive.[46]

Guns. Finally, despite the popular clampdown on using guns, in reaction to the violence of guns in the cities and schools, throughout the United States, an increasingly vocal movement has developed that sees gun ownership as a privacy issue. This movement embraces not just the National Rifle Association (NRA) and other gun clubs, but involves many civil libertarians, especially those in the Libertarian Party, who feel their personal privacy and Second Amendment rights are being threatened by efforts to control guns. They believe the effort to register all guns and the crackdown on gun dealers via restrictions and higher licensing fees is the first step to taking guns away from citizens altogether. They consider gun ownership essential in a free society, since they enable the individual to protect him or herself from criminals and other threats, such as when the increasingly overburdened police are unable to provide protection. Further, they see gun ownership as a source of protection from the danger of an overly regulated, big government, totalitarian society that controls the individual.

For those making this privacy argument about guns, the tragedy in Waco, Texas, was a kind of cautionary tale about the dangers of big, intrusive, government. While most of the nation dismissed David Koresh and his followers as a bunch of religious wackos who obstinately refused to come out, which provoked the Alcohol, Tobacco and Firearms troops (ATF) to eventually lose patience and charge in, the progun privacy advocates see the raid as an especially blatant invasion of personal privacy rights. In their view, there was nothing wrong or illegal about the group owning guns for their own protection; they made no secret of it. Prior to the face-off, Koresh even invited some local law enforcement officers to come over to see his gun collection, so the authorities could have easily checked any reports about illegal gun ownership or child molesting which triggered the raid, in a much more informal, cooperative way, including even arresting Koresh on the street in town. Thus, these advocates feel the ATF and other government agents shouldn't have invaded Koresh's property in the first place, since he was on his private property. It should have respected his privacy rights as a citizen.

In turn, unless the social conditions contributing to this reaction change—notably the spiraling crime problem, the growth of big government, the fear of others in a society where traditional values and trust are breaking down—those advocating gun ownership as a privacy right, and as a necessary form of individual self-protection, are likely to increase in numbers.

Notes

1. Harris-Equifas, *Health Information Privacy Survey 1993,* Conducted for Equifax by Louis Harris and Associates in association with Dr. Alan Westin,

Columbia University (New York: Louis Harris and Associates, 1993), 18, 20, 42, 89, 92.

2. Sheri Alpert, "Medical Records, Privacy, and Health Care Reform." Paper presented at the Third Conference on Computers, Freedom, and Privacy, Burlingame, CA, March 9–12, 1993.
3. Prepared remarks of Janlori Goldman, Director, American Civil Liberties Union, Privacy and Technology Project, presented to the American Health Information Management Association's (AHIMA) Symposium on Confidentiality and Health Care, Washington, DC, 15 July 1993; and Statement of Janlori Goldman, Director, American Civil Liberties Union, Privacy and Technology Project, before the House Government Operations Subcommittee on Information, Justice, Transportation and Agriculture, Regarding the Confidentiality of Health Records, 4 November 1993.
4. Goldman, presented to AHIMA, 6–7.
5. Ibid., 8–9.
6. Goldman, presentation to the House Government Operations Subcommittee on Information, Justice, Transportation, and Agriculture, 5–6, 13–14.
7. Alpert, 7.5.
8. Daniel Z. Sands, MD., "Medical Information and Privacy," Program and Position Papers, *The Third Conference on Computers, Freedom, and Privacy*, March 9–12, Burlingame, CA, 7.9–7.10.
9. *Dr. K. et al. v. State Board of Physician Quality Assurance,* 98 Md. App. 103, 632 A.2d 453 (Md. App. 1993), cited in Lexis 165, 1–10.
10. *Whalen v. Roe,* 429 U.S. 589 (1977).
11. *In Re Search Warrant (Sealed),* 810 F.2d 67, cer. denied 483 U.S. 1007 (3rd Cir. 1987).
12. *Dr. K.*, in Lexis, pp. 19.
13. *State v. Poole,* 499 N.W.2d 31 (Minn. 1993); 32–35.
14. *Stone v. City of Stow,* 593 N.E. 2d 294 (Ohio 1992), 295–301.
15. *Heller v. Norcal Mutual Insurance Company,* 21 Cal.Rptr.2d 135 (Cal.App.5 Dist. 1993), 137–144.
16. "Victims Can Now Get Rapists' HIV Status," *San Francisco Chronicle,* 4 July 1994, A-16.
17. Christine Spolar, "Privacy for Public Figures," *Washington Journalism Review,* (June 1992): 20–22.
18. "A Ruling on Doctors with AIDS," *Newsweek,* 6 May 1991, p. 64.
19. *Doe v. Roe,* 599 N.Y.S. 2d 350 (A.D. 4 Dept. 1993), 351–57.
20. *Doe v. Town of Plymouth,* 825 F. Supp. 1102 (D. Mass. 1993), 1104–1112.
21. *Long v. American Red Cross,* 145 F.R.D. 658 (S.D. Ohio 1993), 659–68.
22. *Watson v. Lowcountry Red Cross,* 974 F.2d 482 (4th Cir. 1992), 483–84.
23. *Doe v. Johnson,* 817 F. Supp. 1382 (W.D. Mich. 1993), 1385–1400.
24. Shannon P. Duffy, "AIDS-Infected Lawyer Sues Law Firm; Alleges Illness Led to Firing," *The Legal Intelligencer* (23 August 1993): 1.

25. *Privacy Journal,* July 1993, citing guidelines published in *U.S. Law Week,* sect. 2, 15 June 1993, and *California Daily Opinion,* 10 June 1993.
26. Don Mayer, "Workplace Privacy and the Fourth Amendment: An End to Reasonable Expectations?" *American Business Law Journal,* 29, (Winter, 1992): 625–63.
27. Loren Tompkins and Teresa Mehring, "Client Privacy and the School Counselor: Privilege, Ethics, and Employer Policies," *The School Counselor,* 40 (May 1993): 335–42; 336.
28. *Tarasoff v. Regents of University of California,* 17 Cal. 3d 425 (1976).
29. Tompkins and Mehrin, 337.
30. Sharon Begley, "Blood, Hair and Heredity," *Newsweek,* 11 July 1994, 24–25.
31. Begley, 25.
32. Dan L. Burk, "DNA Identification Testing: Assessing the Threat to Privacy," *University of Toledo Law Review,* 24 (Fall 1992): 87–102; 88.
33. Ibid., 89–90.
34. Ibid., 95–96.
35. Sonia M. Suter, "Whose Genes Are These Anyway?: Familial Conflicts Over Access to Genetic Information," *Michigan Law Review,* 91 (June 1993): 1854–55, 1873–74, 1881–82, 97.
36. Ibid., 1891–93.
37. Carol Lee, "Creating a Genetic Underclass: The Potential for Genetic Discrimination by the Health Insurance Industry," *Pace Law Review,* 13 (1993): 189–228; 191–93.
38. Philip Reilly, "ASHG Statement on Genetics and Privacy: Testimony to the United States Congress," *American Journal of Human Genetics,* 50 (1992): 640–42.
39. Sam Fulwood III, "Fears for Privacy If Clinton Starts Medical Data Bank," *San Francisco Chronicle,* 25 August 1993, A-8.
40. *Academic American Encyclopedia,* S.V. "Privacy, Invasion of," (Grolier Electronic Publishing, 1993): online on Prodigy.
41. *Dahl v. Secretary of the U.S. Navy,* 830 F. Supp. 1319, 1993 U.S. Dist. Lexis 12102.
42. *Steffan v. U.S. Court of Appeals for the District of Columbia Circuit,* 8 F.3d 57, U.S. App. Lexis 29521.
43. *Dahl,* Lexis, 1–2, 65.
44. *Steffan,* Lexis, 1–3, 41–42.
45. "Lawmakers Hear Views on Lesbian's Camp," *San Francisco Chronicle,* 7 July 1994, A-16.
46. Interview with Dale Gieringer, Coordinator of California NORML, San Francisco, California, 11 December 1994.

Chapter 10

How Big Guv.Doc Is Watching You

From Surveillance to a Data Base Society

In the 1950s and 1960s, the big concern of privacy and individual rights advocates was that big government was looking for those it regarded as Communists, radicals, and other malcontents, who wanted to bring down the government or radically change it. Then the concern was that this crackdown was increasingly subverting personal liberties, rather than catching presumed subversives. Now the concern about government is focused on monitoring the phone lines, cross-matching data bases and selling information to big business which is using this for marketing purposes. However, though the reasons why the government is watching and sharing information have changed, the basic concern of privacy advocates is much the same, namely that the government will make use of new technologies that give it a greater ability to control and interfere more in everyone's life.

As a result, the battle over government record keeping and snooping has continued in various venues, which include keeping records in various types of data bases, surveillance; the battle over what information the government must and cannot disclose under freedom of information laws; what the government must reveal and can conceal in the courts; and regulations affecting privacy in the schools. It is a difficult, complex, ever changing area, since government policies and practices vary widely from state to state, at different levels of government, and in different agencies.

But generally, the main thrust, as we shall see here, has been for the government to gain more power to use increasingly powerful technologies to investigate what everyone is doing—in part due to deepening social concerns about crime and other breakdowns of the social fabric. Yet, at the same time, internally, the government is taking steps to protect the privacy of its own staff and operations from outside surveillance by various organizations, individuals, and members of the media. For example, it is using Freedom of Information Act exemptions to protect the privacy of government staff members when individual citizens and members of the press may seek information under this act. When they ask, they find that some of this information is withheld due to privacy considerations, which in some cases has led to appeals and law suits.

The Growth of Government Records and Data Bases

The Push for a National ID

Today the dangers inherent in creating a national identity card have come to the fore, as more and more data bases contain increasing amounts of information and are increasingly linked together through computer matching. The pressure to create such data bases has increased since the early 1990s, possibly using the social security number as a universal identifier. There are serious fears that a national ID could be easily misused without the necessary privacy protections, or if such protections will even work, given the potential for leaks and abuses in a large, complex system. For example, among the potentials for misuse are these:

A con artist could find out one's ID number, and beyond the fraud already possible with credit card, bank account, and other numbers, could use that number to access complete financial data on someone, tap into medical records, perpetrate welfare fraud, and use that number for committing crimes, before the real ID owner discovers this.

Already criminals have used social security numbers to get access to credit cards and run up hundreds or thousands of dollars in bills, and criminals could wreak even more havoc with a universal identifier.

There could be even more and bigger mistakes than there are now, creating even more problems for victims, since in the past mistakes in government records have resulted in people not getting benefits or getting billed repeatedly for money they don't owe, with errors taking months, even years to correct.

Thus, the concept of a single identifier frightens many, given the potential for multiplying fraud and error, if that number falls into the wrong hands or gets snarled up in a government mistake.

As two representatives of the American Civil Liberties Union (ACLU), Janlori Goldman, then Director of its Privacy and Technology Project, and Lucas Guttentag, Director of its Immigration Task Force, commented in a statement to the House Subcommittee on Social Security about these concerns:

> Over the past fifty years, the SSN has evolved from a single-use identifier to the identification number of choice for the public and private sector . . . [Now] it is possible to instantly exchange, compare, verify and link information in separate data bases, often without the knowledge and consent of the person divulging the information. Such a storehouse of information, inevitably made accessible to federal agencies, state governments and private sector interests, presents a very real potential for abuse.[1]

Besides the potential for criminal access and mistakes, Golden and Guttentag suggested other abuses. For example, the government could use this computerized and matched information to track the transactions and movements of millions of people, including political activists; and this information could be used in a discriminatory manner by employers and law enforcement.

So how did we get to this state? Originally, the social security number was created by the 1935 Social Security Act to help the Social Security Administration keep track of social security contributions. Covered workers got an account number, reported this to their employers, and then their employers advised the Internal Revenue Service (IRS) about the wages paid and taxes withheld from their employees using this number.

Gradually, the number became used for more and more purposes. For example, in 1943, President Roosevelt encouraged all federal agencies to use it when assigning account numbers to individuals for better record keeping. In 1961, the Civil Service Commission began using it to identify all federal employees. And in 1962, the IRS began requiring this number on individual tax returns. Then, in the mid-1960s, as computers spread, the number was increasingly used in public assistance programs. Later, in the 1970s, many private companies began to use the SSN, too, for credit applications, insurance, and employment. It even became used for enrolling in college or providing ID to cash a check.[2]

But now there are new pressures for a national ID card to deal with current social issues, such as illegal immigration, gun control, and the push to create a national health program. So privacy advocates are mobilizing to keep the government from creating a single national identifier, subjecting everyone to increasing government control and monitoring, which threatens fundamental democratic rights.

To avoid abuse, as the use of this single ID spread, when Congress passed the Privacy Act of 1974 it included prohibitions to prevent the SSN from becoming a national identifier—such as no new uses unless Congress authorized them. Even so, through the 1970s and 1980s, Congress enacted many new programs using the SSN, such as requiring dependent children claimed on tax returns to have an SSN.[3]

The Problems of Computer Matching and "Smart" Cards

Meanwhile, as the struggle over the national ID card goes on, another fight is brewing against the government using computer matching and "smart" cards, as computerizing and digitizing data becomes increasingly efficient.

Computer Matching and Mismatching

In computer matching, which goes back to the early 1970s, the computer compares two or more sets of computerized records to find individuals whose names or identifying numbers are in more than one file. Most commonly, different government agencies have used this method to look for fraud, error, or abuse in government programs (e.g., the double-dipping welfare recipient) or to determine whether a person applying for or receiving benefits is entitled to them or should be excluded (say if the agency discovers a person has more money in a bank account than permitted to get benefits under a particular program). In this way the government can eliminate fraudulent claims and reduce waste. Supposedly, according to watchdog government agencies like the Office of

Management and Budget, computer matching has led to substantial savings and the recovery of overpayments in federal benefit programs.[4]

But despite such savings, the downside is the cost to personal privacy from the combining of these records. Though matching itself may not produce a single national pool of information that creates a national ID, it furthers the process of creating this ID, since it brings together a vast array of material on a single individual.

While many of us may agree that privacy shouldn't be used to cover up dishonest behavior and that matching can be used to evaluate or verify that people are receiving what they should for government programs and not more, the problem is that matching is commonly used for purposes that go beyond pulling up discrepant records to identify dishonesty and fraud. For example, mistakes can be compounded when records are matched together and these combined records added to a still more comprehensive file. Also, records gathered for one purpose can be used for another, such as being resold for private use, unless privacy protections are in place to limit how information is matched and subsequently used.

For example, consider this example, described by sociologist James B. Rule. The Treasury Department has a system that records the names of all those arriving in the country when they cross the border. The Treasury passes this data on to many other agencies, including the State Department, IRS, FBI, and CIA. They then use this data to trace the past movements of people or keep track of their current movements.[5] While such information may prove useful if one of these individuals later turns out to be a terrorist, is accused of a crime, or seeks to remain illegally in the country, this pool of data can subsequently create problems for the other people who remain in the country legally and don't participate in illegal activities, which is the vast majority of the people on whom data is collected. These problems can develop as the data is moved from file to file and combined with more and more data from other agencies, if wrong data gets entered or important data is left out along the way.

There is also the danger of targeting people for surveillance who have not yet done anything wrong and pulling together vast files of data on them from many sources. This is like the modern-day computerized version of Hoover's FBI files. When he headed the FBI, he built up millions of files on people because they were subject to some suspicion or simply because Hoover didn't like them. They might have happened to go to a meeting deemed to be subversive, associated with the "wrong" people, or happened to be on the "wrong" side of the political spectrum, from Hoover's point of view. Rule fears this might happen again. As he points out, in 1967, the FBI started what could become a modern equivalent of Hoover's files when it launched the National Crime Information Center (NCIC), a computerized data base to keep track of everyone coming into contact with the criminal justice system, from arrest through conviction, sentencing, and penalty. Over the years, the data base has naturally grown in size, and in 1988, the FBI proposed expanding it even further to include the names of persons "of interest"—people not yet arrested and or not yet wanted for arrest. Should a participating agency ask about any of these people, this would alert all of the other agencies in the system. Even an inquiry in a routine traffic stop might trigger the process. When the FBI proposed this plan, it triggered major protests from civil libertarians, so that then FBI director William Sessions dropped the idea of including this proposed expansion in his $40 million plan for modernizing the NCIC. But, as Rule warns, this idea may come back in some form: "It would be rash to imagine that we have heard the last of the idea."[6]

Unfortunately, as crime and violence, or the perception and fear of them, increase along with fears about other social problems, so does the cry for more law enforcement tools to control an unruly, restive population and restore law and order.

How Smart Are "Smart" Cards?

Meanwhile, as the push for a single identifier increases and more data matching occurs, other high-tech and biotech devices are being used to encode more information automatically. For example, microchips can now make IDs and passports "smart" machine-readable cards. The process is like going through a supermarket scanner, except these devices are reading you. And many do much more than identify people; some are like mini-computers storing huge amounts of information. For example, an optical card made by the Drexler Technology Corporation in California can hold a computerized face photo with up to 1600 pages of text at a relatively small cost—less than $3.00 each when produced in large runs of a million or more cards.

Such "smart" devices are already in place in other countries, like New Zealand, which issued about 1.2 million smart cards to citizens by mid-1992 to keep an ongoing record of all social and health services provided to each New Zealander, and citizens will be using machine-readable smart passports, too.[7]

Soon, too, many companies will be using scanning devices to scan anyone who wants to enter the premises or particular areas to make sure they are who they claim to be. The devices use a process called "biometrics," which takes real-time photographic measurements which can then be used to track individuals from place to place or compare the person presenting him or herself with the image stored. The process is much like comparing a person's fingerprint with one on a card to verify identity.[8] One advantage to this technology is, of course, the improved chances of detecting fraud when a person presents an SSN or other ID. But alternatively, others view this as one more high-tech device for further peering into people's privacy, particularly since people may not even know they are being photographed or tracked by these biometric cameras.

The Battle to Correct or Stop the Record

As the number of records mounts, so does the battle against their proliferation in all areas of record keeping—to eliminate or correct them, or incorporate privacy protections. A key question is how to balance the interests between using these new record-keeping technologies efficiently to protect society and at the same time protect the individual from errors and unfair exposés. That is what much of the current privacy debate is about.

Getting Out of the Vote

One big battle that was won by privacy advocates was over linking the social security number to voting. It began in a small town in Virginia in 1991, after Marc A. Greidinger was repeatedly asked for his social security number—such as when he sought a driver's license, went to open accounts with local utilities, and even tried to rent a video.[9]

The last straw came when he tried to register to vote, but was told the State of Virginia wouldn't register him unless he provided his number. At this point, since he was a lawyer, then working for the U.S. Fourth Circuit Court of Appeals in Richmond, Virginia, he did what lawyers often do. He decided to sue the state, to keep the social security number out of the hands of the voting registrars. Also, he saw his suit, *Greidinger v. Davis,* decided in March 1993, as a symbolic gesture against the growing danger of using the social security number for multiple purposes, thereby increasing the chances of misuse if it got into the wrong hands.

Though Greidinger lost in district court, when he appealed to the appeals court where he worked, he won. The court concluded that the state's interest in using social security numbers to prevent voter fraud infringed too much on the individual's right to vote. Yes, the state might find this data helpful in preventing voter fraud. But the state also disclosed the voter's SSN to private individuals who asked the registrar for vote records, and it had no way to prevent these individuals from using this information for purposes unrelated to voting. And this, the court felt, was unfair to the individual who wanted his or her number kept private, since if he didn't disclose it, he couldn't vote, which unfairly deprived him of this right. Also, there were some good reasons not to have to reveal one's number because of the potential for misuse. Among them, as noted by the court: "For example, armed with one's SSN, an unscrupulous individual could obtain a person's welfare benefits or Social Security benefits, order new checks at a new address on that person's checking account, obtain credit cards, or even obtain the person's paycheck." And so the court sided with Greidinger.[10]

For privacy advocates, the decision was a heartening victory, and some hoped it would contribute to deterring the use of social security numbers for general identification. But as the growing pressure for a general identifier mounts due to the many social concerns noted and the efforts to create a national health care plan, Greidinger's victory might be viewed as more of a single small victory in a continuing war.

Car Wars

Another growing battle arena is at your local Department of Motor Vehicles (DMV), which besides the social security registry is the biggest source of personal information about everyone, for even if you don't drive a car, you can still get an ID card from your local DMV—and you may need this, because commonly DMV IDs are now required by merchants, the police, and others to check someone's identity. A key reason these have become the ID of choice for many is that they include a photo, date of birth, one's presumed current or last address, and fingerprints in the states requiring them.

But while the DMV ID has gained general acceptance for routine government, police, and insurance matters, the controversy has been over whether the DMV can or should release information to commercial users or the public in general and, more specifically, to whom and when.

Before this controversy led to changes mandated by the federal crime bill passed in late 1994 (which now prohibits the release of this information to private individuals and companies), about three dozen state DMV's sold registration information, such as to direct mail companies, which use the data for commercial solicitations, or to companies compiling special directories, like reverse street-to-name directories. It is from the DMV that many big mail and directory houses, like the R.L. Polk Company (which puts out the well-known Polk Directories of names, addresses, and phone numbers, organized by street or number), obtained much of their data.[11]

Should the states be in the business of selling public data for private use? Or should the DMV even be releasing information, particularly home addresses, to the general public? This question became of serious concern in California in 1989 when an obsessed fan of the television star Rebecca Schaeffer got her address from an out-of-state detective agency, which got it by contacting a California agency, which easily got it from a quick request to the DMV. Then, the fan went to her address and killed her. The news of Schaeffer's death, and the ease with which the man got her address from the DMV, was electrifying. The incident stimulated a debate in the media and the California legislature over whether DMV data should be made public. This resulted in a bill, passed in 1990, which restricted the right to obtain this information to certain individuals and for specified purposes, such as registered process servers needing to serve court papers and certain approved investigators after they post a large bond of about $50,000, which costs $250 a year to obtain.[12]

In response, the investigative industry has launched a fight against these restrictions, as limiting legitimate investigative inquiries. This fight has been led in California by the California Association of Licensed Investigators (CALI) which is trying to get the law changed. Meanwhile, other states, influenced by developments in California, considered their own restrictions on giving out DMV information to the public and the private enterprise. On the national level, Representative James Moran introduced a bill, and Senator Barbara Boxer an amendment to President Clinton's Crime Bill, to prohibit access to DMV records nationally. After some discussions, meetings, and revisions, these proposals became the Driver's Privacy Protection Act of 1994 which was enacted as part of the federal crime bill that passed in August 1994 and was signed into law to become effective in January 1995.[13] What this legislation means is that DMV records cannot be sold for ordinary commercial purposes or generally accessed by ordinary citizens, although they can still be obtained for certain restricted uses, such as for use by law enforcement, insurers, businesses verifying the accuracy of personal information submitted to them, and investigators using it for certain purposes, such as serving court subpoenas. Now all states must adhere to these guidelines, although they can provide more restrictive access if they wish, as is currently the case in California in response to the Schaeffer killing.[14]

Crime Beat

Crime record data is another source of discussion. Crime data can sometimes gets lost from view until too late, because it isn't accessed or is scattered in different files. Another problem is that incorrect or outdated information on the ordinary citizen may be called up or leaked out of the system, which can be very damaging. A good example of the former is the long rap sheet of Richard Allen Davis who killed a young girl, Polly Klaas, which wasn't called up by the police when they briefly stopped him for questioning. They let him go, whereas if they had checked, they might have arrested him that night, saving Polly's life, since she was still alive, tied up nearby. By contrast, when damaging information about the ordinary individual is released inappropriately to private parties, it can harm that person's reputation and interfere with his or her right to credit and employment.

A key problem is that the criminal justice records include data from all levels of the system which keep records of arrests and convictions—local police departments, prosecutors, courts, probation departments, prisons, parole boards, U.S. Attorney's offices, and the FBI. Much of this information is also combined nationally into the National Crime Information Center (NCIC), which includes dispositions of any criminal charges too. However, not all of this information is up-to-date, since record keeping varies from jurisdiction to jurisdiction. Also, confidential data can often leak out of the system, including information on many currently law abiding citizens who have records of past misdeeds. This can include even brief encounters with the law that can sound incriminating though they aren't (like being briefly arrested, then questioned about a crime, and released). Just consider all the information leaks from the police in the O.J. Simpson case, much of which contained incorrect information. Similarly, records about ordinary citizens can be leaked, too, creating embarrassment and tarnished reputations, even when the data is incorrect.

The Problem of Data Leaks

The data leaking problem is a serious one, especially when incorrect records are misinterpreted by those outside the system. For example, the Bureau of Justice Statistics reports that about a quarter to a third of the total workforce has a criminal history record,[15] which includes both arrests which did and did not result in a conviction. This arrest and conviction data is widely available, not only within the criminal justice system. As privacy expert Evan Hendricks, publisher of the *Privacy Times* notes, conviction data is generally available to private employers, and the FBI is authorized by Congress to disclose criminal history records to a variety of private organizations, including insured banks, portions of the securities industry, the commodities industry, and day care centers.[16]

Almost all states (47 as of 1990) prohibit releasing information on past arrests which did not lead to convictions for noncriminal purposes to avoid unnecessarily tarnishing a person's reputation, such as when employers evaluate job applications or when professional boards review background data for licensing purposes. But leaks still occur. A key time this happens is when employers, the most common users of criminal justice records after law enforcement, check on job applicants.[17] Then, they may use that arrest data, even though it did not result in a conviction, to discriminate against an individual seeking employment.[18]

However, apart from the problem of leaking information that shouldn't get out, the trend has been for state legislatures to approve the release of criminal records to private groups, usually for job and career related purposes, while the laws protecting this data vary widely from state to state. Though Congress tried to enact federal legislation in the 1970s to set national standards for disseminating state criminal history information, this failed. The result has been both a great diversity of laws in the states and "a steadily increasing volume of authorized noncriminal justice use." For example, according to the Bureau of Justice Statistics: "In several states, including California, Minnesota, Pennsylvania, and South Carolina, noncriminal justice traffic is greater than total criminal justice use of the criminal record systems, and in several other states, noncriminal justice use is 40 percent or more of total system use."[19]

In fact, these policies and practices vary so widely that in some states, such as Florida and Wisconsin, anyone interested in knowing someone's criminal history for any purpose can readily do a check (including, say, a woman who wants to check out a prospective date). By contrast, in other states, like Tennessee, noncriminal justice access is very limited, and it is even considered a criminal offense for nonauthorized people to access this data.

Juvenile records, too, sometimes get spread too far, though they are supposed to be confidential by law in every state, and many states permit people to seal or expunge their juvenile records when they turn eighteen or twenty-one. Still these records are widely disseminated, not just among criminal justice agencies, but to other organizations dealing with juveniles, such as schools, clinics, and social service agencies.[20]

So should these data be readily available or not? On the one hand, not knowing risks the real danger of an employer hiring someone who may be a threat to the business (such as a man with a string of arrests for theft, even though he wasn't convicted) or of a community having someone move in who may be a threat to the neighborhood (such as the accused child molester who isn't prosecuted because of insufficient evidence from many very young children). Employers and neighbors may rightly want to know if their business or children are truly threatened. But on the other hand, people who have not been convicted or have served their time for a past offense may hope to get on with their lives, without the stigma of the past following them everywhere.

The recent trend, however, has been to release such discrediting information should the type of activity the person has previously engaged in pose a threat to the community. An example is newly passed legislation in 1994 in California that provides a 900 number operated by the Department of Justice that members of the community can call to find out if a person has been convicted of a sexual offense involving children. However, this information may only be used to protect a child at risk and not for any other purpose, in order to protect the privacy rights of the registrant. A caller using this number for any other purpose can face civil and criminal penalties.[21]

The Wrong Data Dilemma

The problem of releasing stigmatizing data is compounded when it is incorrect or outdated, causing a person embarrassment or upheaval in their lives. Even the Bureau of Justice Statistics which collects and publishes this data recognizes the problem, noting in a 1992 review of state privacy and security legislation that: "While 52 states have adopted at least some standards for accuracy and completeness that reflect standards in the DOJ regulations, there is little question that the quality of criminal history data falls short of satisfactory. Disposition reporting—or the lack of reporting—remains the most serious deficiency, especially in terms of court disposition reporting."[22]

Supposedly, FBI regulations do permit an individual who believes his crime records are wrong or incomplete to ask the police or other criminal justice agency contributing this information to correct or update it. Then the FBI is supposed to make the changes requested by this agency. But there is a problem in getting this data actually changed, because the system is so overloaded. For example, privacy expert Hendricks notes that "getting a contributing agency to forward a rap-sheet correction to the FBI can be something of an ordeal. Overburdened or uninterested police officials may simply not want to be bothered, and the burden of proof to substantiate the correction—for example, by producing a copy of a court record showing the disposition of an arrest—is usually upon the subject of the record."[23]

Still, it can be done, and it is probably a good idea to get any incorrect incriminating data off the record to avoid unnecessary problems should the individual later have an encounter with the police or the courts or have an employer check his or her records for a job. However, many individuals don't know they have a record or that they can correct it. Or they may think the record was erased when it wasn't—an experience I had myself. This occurred about ten years after I was cited for trespassing with about four dozen people having a costume party in an abandoned government building. In the middle of the party, the police arrived, after being alerted by a security guard, and we were all cited for trespassing. After we went to court, we went through a brief diversion program (for example, I turned in an essay on trespassing law), and after this the citation was supposed to be eliminated from our arrest records. But they didn't tell us that we each had to send a letter requesting that the record be removed. As a result, I discovered it was still there about ten years later when I applied to be a member of the San Francisco civil grand jury, and I was one of the thirty potential jurors selected. As we waited in a courtroom before the drawing to determine which fifteen jurors would be selected, the judge suddenly called me into chambers and asked me about my earlier trespassing "arrest." In this case, I was able to successfully explain what happened, so I remained in the jury pool, although I was not actually selected. But if I hadn't been asked about this, I wouldn't have known this potentially damaging information was still there in my record.

The "Can't Get It or Change It" Problem

Another problem is when one can't find out information or change it, because law enforcement won't provide the information or amend the files, claiming it doesn't have to do so because it is exempt. According to legal scholar Gregory Firehock, this is because of the government trend to protect even incorrect records held by law enforcement.[24]

This inability to change records is exactly what happened to "John Doe," when he tried to get some records purged from his FBI files. But the FBI refused, and tried to fight, though unsuccessfully, and the *Doe v. FBI* case was decided in 1991.[25] Doe had gotten these records because he had been very active politically in the late 1960s and early 1970s and had built up a file as a radical troublemaker, though he later became a well-respected law-abiding citizen who had a distinguished career in psychiatry.

But when Doe applied to the state of Michigan to expunge his past records, and the Michigan court agreed, Doe ran into problems. Since the court felt that Doe's steady employment and lack of subsequent convictions showed he had been "rehabilitated," it asked the FBI to expunge his records, so by law Doe would no longer be considered to have been convicted of any crime. But the FBI did not do this. It did delete references to Doe's prior arrest and nolo contendre conviction for possessing an explosive device, which had resulted in five years probation, a small fine, and sixty days of community service, but it continued to keep his records in its Central Records System.

Unfortunately, leaving these records there was like a waiting grenade, which finally went off in 1985, when Doe applied to the Social Security Administration (SSA) when it advertised a Deputy Medical Officer position. Eventually, Doe was selected as the most qualified person and his application was approved by the Health and Human Services Department, which is in charge of the SSA. But when the Office of Personnel Management, which approves high-level positions, did its standard FBI background check, this turned up the CRS records, including information about Doe's earlier arrest on "bombing" charges, along with details about his nolo contendre plea, incriminating address book, attendance at a protest rally, and subversive remarks on a radio talk show.

Whether or not the records themselves resulted in Doe not getting the job, Doe now knew the records were still there and wanted them out. So he wrote to the FBI requesting this, pointing out that much of this information was incorrect. But the FBI refused, claiming its records exempt under the law enforcement exemption of the Privacy Act. It was only willing to put a copy of his expungement request in its file and add more complete information about his arrest and conviction, but that was all.

Unsatisfied, since this damaging information would remain, Doe sued. But eventually, the Washington, DC Court of Appeals sided with the FBI, agreeing that the records could remain as exempt for law enforcement purposes. Further, the court said the FBI didn't have to continuously update old files, because of the administrative and investigative burden of doing so, which would interfere with its ability to investigate current matters. After all, as the court noted, the FBI received approximately 2.3 million name-check requests in 1985, the year Doe encountered his own problems with the FBI records.[26]

Thus, if there is information in your file and the FBI or other law enforcement agency wants to keep it there, you may find it hard to get it removed.

Crime Watch and the Media

The existence of all these criminal records raises the question of accessibility to the general public and to the media, which can gain access to anything available to the general public. Before the widespread use of computers and data bases, all of these records were on file where the records were originally created, and anyone could look through by searching record books or lists by chronological order or by the name of defendant, unless any records were sealed. But the effort of going to a particular location to check records meant that most records were untouched.

However, with computers and data bases, linking law enforcement agencies and courts, a few key strokes can make this information instantly available. If we add the attention of the media, and the popularity of modern news entertainment shows featuring a strong dose of crime stories like *Current Affair, Hard Copy,* and *Inside Edition,* the potential for revealing not only present but long buried criminal record data is huge.

Suing the Government for Releasing Private Information

If there were clearer guidelines about how to achieve this balance, perhaps this might cut down on the problem of the individual suing the government for invading their privacy when their records are inappropriately revealed, and sometimes winning substantial damages.

This is what happened when Elvis E. Johnson of Texas sued some IRS agents for disclosing private taxpayer information about him, in the *Johnson v. Sawyer*[27] case, decided in 1993. This tax information was made confidential when Congress, as part of the Tax Reform Act of 1976, removed tax returns and the information in them from the realm of public documents and provided criminal and civil sanctions for the unauthorized disclosure of this information.[28]

While these policies have generally worked to keep tax information confidential, the government itself has had to pay for inappropriate disclosures, as in the Johnson case. This began after Johnson entered into a plea bargain and was convicted in a tax case. Wanting to use the settlement to show the power of the IRS to help convince other taxpayers to pay, several IRS officials put out two press releases about Johnson's conviction and plea bargain, which included information on his private life, as well as his tax return. Eventually at least twenty-one newspapers published his story based on this release—a publicity coup for the agency, which contributed to its problems in court.

As Johnson pointed out in court, taxpayer information is confidential, and the IRS is not supposed to release federal tax returns to the public, which includes not releasing information about the taxpayer's identity, amount of income, any deficiencies, and whether that return is being investigated, except under very special circumstances, such as when the facts have already become a matter of public record. But instead, the IRS agents put much more in the press release than in the official court record, such as Johnson's age, home address, and official job title at the American National Insurance Company, which came from his confidential taxpayer file or from the IRS investigation of him.

Unfortunately, all of this information slipped in because after Johnson pleaded guilty, one agent, Stone, contacted the public affairs officer, Sally Sassen, with the news so she could prepare a news release. But he didn't mention there was any proscription on publicity, and after she wrote up the release, she disseminated it without checking on the accuracy of the release or whether she could properly use this information.

Then, making matters worse, the information hit the news just as Johnson's otherwise exemplary business career was "on the eve of achieving its pinnacle," at his company. Although the president and other board members of the company were aware of his tax troubles and impending guilty plea, they had asked him to remain with the company, and he was considered the "heir apparent to the CEO-ship." But when the story based on the release hit the media, they questioned his continued employment instead with the full board, which in turn asked for his resignation. The public airing of a matter that might have otherwise been downplayed in the company was just too damaging to Johnson's reputation, so he had to go.

Thus, the court agreed that the IRS agents had spread damaging information, and concluded that the government, just like any reasonable person, should not "publicize embarrassing or damaging private facts about another person."[29] The decision was worth about $10 million to Johnson.[30]

Revealing and Concealing Records

While one problem is that of leaky government records, the opposite problem is when the government won't release information it has, claiming it would reveal too much about someone or something in the government. Disclosure laws, such as the federal Freedom of Information Act and local government sunshine laws, require the government to open its files. Sometimes, however, the government claims an exemption to protect someone's privacy or some sensitive information. So this is still another privacy battleground—what the government has to reveal versus what it can conceal. It's an ironic counterpoint to the battle over keeping one's private life from the government and keeping the government from revealing that information.

Most commonly, these struggles are over law enforcement and IRS documents, since these agencies are more likely to withhold sensitive investigative information, claiming they need to keep it secret to protect the identity of their agents or operations. And generally the government wins in these cases, by showing it needs the secrecy to avoid compromising its employees or activities.

Battling the IRS

In one such case, decided in March 1993, the Church of Scientology of Texas tried to get information from the IRS when it sent two letters in December 1990 requesting information under the Freedom of Information Act. The letters asked for any records referring to the Church, Scientology, or Dianetics since 1974. Though the IRS had almost 2200 pages of records and released some in full, it only released portions of other records and held back some records, claiming they were exempt from disclosure under the FOIA.

What were these records the IRS held back? The Church tried to find out, and after exhausting its administrative appeals, it sued to get the IRS to release the records. But the IRS resisted, claiming it could withhold records relating to its internal personnel rules and practices, those containing taxpayer return information, or those revealing the identities of protected individuals, such as witnesses, jurors, and service employees. It also claimed certain internal or interagency memos, letters, and personnel and medical files were exempt.

After weighing the individual right of privacy versus the FOIA's goal of opening up government agencies to public scrutiny, the U.S. District Court eventually decided that the IRS could keep the withheld material private. A key factor was the IRS's concern that the public identification of these employees might "subject them to harassment and annoyance in their private lives," and thus invade their own personal privacy. Also, the court was concerned about what the church might do, given its past history in the courts, which reflected a high "degree of animosity between the CST and the IRS,"—another reason to keep the personal information of IRS employees confidential. Then, too, the court felt that several other exemption provisions could permit the agency to withhold information, such as an exemption to keep records confidential to avoid interfering with an investigation or presenting a case. Additionally, agencies were permitted to withhold documents that contained identifying information about actual or potential IRS contacts or lower level government employees, particularly if the disclosure might subject these employees to "harassment and annoyance." Thus, any records with their names, addresses, social security numbers, or personal information were exempt.

But then, since the IRS had withheld too much, such as full documents with some exempt data, it had to go back to eliminate the identifying data in these documents where it could, and turn over the rest to the church. And the burden was on the agency to show it couldn't segregate a particular document for this partial release. Then, it had to release all nonexempt portions of these documents.[31]

Thus, on the one hand, the privacy of the IRS operations and its agents were protected. But, on the other hand, the agency had to be as open as possible and turn over what it could.

Taking on the FBI, CIA, and the Police

Individuals trying to get information from the FBI, CIA, and local police agencies have run into similar claims of protecting the privacy of individual witnesses, informants, employees, and others involved in the investigation. In the cases that have ended up in court, the government has won. Perhaps contributing to the government's success is the fact that the individuals trying to get information have been convicted prisoners, trying to learn about the investigation in order to reverse their fortune—or perhaps more accurately, misfortune—in the criminal justice system.

This is what happened to Alvie James Hale, Jr., who was convicted for kidnapping and killing William Jeffrey Perry in Oklahoma. He was sentenced to death by the state of Oklahoma in 1984, but claimed he was really innocent. He argued in the case of *Hale v. U.S. Department of Justice,* decided in August 1992, that what really happened was that Perry had concocted an elaborate plot to stage his own kidnapping to extort money from his parents for gambling debts and drugs. Then Perry got three people to help him, but when he changed his mind in the middle of the staged kidnapping, one participant, Nicky Johnson killed him for real and buried the body on Hale's father's property, while Hale was elsewhere making the ransom calls. That's why, as he battled the death sentence, Hale wanted the government's information on Perry and his murder, particularly any evidence that might incriminate Johnson, since he believed the FBI failed to disclose this to protect Johnson as its informant. So, under the FOIA, he claimed, he should get this information.

But after the district court turned him down, so did the Circuit Court of Appeals, noting that the FBI was justified in not releasing any information identifying its confidential sources. After all, the sources had been assured of confidentiality, and as the court noted, the identities of third parties who are interviewed or whose names surface in a criminal investigation can be excluded from disclosure to "prevent embarrassment and harassment and to enable the FBI to gather the information it needs." Thus, since Hale couldn't show any sufficient public interest to overcoming the FBI's claim to keep this information confidential the FBI didn't have to disclose this information. His arguments about the fairness of a *particular* trial and his unsupported suspicions of what might have happened were not justification enough.[32]

Beatrice Maynard similarly struck out when she tried to get CIA documents about the disappearance of her former husband Robert Thompson during a flight over Cuba over 30 years before in December 1961, in the case of *Maynard v. C.I.A.*, decided in February 1993. She made her request in January 1987, suspecting he had worked for the CIA, since he had distributed anti-Castro leaflets before he disappeared on his flight. But when she finally got about 30 pages of information, a critical memo from December 1961 had a paragraph with heavy deletions.

What did this mystery paragraph contain? The CIA wouldn't tell her on the grounds it would "reveal the identity of an intelligence source or disclose an intelligence method," and thereby create a risk that a "hostile intelligence organization" might "neutralize the use of those methods" thereby causing a loss of intelligence. And the U.S. Court of Appeals judge agreed.[33]

Much the same result has occurred when individuals have tried to get information on investigations from their local police department. The privacy of informants and witnesses not revealed in open court has been protected. For example, the Maryland Committee Against the Gun Ban discovered this when they wanted to look at a report by internal investigators in the police department about the conduct of police who had served a subpoena on the committee. Although the Maryland Public Information Act provided that all persons should have "access to information about the affairs of government and the official acts of public officials and employees," it also included a privacy out—"unless an unwarranted invasion of the privacy of a person in interest would result." Thus, though the committee might get most of the report, they couldn't get information on the officers who were investigated and on the witnesses who were promised confidentiality in giving their testimony.[34]

Should people be able to know the witnesses, informants, and investigators lined up against them? There are arguments on both sides, but generally, informants, secret witnesses, and agents can maintain their confidentiality for their own protection. As a result, the individual who wants to find out, even if he thinks an informant or secret witness lied or gave incorrect information about him, cannot discover who gave the information against him in an investigation, unless their testimony is aired in open court.

When the Interests of the Government and the Media Collide

When the media find out information from the government it can usually print it, as noted. But what about the opposite situation, when the government has information the media wants, but doesn't want to release it. Just as private individuals have done in taking on the government to get information, so has the media, using the Freedom of Information Act (FOIA) to open up government records. But to get it officially when the government doesn't want to release it, the media seem to be treated much like anyone else—and the privacy rights barrier often prevails.

This was what happened in the long, convoluted *McDonnell v. U.S. of America* case, decided in September 1993. Two authors, Robert J. McDonnell and Frederick N. Rasmussen tried to get information from the Navy on the Morro Castle disaster, which occurred back in 1934, when a fire broke out on an ocean liner off the coast of New Jersey. They hoped to write a book about the unusual circumstances surrounding the tragedy in which over one hundred people died. For example, just hours before the fire, the captain of the ship died; there was about an hour delay between the outbreak of the fire and the sending of an SOS signal; and there were intimations of foul play. In fact, after an FBI investigation, a federal grand jury returned indictments against the owners and certain ship officers, charging them with willful neglect of duty. The chief officer and ship engineer were convicted for negligence, though their convictions were overturned. Twenty-five years later, one author, Thomas Gallagher, in *Fire at Sea*, concluded that the fire was deliberately set by the ship's radio officer.

To find out what really happened, in June 1985, the two authors began searching for information. But after several years of corresponding with the FBI and Navy and getting some documents, the authors felt the FBI and Navy were still holding back key documents dealing with the investigations of key figures in the disaster. Thus, eventually they filed an FOIA suit to get this information. However, after long arguments over such details as whether McDonnell followed the required administrative procedures before filing suit or if he could add a freedom of the press claim to the suit (which he couldn't), the U.S. Court of Appeals turned the authors down. The key reasons were that some of this material was classified to protect the secret cryptographic code used, and should remain so despite the passage of time; that the records of the secret federal grand jury were normally kept secret and should continue to be without a special court order which McDonnell didn't have; and that the government could withhold the records of one man who was a juvenile at the time, even though he was long since dead (over 30 years), especially since these included medical records. Further, the court felt the government could exempt from disclosure various records compiled for law enforcement purposes, such as the names of FBI and Navy law enforcement personnel, and any third parties who gave information or were named during the investigation.

Thus, even though the disaster had happened over fifty years before, the government could still conceal the names of law enforcement personnel, and the identities of suspects, witnesses, and others interviewed during the investigation. For, as the court noted: "while the privacy interest of those involved in a criminal investigation may become diluted by the passage of time . . . the potential for embarrassment and harassment may endure for many years." Besides, the individuals who spoke to the government had been provided with confidentiality at the time. Thus, the information remained as buried as the Morro disaster.[35]

Thus, even when the government has been required to release some information it may still be able to withhold other material, such as when the *Boston Herald* tried to get some salary and employee discipline records from Amtrak, a heavily government regulated and unionized industry, in the case of *News Group Boston, Inc. v. National Railroad Passenger Corporation,* decided in August 1992. U.S. District Court agreed the paper could get information on the nature of the employee's offense, the original discipline imposed, the disposition of the case, and job titles and payroll information. But it couldn't get names and addresses in order to protect employee privacy rights.[36]

The irony is that as the government is collecting more and more information about us, with the supporting technology and laws to help it do so, it also seems to be getting better at withholding information from the public and the media, even though open information and open meeting laws are proliferating. That's because when private citizens or the media try to find out, the government uses privacy arguments to keep the information closed, and generally, the courts are supporting the government's right to conceal information about the identities of its employees or third parties in its investigations.

This trend has been growing during the 1990s, as Deckle McLean, an associate professor of journalism at Western Illinois University, noted after reviewing a series of FOIA cases from the 1960s through 1992. Before 1989, he notes, the states and federal courts were much less likely to give privacy exemptions, and only did so for more restricted purposes. But since then, the courts have been much more likely to keep the requested information private—in about 80 percent of the federal cases and about 50 percent of the state cases between 1989 and the middle of 1992.[37]

Why the change? According to McLean, the big difference is the growth of computerizing and compiling information into data bases. As a result, the courts have finally realized the need to catch up with the new record-keeping technology and adapt the law accordingly.

Thus, they have reinterpreted the meaning of the federal Freedom of Information Act (and the state versions of this act), which initially was usually interpreted to guarantee openness. But now, increasingly, the courts have been saying that the purpose of these acts is to assure that citizens can see how their government agencies work—what they are up to. Then, using this new interpretation, the courts have said that information which does not bear on the way the agency operates does not have to be disclosed under the FOIA, such as personnel data in government files. So the government doesn't have to release this information and can protect the privacy of all of these people, who are much more open to scrutiny because of the computerization and compilation of these records.[38]

Paradoxically, then, the growing privacy protections sought by the government in these FOIA suits is a reaction to the loss of privacy due to the government's own data collection process. As a result, as the media have sought openness, they have come up against this privacy barrier, in which the laws once passed to assure government openness are now being used to hold back information, using the privacy exemption to prevent its release. So, ironically, though the federal and state freedom of information acts were originally passed to provide access to the workings of government, the government agencies using these acts have hidden behind the privacy exemption, ostensibly to protect their own privacy and the privacy rights of the individuals in the agency, even though these individuals may have no objection to the release of this information about themselves, as noted by Kimera Maxwell and Roger Reinsch at the Emporia State University in Kansas.[39]

So who does the FOIA really protect, they ask. When the act was first passed, its primary purpose was "disclosure, not secrecy," to guarantee each person the right to know about the business of his or her government. Congress and the courts were supposed to have the responsibility of determining whether the information could be withheld, not the agencies. These agencies were required to disclose all of their records unless specifically exempt. But since then, the agencies have tried to keep their records closed by defining their exemptions broadly, or have used excuses to keep from giving out information, such as "We can't find the material," charging high fees, or instituting long delays to discourage people from accessing records.[40]

Employee Blues

Another arena for conflict is the power of the government versus employee rights in some government—union/large company cases over who has access to information on employees. Can the government keep it private, or can the union or company find out what they want to know in these bureaucratic privacy battles between the Freedom of Information Act and the Privacy Act, bringing different arms of government and different bureaucracies to the frontlines. Often it's a toss up, depending on circumstances.

It's a Secret

In a few cases, the unions have found their way blocked in getting names or background information on union members when they wanted this information to better organize or represent them. This occurred in the *Federal Labor Relations Authority v. U.S. Department of Commerce* case, decided in April 1992. The union representing National Weather Service employees in Maryland wanted to get all the names, duty stations, and locations of all employees receiving outstanding or commendable personnel evaluations. But after it made its request in 1986, the National Weather Service didn't want to release these names, citing the Privacy Act and the FOIA exemption. Ultimately the U.S. Court of Appeals agreed. Even if the employee evaluations were positive, the court felt the employees had an interest in keeping this information private, since disclosing even favorable information could embarrass an individual or incite jealousy in coworkers. And, of course, a list identifying those who received high ratings would reveal by omission the identities of employees who did not receive them, thereby invading their privacy, said the court.[41]

But You've Got to Tell

Yet in other cases, the unions were able to get addresses, when they were able to show a compelling reason that it was in the public interest to reveal this information. For example, in the big *Federal Labor Relations Authority v. U.S. Department of the Navy* case, decided in March 1992, the union took on several different Navy agencies in the states of Washington and California involved in sales, publications, and printing, education, and running an air station and hospital, plus the U.S. Departments of the Interior and Labor—and it won! In each case, the labor unions claimed the agency was engaging in unfair labor practices by refusing to divulge the home addresses of their workers, which the unions wanted, so they could send mail free of employer supervision and interference. Here, the U.S. Court of Appeals agreed with the unions, observing that the Federal Service Labor-Management Statute requires the federal agencies to disclose information to the employee's unions. Then, after noting the conflicting acts (the Privacy Act generally prohibits disclosure and the FOIA requires disclosure), the court decided to require disclosure, particularly since most circuit courts hearing these cases decided this too. Its reason for this decision was that the "strong public interest in assuring the integrity of the collective bargaining process" was more important than "the employees' interest in keeping their home addresses private."[42] So score one for the unions this time!

In turn, these contradictory decisions seem to be almost guaranteed by the conflicting laws—the Labor-Management Statute requires disclosure; the Privacy Act prohibits it; and the FOIA requires disclosure as an exception to the Privacy Act, except when an exemption can be used to prevent disclosure. The laws are like a thicket of contradictory instructions which take effect under different conditions. So it is no wonder that the question of whether to release this employee information or not "has been litigated many times before,"[43] as the court deciding for the U.S. Navy noted.

So what's the difference? Why should the unions win in one case, but not in others. The result seems to depend to some degree on where the case is tried. In some jurisdictions, the trend has been to favor disclosing information, in others to support concealment. Or, as the court deciding the big Navy case in Washington and California noted, highlighting this problem of making a consistent decision: "Other circuits have ascribed wildly different weights to the strength of the privacy interest in one's home address."[44]

Thus, with the laws in conflict, the outcome could easily go either way in future cases, depending on what the judge considers more important—the employee's right to privacy or the union's right to know.

Battles within Battles

When other types of battles are going on, like employee strikes or claims of sex harassment, there may be privacy battles as well, as when the government is asked to release some information from its records, but wants to keep confidential employee or witness names and records. Here, too, the Privacy Act or privacy exemptions seem to outrank the power of the FOIA or state open records acts.

For example, after the 1981 air traffic controllers strike, about two hundred controllers who lost their appeal for reinstatement and did not settle, hired a lawyer who tried to get information under FOIA about the reasons why the government reinstated and settled with other employees. When the Federal Aviation Administration (FAA) refused to turn over this information, the lawyer sued to get these documents in the

Norwood v. Federal Aviation Administration case, decided in August 1993. He did get some information, since the U.S. Court of Appeals agreed he was entitled to discover whether the administration handled the strike in a "fair and consistent manner," and he could obtain general legal and financial information showing why the reinstated controllers were able to get the FAA to reinstate or settle with them. But the agency could redact identifying information on the controllers, including their names, previous and current locations, addresses, and social security and other identifying numbers.[45]

Other Skirmishes

Besides these hard-fought cases in the courts, there have been other recent conflicts at the public–media–legislative level to get the passage of laws or institution of certain government policies, since today a great many policy decisions and the activities of most government agencies have some impact on personal privacy. As a result, increasingly, privacy considerations are being reviewed in the early stages of government decision making.

For instance, in developing plans for the coming information highway, the federal government has set up a national task force to debate and develop privacy protection policies. So perhaps in future years, these issues will be less likely to be settled in the courts than through a spirited public debate.

For example, this increased concern about privacy helped influence the post office in setting up its change of address policies. As reported in the *Privacy Journal* in early 1993, the new Postmaster General, Marvin Runyan, reacting to pressure from privacy advocates, softened the U.S. Postal Service's former resistance to including privacy protections in its national address program. Originally, the post office took the change of address forms people filed, created computerized lists of address changers, and turned these over to private mailing companies, so the companies could update their lists before making mass mailings. But as revealed in hearings before the House Subcommittee on Government Information, these companies were not just updating existing lists. Additionally, they were putting together lists of "recent movers," to target them for special mailings. In response, Runyan sent off a conciliatory letter to the subcommittee, noting the individual's privacy interest in his or her name and address, and stating that he would thereby clarify and strengthen the "privacy notice on the next printing of change-of-address order forms." And still another change resulted from these subcommittee hearings and public objections—the U.S. Postal Service would no longer create a data base of New York City names, addresses, and apartment numbers by having letter carriers copy information from apartment letter boxes.[46]

Also, the IRS decided to voluntarily incorporate some additional privacy considerations in its policies. Though legally it didn't have to do so, it decided that it would now cover up the social security numbers on the mailing labels it used to send forms to taxpayers. It was a change privacy advocates very much wanted, since if visible, these numbers could easily be used for illegitimate purposes by anyone seeing the form.

Likewise, even before the 1994 Driver Privacy Protection Act was added to the Crime Bill, some state Departments of Motor Vehicles backed off in the information they collected or used about people. For example, in Massachusetts, the DMV, which became a defendant in a lawsuit seeking to restrict its disclosure of social security numbers, decided to stop collecting these numbers, which it hadn't been using for many years.[47] And as previously noted, California legislators passed their own strict law regulating the release of personal addresses on records to most private individuals and companies, with limited exceptions, that was, as of 1995, stricter than the federal guidelines. For example, process servers and private investigators must post a $50,000 bond to be registered to get DMV information for approved purposes!

And so the battle goes on, primarily by lobbyists, legislators, and representatives of the administration, trying to work out a policy to balance privacy and other concerns, such as for efficiency and economy. A goal is to work out agreements and guidelines to help avoid the need for court involvement. But if these arrangements can't be settled or there are further disagreements, these matters could well become the court cases of tomorrow. Then judges rather than government officials, legislators, and the public will end up making the final determination, as they have in many other battles that have come to court.

Notes

1. Janlori Goldman and Lucas Guttentag, "The Social Security Number and a National Identifier," Presented before the House Committee on Ways and Means, Subcommittee on Social Security, 27 February 1991, 1.
2. Ibid., 1–2.

3. Ibid., 4–7.
4. S. Rep. No. 516, 100th Cong., 2nd Sess. 2 (1988).
5. James B. Rule, "Where Does It End? The Public Invasion of Privacy," *Commonwealth* (14 February 1992): 14–15.
6. Ibid., 14–15.
7. Alexander Besher, "How Smart Are 'Smart Cards?'" *San Francisco Business,* April 1992, 8.
8. Paul Robinson, "Biometrics," *Computer Privacy Digest* (4 March 4 1994): 4.
9. Michael deCourcy Hinds, "Privacy Fight Focuses on Social Security Numbers," *New York Times,* 25 March 25 1993.
10. *Greidinger v. Davis,* 988 F.2d 1344 (4th Cir. 1993), 1345–53.
11. Leslie G. Foschio, "Motor Vehicle Records: Balancing Individual Privacy and the Public's Legitimate Need to Know," *Privacy and Publicity,* (1990) 35–40.
12. Author interview with Sam Brown, licensed private investigator, San Francisco. Author of *Private Eyes* (with Gini Graham Scott; Boulder, Colorado: Paladin Press, 1994), October, 1994.
13. Eddy L. McClain, "Federal Crime Bill Update," *CALI Newsletter,* Vol. 28 No. 2, October/November 1994, 13.
14. "President Clinton's Crime Bill; Driver's Privacy Protection Act of 1994," Provisions of Bill in *CALI Newsletter,* Vol. 28, No. 2, October/November 1994, 15–16 and discussion with Kristin King, Legislative Assistant, Congressman James Moran, December 12, 1994.
15. Bureau of Justice Statistics, State Criminal Records Repositories 1 (1985); SEARCH Group, Inc., *Criminal Justice Information Policy: Privacy and the Private Employer,* cited in Evan Hendricks, Trudy Hayden, and Jack D. Novik, *Your Right to Privacy* (Carbondale, IL: Southern Illinois University Press, 1990).
16. Hendricks et al., 45.
17. *Criminal History Record Information: Compendium of State Privacy and Security Legislation, 1992,* Bureau of Justice Statistics, U.S. Department of Justice, Washington, DC, 4.
18. Hendricks et al., 47–48.
19. *Bureau of Justice Statistics,* 8.
20. Hendricks et al., 51–52.
21. California Penal Code, 1994.
22. *Criminal History Record Information,* 7.
23. Hendricks et al., 49–50.
24. Gregory R. Firehock, "The Increased Invulnerability of Incorrect Records Maintained by Law Enforcement Agencies," *The George Washington Law Review,* 60 (June 1992): 1509–52.
25. *Doe v. FBI,* 936 F.2d 1346 (C.D. Cir. 1991).
26. Firehock, 1517–30.

27. *Johnson v. Sawyer,* 4 F.3d 369 (U.S. App. 1993), Lexis 27285.
28. Allan Karnes and Roger Lirely, "Striking Back at the IRS: Using Internal Revenue Code Provisions to Redress Unauthorized Disclosures of Tax Returns or Return Information," *Seton Hall Law Review,* 23 (1993): 924–66; 924–25.
29. *Johnson,* 3–78, in Lexis.
30. *Johnson v. Sawyer,* 760 F. Supp. 1216, p. 1233, cited in Allan Karnes and Roger Lirely, "Striking Back at the IRS: Using Internal Revenue Code Provisions to Redress Unauthorized Disclosures of Tax Returns or Return Information," *Seton Hall Law Review,* 23 (1993): 924–66; 961.
31. *Church of Scientology of Texas v. Internal Revenue Service,* 816 F. Supp. 1138 (W.D. Tex 1993), 1146–62.
32. *Hale v. U.S. Department of Justice,* 973 F.2d 894 (10th Cir. 1992), 896–902.
33. *Maynard v. C.I.A.,* 986 F.2d. 547 (1st Cir. 1993), p. 553.
34. *Mayor and City Council of Baltimore v. Maryland Committee Against the Gun Ban,* 617 A. 2d 1040 (Md. 1993), 1040–48.
35. *McDonnell v. United States of America,* 4 F.3d 1227 (U.S. App. 1993), in Lexis 24140, 1–97.
36. *News Group Boston, Inc. v. National Railroad Passenger Corporation,* 799 F. Supp. 2d. 778 (Mich. App. 1992).
37. Deckle McLean, "Privacy Gaining Heft as an FOIA Exemption," *Communications and the Law* (March 1993): 25–46; 25–27.
38. Ibid., 28.
39. Kimera Maxwell and Roger Reinsch, "The Freedom of Information Act Privacy Exemption: Who Does It Really Protect?" *Privacy and Publicity,* (1990): 83–97; 83.
40. Ibid., 86–87.
41. *Federal Labor Relations Authority v. United States Department of Commerce,* 962 F.2d 1055 (D.C. Cir. 1992), 1056–59.
42. *Federal Labor Relations Authority v. U.S. Department of the Navy,* 958 F.2d 1490 (9th Cir. 1992), 1492–93.
43. *Federal Labor Relations Authority v. U.S. Department of the Navy,* 1492.
44. *Federal Labor Relations Authority v. U.S. Department of Navy,* 1496.
45. *Norwood v. F.A.A.,* 993 F.2d 570 (6th Cir. 1993), 572–75.
46. "Change of Address," *Privacy Journal,* 19, (February 1993): 5.
47. "SSNs," *Privacy Journal,* 19, (May 1993): 7.

Chapter 11

Court Watch

At one time the courtroom had a reserved and restrained atmosphere, with spectators limited to those who could fit in the available seats. Cameras, much less television cameras, were unthinkable. The only images of what went on in court were made by courtroom artists, who sketched, since cameras weren't permitted; and when the idea of videotaping court trials was first proposed in the 1960s,[1] many judges fought adamantly against it. They were afraid that the presence of a camera would undermine the decorum of the courtroom.

But now courts have joined the television-infotainment age, and cameras have become common in many courtrooms. Besides the traditional court reporters who carefully record the official transcripts, a new breed of court reporter has become a TV star. For today the camera in court has not only spawned a phenomenally successful cable TV channel, Court TV, with about 14 million viewers as of 1994, but it has turned some criminals and real-life Perry Masons into stars. And many once private citizens cannot return to a quiet private life, at least for some time, even if they want this. For they have become overnight celebrities, many turning their lost privacy into big bucks fame.

It is as if the courts, once a fairly conservative, decorous institution, have become another type of superhyped talk show, with privacy another information age casualty. While some welcome this new openness, since the public now can see what really goes on in the courtroom, others cringe at the courts surrendering to the media explosion and the packs of press hounds yelping for news in the more sensational cases—like the O.J. Simpson fury that turned some networks into the "O.J. Simpson Channel" for several days, as some media critics joked.

So far the media's and public's thirst to know has been winning, as more and more courts have appeared on candid camera. But a backlash appears to be growing, too, as some judges close their courtrooms to cameras or prevent cameras from showing certain things, such as a woman's face in a rape case, a child in a child molestation case, or the jury in a violent crime case, where there is a fear of retaliation. In turn, sometimes the prosecutors or defense attorneys in sensitive cases may request a closed courtroom, keeping the cameras out, if the judge approves.

So cameras in court have involved one kind of battle, while another struggle has developed over the media's efforts to gain access to certain court documents that the courts have tried to withhold from them—much like the media–government FOIA battles. Another battle is between various parties in a lawsuit to force the other side to reveal personal information and documents, while that side wants the information kept out of court.

The Cameras in the Courtroom Era

It may seem hard to realize today that the constitutional rationale for allowing the camera in the courtroom was the First Amendment public's right to know. That is the view of the media and open court advocates, and generally, when the issue of an open court versus keeping out the media and spectators has come up, the Supreme Court has supported those keeping the trial public.[2]

But initially and today, many have argued against cameras in court as an affront to privacy. The controversy over cameras dates back to the famous Charles Lindbergh child kidnapping and murder trial in the early thirties. The judge banned microphones and cameras in the courtroom, afraid the carnivallike media coverage might bias the jurors against the alleged kidnapper and murderer, Bruno Hauptmann.

Then in 1965, the media came under fire again, when the U.S. Supreme Court overturned the conviction of Billie Sol Estes, a flamboyant, highly publicized con artist. It claimed he didn't get a fair trial because of all the media coverage, which included wires crisscrossing the courtroom and microphones in front of the judge, jury, and attorneys. Further, the Court had some concern that the media coverage might have distracted the participants and affected their ability to pay attention and remember information.[3]

Yet, as television news coverage grew, the pressure mounted to let cameras in the courtroom. So in the late 1970s, experiments began with introducing cameras—California in 1978 and Florida in 1979. Many disparaged these initial experiments, especially judges, prosecutors, and defense lawyers. According to Boston professor Susanna R. Barber, author of *News Cameras in the Courtroom*, they argued that the cameras would be "physically disruptive, distracting, and detrimental to the dignity and decorum of the courtroom." And some complained that the cameras would turn the parties, judges, and lawyers into actors, playing and emoting to the cameras, and that the jurors would be swayed by public opinion.[4]

However, those arguments were quickly discredited. As in Florida, the courts typically used a single camera in court for each trial, and the media organizations pooled their coverage. As a result, researchers studying the cameras' effects soon found that they did not "have a significant impact on judges, witnesses, lawyers, and other participants."[5] So increasingly, since the 1980s, cameras have moved into the courtroom.

Yet, as more courts have become hooked up to cameras, in forty-seven states as of 1993, anticamera advocates have raised key privacy arguments to keep cameras out. Most notably, they have expressed concerns about invading the privacy rights of witnesses, especially victims of physical and sexual abuse; and they have cited the damage to the reputations of defendants. Conversely, the camera supporters argue that the participants in a trial surrender this privacy right, because by being in a trial, they have become public figures of interest to the public, especially in a criminal trial.

So the battle has been joined, although for the anticamera advocates it has largely been a losing cause, though judges have closed selected trials to protect victims, witnesses, and jurors in especially sensitive or dangerous cases. The privacy argument has generally been considered weak, and if mentioned at all, it has generally been combined with concerns about the dangers of pretrial publicity or juror prejudice, according to Barber.[6]

As a result, the general practice that has developed in almost every state has been to let the judge decide on a case-by-case basis whether or not to permit cameras. In some cases, the judge may decide on his or her own; in others, the judge invites the parties and witnesses to make a request if they want to stop the cameras, and then, it's up to the judge. Depending on the situation, the judge might ask that the cameras be turned off at certain points in the trial, excluded entirely, or left on through all the proceedings. The particular arrangement depends on the state. Although forty-seven states do allow some form of camera coverage, as Barber notes, in twenty-six states, anyone wanting to bring a camera to court has to get the prior consent of the court or the judge, while many other states require an advance notice of TV coverage plans. In addition, some states have rules that prohibit or limit coverage of certain types of cases or participants."[7] Only three states prohibit cameras entirely—Indiana, Mississippi, and South Dakota.[8]

According to Barber, one of the cases which triggered these special privacy concerns was the famous Big Dan's barroom rape trial in 1984 in Fall River, Massachusetts. It's the case which was later the subject of the 1988 Oscar-winning film *The Accused* starring Jodie Foster. The coverage was a forerunner to today's media circus. Briefly, what occurred is that a woman, who went into Big Dan's bar for a drink, was gang raped on the pool table, while onlookers cheered on the rapists. The case attracted widespread public interest, and numerous broadcast media organizations covered it, including Ted Turner's Cable News Network. A central camera in the courtroom was used to provide pooled coverage for the different news groups. Within a few days, the victim's name was broadcast nationally, and the print media soon followed suit, leading to widespread discussion that the victim had been raped twice, first by the rapists, and then by the media.[9]

In turn, the spirited public debate over cameras in the courtroom after this case contributed to the development of the current guidelines in most states which now allow audiovisual coverage, but with varying guidelines about what can be recorded, televised, or photographed, setting the stage for the ever-present court TV of today.

Releasing Information to the Media and Reporting on the Courts

While the media can generally write about anything they learned about legally if they are largely accurate in what they say, there have been many court cases over whether the information should have been released in the first place, and if the media is using the court documents accurately or in a misleading way, thereby giving a false impression of someone.

Generally, once something has occurred in a courtroom or is part of the official public record, prosecutors and lawyers are free to report it, if what they say is accurate. For example, Stephen Buckley discovered this in the *Buckley v. Fitzsimmons* case, decided in January 1992. After he was tried and sentenced to three years in jail, he tried to claim he was unfairly tried and convicted, because a press conference and the publicity that followed "deprived him of a fair bail hearing and trial." He felt it unfair that the judge refused to dismiss the prosecution's case because of prejudicial publicity. He claimed the prosecutor himself had defamed him by announcing during a press conference that he had been indicted. But the U.S. Court of Appeals turned him down, saying that the prosecutor was immune from suit in conducting a press conference, just as in presenting evidence in court, since he was merely acting as a public official informing the public about what was going on in a matter open to public.[10]

By contrast, while accurate reporting about what happened in court may be fine, the press or anyone else cannot use court records to mislead, as one reporter and publisher discovered in the *Kumaran v. Brotman* case, decided in June 1993. Sampath Kumaran had formerly worked as a substitute schoolteacher and security guard, and he also spent quite a bit of time filing lawsuits. After a *Chicago Tribune* reporter noticed this, he wrote a mocking article: "Having His Day in Court is Virtually an Everyday Event for West Sider," noting the many ways in which Kumaran claimed he had been wronged in about two dozen lawsuits which he had filed since 1980.

The basic thrust of his article was that Kumaran filed unwarranted suits to get settlement money, such as when he sued the People's Gas Company for $1 million because it shut off his heat, sued the Illinois Bell Company because it "wantonly" gave him a defective telephone line, and sued two airlines, Kuwait Airways and Air India, because the first had bumped him from a flight and the second had lost his luggage. Then, too, he had sued his employers, claiming they had fired him as a security guard because he was an East Indian, and he had sued the State of Illinois for denying him unemployment benefits while he was between jobs as a substitute teacher. To further bolster his view, the reporter quoted several lawyers and defendants who questioned Kumaran's integrity in filing the suits, including one defendant who commented: "This guy's just working a scam," and another who observed, "Basically, he's figured out the system, that it's cheaper to settle than to try a case."

Not surprisingly, angered at being accused of filing unwarranted suits for settlement money, Kumaran filed another suit against the reporter and publisher, claiming that the article not only defamed him and invaded his privacy, but was designed to "ridicule him, deprive him of his livelihood, and pressure him to leave the country," as well as incite "public hatred" and cause him to lose "employment opportunities."

Unfortunately for the reporter and publisher, the Appellate Court of Illinois agreed Kumaran might have a case. Although the reporter and publisher claimed that the article "was a privileged account of judicial proceedings," the court felt that rather than just report on what was in the court record, the article presented a biased, selective report to make Kumaran look like a scoundrel. However, he did have other factors in his background that made him seem like a respectable, upstanding citizen. For example, about three years before the article appeared, Kumaran had been a substitute teacher in good standing at two suburban high schools. Thus, the court felt it only fair that Kumaran should have a chance to present his case against the reporter and the paper; and since he was a private person, not a public figure, he only had to show they had acted negligently, not with actual malice, in publishing this article about him.[11]

Protecting Sources

Another big point of dissension between the media and courts is the media's protection of their sources. At times, reporters and writers have gone to jail over this principle, rather than reveal who told them what, because typically, they promised their source confidentiality. In many cases they feel their source may be in danger from retaliation if their identity becomes known. Their response is much like that of prosecutors and law enforcement people protecting witnesses and informants, although the latter have the government's power behind them, and generally, the courts support protection of witnesses' and informants' privacy.

Generally, these source issues come up in criminal cases, where a writer has interviewed a witness or party to the case for a book or story, and has some confidential information not published in the story, usually background notes, tapes, or transcripts. When this becomes known, one of the lawyers wants to get this—usually it is the defense lawyer to help his or her client, but sometimes the prosecution may seek this information too.

Many times writers simply go to jail, particularly when they can't afford the lawyers to challenge the judge's request on freedom of the press or other grounds. But in some cases, when a major media organization claims confidentiality, it may be able to work out a compromise, in which the court gets much of the information it wants, while the media can block out the names and identifying data of confidential sources.

For example, in one representative case, Rik Scarce, a sociology doctoral student in Spokane, Washington, was sent to jail in handcuffs after a brief contempt hearing. The events leading up to the judge's decision were these: He had done some research on the radical environmental movement, and federal investigators believed he had interviewed two or three people suspected of raiding and vandalizing laboratories and fur farms in Oregon, Michigan, and Washington in 1991 and 1992. In February 1993, the federal prosecutors subpoenaed him to testify before a grand jury about his discussions with one suspect, Rodney A. Coronado, whom federal agents believed was behind a 1991 Washington State University lab raid in which radical environmentalists released twenty-three animals and caused $150,000 in damage. But Scarce refused to testify, claiming his sources were confidential and he was protected by the First Amendment as a writer and scholar. The privilege in Washington applied to members of the press in civil and criminal cases, and he felt it should apply to writers and scholars too. But unfortunately for Scarce, the court rejected his arguments and sent him off to jail.[12]

By contrast, when CBS was subpoenaed to supply a videotape by a defendant and refused in the *United States v. Sanusi* case, decided in December 1992, it was able to work out a deal. The case began when a team of U.S. Secret Service agents arrived with a search warrant at Babatunde Ayeni's apartment in March 1992 and searched for evidence of credit card fraud, such as fraudulently obtained credit cards, lists of names and account numbers for such cards, false IDs, and incriminating bank records. Though they didn't find any evidence of fraud, they did find a color photo of Anthony Sanusi, who was subsequently charged with fraud along with Ayeni and eight other defendants. Meanwhile, during the search, a CBS News crew arrived and filmed for about twenty minutes.

Later, when Sanusi, who wasn't at the raid, found out about the CBS crew, he tried to get a copy of the tape, thinking it might have information he could use to dismiss the indictment or better defend himself in a trial. But since CBS didn't want to give up the tape, which it hadn't yet broadcast, it fought to quash the subpoena to turn it over. CBS was able to work out a deal. Besides its large resources, CBS also had behind it a local New York law that provided for a newsgather's privilege for material obtained confidentially and nonconfidentially, much like the press privileges provided in other state laws. Thus, the U.S. District Court decided on a compromise, in which it recognized both CBS's newsgathering privilege to quash the subpoena, and the defendant's argument to defeat this privilege because the tape might help him defend himself in a jury trial, since it showed that the agent's exhaustive search of the apartment revealed no evidence of fraud. Though Sanusi could argue this is what happened without the tape, the court felt the tape's impact on the jury could be especially compelling, in showing "the government's zeal to arrest him and its failure to produce any evidence after tearing apart his home." Thus, the court decided that CBS had to give up the tape to help Sanusi, particularly since its crew had filmed without asking permission at the apartment, so in effect CBS was filming illegally. Yet, at the same time, to protect the privacy of the confidential source which CBS agreed to protect at the government's request, CBS was permitted to obscure the identity of that source on the tape it had to turn over.[13]

Protecting Juveniles and Rape Victims

Although the media has faced its own battles over printing the names of rape victims and juveniles, the courts and participants in court hearings have been struggling, too, with what to do when juveniles and rape victims turn up in court. Should they inform the public or protect the individual's identity? When juveniles are involved in sensitive sex and criminal cases, the general policy is to protect the juvenile and keep his or her name out of the media, with the decision left up to the judge. The judge, in effect, has the power to stop the presses or the cameras, with a restraining or gag order preventing anyone from publishing or broadcasting that juvenile's identity. Usually judges have been likely to do this when the juvenile is a victim rather than an offender.

For example, in the Michael Jackson child molestation case, the thirteen-year-old boy's identity was carefully concealed in court records and news reports, and whenever the television cameras showed the boy, say leaving a hearing, his face was carefully blocked from view. By contrast, courts are less concerned about keeping the name of offenders from the public, particularly with the growing tide of juvenile crime, and more stories about them are appearing in the media. Indeed, more older juveniles are being charged and tried as adults, and even younger ones accused of very serious crimes, such as Eric Smith, the then 13-year-old boy accused and subsequently convicted of the second degree murder of an 8-year-old boy.

But when the courts do try to protect juveniles, at times some members of the media have protested that this is unfair, a prior restraint on press freedom. But, as often occurs in these court and law enforcement versus media struggles, the court and law enforcement officials win in the name of privacy.

This is what happened when a circuit court in Illinois issued an order prohibiting an Illinois newspaper, the *Champaign News-Gazette,* from disclosing the identities of two minors who were victims of physical and mental abuse in the *In Re Minor* case, decided in June 1992. The juvenile court held hearings on providing shelter and care for the two juveniles, when a *News-Gazette* reporter wanted to cover the proceedings. But at the door, he had to sign a pledge not to reveal the juveniles' identity. Though he grudgingly signed and was admitted, the newspaper appealed, claiming this was "an unconstitutional prior restraint" on the freedom of the press and that the general public had a right to know "what is transpiring in its courts."

But the Illinois Supreme Court agreed with the court, noting that a juvenile court act permitted the court to prohibit anyone in the court from "further disclosing the minor's identity," though if the media learned the minor's identity through other legal means the court might not be able to do anything. Moreover, the court emphasized there were some very compelling reasons for concealing their identities, since publicly identifying them could adversely affect them for the rest of their lives by causing "continuing emotional trauma" and interfering with the long and difficult healing process. Besides, this was the general policy in other courts, and in this case, they were victims of child abuse, not juvenile delinquents, so they were especially worthy of court protection, unlike criminal offenders.[14]

Similarly, the courts have become generally protective of the identities of rape victims, requiring cameras to block out their faces when they testify, forbidding reporters at the hearings or trials from revealing their names, and sealing court records to keep reporters or others from finding out their names and identifying details later.

This is what happened in the *Deborah S. v. Diorio* case, decided in February 1992. Deborah S, a New York City resident, had gone out on a date with Charles Diorio, and when she tried to tell him no, he wouldn't take no for an answer, and his sexual advances turned savage. He pulled out a knife, threatening to cut her or her clothing if she didn't submit. After he was ultimately convicted of three violent felonies, Deborah S took him to court, too, seeking compensatory and punitive damages.

She won, and though she didn't request anonymity in her suit and began her action before a New York law was passed requiring confidentiality of the identity of sex victims, the New York City Civil Court sealed her file and omitted her last name and residence address anyway "in the interest of justice" to protect her privacy, citing the new law. Even though Deborah S's situation occurred before the law passed, the court felt it only fair that it apply to her, because of the severe trauma she had suffered.[15]

In addition, besides preventing their names and identities from being revealed in court records, rape victims can now typically keep out information about their past sexual activities. At one time, many defendants tried to bring in this information to show the woman probably consented, because she had an active sexual history; or they tried to turn the jurors' sympathy against her by presenting her as a promiscuous, immoral person. But now they can't do this. In fact, in some cases, to avoid inflaming the jury, judges will even exclude information that the victim had previously participated in the public sex industry, which might otherwise not be considered private activity and therefore could be presented in court.

That's what happened to M.G. from Alaska after she was raped by Kenneth Wood, who was convicted in the case of *Wood v. State of Alaska,* decided in February 1992. The rape occurred in 1983, about six months after M.G. met Wood, who lived nearby while she was living with her then boyfriend, Bob Berube. She and Wood soon became friends, and saw each other frequently over the next six months, in what Wood claims was a sexual relationship, though M.G. says it wasn't. Meanwhile, M.G. was going through a rocky on-and-off relationship with Berude.

Then, in April 1983, the relationship with Wood turned into rape. M.G. was visiting a friend when Wood showed up and wanted to talk about their relationship. Though M.G. didn't want to talk about it, and was at this time trying to drop Wood out of her life, he was insistent. Finally, he persuaded M.G. to go with him to get cigarettes, and as they drove along, they began to argue and M.G. asked him to take her home. When he refused, she tried to jump from the moving car. Wood stopped her, hit her, and at one point, pulled out a gun and threatened to use it. Eventually, they ended up at the home of a male friend of Wood's, where M.G. says, Wood told her to go into the bedroom and take off her clothes, and he forced her to have sex, saying he wouldn't hurt her if she did. Subsequently, she told her then boyfriend and the police.

Wood was eventually convicted of sexual assault, and in appealing his conviction, he argued that the judge had unfairly prevented him from presenting evidence about M.G.'s racy past which might have showed he wasn't guilty, including that she had modeled in men's magazines, acted in pornographic movies, and showed him nude photographs of herself from men's magazines. But the U.S. Court of Appeals agreed that although her porn and modeling career were not private acts, the judge still could keep this information out of court because it might bias the jury against her as "an immoral woman," and so base its decision on that hostility rather than on the facts of the case. So Wood's conviction remained.[16]

Presenting Personal Medical Information in Court

Though medical records and meetings with doctors and therapists are considered very private, as discussed in chapter 9, what happens when that information might be evidence in court to help a defendant prove innocence, might show a plaintiff in a civil suit has suffered emotional distress, or might show someone would be an unstable parent in a custody case? In such cases, can medical records or notes be used? In general, such records are considered inviolate, the product of a confidential relationship between doctor or therapist and patient, and the victim can obtain damages if a doctor or therapist reveals such confidential information. In some cases, however, there are exceptions and the records can be pulled into court.

Can't Use It—It's Confidential

A New York attorney representing a car accident victim encountered his own records roadblock when he tried to get them in the case of *Hanig v. State Department of Motor Vehicles,* decided in February 1992. His female client was hit by a car driven by Frank Jordan (not the Mayor of San Francisco), and when he tried to get the DMV record on Jordan's license application, he found that Jordan's responses to one question: "Do you have, or are you currently receiving treatment for, any disabilities?" were covered over, followed by a list of serious disabilities, including epilepsy, fainting or dizzy spells, and having a mental disability. The document ended with the note that this covered-up information was considered confidential under New York's Freedom of Information Law.

Concerned that the concealed disability might have affected Jordan's driving that fateful night, the attorney repeatedly appealed the decision and finally sued the DMV to get this information. But the New York Court of Appeals turned him down, too, noting that medical histories, like certain other personal information, such as employment and credit histories, were exempt from mandatory disclosure. It was private information and should remain so.[17]

Conversely, this protection policy can sometimes protect individuals who want to keep their records private and out of court, as Julie Bosson found. She was able to keep her own mental health records out of court when she sued the Children's World Learning Center in Texas on behalf of her son K.P., in the case of *K.P. By And Through Bosson v. Packer,* decided in March 1992. She sued for her son because she claimed another child at the center performed a sexual act on him, causing him psychological and emotional damage and medical expenses, as well as her own loss of his companionship, love, and affection.

In response, the Center raised questions about her own mental health and sought to see her mental health records, which Bosson didn't want to disclose. Did she have to? If she had been a patient, claiming damages herself, then she would have to show them, because her own mental condition would be an issue. But since she was only suing on behalf of her son, as her son's "next friend," and not seeking individual damages for herself, she could keep her records private.[18]

In turn, since medical and therapeutic records are considered so private and are generally not permitted in court without consent or special exceptions, a patient can often gain damages if a doctor or therapist reveals such confidential information without permission. That's what happened when Diane Renzi sued her psychiatrist, Dr. Helen Morrison, in the case of *Renzi v. Morrison,* decided in June 1993, because Morrison revealed her confidential communications in a custody hearing when called as a witness by Renzi's husband.

The case started in August 1983 when Renzi's husband filed a petition to dissolve their marriage and sought temporary custody of their two-year-old daughter. When Renzi soon discovered that her husband had contacted Morrison, and that Morrison had told him about her psychological tests and evaluations, Renzi wrote to Morrison, asking her not to disclose any confidential communications, advising her these were protected from disclosure under the Mental Health Act in Illinois. But even so, Morrison voluntarily appeared at the custody hearing and offered to testify for Renzi's husband. Despite Renzi's objections, the judge invited Morrison to testify, and her testimony about Renzi's emotional health helped tip the balance, so the judge awarded temporary custody to Renzi's husband.

Renzi sued, and though Morrison claimed she was immune from any liability as a witness in a trial proceeding, the Appellate Court of Illinois agreed Renzi had a case. After weighing the conflicting rights, witness immunity and doctor–patient confidentiality, the court sided with Renzi, since Morrison was Renzi's psychiatrist and she was hired to treat her. Worse, she "appeared voluntarily and offered to testify for Renzi's husband"; she wasn't even appointed by the court or ordered to testify. Thus, the court concluded she could be held liable for damages, and now it was up to a jury to decide.[19]

It's in the Record

Yet, at other times, medical/mental health records can be introduced and revealed, can't be sealed, and are open to anyone who wants to see them. One time is when someone files a suit charging malpractice causing mental or emotional harm. Then, he or she usually has to reveal the records to show the psychological and other damage despite any psychological harm from revealing the records. Or if someone's records have already been opened to the public in court, it may not be possible to seal them again. Sometimes in complicated cases, the judge or jury may decide what gets revealed or concealed, as the public knowledge/personal privacy arguments are fought on both sides.

For example, Joseph Street had to open up his wife's medical records after he sued several physicians, the university hospital, and others, claiming the doctors had breached the confidential patient–doctor relationship and presented private information in a malpractice suit he filed against Dr. Leslie Hedgepath in the Washington, DC case of *Street v. Hedgepath*, decided in June 1992. He had originally sued Dr. Hedgepath for failing to diagnose his wife's cancer, which resulted in her death, and the case ended with a hung jury. He now filed this additional suit because during the trial, Dr. Hedgepath had called on these doctors, who had also treated Mrs. Street, to support his side of the story, that he had not been negligent and had not caused her injuries leading to her death. Their testimony was effectively compelling. For example, one doctor claimed her cancer had already spread through her body and she had a very bad tumor that was often fatal even though very small, so she couldn't have been saved anyway. Eventually, the jury couldn't decide if Dr. Hedgepath was negligent or not, resulting in a hung jury and a mistrial.

That is when Street sued, claiming the doctors had breached Mrs. Street's confidential relationship with her treating physician, because they talked about her treatment with the defense attorneys and at the trial. But had they breached this special relationship? Even though the District of Columbia had passed a law preventing doctors from testifying about their patients' condition without their consent, the District of Appeals Court concluded it was fine to introduce this medical testimony, since Mrs. Street's surviving spouse had sued based on what had happened to her. So that meant that he had in effect waived any privilege against disclosing relevant medical evidence, and gave his implied consent to disclose any confidential medical information relevant to the case.[20]

Can You Say It?

Another question relates to whether someone can be liable for revealing evidence in court, and whether he or she can use that information later. The general rule is that one is "immune" or protected from liability for whatever one says in court, and once these statements are part of the court record, anyone can publish those statements later. Also, when a person is involved in a legal case, their name generally can be released to the public, and they can't keep their name out of the record, unless there are special exceptions (such as a juvenile or rape victim, in which case the judge will seal the record).

However, a suit cannot be initiated mainly to discredit someone in public or use the litigation discovery process (which is designed to bring out facts about the case, and perhaps encourage a settlement) to maliciously send out defamatory information about someone to others not involved in the litigation. The following examples illustrate these battles over who can say what, when, and to whom.

Who's Immune? I'm Immune, You're Immune. Typically, participants in both criminal and civil cases are given immunity for what they say or present as a document in court so they can freely give evidence. Then, once something is in the public record, anyone can report it, unless there are special exceptions as noted and the judge seals the record. That's the essence of an open democratic society in which government processes are kept open for the public to know, and generally those who want to keep information about themselves from being included in the public record or sealed later have lost.

For example, Babette J. Spitler, one of the preschool teachers originally named as a defendant in the notorious McMartin Preschool child molestation case in Los Angeles found this out when she objected to statements made about herself during some hearings on the case. In the original case, one of the longest and most expensive trials in the Los Angeles area and in U.S. history in the mid-1980s, the McMartins and several child care workers were accused of molesting numerous children, even taking some of them to bizarre satanic rituals. Eventually the case resulted in a hung jury and mistrial, mainly because much of the testimony from the children who were interviewed by therapists seemed questionable, subject to suggestion and false beliefs implanted by the interview process.

Though the matter was officially closed in January 1986, when the newly elected district attorney, Ira Reiner dismissed charges against the five codefendants, Spitler sued the child care professionals in the investigation for defamation in the case of *Spitler v. Children's Institute International,* decided in December 1992 . She claimed that the professionals had made defamatory statements about her in the preliminary hearing on the case and then these were republished in the legislative proceedings. Also, she objected to statements one of the professionals, Kathleen "Kee" MacFarlane, made to a U.S. congressional subcommittee investigating child abuse nationwide; and she objected to statements MacFarlane made to ABC journalist Wayne Satz about what she would say at the preliminary hearing. But the Court of Appeal concluded that the Children's Institute and MacFarlane were "absolutely immune" from any liability, because they had been asked to evaluate the McMartin preschoolers for possible sexual abuse and then report their findings in court.[21]

Similarly, Jerome Wagshal from Washington, DC was unsuccessful when he sued arbitrator Mark Foster, who was assigned to help arbitrate his suit against the manager of some real property he owned, in the case of *Wagshal v. Foster,* decided February 1993. The problem began after the judge hearing Wagshal's Superior Court suit tried to settle it by assigning it to an arbitrator under the court's Alternate Dispute Resolution (ADR) program. Wagshal objected to the first arbitrator, so the court appointed another, who happened to be Foster. After Wagshal objected to Foster too, Foster asked the judge for permission to withdraw. But before he did step down, Foster suggested that the court might "remonstrate" with Mr. Wagshal about his obligation to participate in mediation, implying that Wagshal's attitude was interfering with successfully resolving the case. About six months later, though a third evaluator finally settled the case, Wagshal sued Foster, claiming that Foster had contributed to the less than satisfactory settlement Wagshal received. Wagshal's rationale was that Foster expressed his opinion about the case to others, including the judge, reflecting "unfavorably upon the merits of Wagshal's claims." But the U.S. District Court sided with Foster and dismissed the case, observing that court-appointed arbitrators, mediators, and others involved in alternative dispute resolution programs are immune from prosecution, as are other officials of the court when doing their job. After all, when Foster expressed his opinion about the merits of the Wagshal case, he was simply acting in his official capacity, as he was hired to do. So, if Wagshal didn't like his opinion, too bad, Foster was immune.[22]

Naming Names

Can you keep your name out of court proceedings? Probably not. Typically, judges only seal the record or find ways to conceal the person's identity in the case of juveniles, some rape victims, and special cases. But most parties, even nonparticipants named in documents, have their names in the record, so the public and press can generally see whatever any documents have to say about them.

That's what some Florida "John Does" discovered after they were named on an alleged prostitute's client list discovered in a widely, and wildly, publicized case: *Post Newsweek Stations v. Doe,*[23] decided in February 1993. The case hit the media circuit in July 1991, when the Broward County sheriff began investigating charges that Kathy Willets, a willowy blonde, and her husband, Jeffrey Willets, the County Deputy Sheriff, were operating a prostitution scheme.[24] It was like the Miami Vice version of Beverly Hills madam Heidi Fleiss.

After police officers, with a warrant, searched the Willets' home, they found business cards, lists, and a Rolodex containing customers' names and sexual preferences. They also found a tape recorder connected to the Willets phone and tapes used in the scheme. Soon after, the state charged Kathy Willets with prostitution, her husband with living off the earnings of prostitution, and both with unlawfully intercepting phone conversations.

So who were the customers? The *Miami Herald* and other media wanted to know, so they filed suit asking the trial judge to release this information from the records seized in the Willets' home. But the customers didn't want to be identified, and the attorneys for five of them tried to keep the material out of court. At first the judge agreed, but in the discovery phase, when the Willets sought to get information about the materials taken from their home and the material held by the state, which is supposed to be available to the public, the attorneys tried again to keep the records closed. But the Florida Supreme Court went along with the strong Florida law, which much like the approach in most other jurisdictions, favored keeping the court records open, except for special exceptions (like protecting the confidential identity of a blood donor in an AIDS case or preventing the disclosure of psychiatric counseling). But the court didn't think the johns deserved any special consideration, since their names had turned up in connection with the commission of a crime. And so their names were finally released.[25]

But You Can't Use a Court Case to Defame

Yet, though records are usually open, one big exception is that you can't take advantage of the legal process to sue someone so you can then use the case to spread damaging information about them—and you can't go all out in publicizing this information to third parties to get back at someone maliciously.

That's what the Aetna Life Insurance Company and its law firm discovered when they tried to discredit Dr. Stanislaw Burzynski, a doctor and researcher in Houston, Texas, who provided what they considered a worthless treatment for cancer, and for which they didn't want to pay. However, Dr. Burzynski sued them with some success, because they spread around information to discredit his unconventional therapy techniques, in the case of *Burzynski v. Aetna Life Insurance Company,* decided in August 1992.

One especially controversial technique was Burzynski's method of injecting substances distilled from human urine, which he called "antineoplastins," into the body. Supposedly, these substances would "reprogram" cancer cells to function normally. In support of his theories, Burzynski appeared on numerous national TV programs, including *20/20* and *Sally Jessy Raphael.* But the Food and Drug Administration (FDA) was still skeptical, and in 1983 it barred him from interstate transactions involving his treatment. In 1988, the Texas Department of Health ordered him to stop treating cancer patients without FDA approval.

That's why Aetna refused to pay for these treatments by one of Burzynski's patients, and after she died, Dr. Burzynski, who was still unpaid, took over her case and pursued her claims against Aetna. In response, Aetna struck back, suing Dr. Burzynski, and they not only charged in a Racketeer Influenced and Corrupt Organizations Act (RICO) conspiracy suit that he fraudulently induced Aetna to pay insurance claims, but during discovery, Aetna sent out mailings about him to dozens of other insurance companies that might have paid or might currently be paying claims for his treatments. In the letter, they sought information about Burzynski and suggested he was a fraud. Among other things, the letter ominously noted in italics: "*This letter is to warn you of potentially fraudulent claims for insurance reimbursement that may have been made to your company.*" Then, after asking for information on any claim history the company may have had with Dr. Burzynski, the letter went on to label his antineoplastin treatment as "worthless," noted the 1983 FDA action against him, listed unfavorable reports on the treatment from the medical community, pointed out that Dr. Burzynski hadn't gotten FDA approval for the drug, and stated that a Texas grand jury was currently investigating his operation.

Though such statements might be true, the U.S. Court of Appeals decided the letter and mass mailing was just too much, since it went beyond the usual disclosure privilege in discovery. As a result, it felt that Burzynski might have a basis for showing that Aetna and the law firm had injured him by among other things interfering with his business relationship and promoting a conspiracy against him when it sent out this discrediting material. In short, the court felt that Aetna had gone too far in purposely exploiting the discovery privilege for "ulterior, malicious motives" by sending out "defamatory material" to parties with no legal interest in the litigation.[26]

If Dr. Burzynski's treatment did turn out to be worthless or even harmful, this might be a defense the insurance company could use at its trial. But the court didn't feel it fair to make this assumption at this point. So neither should the insurance company in its letter.

It is also dangerous to use the possibility of litigation as a basis for spreading discrediting information about someone. An example of this occurred when a court thought Lorelei Trenfel might have a claim for defamation against her former accountant and attorney when they spoke disparagingly about her with her mother and brother, who were thinking of suing her for mismanagement and fraud in a family auto dealership dispute, in the case of *Trenfel v. Jasper,* decided in March 1993. The problem began in 1986, when Lorelei's parents ousted her brother as general manager of the family's Toyota car and truck dealership in San Diego, and put her in charge. But in 1987, soon after her father died, her mother had a change of heart and fired Lorelei and tried to put her brother in charge again.

In response, Lorelei not only sued her mother, but she sued her accountant Kevin Jasper and attorney Howard Silberman, since they told her mother and brother she had mismanaged the company, and they claimed she was stealing money from the dealership and might be involved in criminal activity. But Lorelei claimed they knowingly made these false charges because they thought they might be replaced at the dealership. Since she didn't do these things, she claimed, they had defamed her by their remarks.

Had they made their remarks during a judicial proceeding or even if they had been seriously contemplating one, they could have said what they did, because they would have a special "privilege to defame" in speaking to others in connection with taking steps to initiate legal action. But if not, they wouldn't be protected and Lorelei might have a case against them. They couldn't, as the court put it, use just "the bare possibility that the proceeding might be instituted . . . as a cloak to provide immunity for defamation when the possibility is not seriously considered."

Unfortunately, it wasn't very clear whether a potential lawsuit was "actually contemplated" when Silberman and Jasper said what they did. So, since the court couldn't decide whether they made a "good faith communication about prospective litigation that was contemplated for legitimate purposes" or were just trying to promote "their own economic self-interest" at Lorelei's expense, it sent the case back for trial. If they had said what they did in connection with contemplated litigation, they were home free; if not, they might be liable. It was up to the jury to decide.[27]

Checking for Weapons

Finally, in today's climate of gang violence and fear of crime, the question of whether weapons checks in the courtroom before people enter are acceptable or an invasion of privacy has become a matter of controversy, too. It would seem, though, that it's probably fine for the courts to do these checks.

For example, the matter became an issue in New York, when the Legal Aid Society of Orange County sued the chief administrator of the New York courts to challenge the constitutionality of using magnetometers to search for weapons that might be in the possession of people who wanted to go into the county family court. As it turned out, it was constitutional, in the case of the *Legal Aid Society of Orange County v. Crosson,* decided in 1992. The U.S. District Court regretfully acknowledged that the growing dangers of modern society had made protection and security a priority, so the concern for privacy had to give way. As District Judge Goettel, deciding the case in U.S. District Court observed: "Sadly, newspaper headlines record daily our society's growing willingness to do violence, against those we live beside, those we do not know, and even those whom we love. Courts, long viewed as bastions of justice and security, now struggle against the same violence that invades our schools, roams our streets, and tears at the very fabric of our society threatening to rip it apart."

Thus, the judge found it reasonable to use these magnetometers, especially since family courts may have a greater potential for violent outbursts due to the highly personal and emotional issues involved. He felt, as did other courts, that the use of these devices involved a very "minimal invasion of privacy," since the person being checked simply passes through the magnetometer quickly, and there are no "personal indignities or humiliations" of physical searches or any need to detain people in doing these searches. Accordingly, he felt this device a good choice as a security measure that was now unfortunately necessary to protect the courtroom, observing that: "Protecting judicial officers and members of the public from the omnipresent threats of violence that surround our public institutions involves greater security efforts and vigilance than ever before."[28]

So, ironically, while the courts have become more open to the public because of the media and the open records laws, the courts have increasingly been checking up on people entering the courtroom, too, using security devices like the magnetometer to check. Thus, in the courts, increasingly there is less privacy, as in other areas of society, today.

Notes

1. *Estes v. Texas,* 381 U.S. 532 (1965).
2. Susanna R. Barber, "The Big Dan's Rape Trial: An Embarrassment for First Amendment Advocates and the Courts," *Privacy and Publicity,* (1990) 63–81; 67.
3. J. Stratton Shartel, "Cameras in the Courts: Early Returns Show Few Side Effects," *Inside Litigation,* 7 (April 1993) 1, 21–26; 1.
4. Barber, 64.
5. Shartel, 22.
6. Barber, 66.
7. Ibid., 71–2.
8. Shartel, 21.
9. Barber, 69–71.
10. *Buckley v. Fitzsimmons,* 952 F.2d 965 (7th Cir. 1992), 965–67.
11. *Kumaran v. Brotman,* 617 N.E.2d 191 (Ill. App. 1 Dist. 1993), 192–203.
12. "Student Jailed for Refusing to Identify Sources," *The News Media and the Law,* (Summer 1993): 35.
13. *United States v. Sanusi,* 813 F.Supp. 149 (E.D.N.Y. 1992), 151–60.
14. *In Re Minor,* 595 N.E.2d 1052 (Ill. 1992), 1052–57.
15. *Deborah S. v. Diorio,* 583 N.Y.S.2d 872 (N.Y.City Civ. Ct. 1992), 876–81.
16. *Wood v. State of Alaska,* 957 F. 2d. 1544 (9th Cir. 1992), 1545–52.
17. *Hanig v. State Department of Motor Vehicles,* 588 N.E.2d 750 (N.Y. 1992), 753–54.

18. *K.P. By And Through Bosson v. Packer*, 826 S.W. 2d. 664 (Tex. App.—Dallas 1992), 665–68.
19. *Renzi v. Morrison*, 618 N.E.2d 794 (Ill. App. 1 Dist. 1993), 796–97.
20. *Street v. Hedgepath*, 607 A.2d 1238 (D.C. App. 1992), 1240–46.
21. *Spitler v. Children's Institute International*, 14 Cal.Rptr.2d 197 (Cal.App. 2 Dist. 1992), 198–202.
22. *Wagshal v. Foster*, 142 LRRM 2965 (1993), 2965–66.
23. *Post-Newsweek Stations v. Doe*, 612 So.2d 549 (Fla. 1992).
24. "Court Releases Names in Prostitution Probe," *The News Media and the Law*, (Winter 1993) 16.
25. *Post-Newsweek Stations v. Doe*, 550–52.
26. *Burzynski v. Aetna Life Insurance Company*, 967 F.2d 1063 (5th Cir. 1992), 1063–66.
27. *Trenfel v. Jasper*, 16 Cal. Rptr. 2d. 913 (Cal. App. 4 Dist. 1993), 915–21.
28. *Legal Aid Society of Orange County v. Crosson*, 784 F.Supp. 1127 (S.D.N.Y. 1992), 1128–31.

Chapter 12

School Gaze

From elementary school to college, school has become a privacy battleground, primarily in high school and university. Mainly, these conflicts have occurred on four main fronts: the effort to keep schools safe from crime and drugs; efforts to control, shape, or punish different types of student behavior; the school–media conflict over what the media can cover and publish; and the struggle over what a school can say when it is trying to terminate or has terminated a teacher or staff member.

Most of these battles affect areas of society already featured in separate chapters. But since the school is a kind of special preserve, a world unto itself of students and teachers, I will discuss these school privacy issues separately.

Schools as "War Zones"

As we saw in earlier chapters, there has been increasing surveillance in other areas of society due to concerns about crime and drugs, and this has carried over into schools and colleges. Like a microcosm of society, schools have been invaded by these same problems, resulting in the airportlike screening devices and police practices that have become a daily routine in many schools. In many communities, as widely reported in the news, even elementary schools now have check-in stops through which students have to pass, so they can be checked for weapons. If any turn up, they will be confiscated, and the student will sometimes be charged with a crime or suspended from school as well. In many schools, principals and teachers now do occasional locker checks for illegal drugs, stolen property, or other evidence of a crime. While these surveillance and search practices have been challenged in some localities, the lower courts have generally given them the green light, feeling the added security measures were justified given the risks of these dangerous times and the need to protect students from these dangers. In fact, in some jurisdictions, there are moves to make carrying a concealed weapon into a school a felony, and in some states (such as California) it now is a felony for both adults and juveniles.

Meanwhile, there are efforts around the country to make juveniles more accountable for what they do, including no longer sealing the juvenile's record. For example, in California, after the Polly Klaas murder and Richard Allen Davis's conviction, Mike Reynolds, another California father whose daughter was raped and killed, got renewed support for the supertough "three strikes and you're out" measure that he proposed, which had languished in political limbo for about two years. Legislators were able to push it through quickly and it was the first of several similar proposals signed into law by Governor Pete Wilson. One of its provisions now opened juvenile records and allowed convictions as a juvenile to count toward the "three strikes," in this law, which provides for life sentences for three-time losers, who have previously committed at least two violent crimes.[1]

Thus, increasingly, popular opinion is urging a stepped-up watch on juveniles generally, as well as in the schools, given the rising concern about juvenile crime, thereby justifying the crackdown on juvenile privacy because of the need to protect the general public and juveniles from one another. Then, too, besides just protecting students from danger, the schools argue that they need this added surveillance and control to keep the school environment conducive to learning.

Controlling and Checking Student Behavior

Besides the surveillance crackdown to control violent crime, school controls to deal with discipline and drug problems have also been tightening, resulting in other erosions of student privacy.

The Roots of the Decline of Student Privacy Rights

The roots of this stepped-up search and surveillance go back to the early 1980s, when discipline and drug problems began to become increasingly severe. But when parents and civil libertarians responded by protesting these actions, in many cases in the courts, school officials generally won. As a result, increasingly they gained the opportunity to investigate and search, if they had a reasonable rationale for doing so.

In 1984, there was a precedent setting case from New Jersey decided by the Supreme Court, *New Jersey v. T.L.O.*[2] It began when a principal searched a high school student's purse, suspecting marijuana, although she objected that her purse was private. After she and her parents challenged the matter and the case wound up in the Supreme Court, the court supported the principal, agreeing that school officials have a right to search a student or his or her property without a warrant. They just need reasonable grounds to suspect the search might turn up evidence the student had violated or was violating the school's rules.

This decision helped to give principals and other school officials the right to check up on and control most of what was happening in the school, given the school's need to maintain an environment conducive to learning. This right includes searching student lockers (since they might contain contraband or drugs) and monitoring student speech and publications (since they might contain discriminatory or defamatory content).

The crackdown on speech and publication has in turn led to the big censorship-political correctness battle in the news today. Those arguing for personal privacy and freedom of speech are on one side, while those seeking to protect the sensibilities of minority and disadvantaged groups or to protect children from erotic and satanic writings are on the other. The PC/censorship battle is too extensive and complicated to deal with here in any detail. But the basic privacy issue is that principals and teachers are increasingly seeking to control private student behavior, including what they say and do and what groups they may associate with, in response to pressures from both liberals and conservatives. While the liberals have been trying to protect minorities and disadvantaged groups from insults and discrimination, the conservatives have been trying to keep anything they consider too sexual or satanic—including fantasy and traditional folk stories about witches and goblins—out of the schools. And here too, privacy advocates claim, schools are generally clamping down on both sides, shutting off debate, and trampling on student privacy rights in the process.

In turn, since the *T.L.O.* case, the right of the schools to control student speech and behavior has been supported by some key court decisions in the 1980s. For example, in 1988, the Supreme Court decided in the *Hazelwood School District v. Kuhlmeier* case that school officials can impose reasonable restrictions on the content of a student newspaper, which in this case included excising two objectionable pages.[3] Similarly, in a late 1980s California case, *Leeb v. DeLong*, the California Appeals Court agreed that a school principal and other school officials could prohibit students from distributing an issue of a newspaper they thought was possibly defamatory because of what the students had said about someone. The court took the position that the school district could censor official school publications they reasonably thought might have any defamatory content, because this put the school at risk for a legal action against it. But they could not censor for merely taste or educational reasons.[4]

Since then, the schools have generally expanded their efforts to check and shape student behavior in other ways, with court support when challenged, in the name of protecting students from crime, violence, drugs, and recently, even disturbing ideas. As a result, as the power of the school to investigate and control has increased, the student's personal privacy has declined. It's a sad trade-off in reaction to the dangers and conflicts of our times.

The Trend to Increased School Checking and Control

The irony is that one reason why principals and administrators can check and control more is to preserve the learning environment at a time when teachers have increasing discipline problems with kids who have little interest in learning. Still, school officials try, and in some cases protesting students and parents have taken their invasion of privacy complaints to court—or to the court of public opinion.

Such a battle erupted when a high school vice principal in Mt. Olive, New Jersey caught two high school freshmen with computer disks containing copies of the *Jolly Roger Cookbook*, describing techniques for hacking on computers. Taking the position that they could censor any document or material they considered inappropriate, the administrators confiscated the disks from the students, notified their parents, suspended the students for three days, and contacted the police who investigated further. Though the matter never ended up in court, it outraged civil libertarians, who commented angrily on the censorship and punishment of the students. For example, in one outraged bulletin board posting on the *Computer Underground Digest*, Jeff Kosiorek commented:

> Where do school officials get the right to censor any type of publication a student may have in his or her possession? Furthermore, how can they punish these youths when even the investigating officer, Detective Joseph Kluska, said, "It's not illegal to know how to do these things." The students were not in anyway using the information found in the cookbook for illegal activities, yet they are being punished only because the vice principal, John DiColo, deems them inappropriate.
>
> In a school where they profess the merits of the American Constitution and the rights protected therein, the hypocrisy is absurd.[5]

Yet, despite such gripes, school administrators generally can use such tactics by claiming they are trying to preserve order and an appropriate learning environment. Furthermore, they generally can take action, such as suspending a student, even when a student engages in illegal activity outside school, or is just accused of it.

One student found this out when he sued a high school principal for invasion of privacy, civil rights violations, and slander, in the case of *Durso v. Taylor*, decided in January 1993. The conflict began after Eric Taylor, then a sixteen-year-old high school student in Washington DC, was arrested for allegedly raping another student at his home. The police appeared at his high school on a warrant, and as about twenty students watched, the police escorted him away in handcuffs. The next day, the high school principal, Michael Durso, told Taylor he couldn't return to school until Durso had spoken to Taylor's mother. The next day, in meeting with them, he encouraged Taylor to transfer to another school. At first, Taylor agreed and studied at home for about two weeks. But after a hearing officer decided Taylor should return to school and Taylor did, Durso at first refused to admit him. However, after Taylor's mother appealed to him, the superintendent ordered Durso to admit him, so Taylor returned, accompanied by a student demonstration and media coverage. Eventually, the criminal charges against him were dropped, and he graduated with his class.

But the question lingered: Could the principal suspend a student accused of a crime without a hearing, or use an incident that occurred off school property inside an individual's home to control a student in the school? A year after he graduated, when Taylor sued the principal, his suit raised these questions. Eventually, though, the Court of Appeals sided with the school, noting that it had an interest in ensuring an environment that would not be disruptive in educating its students. Also, the court agreed that Durso did not have to hold a formal hearing before suspending Taylor, even though there should usually be one before a student was suspended to provide due process rights. However, the school could immediately suspend a student if it felt his presence posed a danger to others or disrupted the school environment. Thus, Durso's informal meeting with Taylor and his mother was enough, though perhaps Durso might have invaded Taylor's privacy in making comments to the media about the case, and it would be up to the trial court to decide if he did or not.[6]

Yet, while the trend is toward increasing power to check and control, there are still limits on how far teachers and administrators can go, especially in a college or university setting, where students seem to have more rights than in the lower schools. For example, though schools have gained the power to search for suspected illegal drugs (such as in student purses and lockers), they cannot just engage in suspicionless random drug testing, particularly at the college or university level, at least in some states.

For example, the University of Colorado was turned down when it tried to do this in the case of *University of Colorado v. Derdeyn,* decided in November 1993. The university had established a random urinalysis-drug testing program in 1984 for intercollegiate student athletes, and all students were required to submit to testing, or they couldn't participate in intercollegiate athletics. David Derdeyn and other student athletes protested the policy, because like many students they objected not only to the random suspicionless testing, but some of the procedures used. One that was particularly offensive was observing students during the act of urination to be sure no one cheated, and the penalty for a first positive included suspension from the current competitive season. In fact, the process was so embarrassing that one female student testified that the students called being selected for the team as being on "the pee team."

Even the Supreme Court of Colorado agreed this testing program was a bit much. It pointed out that the students had not really consented to participate in it, and in the absence of their voluntary consent, it felt the random, suspicionless testing was too invasive, a violation of both the Colorado and U.S. constitutions. Even though the university claimed the students had signed consent forms advising them about the program, so they had a "diminished expectation of privacy," the court felt the students did not really consent voluntarily, since they had to sign to participate in athletics. In addition, the court felt that university students should have as much privacy protection as anyone else; they shouldn't have less protection "simply because they are university students." Further, it emphasized that in this day and age, a college or university cannot use the "in loco parentis" claim to deprive students of their constitutional rights, say by doing unwarranted or random searches without probable cause.[7]

The School Meets the Media

Though the media can largely write and broadcast what they want, if largely true and obtained legally from open and public records, the schools, like various government bodies, have tried to restrict access to records and meetings. But often the press has been able to force open these meetings. One time was when the *Ann Arbor News* and other newspapers wanted to cover a meeting of the Board of Regents of the University of Michigan, which was considering hiring a new president, in the case of *Booth Newspapers, Inc. v. The Board of Regents of the University of Michigan,* decided in September 1993. After the current president resigned in 1987, the Board of Regents pulled together a list of potential candidates and began the winnowing process, using numerous phone calls and informal group meetings. But it avoided having full meetings, since these would have to be public under the Michigan Open Meetings Act. In this way, it reduced the original field of 250 candidates to twelve, whereupon the Presidential Selection Committee began making confidential visits to the candidates' home cities to interview them, reducing the field still further to two. Finally a nominating committee decided on one candidate, Dr. James Duderstadt, who was elected president.

But the *Ann Arbor News* and other media objected, claiming the Board of Regents had violated two openness in government laws: the Open Meetings Act and its state Freedom of Information Act. So now it wanted the courts to force the board to open up its records about who was considered for the presidency, how they were selected, and where the regents traveled to interview candidates. Eventually the Supreme Court agreed that the university had been excessively secretive, should have had open meetings, and had tried to evade doing so by its informal decisions and conferences, which achieved the same result as if the entire board met publicly and formally voted. However, as a public body, it couldn't do this; it had to hold all its deliberations in an open meeting, couldn't conduct closed interviews, and couldn't conceal the identities of the candidates interviewed, even if they requested privacy. The public's right to know about the qualifications of candidates for public positions and the hiring procedures of public officials was more important. So the board had to disclose the requested information to the press.[8]

Employment in the Schools and the Public Right to Know

This conflict between public knowledge and individual privacy is also played out in school employment privacy cases. Like other employees, teachers, counselors, and other school personnel frequently want to keep employment information private; such as when they are accused of poor performance or want personnel records kept confidential. But since most schools are public institutions, and school personnel are viewed as a role models for children and others, there is more support for opening up the records as well as meetings. Also, when school personnel sue, because something adverse has been revealed about them, they often find there is little they can do, since the administrators, as well as the schools, are considered immune if they are just doing their job. But if they spread lies and innuendoes, they may exceed the scope of this immunity, and then they might be found liable for defamation or invasion of privacy.

Lawrence Levine discovered this wall of immunity when he sued the New York City Board of Education in the case of *Levine v. Board of Education of the City of New York*, decided in October 1992. He sued because the Board disclosed information about his mental health. He had worked on and off as a substitute and regularly licensed teacher in New York City, but problems began in 1984, when the Board put him on an involuntary continuing leave of absence without pay for health reasons. Though he was examined from 1984 to 1988 by physicians or psychiatrists from the Board's medical bureau to determine if he was fit for service, they continued to turn him down. That's why finally he decided to sue, claiming among other things that the Board had invaded his privacy and defamed his character. But the Supreme Court said no, because it felt an employer had a qualified privilege to evaluate an employee's performance and potential, and in doing so, the Board had only passed a letter about Levine around to its internal staff. This was fine, because it had to disclose information about his mental health status so it could carry out its own duties in deciding what to do about his case.[9]

Likewise, school psychologist Karen Perkins was unable to keep the public schools from disclosing her sick leave records, in the case of *Perkins v. Freedom of Information Commission,* decided in December 1993. The case began when the New Fairfield Taxpayers Association president Arthur Azzarito sought information on her records under the state Freedom of Information Act. She wanted to learn how many sick days she had accumulated, how much she was paid, and when she last worked. Although the school district initially turned down this request on privacy grounds and Perkins objected to releasing this information, too, the state Freedom of Information Commission ordered the school to provide these records, and so Perkins appealed to the courts.

But the Connecticut Supreme Court turned her down, since the taxpayer's group just wanted numerical data, and the court felt that any information should be disclosed under the Act, unless there was a clear exemption for privacy reasons. Perkins tried to show this, claiming this information might allow the taxpayer's group to know if she was "sickly" or "healthy" by comparing her records with the sick leave days allowed in her contract, leading to a public discussion of her health and her personal embarrassment. But the court felt she was merely speculating about what might happen, and besides, as a public employee, she had less expectation of privacy, because of the public's right to know.[10]

Still, certain personnel records may be considered private, such as when a school employee is involved in a disciplinary case, as occurred in the case of *LaRocca v. Board of Education of the Jericho Union Free School District,* decided in August 1993. It began when Dr. Marc Horowitz, a principal employed by the Jericho Union Free School District in New York was disciplined in a private hearing. When Anthony LaRocca, vice president of the Jericho Teachers' Association wanted to find out what had happened, the school board, superintendent, and Dr. Horowitz fought to keep the details of the hearing private. The New York Supreme Court agreed. Though it recognized the importance of "open government" in a democracy, it felt that the "citizen's right to privacy" had to be respected too. In this case, it felt it important to keep LaRocca's personal employment records private, since the disciplinary hearing had been resolved by a settlement. After all, said the court, if the records of a settlement agreement were made public, then "no educator would ever settle" knowing that the charges, even if unproven, could be revealed to the public and thus have an adverse impact, perhaps irreparably, on his professional's reputation." Instead, the educator would opt for a costly hearing, so the record would be confidential if tried successfully. Thus, LaRocca wasn't able to get the records.[11]

When School Officials Say Too Much

Still, there are limits, when school officials spread around unfavorable information that discredits employees in the eyes of others. If that information is untrue or discriminatory, that's even worse. The discredited employees may not be able to sue the school or school district itself due to government immunity, but they may be able to successfully sue the officials who unjustly said too much.

That's what Girard Petula found when he sued the school districts and two superintendents, James Mellody and Roger Lewis, in the *Petula v. Mellody* case, decided in August 1993. Petula had worked as a school administrator, and when he looked for another job, Mellody and Lewis allegedly made some false and defamatory statements about him to prospective employers, spread this information to numerous school districts, and acted with "fraud, malice, and willful misconduct" to harm him. Did they? If so, they could be held liable for what they said. Conversely, if they were just acting within the scope of their employment in saying what they thought of Petula, like the school district, they would be immune. The Commonwealth Court sent the matter back to the trial court to decide.[12]

Janet Nazeri, a Director of Teacher Education in Missouri, was similarly able to hold both the Missouri Valley College and Dennis Spellmann, vice president of the college, accountable. This occurred when Spellman told a *Marshall Democrat-News* reporter exactly what he thought of Nazeri, in the case of *Nazeri v. Missouri Valley College,* decided in August 1993. Among other things, Spellman stated in their October 1989 meeting that he felt Nazeri was "incompetent, out to get the college, prejudiced against the college, and opposed to church schools having education programs." Additionally, he claimed she had lived for years with a woman "who is a well-known homosexual," and he further stated that Nazeri "left her husband and children to live with [her]." In fact, he added in a subsequent interview that Nazeri was "out to close private colleges" and he "would not tolerate fags on campus." He further accused Nazeri of conspiring with her roommate to use her position to poorly evaluate the college's educational program to achieve her goals.

Although the newspaper did not actually publish these comments, Nazeri charged they became public knowledge anyway. Also, she charged that Spellman continued his campaign against her in various ways, such as by telling the administrative assistant to the Commissioner of Education that he did not want Nazeri to head an evaluation team at the college. His efforts seemingly worked, because a few months later, she was relieved of a number of responsibilities as chair of the evaluation teams, another official was assigned to make a presentation to the Board of Education instead of her, and she felt she encountered public ridicule and a loss of reputation and public respect. Some fellow employees even told her she was too controversial to associate with; and she found that communications she would normally receive were routed around her, so she was out of the loop.

Even the Missouri Supreme Court agreed that Spellman and the school had gone too far in making slanderous defamatory remarks about her. In particular, the court noted that Spellman sought to portray her as "an unchaste woman . . . engaged in illegal and immoral acts, and a person who abandoned her home, spouse and family," and one who "engaged in adulterous and criminal conduct." In addition, he accused her of a "lack of skill and fitness to perform her official duties," portrayed her as "incompetent and prejudiced," and questioned her integrity in suggesting she was "willing to abuse her official position" to perform a "bad program evaluation" in order to "advance her own personal agenda." Further, he insinuated she was a "homosexual and an adulteress" who left her family to engage in "an adulterous and unchaste relationship with a lesbian woman," which was a defamatory statement. It was, said the court, because it was false and homosexuality was still viewed with disfavor, even contempt, by much of the population in Missouri, and was still a misdemeanor in the state. Thus, since the Supreme Court felt Nazeri had a case against Spellman and the college, it would now be up to the trial court to try the matter.[13]

Thus, while what goes on in the school may be somewhat more open to the public, both in dealing with employees and keeping public meetings open, there are still limits to what officials can say or do, including inappropriately spreading around unfavorable and untrue information.

Notes

1. Talk by Greg Houston, Dublin City Council member, running for Mayor of Dublin, supporter of the McReynolds Three Strikes Bill, 24 March 1993.
2. *New Jersey v. T.L.O.*, 469 U.S. 325 (1984).
3. *Hazelwood School District v. Kuhlmeier*, 108 S. Ct. 562 (1988).
4. *Leeb v. DeLong,* 198 Cal. App. 3D 47.
5. Jeff Kosioreki posting, *Computer Underground Digest,* 5, (October 24, 1993).
6. *Durso v. Taylor*, 624 A.2d 449 (D.C. App. 1993), 451–57.
7. *University of Colorado v. Derdeyn*, 863 P.2d 929, Colo. 1993, cited in Lexis 887, 2–28.
8. *Booth Newspapers, Inc. v. The Board of Regents of the University of Michigan,* 444 Mich. 211, 1993 Mich., Lexis 2419, 2–34.
9. *Levine v. Board of Education of the City of New York,* 589 N.Y.S.2d 181 (A.D. 2 Dept. 1992), 182–83.
10. *Perkins v. Freedom of Information Commission,* 228 Conn. 158, 1993 Conn. Lexis 411, 2–31.
11. *LaRocca v. Board of Education of the Jericho Union Free School District,* 602 N.Y.S.2d 1009, 1993 N.Y. Misc. Lexis 415, 1–4.
12. *Petula v. Mellody,* 631 A.2d 762, 1993 Pa. Commw., Lexis 544, 2–12.
13. *Nazeri v. Missouri Valley College,* 860 S.W.2d 303, 1993 Mo. Lexis 88, 1–41.

Chapter 13

Keeping an Eye on the Money

For many people, a big concern with the growing computerization and concentration of data bases is the exposure of their assets. They fear people will discover their assets, sue them, access their credit card and social security numbers fraudulently, and run up bills or worse in their name. Many also fear that the government might confiscate their funds and property for trivial reasons or due to mistaken identity; the media might publish financial information about them; or information in their financial and credit records might be wrong, used to deny them credit or embarrass them. Many additionally worry they may have trouble correcting the problem.

In many cases, they are right to be fearful. One hears about invasion of financial privacy horror stories in the courts and the press. There is even a publication now to help people with these concerns protect their assets: *The Financial Privacy Report*. Meanwhile, the insurance companies are joined in the battle, too, when they try to avoid paying for invasion of privacy claims, while their insurees try to get them to pay. Thus, the battle over financial privacy has been going on intensely on a number of fronts—over consumer and credit issues, over what personal financial information banks can release, over ways to protect assets from snooping and confiscation, and over insurance coverage.

A Bit of History

The growing concern about financial privacy began in the 1960s, when people first began to become concerned about the growing computerization of records and the loss of control of personal information. This occurred as an increasing number of government agencies and private institutions began to collect and exchange more and more information about them.

Though a centralized national database, including income, census, and social security numbers on all U.S. citizens was at one time considered during the 1960s as a means of more efficient government, it was turned down. But still the number of separate databases in government and private industry grew.

Then in the early 1970s, a rising pressure for privacy protection from all this information gathering led Congress to pass a series of acts to protect personal and financial privacy. One, in 1970, was the Fair Credit and Reporting Act, which restricted the activities of the growing number of private credit and investigative reporting agencies which collect and sell financial and credit information about people. Under the act, these agencies could only disclose their records on consumers' credit worthiness to authorized customers (who were supposed to use this only to check credit). Also, the act required these agencies to let consumers review their own records and correct inaccuracies.[1] Soon numerous states followed suit, passing their own consumer protection laws, including California, Florida, New York, and Texas.[2]

Another key act was the Privacy Act of 1974, that established certain guidelines for collecting, maintaining, using, and disseminating personal and financial information. Most notably, it restricted government agencies from disclosing information collected for one purpose for a different purpose, gave citizens a right to access and correct their records, and limited the use of social security numbers for ID purposes.

Unfortunately, though these acts were on the books, in practice, they did little to hold back the increasing collection and dissemination of data. Despite restrictions, many individuals and companies obtaining data from private credit and investigative agencies used it for other than legitimate credit checking purposes. Also, this Privacy Act did little to stem the growing collection and exchange of data from one agency to another; and the social security number continued to be used increasingly as an identifier in gathering and pooling data. The government simply argued that it needed to do all of this computer matching of separate agency records for financial efficiency, so this was a "routine use," and therefore exempt from any restriction on disclosing personal records for another purpose.[3]

Meanwhile, as government policies ironically trampled over privacy rights while passing legislation to protect it, the courts stepped on financial privacy rights, too. An example of this is the 1976 *United States v. Miller* case, in which the Supreme Court ruled that one does not have a constitutionally protected privacy interest in personal bank records held by a bank. Instead, the Court felt that these records have become bank business records, so that the banks can freely release them to government agencies, such as, in this case, to law enforcement agencies seeking these records without a warrant or showing probable cause.[4]

Then, in 1977, this mingling of government records increased even more when the Carter Administration began its "Project Match" program to increase government efficiency, by using computers to compare the names of welfare recipients in the Department of Health, Education and Welfare (HEW) files with the payroll files for Civil Service Commission and Defense Department jobs in eighteen states.[5]

One reaction to these incursions was still more privacy protection laws from Congress, some to protect financial privacy. One such law was the 1978 Right to Financial Privacy Act. Passed as a reaction to the *Miller* decision allowing bank records to be disseminated, it required law enforcement officers to show that the records they wanted were relevant to a particular crime they were investigating. They also had to follow certain due process procedures,[6] so they couldn't just fish for information indiscriminately.

Then, came the Debt Collection Act in 1982, which restricted the federal agencies in the federal debt information they passed on to a private credit bureau. Subsequently, Congress enacted additional controls on computer matching in 1988. It amended the 1974 Privacy Act with the Computer Matching and Privacy Protection Act of 1988, which established that computer matching was not a routine use of data, so agencies couldn't simply swap data about individuals as in the past. Now, before an agency could take any adverse action against someone (such as denying employment benefits), the agency had to write up an agreement indicating the purpose for the match, state the records to be match, do a cost–benefit analysis of the match, and independently verify the results of the match. Though the agency could still match the same type of records, there were now procedural protections, so that individuals were now given better notice and had a right to a hearing before losing any benefits.[7]

In addition, a few other acts in the 1980s added protections in response to the new technologies and markets that developed in this period. Among them: the Cable Communications Policy Act of 1984, the Electronic Communications Privacy Act of 1986, and the Video Privacy Protection Act of 1988.

Yet, ironically, while these laws were passed to protect, other laws were passed taking away certain protections. For example, while the Privacy Act sought to prevent the social security number from becoming a national identifier by prohibiting agencies from requiring an individual's social security number to provide services or benefits, the 1986 Tax Reform Act made the use of this number more likely, since it required parents to obtain a social security number for all children over five to claim them as dependents on their tax returns.[8] At the same time, loopholes in these laws have permitted government and private industry to make further incursions on personal privacy. So these laws are really more an expression of policy ideals than what actually happens in practice.

With these laws as a backdrop, the struggle for financial privacy has continued on four key fronts: over consumer and credit protections, over bank privacy rights, over protecting assets from discovery and confiscation, and over insurance coverage.

Consumer and Credit Protections

The big problem with credit reports is they may be incorrect or released to the wrong people. Often credit cards end up being misused, when people obtain them fraudulently and use them for fraudulent purposes, such as running up charges on someone else's account.

One all-too-common complaint is the bureaucratic slipup, in which the wrong information is entered into a file, say because people have similar names or records are not updated. Then, the person with this incorrect data may not know the error exists. Also, clerks sometimes inaccurately give out information, at times because persuasive individuals, including investigators and crooks, convince them to tell them, sometimes using a pretext to do so.

Still another problem is that those who get the information for one purpose may sell it to someone else for another, such as to direct marketers who use it to make sales calls or send out pitch letters. And now, with the development of computer bulletin boards, on-line services, and the net, financial and credit information can be spread even more widely.

Beginnings

The battle for credit card privacy goes back to the late 1960s and 1970s when America began turning into a credit society. Today, we take credit cards and reports for granted. But before the credit card came into fashion in the late 1960s, credit privacy was much more controllable, since people who wanted credit generally went to a local bank, appealed to friends and relatives, or perhaps visited private loan companies and loan sharks. There was no huge independent credit industry, no huge bureaucracy for credit checks.

I remember very vividly when the credit "revolution" started, because in 1967 I worked in market research for a San Francisco ad agency, then called Foote, Cone and Belding, representing the newly formed California Bankcard Association. This group was made up of about forty banks that had joined together to support this new idea of a private credit card. The banks had found about forty thousand merchants around the state who would provide this credit, which would presumably attract more customers who would spend more money.

At the time, no one thought about the privacy implications. The big question was "Would it work?" Would enough merchants be willing to pay an extra percentage and handle the paperwork to accept these cards; and would enough consumers want to use these cards to make the system viable? I did research on the first commercials, which featured a customer going from store to store, with two or three columns of bankers in sober gray suits behind her. Meanwhile, the voiceover spoke about the power of shopping with the power of forty banks behind you. My job was to test out various claims about the card to learn the strongest selling points, such as "Easy to charge with no other credit," and "Don't have to carry large amounts of cash."

But there was little concern for privacy. The closest any claim came to hinting at the privacy implications of using a credit card was one that said that "a Master Charge card also serves as a handy credit reference." However, at the time, the focus was on how these cards would provide access to cash and credit, with the support of the West's largest banks and stores. No one gave much thought to how the credit card would contribute to growing data bases with information about consumers who had cards, what they spent, where they lived, or how they paid their bills. Nor did anyone seem to consider how credit card fraud would become a big growth industry of the 1970s, 1980s, and 1990s, leading to the privacy backlash against credit reporting and credit card fraud we are experiencing today.

Credit Cards and What Your Credit Report Says about You

The reason the privacy problems involved with credit have become so critical today is because the credit report has become a passport into today's economy. Except for those rare individuals using cash, it is hard not to function without others looking at our credit records for various purposes. For example, some common times people check is when you buy on credit, offer a check, open a bank account, buy or rent property, go into business with someone, or seek higher level employment (though credit information is ideally not supposed to be used for this information). In fact, today, if you try to pay large amounts in cash to get out of the credit reporting economy, say to buy a car or house, you will immediately arouse suspicions about the source of those funds. Maybe it sounds overly dramatic, but some people wonder about money from drugs or crime when they see large amounts of cash offered in payment for something.

Thus, it's hard not to have a credit report, which is a credit history of how you have been spending your money. Even if you don't have a single credit card, you probably still have a credit report. According to the Privacy Rights Clearinghouse, if you have opened a bank account, rented an apartment, bought a car, or have purchased something on the installment plan, someone has probably filed a credit report about you with one of the major credit bureaus.[9] The information in these reports is collected from various sources, including banks, utilities, credit card accounts, and includes your name variations, address, social security number, and employment information. It may even have details on your legal record, such as whether you have been married or divorced, have any arrests or convictions, or have ever gone bankrupt or have liens on any property.[10]

In turn, the credit report has become one of the most important personal references which is used to make life-altering decisions, such as whether you get the house, job, or insurance coverage. A key reason decision makers today rely on this is because this report has become so comprehensive and other references are uncertain in these highly mobile and transitory times. It's hard to believe how powerful this has become in just twenty-five years!

Unfortunately, however, the huge amount of data that is kept, the difficulty of checking all of it for accuracy, and the chance of misfiling data due to similar names or the slip of a keystroke or mouse, means that some mistakes are almost guaranteed to occur. Yet, when they do, consumers often encounter legal barriers that keep them from being fully compensated for any damages they suffer.

For example, according to the Fair Credit and Reporting Act, much adverse information is supposed to drop from the files with the passage of time, such as reports of judgments, accounts place for collection, and records of arrests and convictions, which have to be dropped after seven years. Consumers are also supposed to be notified when there are investigative reports, so they can learn what is in their files and make any necessary corrections. But consumers harmed by wrong information circulated by mistake have little recourse, since they can't bring defamation, invasion of privacy, or negligence actions unless they can show false information was spread about them "with malice or willful intent" to injure them, or that an agency did not make reasonable efforts to correct a false report, according to New York litigator Blair Fensterstock.[11]

However, consumers and privacy advocates seem to have better luck holding credit agencies responsible when these agencies or their personnel disclose information to the wrong person, use confidential information for an inappropriate purpose for which it wasn't gathered, or access data about them without proper authorization. But there are still lots of holes in the system, and it is often hard to gain redress or compensation when these leaks prove damaging. Even so, consumers and privacy advocates have been fighting back, sometimes successfully, sometimes not.

The "Who's Responsible?" Problem

The sheer difficulty of pursuing these cases for little return may be a reason few cases have worked their way up through the courts, though if you talk to almost anyone, you will hear horror stories of problems when the wrong information was incorrectly disclosed and acted upon. Unfortunately, it often can be difficult to pin the blame or determine damages, such as when a landlord doesn't rent you that terrific apartment because the credit report incorrectly shows you owe money. Can you actually hold the creditor that provided the wrong information responsible? It is one of those hard-to-prove cases with uncertain damages. Maybe you wouldn't have gotten the apartment or loan for other reasons. Thus, it's a difficult-to-win case.

The Default Is Yours

A key problem in these battles is holding those in the credit chain of command responsible when things go wrong, as Greg and Mary Henson found in the case of *Henson v. CSC Credit Services,* decided in September 1993. Greg's problem started after a judge incorrectly entered a judgment against him for about $3600. This occurred because Greg had bought a Camaro and sold it to his brother Jeff, who drew up a security agreement with the Cosco Federal Credit Union. But when Jeff subsequently didn't meet his payment schedule, Cosco took both Greg and Jeff to court. After it obtained a default judgment, the judge entered the judgment, only supposed to be against Jeff, against Greg, too. Though Greg contacted Cosco to correct their records and drop his name from the default judgment, Cosco didn't do so, until Greg filed suit against them. In the meantime, the two credit reporting agencies, Trans Union and CSC, picked up the information about the judgment and published it, so that Greg had credit problems. He was denied credit, had to pay more interest on loans, and, he claimed, suffered "public humiliation and embarrassment."

In his suit, Greg argued that Cosco and the two agencies were at fault, since they failed to correct their records in a timely manner, as required by the Fair Credit and Reporting Act. But he ran into the "who's responsible?" problem, since unfortunately, as the court noted, the report was not inaccurate, because the court did enter the judgment against Greg as well as Jeff. Moreover, the agencies only had to use "reasonable" procedures to insure "maximum accuracy." They didn't have to seek to discover or provide additional data about the clerk's incorrect entry, since the court felt that would be too much of a burden on the agencies. Instead, the court felt the agencies should be able "to rely on public records without extensive inquiries" into their accuracy.[12] So Henson's claim for damages fell through the "who's responsible?" crack.

It's True: True Reports Can Be Reported

In other cases, where consumers have protested the passing of true information from one organization to another in the credit checking chain, they have struck out. Raymond J. Francis, for example, discovered this when he sued Dun and Bradstreet in the *Francis v. Dun & Bradstreet* case, decided in February 1992. He sued for defamation, interference with prospective economic advantage, injurious falsehood, and emotional distress, because Dun & Bradstreet had passed on information in its credit report that suggested he was responsible for the bankruptcies of his two prior businesses.

Francis had not had a very successful business experience. In the 1970s, he had started a potato chips company, Crisp International, which went into bankruptcy in 1982. Soon after, he became president and chairman of the California Trim Plan, a diet business, which also landed in bankruptcy court in 1985. Unfortunately, Dun & Bradstreet knew about these failures, and though Francis asked the company not to mention the bankruptcies, since they were affecting his credit, Dun & Bradstreet refused and published the information anyway. However, legally, they were entitled to do so, since for credit purposes, Francis' past ventures, including his failures, were open for publication; he couldn't escape his past. If the information was true, no matter how unfavorable, Dun & Bradstreet could print it; there's no defamation in speaking the truth. Thus, Francis was unsuccessful in his suit for, as the court concluded: "Credit reports are sometimes unflattering, but they are necessary in modern society."[13]

In short, as a credit-using society, we need credit reports. They have become the economic equivalent of arrest records that can follow us forever. Thus, as much as we might like to put an unfortunate chapter from the past behind us and restore our good name, in many cases we can't.

Wrong Name, Wrong Number

However, while most collecting and sharing of true credit data is widely accepted for making credit related business decisions, if the information is wrong, for whatever reason and the victim reports this, it should be corrected. As a result, if the credit reporting agency doesn't take reasonable and timely actions to correct it, it can be held liable for damages.

That's what happened when Sherri Lynn McWilliams got mixed up with Sherri Lou Mitchell. Her life became a nightmare for a couple of years, because the credit reporting agency that collected the data wouldn't correct it in the case of *Mitchell v. Surety Acceptance Corporation*, decided in November 1993. The nightmare began when the United Bank of Grand Junction, Colorado, mistakenly disclosed Sherri *Lynn's* name to a woman named Sherri *Lou* McWilliams, who began to use Sherri *Lynn's* social security number and savings and checking account information to take money from her bank and engage in a series of business transactions, leaving Sherri Lynn with a trail of debts.

The trail started with an insufficient funds returned check for $88 which Sherri Lou passed at Safeway in December 1986. Safeway soon referred the item for collection to Surety, an Arizona debt collection agency, and after Surety failed to find Sherri Lou in the Phoenix area, in January 1989 it asked the TRW credit bureau to try to find her through skip tracing. Meanwhile, by December 1989, though TRW still hadn't found her, Sherri Lou surfaced again in a Phoenix auto accident, where she gave the investigating officer Sherri Lynn's social security number.

Soon after, accounts of this accident and Sherri Lou's bad check ended up on Sherri Lynn's credit report. When Sherri Lynn learned of these entries a couple of months later, she disputed them, but after TRW verified the Safeway check debt, Surety sent Sherri Lynn a demand letter asking her to repay this. Even though Sherri Lynn insisted: "I'm not Sherri Lou, so I'm not liable for the check," Surety continued to claim she was responsible, and showed no interest in reinvestigating the matter or deleting the information Sherri Lynn claimed was inaccurate. Instead, as the company tried to collect the debt, Sherri Lynn claimed that its agents "harassed, annoyed and ridiculed" her, told her "she would have no further problems" if she paid her debts, and accused her of lying. She found one agent, Tim West, who sent her the demand letter, especially offensive when she called him to try to put the matter right. When she explained that this other Sherri was using her social security number, that the stress was aggravating her MS condition, and that the mixup had cost her the chance to buy a house and get a job, so that she was beginning to feel "life was no longer worth living," he just laughed at her. As she told the court: "He did not believe a word I said. He only implied that I was lying by laughing and. . . . He obviously thought I had made up the entire story." Even when Sherri spoke to West's supervisor, that did no good either. His supervisor told Sherri the same thing—just pay up. Since neither of them believed her, they didn't check out her story or take the number of the police officers who had investigated the traffic accident and so could verify her story.

Eventually, the U.S. District Court in Colorado agreed that Sherri might be able to hold Surety liable for its agents' actions by showing that the company's conduct was "atrocious or utterly intolerable in a civilized community." So the court sent the case back to the jury to give Sherri a chance to show this and perhaps collect for her suffering if she could so convince the jury.[14]

Banks, Other Financial Institutions, and Privacy Rights

The privacy of bank records has become another battlefield over who owns the records—the individual providing the bank with financial information about himself, or the bank which has added this information to its own data base.

The roots of the current status of bank records and what banks can do goes back to 1970 when Congress passed the Bank Secrecy Act. Ironically, this Act was not really intended to promote bank secrecy but to make bank records available to the Secretary of the Treasury and help law enforcement agencies doing investigations.[15] In fact, the Act also did anything but promote "secrecy" because it contributed to compiling huge amounts of information about each customer, since it required banks to keep microfilmed copies of all transactions of $100 or more for at least five years. As a result, the banks made copies of all transactions, since it was less expensive to copy everything than to sort checks.

Then, in 1976, the privacy of bank records suffered another blow, when the courts ruled in the *United States v. Miller* case that the government could subpoena bank records of a customer's financial transactions without notifying the customer. In this case, Miller had been a moonshiner, distilling spirits without paying tax, and the decision against him gave the government access to banks anywhere. That's because the court deemed that depositor checks and records should be considered part of a commercial transaction, not a confidential communication.[16]

Afterwards, however, a storm of protest from legislators, consumer groups, and even some financial institutions led to a new Right to Financial Privacy Act in 1978. This provided that the government could only obtain records in financial institutions for specific legitimate purposes using certain procedures. In addition, this Act required the financial institutions to keep detailed records about any disclosures. For example, now, the Internal Revenue Service (IRS) couldn't simply secretly get a customer's records, but had to give the depositor fourteen days notice in which to object. If he did, there would be a hearing, and now the IRS had to get a favorable court decision to get the records. The one exception was if there was already court litigation between the government and a depositor. In that case the government could get the records without any special notice.[17]

Another controversy has been over whether the banks can release information to private parties, like credit agencies doing a credit check. Often banks do this as a matter of course when an individual agrees to a credit check by a potential creditor. But it is unclear if the bank can do this when it is not clear if the individual has actually consented or not.

Trent Hickson discovered this uncertainty when he sued his bank, Home Federal of Atlanta, for invading his privacy among other charges, in the case of *Hickson v. Home Federal of Atlanta*, decided in September 1992. The problem began in 1984, when Trent purchased some property in Georgia with a $64,000 loan from Homebanc, and gave Homebanc a promissory note. This included a security deed to the property, which permitted Homebanc to foreclose if Hickson should sell or transfer any part of the property without Homebanc's prior written consent. Unfortunately, after several years of leasing the property to various tenants, Hickson did transfer the property without consent, when he moved to New Jersey and transferred the property to a New Jersey corporation in 1990. After he did, Homebanc began to foreclose on the property, and when Hickson stopped making payments on the note, Homebanc reported this to a credit agency, which Hickson claimed, interfered with his ability to engage in business.

Had Hickson agreed to a credit check by another potential creditor, the disclosure would be fine. But since he hadn't, it wasn't clear whether the bank's release of financial information to a credit agency invaded his privacy or not, and there was no state law or court ruling that provided the answer. So the Georgia District Court sent the case back to the trial court to decide.[18]

One result of all this uncertainty is that some legislators have proposed legislation or amendments to laws to clarify what records financial institutions can release under what circumstances. Texas legislators, for instance, passed a law, dubbed the "Texas Financial Institutions Privacy Act,"[19] that provides financial institutions, from state and national banks to savings and loans (S&Ls), with guidelines on information they can disclose about their depositors, owners, borrowers, or customers. The act was designed to help the banks and S&Ls know what to do when they were asked for records by litigants or the government, while their customers wanted to keep their affairs private. Now, they could know how to respond appropriately and avoid liability for customer suits in releasing records.[20]

For example, the act specifies the procedures the banks and S&Ls should follow when they get a request, such as a subpoena for records in a case in litigation or in a criminal investigation. Generally, the bank or S&L has to produce these records, but it must follow the proper procedures, so there are only limited privacy protections. However, many of the procedures to be followed are not clear, according to two Texas lawyers, Leonard Plog and Don O'Bannon, Jr., writing about this act and similar acts in other states, such as Louisiana, Maine, and Nevada. Also, as they point out, there are few safeguards for the depositor if information is disclosed inappropriately without consent, since there is no penalty provided in the act, as in other states with financial privacy acts. Thus, there is little remedy for this disclosure, apart from hiring an attorney to initiate expensive legal procedures, such as a motion to quash or for a protective order to keep the records from being released.[21] So for all practical purposes, there is very little privacy in one's financial records in a bank or S&L.

The Danger of Having Assets Discovered and Confiscated

In some cases, the lack of privacy protections for assets can spell personal disaster, in that, once discovered, these assets—money, stocks and bonds, real estate, and other financial assets—can be confiscated by the government. This has occurred because of recent federal legislation and legislation in some states permitting law enforcement officers to confiscate funds and property believed to be earnings from the sale of drugs. In fact, in many jurisdictions, the funds can be taken before a person has been tried or even charged with the crime; just the suspicion of drug earnings—say, due to a tip from an informer—sometimes has been enough. Then it has been up to the individual whose property has been seized to *prove* it hasn't been used in drug dealing. And in some cases, individuals only marginally involved with drugs have had property taken—such as the mother whose son, without her knowledge, is selling drugs to a few friends in her home.

Even recent laws requiring hearings before real estate is seized have done little to stem the tide of confiscations when police and federal agents have been able to find personal assets. The laws often just slow down the process; then, after the person explains his or her side of the story, the officials still take the property.

Some of the more poignant cases have been turning up in the papers from time to time, like the case in Placerville, California, mentioned in an earlier chapter, where Bryon Stamate's property was seized after he grew a few marijuana plants for a longtime companion who was suffering from terminal cancer, and since she didn't want to testify against him, she committed suicide. Eventually, after a long and drawn-out legal proceeding and trial, at which he was found guilty, he did get his home back, but he lost about $25,000 in fines and costs.[22]

Meanwhile, a publication called *The Financial Privacy Report* edited by Michael Ketcher has been monitoring these confiscation cases around the country. It reports that over $1.2 billion worth of cars, homes, bank accounts, and businesses were confiscated in 1992 alone from people not yet convicted of anything, up from about $700,000 confiscated in 1991—an increase of about 70 percent.[23] Those targeted have included not only those suspected or accused of growing, manufacturing, or selling drugs, but their landlords and the lawyers representing them (supposedly because their fees have come from drug money). On another front, the *Report* reports that bills have been introduced to Congress to extend these seizure laws to medical professionals who don't comply with federal regulations, such as those accused of Medicare fraud; to computer bulletin board operators who might unknowingly have terrorists using their boards for criminal activity; and to international businesspeople and investors who might obtain money from drug sales.[24]

One of the most dramatic examples of those caught in the web of these police raids and confiscations is Don Scott of Los Angeles County, killed in a police raid. Scott, a 61-year-old retiree, woke up early one morning in October 1992 to find twenty-six DEA agents, L.A. County sheriffs, and National Park officers pounding down his door. As his wife ran downstairs, she confronted angry men with guns pointed at her and pleaded: "Please, don't shoot me. Don't kill me." But it was too late for Don. When he came out of his upstairs bedroom with a gun over his head, the police screamed at him to lower his weapon, and as he did, they shot him dead. What provoked all this commotion was that the police were searching for marijuana, which one officer claimed to have spotted from a helicopter high above Scott's ranch. They never found any marijuana, but they still seized the ranch while they checked. The case received so much publicity that Scott's widow got the house back after no marijuana was discovered. But Scott was dead, and the police appear to have gotten off without any penalties, since no charges were ever filed against the police by California prosecutors.[25]

Mrs. Eula Martin's children and grandchildren were similarly unlucky, though they just lost their property, not their house, according to *Financial Privacy Report* editor Mike Ketcher. Their saga through the justice system began when the police accused Mrs. Eula Martin, a 69-year-old grandmother from Bakersfield, California, of drug dealing. Though she did not live with her children and was not involved in any business with them, legitimate or illegitimate, the police went after the property of her children and grandchildren. Soon after they charged Eula, the police confiscated a beauty parlor that belonged to her daughter, who live in Petaluma, California, over 200 miles away. They also took over the businesses that belonged to Eula's two grown grandsons, who lived in different cities. One lost his concrete-cutting business, the other lost his construction and tour boat businesses. The officers claimed that these relatives helped to launder money for Eula, and then took away the books for the family's construction business. As a result, the family members had no way to prove they had paid for the confiscated cars, home, business equipment, and other property with legitimate funds, until they paid $5000 to copy their records. The family eventually got most of their property back, but only after three years of expensive and time-consuming courtroom battles.[26]

Recently, the outcry over some of these more excessive confiscation cases has resulted in some court decisions to protect people's property, when they haven't yet been charged or convicted of anything. For example, according to *The Financial Privacy Report,* in June 1992, the U.S. Supreme Court ruled in the *Austin v. U.S.* case, that seizing property totally out of proportion to the severity of the alleged offense might violate the Eighth Amendment protection against "excessive fines." But in practice, that doesn't mean much change for most confiscations, since the Court didn't clarify how much property confiscation is too much. Then, too, once someone's property is seized, he or she still has to post a bond—typically 10 percent of the value of the seized property, and has to hire a good forfeiture lawyer to fight to get his or her property back, which can be a very expensive undertaking. Another legal hurdle is that the individual has just ten to thirty days to file a legal challenge, and during this period is in the difficult position of being forced out of the house, losing access to funds in seized bank accounts, and if in business, having the business placed under government wraps.[27] Thus, once any assets are discovered and seized, getting them back can be a long expensive procedure if the individual can even get them back at all.

"Most people find the ordeal so arduous, tedious, and expensive," says Michael Ketcher, editor of *The Financial Privacy Report* "that they just throw up their hands in disgust, let the cops have the property, and get on with their lives the best they can." Indeed, as Mr. Ketcher points out, "the vast majority of these cases are probably below $10,000 to $50,000, and at that size of a loss, it's not worth the money it takes to hire a lawyer and fight the case."

The Supreme Court did try to provide some additional protections in December 1993 in its ruling on the *U.S. v. James Daniel Good Real Property* case, in which it ruled that a hearing was required before the government can seize any real estate. But the ruling still doesn't provide any protections to nonreal property seizures, such as of bank accounts, stock brokerage accounts, mutual funds, cash, and other property. As a result, according to *The Financial Privacy Report,* there are over 5000 of these nonreal estate property seizures each week, which adds up to about 250,000 seizures a year.[28]

Thus, if the government or law enforcement officials can find your assets and has reason to suspect criminal activity, even if incorrect, they can potentially take those assets, either before or after a hearing. Then it can take months, if not years, and much expense to get them back, if ever.

Keeping Your Assets Private—and Protecting Them from Being Confiscated

All these developments—the huge amount of credit data collected, the leaks in the system, the ability of the government and litigants to get personal bank and S&L records, the possibility of having assets discovered and confiscated due to suspicions of criminal activity—mean there is really very little financial privacy and protection.

As a result, some individuals have taken special steps to protect assets, and a number of organizations and publications have grown up to help them do so. One of the most influential of these publications is *The Financial Privacy Report,* which provides readers with a monthly bulletin of recent privacy news. It highlights laws and rulings that can affect their assets and offers suggestions on what readers can do conceal and/or protect their assets.

For example, in response to a rash of seizures of homes and other property for selling or growing small quantities of dope, or having a relative doing this, *The Financial Privacy Report* provided a series of tips on how to shield real estate from police seizure. Some tips: "Don't own, rent . . . Don't allow any illegal activity on your property.. . . . Borrow heavily against your property. . . . Don't tell even the tiniest, little white lie on your mortgage applications. . . . Make sure you can document the source of your mortgage payments." Then, the article went on to suggest what landlords could do to make sure their tenants weren't involved in illegal activities and how to evict them if they were.[29]

Then, too, other suggestions include ways to shield one's assets from lawsuits, a major concern in a litigious society. "My number one rule of financial privacy," says Ketcher, "is to say as little as possible to anyone seeking financial information, including stockbrokers, financial planners, and bankers.[30] He also suggests using a mail drop to discourage would-be litigants and government investigators,[31] and keeping where you live ambiguous.

He cites the example of one man who concealed where he lived and what he owned from just about everyone. He used a series of mail drops in various states, registered his car in one state, had a personal bank account in another state, and had his business mail sent to still another state. And sometimes, he used a few foreign mail drops and occasionally sported an alias, to keep anyone thinking of finding or following him away.[32]

Then, too, in various issues, *The Financial Privacy Report* has recommended using a low-profile investment approach to avoid stimulating the envy and possible attack of not only vicious criminals but of IRS auditors and litigants. As editor Mike Ketcher observed in the publication's maiden issue:

> A low profile will not only help you avoid tax audits and protect your assets from lawsuits, but it will also protect you—and your family—from vicious criminals. . . . We are living in an age of envy. It is an age in which wealth—or any kind of advantage—is not merely coveted, it is resented. It is resented to the point of destruction.
>
> [Thus] it's no longer safe to ostentatiously display your wealth. . . . It's also unwise to have your name and address in too many public records.
>
> [Also] envy pervades our system of civil justice. People now sue at the drop of a hat, and large financial settlements are granted. . . . Just as money or property can make you the target of vicious criminals, or a rapacious tax system, it can also make you a target of a lawsuit.[33]

Some may find such measures like papering over one's identity with a mail drop, staying out of the public records, and maintaining unclear living arrangements extreme. But as we become more and more a high-tech, information-saturated, media suffused, target marketed, surveillance society, more and more people are seeking some measure of anonymity. They are looking for ways to shield themselves and their assets from the various incursions that have become a generally inescapable part of living in the modern day world.

In fact, Michael Ketcher feels things are getting worse. As he commented: "The U.S. government is trying to criminalize financial privacy. They are using the threat of drug dealers and other criminals as an excuse to control and monitor the rest of us." How? According to Ketcher,

> "It is no longer sufficient to simply pay your taxes. You must also file all sorts of forms, showing virtually every substantial transaction and business dealing you are involved in. And there are huge penalties for failing to file some of these forms. Say if an individual takes $10,000 in cash or monetary instruments out of the country and doesn't file a Form 4790 to report it, that person could not only have the $10,000 seized, but also be liable for a criminal fine of up

> to $100,000, and even face a possible prison sentence. There may be no other crime involved. Simply failing to file the form is a criminal action in itself.[34]

Unfortunately, when these financial privacy cases end up in court, those trying to protect themselves often can't win. Another difficulty is that litigation can make one's entire financial life an open book. That's what William Cook found when he guaranteed the payment of an Ohio funeral home's bill for his son's funeral in the case of *Cook v. Carrigan & Mains Funeral Home,* decided in March 1992. When he didn't pay, the funeral home took him to court. Later, when they tried to collect and got a court order requiring him to come to court to submit to a debtor's examination, he objected, claiming the examination invaded his privacy and Fourth Amendment rights. But the court turned him down, noting that a judgment creditor has a right by law to make such inquiries to find out about the debtor's property, income, or other means of satisfying the judgment if he hasn't paid.[35]

In reaction to these developments in which the courts, Congress, and law enforcement haven't provided much protection for people battling IRS auditors, litigators, and others who collect financial information, there has been a growing search for other forms of protection. According to Mike Ketcher, many middle-class people are taking matters into their own hands, seeking more secure methods. The Swiss Bank account is just one of a growing number of alternatives. At one time, people used to think of Swiss banks as the destination of choice for depositing secret assets. But now, all sorts of foreign offshore banks have sprung up that are not only "tax havens" but a place to protect financial privacy, and the small offshore nest-egg is becoming more and more popular. A key reason, says Mike Ketcher, is because "an individual U.S. taxpayer isn't required to report their foreign bank accounts if the total of their foreign financial accounts remains below $10,000 throughout the year."

Meanwhile, a whole cottage industry of special books, reports, and newsletters on techniques for protecting privacy have sprung up since the late 1970s. They describe in more detail all of these strategies for avoiding police seizures, shielding assets from the IRS, keeping bank and credit records more private, putting valuables in private and safe places. These resources and publications have become part of the growing industry of protecting personal financial assets in an era of big government, big business, and Big Brother.

The Battle for Insurance: Who Pays in These Privacy Cases?

So who pays for all this litigation over invasion of privacy claims? Numerous insurance companies have ended up in court over such questions, when they have resisted being involved in privacy litigation or paying if an insuree loses. In turn, some insurees have fought their own insurance companies, claiming the insurer isn't doing enough to fight for his or her claim or is settling too low.

Close to a dozen cases ended up in the appeals and district courts in 1992 and 1993, and undoubtedly many more are still in their early stages. Generally, these cases seem to come down to reading the bottom line on the insurance contract—does the insurer provide coverage for invasion of privacy claims or not? Commonly, at least in these cases, there is no coverage, and so the claimant generally loses in court.

For example, the Coit Drapery Cleaners and their manager in San Mateo County, California, discovered this when they sued their insurer, after the insurer wouldn't defend or pay compensation, when a former employee charged that the manager had sexually harassed her and wrongly fired her in the case of *Coit Drapery Cleaners v. Sequoia Insurance Company,* decided in May 1993. There was no coverage since the court of appeals found these "intentional acts" and the employer's insurance policy excluded such acts. So the cleaners and their manager had a no-win case.[36]

Similarly, employer Steve Tarris and Comprehensive Health Care Associates found they had no coverage either when several women sued him and the company for sexual harassment, sexual assault, sexual discrimination, invasion of privacy, and other wrongs in the case of *Old Republic Insurance Company v. Comprehensive Health Care Associates,* decided in September 1993. The Old Republic and Unigard Security Insurance Companies refused to defend them in these lawsuits or pay when they lost. Here too the California Appeals Court agreed there was no coverage, since all of the claims charged against the company were specifically excluded from both policies.[37]

Just about the only time the insurance companies have had to pay in these invasion of privacy cases is when the agreement specifically says so. That's what happened in Pennsylvania, when the Sun Insurance Company had to cover two physicians, Kakkadasm Sampathacar and

Pannathpur Jayalakshmi, after they lost a suit by a former patient Kathleen Golden for invasion of privacy and breach of a confidential relationship, after they did a chemical face peel to remove wrinkles in the case of *Sampathacar v. The Sun Insurance Company*, decided July 1992. The chemical peel itself was fine, but then they permitted photographs and facts about her to be published in a newspaper ad without her permission. She objected and sued successfully. But did Sun have to pay? In this case, the policy specifically stated the company would cover any loss where the insured had to pay due to a personal injury, including an invasion of privacy, and there were no limits of coverage stated in the policy. Thus, the insurance company had a duty to defend, and if it lost, to pay the bill, whatever it was.[38]

Likewise, the International Insurance Company had to cover some claims against the city of Birmingham, Michigan, including invasion of privacy claims, because the policy covered this in *Guaranty National Insurance Company v. International Insurance Company,* decided in June 1993. The city incurred these expenses after Richard Rosenbaum and two others in his company sued the city and several city police officers and prosecutors for conspiring to harass them in making a false arrest, as well as malicious prosecution, interfering with their business, and invading their privacy from 1981 to 1982, since they believed the company was involved in criminal activity. The jury agreed the plaintiffs were harassed, awarding them about $3 million in damages, and the city paid them a $1,250,000 settlement. However, when the city tried to collect from its insurance company, International Insurance tried to get out of paying its share, claiming the city wasn't covered for these claims, leading to the suit filed by the city's other insurance company. But eventually, the circuit court said International did have to pay, since the policy did not exclude an intrusion into the private affairs of others. So, because the courts generally construe these insurance exclusion clauses in favor of the insured, the courts agreed that the city and its other insurance company could collect.[39]

Thus, generally if the insurance policy says so, you are covered for invasion of privacy claims; if it says you aren't you're not; and if it doesn't say anything or it's unclear whether you are covered or not, you probably are, since contracts when unclear are generally read by the courts to favor the least powerful party—in this case, the insured. These court cases basically come down to reading the policy to determine if the insurance company has to pay or not.

Notes

1. Jerry Berman and Janlori Goldman, "A Federal Right of Information Privacy: The Need for Reform," *Washington, D.C.*, Benton Foundation (1989), 20–21.
2. Blair C. Fensterstock, "The Public and the Fair Credit Reporting Act," *Privacy and Publicity,* edited by Theodore R. Kupferman, Wesport, CT: Meckler, 1990,1–13; 2.
3. Berman and Goldman, 13–14.
4. *United States v. Miller,* 425 U.S. 345 (1976).
5. Berman and Goldman, 15.
6. Ibid., 21.
7. Ibid., 20–21.
8. Ibid., 16.
9. "How Private Is My Credit Report," *Fact Sheet No. 6* (November 1992), San Diego, CA: Privacy Rights Clearing House, Center for Public Interest Law, University of San Diego.
10. "How Private is my Credit Report," Fact Sheet No. 6, November 1992, San Diego, CA: Privacy Rights Clearing House, Center for Public Interest Law, University of California, San Diego.
11. Blair C. Fensterstock, "The Public and the Fair Credit Reporting Act," *Privacy and Publicity,* 1–13, 2.
12. *Henson v. CSC Credit Services,* 830 F. Supp. 1204, 1993 U.S. Dist. Lexis 12700, 1–6.
13. *Francis v. Dun & Bradstreet,* 4 Cal.Rptr.2d 361 (Cal.App. 4 Dist. 1992) 362–65.
14. *Mitchell v. Surety Acceptance Corporation,* 1993 U.S. Dist, Lexis 16924, 1–16.
15. Roy L. Moore, "The 1978 Right to Financial Privacy Act and U.S. Banking Law," *Privacy and Publicity,* 187–207; 189.
16. *United States v. Miller.*
17. Moore, 190–205.
18. *Hickson v. Home Federal of Atlanta,* 805 F. Supp. 1567 (N.D. Ga. 1992) 1569–74.
19. More technically, the act is called the "Adverse Claims to Deposits—Disclosure as to Amount Deposited—Subpoenas and Production" Act.
20. Leonard H. Plog II and Don T. O'Bannon, Jr., "Texas Financial Institutions and the Consumer's Right to Privacy," *Texas Tech Law Review,* 24 (1993): 831–67; 833–35.
21. Plog and O'Bannon, 835–36, 842–43.
22. Interview with Ed Rosenthal.
23. *The Financial Privacy Report,* 3 (July 1993): 1.

24. Ibid., 2 (November 1992): 1–2.
25. Ibid., 3 (July 1993): 1.
26. Interview with Mike Ketcher, editor, *The Financial Privacy Report,* April, 1994.
27. *The Financial Privacy Report,* July 1993,The 2–3.
28. Ibid., 14 (January 1994): 1.
29. Ibid., 3–5.
30. Ibid., 3 (June 1993): 1–4.
31. Ibid., 3 (April 1993): 1.
32. *The Financial Privacy Report,* 3 (June 1993): 1–2.
33. *The Financial Privacy Report,* 1 (August 1991): 1–3.
34. Author interview with Mike Ketcher, June 1994.
35. *Cook v. Carrigan & Mains Funeral Home,* 607 N.E.2d 466 (Ohio App. 2 Dist. 1992), 467–68.
36. *Coit Drapery Cleaners, Inc. v. Sequoia Insurance Company,* 18 Cal.Rptr.2d 692 (Cal.App. 1 Dist. 1993).
37. *Old Republic Insurance Company v. Comprehensive Health Care Associates,* 2 F.3d 105, 1993 U.S. App. Lexis 23747, 1.
38. *Sampathacar v. The Sun Insurance Company,* 25 Phila. 593, 1992 Phila. Cty. Rptr. Lexis 136, decided 21 July 1992, 14, 17.
39. *Guaranty National Insurance Company v. International Insurance Company,* 994 F.2d 1280 (7th Cir. 1993), 1282–85.

Chapter 14

The Selling of Personal Privacy

Personal privacy has become a mushrooming business, resulting in all kinds of products and services. For those trying to learn about others, some popular products include sleuthing equipment, on-line searching services, and personal phone and address records, especially popular with telemarketers and direct mail companies. In response, those trying to protect themselves have a whole range of products and services, too, including mail drops, call blocking devices, and services that ask direct mail organizations to remove their client's name from a mailing list.

Generally, such battles are occurring in the media and in the realm of public opinion, rather than in court, as complaints against a particular company are aired and consumers sometimes vote or threaten to vote with their pocketbooks. Then, if the public and media protest is strong enough, the company using or planning to use a particular marketing approach will back down.

That's what occurred when Lotus, the giant software firm, planned to put consumer data on disk and sell it to direct marketers, so they could better target prospects. But the public outcry was so great that Lotus feared a backlash against its other products, so it didn't introduce the product in the market.

The other major battle arena has been in the legislatures in many states and in the offices of state officials charged with establishing and implementing consumer policies. As a result, due to these earlier battles, based on extensive lobbying, politicking, and media/public input in the late 1980s and early 1990s, the basic guidelines governing the telemarketing industry have been established regulating how and when marketers can call or send mail, what sources they can use for marketing data, and how they can avoid harassing and invading the privacy of those they contact. So far, just about the only types of cases that have ended up in court are those where a customer has a conflict in a retail store, say because employees were snooping on her as she dressed or because a store gave out embarrassing information about her.

Shop Watch

Today shopping under surveillance has become commonplace, as storeowners seek to protect themselves from shoplifting and discourage robberies with videocameras. As a result, now both overt and covert videocameras are very common in stores, banks, and shopping malls, and generally it is perfectly legal to watch and make videotapes. But sometimes even customer watching can go too far, when it goes beyond making sure the customer is there to look or buy, and not commit a crime, to watching for purposes of enjoyment.

Typically, in these overzealous watching cases, attractive women, either customers or store employees or both, are the victims of overly watchful employees. As one former security guard at J.C. Penney's told a newspaper reporter after a former employee sued Penney's for this problem: "I would say it's everywhere. It's very common that you have younger men working with younger attractive women, and there's a little bit of voyeurism when you have these cameras set up. It makes it very easy, especially when you have very lax supervision."[1]

Yet, while such peeping employee cases may be rare, the power of in-store surveillance equipment is so great with its power to zoom in and out and provide extreme closeups, (e.g., read the serial number on a dollar bill), that even when customers aren't getting undressed, the equipment can potentially be used for other invasion of privacy purposes.

Needless to say, the stores, as much as the customers want to stop the misuse of this surveillance equipment, because if customers think they are being watched inappropriately by snooping employees, the stores not only risk potential lawsuits, but the loss of customers.

Furthermore, this concern with security can result in problems if the store too enthusiastically spreads information about a customer it believes may be engaged in illegal activity. While it may be fine to warn other stores so they can protect themselves against such customers, if they spread the news too far, or are wrong, there could be damages for defamation and invasion of privacy.

This is what happened at a Texas mall, in the case of *Mitre v. Brooks Fashion Stores,*[2] decided in August 1992, and *Mitre v. Le Plaza Mall,*[3] decided in July 1993. Gonzalo Mitre and Monica Canseco were shopping with Olga Verduzco at the La Plaza Mall, when Verduzco attempted to pay for clothing with some hundred dollar bills. Believing the bills were counterfeit, a store clerk advised a mall security officer, who held Verduzco while a local police officer called a local financial institution to check if the bills were counterfeit. Though the bills weren't, before the officer discovered this, the mall security officer got photos of Mitre and Canseco from Verduzco, made copies, and distributed them to the shops in the mall, advising them that Mitre and Canseco were passing counterfeit bills.[4] In turn, many shop owners posted flyers accusing them of passing counterfeit bills in their shops.

That's what got them into trouble. The Texas Court of Appeals agreed that it was an invasion of privacy and defamation to post the flyers and the stores were negligent in doing so, particularly since they displayed the photos prominently so that any shopper, not just their own employees, could see them. Also, they told anyone who asked that the people in the photos were passing counterfeit bills. Making things worse, many people who knew Mitre and Canseco saw these photos and heard these accusations.[5]

Additionally, the court felt the mall could be negligent, even be shown to have acted with malice. Although the mall had a right to spread the flyers around to its stores, the problem was that the mall security officer who went around distributing the photos only commented that she believed counterfeit bills were being circulated. But she did not state that she believed and had no reason to doubt that Mitre and Canseco were the ones passing the bills. As a result, it wasn't quite clear what she really believed, so she left the impression they were guilty when they weren't. So again, Mitre and Canseco might be able to show they had been defamed and suffered emotional distress due to the negligent, even malicious, actions of the mall.[6] In both cases, it would be up to the jury to decide if the stores and mall were actually liable and if so, of what, and what the damages would be.

The Dynamics of Creating New Privacy Products: The Struggle to Reveal and Conceal

Thus, as efforts to both reveal what others are doing and protect privacy have become so much a part of everyday life, both the snooping and privacy protection industries have grown in tandem. This process is like the evolving ability of liars and deceivers, which I wrote about in my book *The Truth About Lying.*[7] Researchers have discovered that the ability to deceive helps an organism survive, so the genetic capacity for deception has evolved through natural selection. As psychologist Charles Bond and his co-authors note, "for hundreds of generations those who are the most cunning have left the most offspring, while those who are less cunning have left fewer, so the ability to deceive has increased in the gene pool."[8] Concurrently, the ability to detect deceivers has evolved too, with the better detectors having a survival advantage as well (such as the wilier wolf being better able to find the rabbit trying to hide). But the ability to deceive has always remained just a little ahead, while the detectors keep trying to keep up—like the concealers and revealers in the privacy game.

Much the same kind of process has occurred in the privacy arena as more sophisticated technologies to reveal what people are doing or protect privacy have developed, with the same kind of leapfrogging effect. A similar process goes on in the legislative and courtroom arenas over what can be legally used to reveal or conceal.

Two recent examples, to be discussed further in Chapter 16 on high-tech privacy, are the hotly fought caller ID and cryptography battles. In the caller ID battles, the ID advocates want caller ID so that people receiving calls can see a display indicating who is calling, which could discourage harassment or criminal calls, while ID opponents argue that the ID display will invade the privacy of the callers by revealing their numbers. One solution in some states approving caller ID has been caller ID line or per call blocking, so the caller can block out his or her number, and then the recipient can choose whether to receive blocked-out calls. The result has been another layer of technology in the struggle between revealing or concealing information. And more are on the way, such as callers using phone patches and surrogate numbers to conceal their unblocked identity.

Meanwhile, in the cryptography arena, as designers of cryptographic codes and devices have tried to improve these so users can be more secure in sending information privately to others. But in reaction, as they do, others have been seeking ways to break these codes to get this information—say through industrial espionage to obtain secret product development information. But then these code-breaking efforts have led to efforts to create even securer encryption devices.

The New Privacy Products

Given this growing interest in protecting privacy and revealing information, there are a growing number of catalogs and specialty stores offering both snooping and privacy protection products. These are available both to the professional in the field and to the individual who wants to put up spying or detection equipment around his home or office. Additionally, firms offer all sorts of alarms and security perimeters to keep invaders out, or notify police or security firms if they get in.

It has become very much a spy-eat-spy world, and when I attended one of the many security industry shows (this one by the American Society for Industrial Security), I saw hundreds of booths with the latest in industrial and home security devices. Among them were super zoom cameras—ideal for detecting shoplifters and thieving employees, or for observing someone's house for evidence of illegal or fraudulent activities, such as strenuous physical activity by someone filing a claim for disabilities. I also saw all sorts of audio and computer register devices for monitoring sounds in a room and picking up E-mail messages sent by computer. Plus there were many booths for organizations and training institutes for people in this burgeoning industry.

Here I'll briefly highlight some of the major new privacy products which are becoming more technologically sophisticated each year, like ever-improving weapons, used by the opposing sides in the privacy war to better conceal or reveal information.

Untappable Phones. These phones are growing in popularity in all sorts of industries—finance, medical, chemicals, airlines, law, insurance, automotive, and colleges and universities. They have been developed since conventional phones with wires are simple to tap, and the information traveling on microwave, satellite, facsimile, and cellular phones are easily picked up too. Thus, the new strategy is increasingly to use ciphering systems to preserve confidentiality, or to use untappable phones, with a built-in encryption system.

Supersensitive Cameras. These not only zoom in for closeups, but use high performance infrared sensitive film for taking photos in low light and infrared illuminated situations. Some cameras are especially small, so you can conceal them in your hand or a pocketbook; others are designed with a prism lens so it looks like you are pointing the camera in one direction but you take the picture in another. And all sorts of concealment devices are available to hide the camera, such as attractive indoor and outdoor housings for cameras, so unwary visitors can't tell a camera is watching. For example, what looks like an ordinary lighting fixture may have a smoky dome concealing a camera. Some look like an attractive artwork on the wall. Other popular designs for concealing cameras include video recording briefcases, large wall clocks, and smoke detectors. Cameras can even be concealed in ties and tie clips, fenceposts, air vents, and garbage can handles, say to film someone in an alley.

Optical Card Systems for Storing Data. These small wallet-sized cards are like walking books, with about one thousand times as much information as the old credit card. In fact, these small cards can not only store up to about eight hundred standard typewritten pages as of 1990, more today, but they can store images, such as photographs, drawings, fingerprints, X rays, anything that can be put into alphanumeric or digital form. Besides being used for access systems to determine who gains entry where, they are being used to contain a person's complete personal medical history, employment data, and other personal information. So, if you think you have problems when you lose a credit card, consider what will happen when you lose one of these.

Audio Listening and Data Recording Devices. Besides the standard bugging and detector devices to get rid of wiretaps on phones or bugs planted in the rooms (usually illegal for individuals to install), there are all kinds of audio enhancement equipment. For example, you can use a supersensitive microphone to hear through hard surfaces, like walls, and with long-distance microphones and audiotelescopes (a parabolic mike that looks like a small satellite dish), you can pick up sounds from a distance, up to one hundred yards and beyond with some systems. Then, too, if you want to know everyone who was called from your phone, you can obtain phone logging devices that make a record of all outgoing calls including number called, time, date, and length of call (often used by employers who want to check if employees are making private calls on company time). Or for extra concealment when you talk, there are telephones with built-in voice changers, so you can disguise your voice by making it sound higher or lower. You can also get a scrambler that attaches to almost any phone, even pay phones, and electronically converts normal speech into unintelligible scrambled sounds, so only someone with another scrambler can figure out what you are saying.

Tap and Bug Detection Devices. Want protection against all of these tapping and bugging devices? There are tap and bug detectors, even portable ones you can take with you to "sniff out" hidden transmitters in homes, offices, cars, and other rooms. The detector picks up the signal coming from a wall or appliance. Then using headphones to listen to the signal source while you tap on the wall or play music in the room, you can determine if this is a real bug, rather than just a local radio station reflected by a wire in the wall. If real, you will hear the sound of your tapping or music through the headphones.

Psychological Tests, Drug Testing Programs, Personal Profile Reports. These tests and reports are sold in a variety of versions by different companies to give the employer a detailed picture of the employee before or after hiring. While there have been numerous fights about what's legal, discussed in Chapter 5, generally employers can use these tests, and more and more are doing so. Some administer the tests themselves, others use an outside testing service such as Equifax, Stanton, the London House, and Baker Systems, which provide the materials and conduct the test. Some of these outside services also provide a detailed credit report with information that might impact on job performance, such as a list of creditors and how financial obligations are met.

Personal Monitoring Equipment. These include items like tags and brackets that are placed directly on the person's body or clothing to indicate where he or she is. Still, not all personal monitoring devices are necessarily invasive, though they do keep track of what people are doing. Sometimes, these devices can be personally freeing or a source of safety in certain circumstances. For example, take the tag attached like a wristwatch to a patient with a tendency to wander. As long as the patient remains where he is supposed to be, the system to which it is linked electronically remains silent. But once he goes through a door he shouldn't and wanders off, it sounds the alarm so he can be quickly retrieved. The advantage of using such a device is that before he wanders one doesn't have to restrict or personally observe him. This technique is also used on infants to detect when someone is trying to abduct them from a hospital or a home.

Unique "Eye" and Other Identifiers. Besides fingerprinting and DNA, the privacy industry is creating other unique personal identifiers through a technology called "biometrics" identification. One method is using the "eye" as an identifier. It's claimed to be more accurate than fingerprinting, since the chances of a duplicate eye pattern are one in a million using one eye, or one in a trillion using both eyes. The way the technique works is you peer into an eyepiece device; then the system compares the pattern in your retina to those of others in the system to determine who you are. Another new method is the hand identifier. You stick your hand in a hand-reading device that determines if the pattern on your hand matches one that is previously enrolled in the system. Commonly, these techniques are used by large companies for access control and to determine employee time and attendance.

Special Celebrity and Executive Protection. In today's dangerous fishbowl age, celebrities, top executives, and other VIPs are increasingly using special security and privacy protection services to protect them from stalkers, kidnappers, and overly zealous fans and protestors. Besides providing security guards for day-to-day protection and at special events, these companies also analyze threats from cranks and design a response strategy to protect the VIP. Since VIPs often travel extensively, these companies commonly have contacts all over the world. Then, too, some of these companies provide PR services, since VIPs may need the help of PR people to bury an unfavorable story.

Products to Create Privacy in a Non-Private World. Still other products—many in the gift and novelty category—are designed to provide a feeling of privacy in an increasingly less private world. One example is what one company calls "Cubicle Cues," message cards for people who don't have a private office, just a cubicle or desk in a larger space. The cards are designed to give them the sense of control and privacy that comes with such an office, since the employee puts up the appropriate message outside his or her cubicle or on his or her desk, indicating the desire to be contacted or not (for example, signs that say "door closed," "door is open," or that specify when the person will be available). A key reason for using these cards, according to Stacey Wolf of Atlanta, Georgia, who designed them, is that, by creating worker privacy, these signs help to improve productivity and morale.[9]

Privacy Protection Services: Mail Drops and Private Phone Lines. The mail drop and voice mail services are booming, too, partly because they offer convenience—and for many, because of the privacy they provide. There are thousands of mail drops, from franchised operations like Mail Boxes, USA, to local operations; and a key privacy advantage is that, barring a subpoena, private mail drops don't have to give out addresses, including business addresses (which the post office does). Also, voice mail services not only give the aura of having an office, but can be a barrier against someone knowing and calling one's home number or using that number to access other information stored on a data base by home number.

Organizations, Training Programs, Publications, and Catalogs of Materials in the Security/Privacy Industry. As the industry grows, so does the number of organizations, training programs, magazines, newsletters, and journals, some of which are international. There's a detailed list in the Appendix.

Among the major privacy organizations are: Privacy International, which debates current privacy issues and recommends policies; the Electronic Frontier Foundation, in the forefront of fighting for civil liberties on the net; the U.S. Privacy Council, a coalition of individuals and groups seeking to strengthen the right of privacy; and the Privacy Rights Clearing House, which collects information on privacy issues, including current federal and California legislation.

As for the major security organizations, these include: the American Society for Industrial Security, the largest association of security professionals with over 20,000 members; Asisnet, a computerized briefing service that summarizes new security stories; and the National Computer Security Association.

The major privacy publications, most cited in this book, include: *The Privacy Journal, The Financial Privacy Report, The Privacy Times,* and several electronic publications delivered by E-mail—*The Computer Privacy Digest* and *The Privacy Forum Digest.* The growing number of security publications includes: the *International Security Review*, featuring the latest information on high-tech security devices; the *Security Law Newsletter*, which includes reports on lawsuits involving alleged lapses in security or privacy invasions from security measures like employee drug screening or lie-detector tests; *Security Management*, published by the American Society for Industrial Security; the *Security Insider Report*, with news and reviews on latest developments; and *Security*, also on current trends and technologies. In addition, there are a number of new publications on the growing information society which cover privacy issues, such as *The Information Society* and *Library Hi Tech News.*

The Battle against the Direct Mailers and Telemarketers. Meanwhile, as privacy products proliferate, the direct mailers and telemarketers have been battling with consumers and the government over the collection and use of marketing data. A key question is who owns and controls the sales and use of this personal information? Some of these questions have been resolved through battles in the late eighties and early nineties, resulting in a legislated or negotiated truce on some issues, providing marketers with guidelines they commonly follow on who they can contact, and how and when—at least by phone, fax, and direct mail. But as E-mail and billboards are growing, there are new questions about what's acceptable and what's an invasion of personal privacy in the case of posting commercial ads on boards and sending sales information to individuals by E-mail.

These growing privacy problems in the use of information by marketers has intensified with the growth of the industry and the growing channels for marketing information, as well as by the creative intrusion into mass advertising by individuals and companies like Laurence Canter and Martha Siegel—two lawyers who sent out advertisements about their immigration services to about 5,000 newsgroups, resulting in hundreds of angry newsgroup members flaming them on their E-mail for the invasive advertising. A few statistics show its tremendous growth: By 1989, the direct sales market was up to 92 million Americans, up 60 percent from six years before, accounting for about $183 billion in sales for mail-order purchases and donations, according to a report from Marketing Logistics of Lincolnshire, Illinois. A key reason for this rapid growth is because marketers have found "junk mail" to be highly cost efficient, with a single mailing drawing ten times as many responses as a newspaper ad and one hundred as many as a TV ad.[10]

Likewise, the telemarketing industry has enjoyed rapid growth. From 1983 to 1992, it zoomed from $56 billion to over $300 billion in sales, while the number of employees expanded from 175,000 to 5 million. Again, efficiency contributed to its growth, since marketers can call people for less than a third of the cost of direct mail, with only a 1 to 2 percent response success rate needed to turn a profit.[11] Automated telephone dialers make it even more efficient, since compared to one live telemarketer making approximately sixty-three calls a day, an autodialer can deliver a sales message to about one thousand households daily,[12] which especially bothers privacy advocates because of the potential intrusiveness of all these automatic calls. On the other hand, ameliorating some of these concerns, about 80 percent of the sales are to business clients, an approach used to save the expense of a personal sales visit—and $10 per call versus about $800 per knock.[13]

Yet, while businesses might find direct mail and telemarketing sales pitches useful for staying up-to-date in the field, many consumers complain about the deluge of direct mail and sales phone calls, and now increasingly E-mail and fax mail, as an invasion of their peace and quiet. This is also an opportunity to be pitched on fraudulent schemes, which cost consumers about $15 billion each year according to a coalition of consumer groups called the Alliance Against Fraud in Telemarketing.[14] About 54 million Americans, about 20 percent of the U.S. population, have been defrauded in this fashion according to the first national survey of telemarketing fraud conducted in mid-1992.[15]

In turn, many of these fraudulent practices trade on getting private information, such as when a caller asks you to disclose your credit card number in return for phony or low-quality products or when the caller asks you to reveal your checking account number to verify a prize or a sale. Then, once the caller has your number he can use it or sell it to someone else to use, to ring up bills in your name or withdraw money from your account.[16]

Certainly, the use of personal information for target marketing can provide great benefit for the customer, as marketers argue. For example, by knowing key marketing information on each potential customer—like the car he or she drives, or whether he or she is a renter or homeowner—the marketer can choose the products or services of most interest to this person and shape a marketing approach accordingly. Though the marketer gets more sales, the customer gets more products he or she is likely to need and want, and many customers do appreciate these targeted contacts.

But it is the potential for mounting criminal abuse and contact with unwilling customers that worries privacy advocates, as more and more individuals become part of this marketing system. For example, as of 1990, the name selling and trading business had become a $3 billion business. Many retailers have gotten into target marketing by creating their own computerized customer data base to target customers for special mailings, phone calls, or in-store pitches by linking the phone number with the customer's identity, address, age, and income brackets, dwelling type, and previous purchases in the store. According to privacy expert Robert Ellis Smith, by the end of 1991, 55 million consumers were plugged into a targeted market system—and probably many millions more are today.[17]

In fact, today just about everyone's private life has become an open book, accessible to almost anyone. For example, in his hard-hitting 1992 book, *Privacy for Sale,* Jeffrey Rothfeder showed how easy it is to get information by getting Dan Quayle's and Dan Rather's credit reports with just a few phone calls and data base searches.[18]

Then, too, besides combining data to create targeted promotional campaigns, some companies have gotten consumer information about their competitors' customers in order to woo them away. For example, as described by Rothfeder, MCI offered its customers discounts on calls if they gave them the names of other MCI subscribers they called frequently. Without telling its customers, MCI looked through its customers' phone bills to find the phone numbers of the people they called who subscribed to its competitors—AT&T or Sprint. Then, MCI mailed promotional pieces to these non-MCI subscribers suggesting that their friend or relative who was an MCI customer felt it was to their advantage to switch to MCI because of MCI's great discounts.[19]

Certainly, some customers think this target marketing and sales pitching is great, since they get information on products they are interested in, such as offers about records and music magazines when they join a record club. As a result, they buy more of what they want, reflected in the higher percentage of sales—maybe 5 to 10 percent of the offers, versus 1 to 2 percent when sales aren't targeted—a win for both marketer and customer.

But among the 90 percent or more customers who don't buy, some are very disturbed by being targeted. They don't like and consider an invasion of privacy the mounds of junk mail in their mailbox, the annoying sales calls from earnest salespeople, or even worse, from machines. And now they are bothered by the cluttered E-mail boxes and junk faxes that tie up their phone and cost them paper.

The Consumer Reaction to Direct Marketing and Telemarketers

The consumer reaction today is like a continuation of the first phase of the reaction in the late 1980s and early 1990s, which led to some state and federal legislation to regulate the more intrusive practices of marketers and to some self-regulation practices by marketing companies.

For example, by the end of 1990, over a dozen states passed laws to ban automatic dialers or limit the hours they could be used. Many others, including Connecticut, Florida, Maryland, and Oregon, clamped down on unsolicited fax-machine ads.[20] And in 1991, Congress passed the Telephone Consumer Protection Act,[21] which among other things, prohibits sending unsolicited faxes and using autodialers to deliver prerecorded taped messages to private residences unless the resident gives a prior consent.[22] In practice, many individuals still get them—I know I do from time to time. But at least they are much less frequent than in the late 1980s and early 1990s, when the telemarketers acted like the telephone goldrush days were there with this new technology.

The public and media outcry was also enough to get one marketing idea scrapped in 1991. This was the plan by Equifax, Inc., the largest U.S. credit bureau and consumer reporting company, and the Lotus Development Company, noted for its software, to create a comprehensive CD-ROM disk with demographic data on 120 million households.[23] The plan was to sell this disk, called the "Lotus MarketPlace:Households," so that anyone could put it in a computer and call up a complete consumer profile, including name, address, age range, sex, marital status, income bracket, shopping habits, and "products or life-style category."[24] Then, marketers could target their desired customer and contact them by phone or mail. What especially disturbed consumers and privacy advocates was that this data was from Equifax's data base of millions of credit reports. Though Equifax wasn't contributing any information about a particular consumer's creditworthiness or purchases, consumers and privacy advocates were concerned by the comprehensiveness of the profile. After a storm of controversy erupted, the fear of a prolonged media battle, growing consumer anger, and lawsuits led Equifax and Lotus to pull back to avoid an expensive and probably reputation-bruising battle. Lotus in particular was concerned about the potentially adverse impact on its other software products and services.[25]

One result of all this consumer advocacy, legislation, and court infighting is that some marketers and companies with their own data bases have started to take steps to protect consumer privacy.

For example, some publishers and list rental managers of magazines have decided not to release their customer and subscriber lists.[26] Other companies are giving customers and subscribers a chance to opt out by indicating that they don't want their name distributed to anyone else. And the major companies that sell mailing lists or compile street address directories with phone numbers, now offer individuals an opportunity to write to them to get their names removed.

Meanwhile, the Direct Marketing Association created its own service, the Mail Preference Service, in 1971, to give customers requesting this the ability to have their name removed from all mailings. Until 1990, only a small number—160,000—knew about this or were concerned enough to write.[27] But since them, as privacy concerns and the awareness of what can be done has grown, by mid-1993, 2.5 million consumers opted out.[28] (To opt out yourself, write to the DMA, listed in the Appendix.)

However, while the DMA's service may help consumers opt out of members' mailings, you still have to contact the direct mail companies who are not members directly. But if you do write, they will remove their name from their own lists and those they rent or sell to others, as will many credit card companies.[29]

The same trend has occurred in telemarketing—a legislative crackdown and new privacy protection policies developed by the marketers. For example, the Federal Communications Commission (FCC) instituted regulations that require telemarketers to take unwilling customers off their lists if asked to do so; and they must keep "do not call" lists of all people who don't want to be contacted. If you ask them to drop your name and they call again, you can file a complaint with the FCC.

Again, the Direct Marketing Association has tried to help, establishing a Telephone Preference Service, which consumers can call to be put on a "don't call list."[30] But, as with its Mail Preference Service, it only works with DMA members. You still have to advise others who call directly if you want them not to call anymore.

The Consumer Opt-Out Movement and the Development of Marketing Guidelines

Meanwhile, to make sure marketers are responsive, a few grassroots organizations have sprung up to help consumers get off mailing and phone lists they don't want to be on.

One is the Stop Junk Mail Association, based in Sausalito, California, which will send your name out to companies.[31] It's also a lobbying group that seeks to educate legislators, corporations, and citizens about the invasiveness of junk mail. Another activist group is Private Citizen, in Illinois, which has about 2500 members. The organization puts members' names on a "Do not call" list which is sent to more than 1100 telemarketing firms, along with a letter that these individuals don't want to be called. Cease and desist, it advises, or pay the unwilling consumer for using his time and telephone. Then, if the marketer calls anyway, the letter advises that the callee expects to be paid $100 for his or her time and effort as a "consultant" in responding to the call. If not, the firm can expect to be sued.[32] Additionally you can obtain books to help you opt out, such as *Stop Junk Mail Forever*, a booklet from the Good Advice Press.[33]

Also, new legislation was introduced, such as the Postal Privacy bill of 1993, which would permit consumers who fill out change of address forms to ask to have their names excluded from the mailing lists which the post office creates from these forms and provides to licensed vendors.[34] Though the bill didn't pass, the post office itself decided no longer to provide these names to marketers for marketing purposes, such as special offers to new movers. Now marketers can only use change-of-address information to update their mailing lists. In addition, the post office decided no longer to provide the new addresses in response to individual change of address requests, except for those made by law enforcement or required for court purposes, due to personal safety reasons.

Thus, in response to all of these controversies and consumer resistance, guidelines are gradually evolving to enable consumers who wish to opt out and stay off lists they don't want to be on, while marketers are voluntarily dropping unreceptive consumers off their lists (which benefits marketers too, since they don't waste their time contacting them). And procedures are being worked out to restrict firms in selling and reselling names.

In turn, this is one arena where the free market has worked fairly well, and few cases end up in court. A good example of this mutual trade-off is what marketers did at a West Covina, California, mall. They set up a shoppers club in which shoppers were sent free Plaza Players Club cards, which they could insert into new ATM-machines to potentially win cash, vacations, and other prizes. But first they had to fill out an application, which asked for personal information, such as their address, ages of family members, income level, reading habits, and plans to purchase cars or jewelry to help marketers target certain products to them. Then, this information was pooled into a big mall data base of customers, with about 13,000 of them after the first four months of operation in early 1993.

Though the collection of this information worried privacy advocates, who feared it might be resold to other organizations, in fact the data was kept in the mall, and most consumers found the approach beneficial. They were quite willing to give up the information asked with the understanding that this data about their buying habits might be sold in return for the possibility of various awards—including a $500 weekly drawing, vacation and gift prizes, and discount coupons. Additionally, they could accumulate credit toward future purchases when they made a purchase at a participating shop, and consumers were free to drop out of the program at any time by turning in their cards at the mall.

Thus, in effect, the marketers created a win-win situation: the customers knew how the information was being used and the rewards for providing it; they could opt in or out of the program at any time; and the marketers limited the use of the information to a small group who used it to better provide products and services to interested customers.

Notes

1. Louis Trager, "When Store Guards Become Voyeuers," *San Francisco Examiner,* 29 August 1993, E-1, E-6.
2. *Mitre v. Brooks Fashion Stores, Inc.,* 840 S.W.2d 612 (Tex. App.—Corpus Christi 1992).
3. *Mitre v. La Plaza Mall,* 857 S.W.2d 752 (Tex. App.—Corpus Christi 1993).
4. Ibid., 753.

5. *Mitre v. Brooks Fashion Stores,* 612–13, 16.
6. *Mitre v. La Plaza Mall,* 754.
7. Gini Graham Scott, *The Truth About Lying* (Petaluma, CA: Smart Publications, 1994), 175–76.
8. Charles F. Bond, Jr., Karen Nelson Kahler, and Lucia M. Paolicelli, "The Miscommunication of Deception: An Adaptive Perspective," *Journal of Experimental Social Psychology,* 21 (1985): 331–345.
9. Letter from Cubicle Cues representative, Stephani Perlmutter, P.S. Associates, 1645 N. Vine Street, Chicago, IL 60614, (312) 751-8436. Cubicle Cues, Inc., 714 Germantown Parkway, Suite 5, Cordova, TN 38018.
10. Jill Smolowe, "Read This!!!!!!!," *Time,* 26 November 1990, 62–67.
11. John Greenwald, "Sorry, Right Number," *Time,* 13 September 1993, 66.
12. Consuelo Lauda Kertz and Lisa Boardman Burnette, "Telemarketing Tug-of-War: Balancing Telephone Information Technology and the First Amendment with Consumer Protection and Privacy," *Syracuse Law Review,* 43 (1992): 1027–72; 1056–57.
13. Greenwald, 66.
14. Terri Shaw, "Dialing for Your Dollars: Calls from Strangers Could be Fraud—or Just a Terrible Nuisance," *Washington Post,* 12 December 1991, T-9.
15. "News Conference Concerning Phone/Fraud Swindles," *Fed. News Service,* 7 July 1992; available in Lexis, Nexis Library, Current File.
16. Kertz and Burnette, 1056.
17. Robert Ellis Smith, "Privacy's End," *Utne Reader* (January/February 1992), 64–68.
18. Jeffrey Rothfeder, *Privacy for Sale* (New York: Simon & Schuster, 1992), 5, 65–70.
19. Ibid., 93.
20. "Too Many Busy Signals," *Time,* 26 November 1990, 67.
21. Kertz and Burnette, 1029–72; 1057.
22. Greenwald, 66.
23. Rory J. O'Connor, "Privacy Flap Kills Lotus Data Base," *San Jose Mercury News,* 24 January 1991, 1.
24. Robert Ellis Smith, "Privacy's End," *Utne Reader* (January/February 1992): 65.
25. "Huge Database Scrapped Over Issue of Privacy," *San Francisco Chronicle,* 24 January 1991, C-3.
26. Lambeth Hochwald, "The Privacy Keepers," *Folio* (1 July 1993): 62–63, 103; 62.
27. Evan I. Schwartz, "The Rush to Keep Mum," *Business Week,* 8 June 1992, 36, 38.
28. Hochwald, 62.

29. "Junk Mail: How Did They All Get My Address?" Privacy Rights Clearinghouse, Fact Sheet No. 4 (October 1992), 2.
30. "Telemarketing: Whatever Happened to a Quiet Evening at Home?" from the Privacy Rights Clearinghouse, Fact Sheet No. 5, November 1992, 2.
31. To join the Stop Junk Mail Association and obtain a mail-reduction kit, write to: 3020 Bridgeway, #150, Sausalito, CA 94965. (800) 827–5549.
32. Greenwald, 66.
33. *Stop Junk Mail Forever* (Good Advice Press, P.O. Box 78, Elizaville, NY 12523). ($2).
34. Bill Glovin, "Privacy Bills Could Restrict Non-Profit Mail," *The Non-Profit Times,* (August 1993): 1, 30–31; 30.

Chapter 15

Keeping Watch on the Joneses—and the Neighbors, Friends, Relatives, Lovers, and Others

The privacy battle is played out on the personal level too, as people check up on neighbors, friends, dates, mates, family members, and others. Sometimes they do so themselves, sometimes with the help of a private investigator, and some are suing in court.

A key reason for the increase in these personal privacy battles is that people today increasingly don't trust each other—and sometimes rightly so. People lie; create an outer image; misrepresent themselves; and easily move, concealing their past or true identity. Increasingly, domestic problems are coming out in the open, too, so that a growing number of parents are suspected of things like child abuse, molestation, or alleged satanic ritual activity. Conversely, parents are increasingly wary of their children, concerned about things like drug use or their children getting involved with dangerous strangers.

Such things were not much of a problem when people lived in more stable, enduring communities, and had more personal and direct knowledge of each other, built up over years of interacting or having mutual friends and acquaintances in the community. Also, shared values, expectations, and behavior helped create a sense of connections and community.

But now, with the breakdown of many traditional institutions, increased mobility, and the loss of community ties, people increasingly want to shield themselves from others, while others, in reaction to this shielding, want to find out what has been hidden. Hence, this central paradox in personal relationships today—a growing desire for secrecy by many combined with the increase in formal methods for checking on others. It's fueled by a general sense of distrust of one another due to recent social changes. The high-tech revolution itself helps to encourage this distrust, because now people can sit behind computer terminals and create new personas in digital space, using their anonymity not only for playful benign purposes, say in games, but to trick and mislead others. Also, many of the traditional attitudes promoting trust have broken down, such as ideals of taking responsibility for one's actions and making commitments to others.

As a result, problems that used to be worked out between individuals, in families, or on the community level have become part of the growing privacy battle, resulting in people being quick to launch their own investigations or take others to court for privacy breaches.

The War between the Sexes: Spying Spouses and Lovers

In the 1940s, 1950s, and 1960s, as the divorce rate went up and before many states had no-fault divorce laws, the primary reason that spouses wanted to investigate each other was to catch a partner in the act as evidence for a divorce action. In turn, these kinds of divorce cases contributed to the growth of the private investigator industry, while giving the field its early seedy image of investigators skulking in doorways and bursting in on trysting lovers with cameras.

Yet, despite the new no-fault divorce laws, many spouses and lovers still check up on each other due to a lack of trust. Another incentive is that such evidence can influence the amount and terms of settlement in divorce and custody cases.

Investigating Domestic Cases

I participated in a few of these investigations myself when I worked part-time as a private eye. In one case, a woman wanted evidence that her former husband was living in a homeless shelter and having drinking problems to show he wasn't fit to maintain custody of their daughter. As it turned out, he was a live-in counselor there, and several other staff members had children as well, so all was fine. Another woman suspected that her boyfriend, who kept promising to divorce his wife from whom he lived apart, was still seeing her on the side. So the suspicious girlfriend hired the agency I worked for to discover what his real feelings were. My job was to wait outside his office building around noontime, see if he met his wife for lunch, and then, presenting to be a prospective client, go to the office where he worked as a stock trader, greet him, and see if he was wearing the Rolex watch his wife had given him for his birthday. Since he wasn't wearing it, just a relatively inexpensive Timex, the girlfriend felt she could rest more easily that the relationship with his wife wasn't that strong.

The investigator I worked for also advised me that he and other PIs had a growing number of women and sometimes men asking them to check out their dates, when they thought the relationship might become serious. They wanted to know more since they weren't sure they could believe what their dates had told them, and sometimes they were quite right. For instance, one woman found the man she was dating was not the $150 an hour CPA lawyer-accountant he claimed to be, but a low-level clerk with high life-style dreams. She broke up with him soon after she got the report.

Many other investigations spring out of the bitter custody, adoption, and child abuse cases recently in the news, with private eyes hired by both sides to find incriminating evidence against the other side, or exculpatory evidence about oneself. The high-profile cases make the news, such as when Mia Farrow accused Woody Allen of molesting their adopted daughter Dylan. But for every big case in the news and courts, hundreds are handled quietly behind the scenes for clients by a growing number of private investigators. By knowing the real truth about their partner or their relationship, the clients can either feel relieved their suspicions proved groundless; or if their worst fears are confirmed, they can take action, such as filing for divorce, filing suit, or perhaps confronting the partner and talking about the problem in an attempt to start again.

Spreading the Embarrassing News

Another way invasion of privacy issues come up in these mates and dates cases is when a person starts spreading very personal information about the mate, lover, or date, such as the man who secretly sets up a videocamera, tapes the couple being intimate, and shares it with a few friends. But if the word gets back to his date or partner, she can often collect for her humiliation, invasion of privacy, and emotional upset. Though such cases are commonly settled by a quiet payment between lawyers, when they end up in court, usually the victimized lover wins.

That's what happened after Susan Hudson divorced her husband, Jennings Gordon, and later sued her own lawyer for malpractice in the case of *Hudson v. Windholz,* decided in February 1992. Even though she had divorced her husband in 1983, they continued to see each other romantically for about another year. Then, around June 1984, while they were still seeing each other, Susan met and began a romantic relationship with Gary Hudson, who later became her new husband. Unfortunately, Jennings was the jealous type, and when he discovered Susan's relationship with Gary, he began to repeatedly harass her in embarrassing ways, including distributing copies of some sexually explicit photos he had taken of her before, during, and after their marriage. Besides sending a copy to Susan, he sent a nude photo of her to two magazines, *Gallery* and *Genesis,* along with a forged model consent form agreeing to publication. Later, after *Gallery* published the photo in its October 1985 issue (two weeks before Susan and he were going to be married), he sent a copy of the issue to Gary, to the bank manager of the bank where Susan worked, and to Susan's mother. He even sent a plant with a photo of Susan to the Hudson home the day of their marriage, and he broke into Susan's car and glued another nude photo of her on the car dashboard.

Enough was enough. Eventually, Susan and her new husband, with the help of a lawyer, not only persuaded the authorities to press criminal charges against Gordon, whereupon the harassment campaign ceased, but won $225,000 against Jennings for their invasion of privacy claim. However, they couldn't get anything against *Gallery,* since they had signed a release letting *Gallery* off the hook in return for the magazine giving them a copy of the forged model consent form for the proceedings against Gordon. Later, they did try to sue their original lawyer Windholz for malpractice since he persuaded them to sign this release to strengthen their case against Gordon, because he didn't think they had a strong case against *Gallery* (since the magazine believed the forged model release was valid and if Gordon himself hadn't personally distributed this issue to Hudson's relatives and employer, she might never have known it even existed, thereby incurring no damages.) Thus, the Georgia Appeals Court quickly dismissed the case, since the Hudsons had reasonably signed the release to pursue their case against Gordon.[1]

Not So Trivial Pursuit

Other lovers have gotten into trouble for too ardent pursuit. That's what happened to Edward Cantor of New Jersey in the case of *Rumbauskas v. Cantor*, decided in July 1993. Cantor fell obsessively in love with an employee he hired, Diana Johnson, who had been seeing John Rumbauskas, whom Cantor also hired. Soon problems began: Cantor not only started making "romantic advances and overtures" to Johnson, but he warned John to stop seeing Diana, ordered Diana to end her relationship with John, and told her if she saw him again, "he would hire someone to kill both of them." Then he hired men to follow and observe them.

After Diana quit, Cantor continued to pursue her, using a number of unique methods to show his love, which she and John experienced as harassment. For example, he put up a two-foot sign on a fence around one of his industrial buildings which said: "DIXU Score E-1 J-0." When Diana still didn't respond, Cantor didn't give up either. Among other things, he threatened Diana's custody of her daughter, threatened John's "job, safety, and life," and even tried to pay John to end his relationship with Diana.

Finally, though, after John contacted the police and they arrested Cantor, the threats stopped, and later John sued Cantor for invading his privacy, describing his various injuries. Among them: he had to take circuitous auto routes to avoid Cantor's harassing surveillance; had to buy a baseball bat for self-defence; and missed some days at work. And yes, the court agreed, he could collect damages for any "injuries to a person" because of Cantor's overzealous pursuit.[2]

Too Candid Camera

Lovers may also find themselves in hot water over too candid cameras when the subject of their secret filmmaking discovers the truth. That's what happened to Dan Boyles, Jr. in Texas when he took secret videotapes of his then girlfriend Susan Leigh Kerr in the case of *Boyles v. Kerr*, decided in December 1992. It began in August 1985 when Dan Boyles, then seventeen, with the help of two friends, secretly set up a videocamera to film him having sex with his girlfriend at his friend's house. Afterwards, Boyles took the tape, and showed it three times to ten friends, who soon began gossiping about the tape to others. Like wildfire, the story spread to both Kerr's and Boyle's friends and to students at the schools they attended—Southwest Texas State University and the University of Texas.

When Kerr found out about six months later, when the two were no longer dating, she confronted Boyles, and he finally admitted what he did and gave her the tape. But though he made no copy, she found the whole experience extremely humiliating and distressing, since friends and even casual acquaintances would approach her at social gatherings and make comments about the video. Some of her friends even dubbed her the "porno queen," and the experience adversely affected her academic performance and made it more difficult for her to relate to men. She eventually saw a psychologist for counseling, too.

Subsequently, she won big in court as well, after suing Boyles and his three friends for negligent infliction of emotional distress. The jury awarded her about $1 million in damages. Though Boyles tried to appeal, after she settled with his friends, the Texas Supreme Court agreed she did have an invasion of privacy action, but she couldn't just claim emotional distress by itself. That's because her lawyer won her case with the wrong legal theory, since he wrongly interpreted an earlier court decision. But even so, sympathetic to her plight, and in the interest of justice, the court sent her case back for a new trial, which she seemed likely to win given the court's opinion that what Boyles did made this a "truly egregious case."[3]

Confessing My Love

Unfortunately, though, because of privacy laws in some states, prosecutors sometimes cannot use clear evidence of an intended crime of passion (or any crime for that matter) that has been secretly taped. That's what happened in the California case of *People v. Otto*, decided in August 1992, when Joe Otto was killed and his younger wife, Brenda Sue and her lover, Marvin Elmer Mark, were convicted of killing him. The court threw out their conviction because a tape of Brenda Sue and

Marvin talking about their love for each other shouldn't have been used as evidence against them.

Ironically, Joe Otto suspected that Brenda Sue and lover Marvin were up to no good and he started taping their conversations to confirm his suspicions. His concern was more than warranted. Not only did the recordings confirm their love and show they were after his wealth, but the tapes captured a conversation showing they were after his life as well. As the California Supreme Court sadly noted, Joe's concerns "proved to be well founded. Within forty-eight hours of the recorded conversation, he was found dead," bludgeoned to death in his own home. Soon after, in investigating, the police discovered the secret recordings and several other taped conversations that pointed right to the two lovers. The tapes convinced the jury, which found both guilty of first-degree murder, and each received a prison sentence of twenty-five years to life.

Could the two be convicted without the tapes? There certainly is plenty of suggestive evidence. For example, before Joe, a sixty-one-year-old electrician with a history of heart disease, married Brenda Sue, a thirty-nine-year-old divorced woman with two grown children in 1986, she confided to a friend that she agreed to the marriage "only because Joe was sick and probably would not live long." In her view, the marriage was a good deal, because she wanted financial security for herself and her daughters, and before she agreed to the marriage, she asked for and got a substantial cash payment. She wanted this because she planned to invest it with her lover Marvin Mark, to whom she had once been engaged, although they dropped their marriage plans since Mark had financial problems. But after Brenda got Joe's prenuptial marriage check for $10,000, she promptly turned this over to Mark, who used it to open a new office and pay off some debts.

A few days after their marriage, as Brenda began telling friends and relatives that she wanted a divorce, the taping began. Though Brenda discovered one device, Joe successfully hid a second voice-activated recorder under his daughter Jolynn's bed, which recorded every incoming and outgoing call, including one especially suspicious call, which Joe played to a police officer neighbor. Among other things, Mark spoke of having "a better plan," throughout the call referred to Brenda as "honey," and signed off saying "Love you baby." Then, the next day, the day before Joe died, Mark spoke about "picking up a set of wheels," and he told Brenda when he would arrive home from the office. "Any changes, let me know," he concluded.

The next day Joe was dead, and though the police found Brenda tied up, claiming two Latino men had broken into the home and possibly killed Joe, they immediately suspected this was a phony story. They found no evidence of a forced entry, burglary, or of Brenda being struck as claimed. Then they found the tape.

But though all the evidence pointed to Brenda and Mark, and the tapes helped to show their motive, evidence of prior planning, and love for each other, unfortunately, the prosecutors couldn't use the tapes, since Joe had recorded them secretly from the phone. As a result, he had illegally intercepted their calls. Had the two lovers been talking in the room together, the tapes would be fine, but on the phone, no. So the lovers had to be set free—and will remain so, unless there is a new trial and they can be convicted without the tapes.[4]

Nosy Neighbors, Landlords, and Tenants

Like the spouses and lovers cases, those involving neighbors, landlords, and tenants typically involve disputes and jealousies that have led to attempts to retaliate with threats and intrusions or gather evidence inappropriately. Then, as things escalate, the warring parties end up in court.

Privacy and "Perversion" in Small Town America

That's what happened in the *Cullison v. Medley* case, decided in August 1993, which is like a Hatfields and McCoys feud. It started when Sandy Medley, an attractive sixteen-year-old from Linden, Indiana, went to the local IGA market to pick up chewing tobacco for her brother Ron. On the way, she encountered Dan Cullison, thirty-four, in the parking lot, who started talking to her. After learning that Sandy had recently broken up with her boyfriend, he commented that she had "pretty lips" and invited her to have a soft drink with him. Sandy declined, saying she didn't think her father would approve, and after she told her father, Ernest Medley, he strapped a .38 caliber handgun to his waist. Then, joined by his wife Doris, son Ron, and Sandy, he stormed over to Cullison's trailer, picking up Sandy's brother-in-law, who was also Cullison's neighbor and relative, along the way. They pounded on the door, waking Cullison, and after he groggily pulled on his pants, they angrily confronted him in his living room about what he meant by his remarks to Sandy. Then, without giving Cullison much chance to explain or back down, Sandy called him "sick" and a "pervert," and her mother Doris shouted "obscenities" and called him "filthy names." Finally, after about twenty minutes, as Cullison began feeling severe chest paints and feared a heart attack, Ernest warned him as the party turned to go against talking to Sandy again, saying: "If you ever talk to my daughter again I'm gonna jump astraddle you and we're gonna put the word out on you."

The incident left Cullison shaken, and afterwards, whether he talked to Sandy again or not, the Medleys spoke against him to others and treated him like a pariah anytime they happened to pass him in town. For example, one time when Ernest, a gun strapped prominently to his waist, saw Cullison at a local restaurant, he glared at him. Another time when Sandy drove past Cullison, she "flipped" him the bird, and once as Doris passed by, she called him a bastard.

Cullison was scared, and soon he had trouble sleeping and eating, had nightmares, became depressed and anxious, had headaches, and continued to have chest pains and panic attacks. He often couldn't work either. Additionally, as the word about him spread around town, he found he was ostracized by many residents, especially by girls in high school. And when he went into town or did go to work, he found people called him names, like "pervert" or "child molester." Cullison even complained that: "I walk down the street, women run screaming from me." Also, he found he would freeze up around women and had become sexually impotent, although a doctor tried to help by giving him a "pep kit," so he could stimulate himself by injecting himself with some chemical stimulators. Even so, according to the Medleys, Cullison continued to sexually harass many young women in town, bothering them with inappropriate remarks and suggestions.

Still, at the much publicized trial, the jury sympathized with Cullison for the various ways the Medleys had hurt his reputation and caused him emotional upset, awarding him $75,000, which included $15,000 in punitive damages against Ernest and Doris. But ironically, because of all the publicity, a few new witnesses stepped forward who cast doubt on Cullison't claims of being afraid of women and impotent. One businessman told Ernest he heard that Cullison had been chasing girls at another local restaurant, and one of these women told Ernest that at the time when Cullison was claiming to be impotent, she had sex with him at least four times and was willing to put it in writing.

Thus, after sorting through the new evidence and considering whether it was true or false, or whether it or some evidence at the earlier trial might have been obtained inappropriately, the Indiana Appeals Court decided there was enough newly discovered relevant evidence to require a new trial. Of special concern was one woman's claim she had slept with Cullison, showing, if believed, that Cullison was not impotent, which would wipe out much if not all of his damage claim, despite what the Medleys had done to invade his privacy by spreading talk about him all over town.[5]

Getting the Goods on a Neighbor

When disputes end up in court, sometimes neighbors may try snooping to get the evidence they need, and like private investigators, they can do so, as long as they follow local and state guidelines for investigations.

That's what happened in an early nineties case from Ohio, *Blevins v. Sorrell,* decided in 1990. It began when Richard and Jennifer Blevins felt their neighbors Homer Sorrell and Chalmers Brewer, Jr. had invaded their privacy with their snooping. They had done so because Richard Blevins was something of a "tinkerer," whose specialty was repairing lawn mowers and painting cars, which made a lot of noise. Also, he and his wife had many visitors, which suggested that they were running a lawn mower and car repair business, which might be a violation of city zoning regulations; if so, the city authorities could shut it down.

To find out, Sorrell and Brewer needed some proof, and they set up their own surveillance scheme, which included a telescope to look at the Blevins' home and a camera to take photos of the activities there. After Blevins put up a privacy fence in response, Sorrell and Brewer placed a platform ladder in a tree to get a better view.

At this point, Blevins tried having an attorney send a letter to Sorrell and Brewer to stop this, but it had no effect; so finally, they sued. But even though they demonstrated how intrusive Sorrell and Brewer had been, using photos to illustrate, and described their high costs in erecting the privacy fence, the trial court decided Blevin's activities were merely a nuisance and told Sorrell and Brewer to knock off any further surveillance. But the court rejected any damage claims for privacy invasion or emotional distress. It felt that Sorrell and Brewer had a "qualified privilege" to check out the otherwise publicly visible activities of Richard

Blevins to determine if he was or wasn't violating the local zoning ordinance. Further, they hadn't engaged in their snooping with any malice, fraud, or bad faith.[6] That's pretty much the general rule for individuals and investigators. Everyone can gather evidence they might use in court against someone else, if they follow the law that applies in their own area, such as by staying on their own or public property or by picking up information only from phones not protected by state or federal privacy laws (like cellular phones).

This is what happened in a more recent, and much more convoluted, California case, *Rubin v. Green,* decided in May 1992. In this case, Gerald Rubin, the owner of a mobile home park, had tapes made to gather evidence to show that an attorney and Norma Green, a member of a residents' committee, were unethically trying to solicit residents to hire the attorney's law firm to represent them on complaints against the park. Though Green and the attorney tried to get the tapes excluded as a violation of their privacy rights, the California Court of Appeals felt it was fine for them to use them, since the tapes were made to gather evidence for possible litigation.[7]

Extending Yourself

Even extensions, like decks, with a view of the neighbors, seem more likely to be approved today, as part of this trend to carve out less privacy. That's what happened when Audrey O'Shea sued her neighbors and architectural review board members in the *O'Shea v. Lesser* case, decided in May 1992. O'Shea objected because her neighbors, the Lessers, were building an open deck and enclosing an old deck. They were doing so in violation of a subdivision covenant, with the permission of the review board, without notifying her and giving her a chance to comment on these plans before the board gave its permission. Not only would the new structure block part of her view, she complained, but now the Lessers could see around her patio wall into part of her home, so that she had to change her own life-style to avoid being watched by them.

Unfortunately, the Supreme Court of South Carolina was not sympathetic. Not only did it feel that the Board had the sole authority to decide on allowing an extension and acted in good faith in considering the extension, but it didn't feel Lesser's ability to see into part of her home sufficiently "blatant and shocking" to be an invasion of her privacy. That's because it felt that such a situation was a necessity for people living together in a community today, noting that: "People who live in organized communities must of necessity suffer some inconvenience and annoyance from their neighbors."[8]

When Landlords and Tenants Disagree

Finally, a few landlord and tenant disagreements over privacy have ended up in court. Here the general rule seems to be that the landlord or owner can make certain reasonable restrictions, though a tenant might consider these an invasion of his personal privacy rights (such as imposing a rule against having pets). But if a landlord tries to be too restrictive (such as prohibiting even very quiet pets in some places) or goes too far in trying to find out what a tenant is doing, that isn't acceptable.

That's why Natore Nahrstedt, a California pet lover succeeded when she sued the board of directors of her condominium association over its pet restrictions in the case of *Nahrstedt v. Lakeside Village Condominium,* decided in November 1992. Though she knew when she moved in that she wasn't supposed to have any pets except for fish and caged birds, she got three cats anyway. Once the association discovered this, they began fining her, eventually upping this fine from $25 to $500 month, and when she didn't pay, they threatened to put a lien on her home. In response, she sued to keep her pets without penalty, claiming they were noiseless, not a nuisance, no neighbors complained, and the fines were unfair, designed to force her to sell her condo at an unreasonable price or get rid of her cats. She felt she should be able to live in her home undisturbed and unharassed, so the condo's restriction on cats unfairly violated her constitutional right to privacy.

Did it? In the view of the court of appeals, a landlord, owner, or tenant association could certainly make reasonable restrictions to protect the "peaceful and quiet enjoyment" of other tenants (such as requiring a leash for dogs), and it noted that various state courts agreed with this approach. But in Nahrstedt's case, it made an exception. It felt that if her cats were as quiet as she said and didn't interfere with anyone, she might be able to challenge the restrictive policy, and the fines against her might not be proper. So the case went back to the trial court to decide.[9]

By contrast, Mary Meacham clearly won her wrongful intrusion privacy invasion claim against her former landlord, who locked her out of her apartment during an eviction battle in the case of *Meacham v. Miller,* decided in March 1992. The battle started soon after she moved into an upstairs apartment in Jackson, Ohio, in August 1989. Though she paid the agreed upon $325 rent each month through February 1990, her landlord Paul Miller received complaints about noise from her apartment, gave her a week to leave, and refused to accept any more rent. A few days later, he shut off her hot water and electricity, and the next day, when she returned to her apartment, she found the locks had been changed, and there was a "Keep out" sign on the door. When she finally found an employee of Miller's who let her in after Miller refused, she saw her belongings in boxes in the front room. After she spent a day in a motel and a couple of days with relatives, she did get back into her apartment for about a month after a local court ordered Miller to let her back in. Finally, she moved in early April.

Unhappy about her treatment, she eventually sued for her expenses and damages, and she won, collecting costs for her many expenses. Among them: her lost groceries because Miller shut off the hot water and electricity, costs for staying in a motel, and the loss of a day's pay due to the lockout. In addition, she won $5000 in compensatory and punitive damages since Miller had invaded her privacy. That's because he had entered her apartment after locking her out without notifying her he intended to enter, and afterwards packed her possessions, as well as changed the locks, without an emergency or other legitimate reason for entering. In the court of appeal's view, Miller's actions were sufficiently intrusive to cause her "outrage, mental suffering, shame, or humiliation."[10]

The Right to Investigate Anyone

Meanwhile, as a sign of the times, the investigation field is a growing, increasingly professionalized field of information pros, who have developed new and better ways to investigate, with access to more and more information on data bases. Here and there, a few sources have become off-limits, such as the department of motor vehicles (DMV) records nationally (except for special cases, like serving subpoenas). But for the most part, investigators have not only gained an increased ability to investigate, but there has been more call for them by an increasingly suspicious and fearful public, which is filing more suits and doing more checking on others. Increasingly, too, they are being used by lawyers to investigate personal injury cases, insurance claims, worker compensation cases, industrial espionage problems, and other matters.

In turn, when the cases against investigators have come to court, filed generally by subjects who don't like being investigated, the investigators usually win, as long as they are using legal methods. Generally investigators try to do this so the evidence they uncover will hold up in court; otherwise, if they obtain information illegally and this is discovered, it can't be used in court. This is like police evidence that can't be used if it is successfully challenged because the police didn't have warrants or overstepped search and seizure rules (one of the big challenges in the O.J. Simpson case).

Philomena Di-Minno Hudson found out about investigators generally winning when she sued one investigator, Dallas Winn, and his company after they investigated her, in the *Hudson v. Winn* case, decided in August 1993. They investigated her after William C. Corbett, Jr. died and left a handwritten will leaving his estate to his sister's descendants. Hudson claimed to be Corbett's common-law wife since 1981, and one of the fifteen heirs, Lula Fowler, hired Regional Investigators to check out Hudson's claim and determine if she had inappropriately removed any assets from the estate.

When Winn investigated in August 1986, Hudson was working as a real estate broker out of her condominium in Houston. Winn approached her, pretending to be a CIA agent who had just been transferred to the area, and he asked her to help him find a condominium. After she showed him several possibilities, they returned to her condominium for drinks. Unfortunately for her inheritance prospects, Hudson began talking about her personal life, and in the course of the conversation, Winn got her to sign an incriminating statement on a notepad in which she said "I have not had sex since 1980 . . . but twice." Though Hudson claimed that Winn had invaded her privacy in getting this information from her, the Texas Court of Appeals supported Winn's efforts, since, as Hudson herself acknowledged, she invited him into her condo, freely discussed her personal life with him, and signed the note freely.[11] Though Winn might have tricked her into talking by his pretence, that was all in the game.

Likewise, John Holder didn't have much luck when he sued the city of Allentown, Pennsylvania in the case of *Holder v. City of Allentown*, decided in August 1993. He sued for invasion of privacy in the course of an employment termination suit, in which he claimed he was terminated for writing a letter to the local paper critical of the council. He added his privacy claim after he learned that some city employees had used the city's Criminal Law Enforcement Assistant Network to obtain his motor vehicle registration number. But even if they did use this network, said the U.S. District Court, his DMV record in Pennsylvania was a matter of public record readily accessible by the public. So there was no case.[12] Now had they done this in California or other states that had closed DMV records to the public (or nationally as of January 1, 1995, when a Crime Bill provision closed DMV records to the general public everywhere), the outcome might have been different. But in Pennsylvania at the time, they were still open.

No Protesting

Yet, while investigators may have more ability to investigate, protestors trying to protest against private citizens have increasingly encountered problems over invading a person's peace and quiet. Though protesters may argue their right to "free speech," the protest victims have been arguing "an invasion of privacy," and increasingly winning, especially in areas where there is a great concern with private property rights.

One such example occurred in Texas, where Dr. Eduardo Aquino and his family lived when they successfully sued a group of abortion activists who picketed his residence in Corpus Christi, Texas, in the *Valenzuela v. Aquino* case, decided in May 1993. The abortionists had been picketing the two clinics where he performed abortions since 1982, and in 1988, they stepped up their efforts by picketing his residence once a week over a four-week period. Each Tuesday, from 4:30 to 6:30 P.M., about a dozen to two dozen protestors walked up and down his street, a suburban cul-de-sac, carrying signs, like: "Abortion is Murder" and "God Gives Life, Aquino Takes Away." Though the protestors didn't block his driveway, interfere with access to his property, or otherwise break any state or city laws in their peaceful protest, Aquino and his family were not only upset, but some family members became ill.

Thus, Aquino sued and he won a permanent injunction which prohibited the picketers from picketing within four hundred feet of his property. Though he initially won $810,000 from a sympathetic jury, eventually an appeals court and the Supreme Court of Texas threw this out to both protect his right to privacy and the protestors' right of free speech. But the court kept the injunction in place, because as it observed, "To those inside . . . the home becomes something less than a home when and while the picketing . . . continues. . . . The tensions and pressures may be psychological, not physical, but they are not, for that reason, less inimical to family privacy and truly domestic tranquility."[13]

Privacy in a Private Club

Finally, just as the home is given special protection as a place of refuge, so is the private club. Although some laws now limit discrimination when clubs are used for business as well as social purposes, if the activities are social only, a private club can generally make its own rules and policies.

Mary Ann Warfield discovered this when she sued a California golf and country club that terminated her membership after she got divorced, in the case of *Warfield v. Peninsula Gold & Country Club,* decided in January 1993. Though she won the country club membership in her divorce settlement, the club's policy was to issue family memberships to adult males only. Its rules even stated that if a marriage ended by divorce or annulment, then all membership rights, privileges, and obligations of membership went to the ex-husband. Thus, though Mary Ann had a wonderful relationship with the club before her divorce, which included using it as a source of contacts for her residential real estate business, now she could no longer do these things, since she no longer qualified as a regular member. The best she could do was obtain a "golfing membership," which the club offered her, to use the golf club facilities.

For Mary Ann this was not enough, and in her suit, she claimed the club was guilty of discrimination against her under the Unruh Civil Rights Act (named for its sponsor Jesse Unruh), which prohibits discrimination in all business establishments. But the California Court of Appeals turned her down, concluding that this was a truly private club. That's because it limited membership to a relatively small number of people from a limited geographical area, unlike large organizations like the Boys Scouts or Rotary Club. Also, it limited the use of its facilities to members and invited guests to promote privacy and intimacy. Thus, the court felt it was up to the club to decide who could be a member and what its policies would be. Accordingly, since Mary Ann was divorced, she was out.[14]

Summing Up

In sum, incursions on personal privacy have increased as more and more people are taking steps to watch and investigate each other on their own or with the help of a growing number of investigators, who have been using increasingly sophisticated techniques to conduct investigations. Yet, a few key preserves of privacy still remain—the private residence and private club. As a result, generally, when these cases come to court, the courts have supported the right of personal privacy over free speech and discrimination claims.

Notes

1. *Hudson v. Windholz,* 416 S.E.2d 120 (Ga.App. 1992), 121–124.
2. *Rumbauskas v. Cantor,* 629 A.2d 1359 (N.J. Super A.D. 1993), 1359–62.
3. *Boyles v. Kerr,* 855 S.W.2d 593 (Tex. 1993), 593–602.
4. *People v. Otto,* 831 P.2d 1178 (Cal. 1992), 1179–83.
5. *Cullison v. Medley,* 619 N.E.2d 937, 1993 Ind. App., Lexis 1011, 1–27.
6. *Blevins v. Sorrell,* 589 N.E.2d 438 (Ohio App. 12 Dist. 1990), 439–41.
7. *Rubin v. Green,* 5 Cal. Rptr. 2d 331 (Cal. App. 4 Dist. 1992).
8. *O'Shea v. Lesser,* 416 S.E.2d 629 (S.C. 1992), 630–33.
9. *Nahrstedt v. Lakeside Village Condominium,* 11 Cal. Rptr.2d 299 (Cal. App. 2 Dist. 1992), 301–11.
10. *Meacham v. Miller,* 606 N.E.2d 996 (Ohio App. 4 Dist. 1992), 997–99.
11. *Hudson v. Winn,* 859 S.W.2d 504 (Tex. App.-Houston (1st Dist). 1993), 506–508.
12. *Holder v. City of Allentown,* 151 F.R.D. 552, U.S. Dist, (1993), Lexis 11484, 2–3.
13. *Valenzuela v. Aquino,* 853 S.W.2d 512 (Tex. 1993), 514–18.
14. *Warfield v. Peninsula Golf & Country Club,* 16 Cal. Rptr.2d 243 (Cal. App. 1 Dist. 1993), 244–50.

Chapter 16

The New Information Revolution and the Battle for Privacy

Now the battle for privacy has shifted to still another battlefield—the new communications technology and information highway. Since this battlefield is so new, the conflicts are just starting to come to court. Instead, most battles are going on in the media, in Congress and state legislatures, at trade and academic conferences, and among business and grassroots lobbyists, who are trying to work out the laws and policies for this new electronic frontier. It is a national dialogue in which the contending parties are using the new medium itself to carry on much of the conversation, through electronic newsletters, computer bulletin boards, the Internet, encrypted messages, and other new devices.

New Technology/New Battlefield

Ironically, this new battle is like a modern counterpoint to the struggle for privacy that started a century ago. Back then, the struggle was triggered by another new technology, the rise of the mass media in the late 1800s. This created the beginnings of the cult of celebrity, yellow journalism, and mass advertising, and made the invasion of privacy become possible on a scale never known before. Today, the scale for invading personal privacy is upped even more with the communications revolution that has created a global electronic information highway and huge digital collections of data, such as a single CD-ROM containing all listed U.S. phone numbers. While the possibilities for enhanced communication and efficiencies of scale are appealing, without privacy protections, anyone's personal data that has gotten into a data base or in a news account anywhere, can be almost instantly distributed to and accessed by anyone all over the globe.

There is a tremendous struggle today to develop the rules of the road, to provide easy access while preserving privacy. Eventually, the policies and plans worked out now will shape the way we live and communicate in the twenty-first century. Perhaps another parallel is to the age of exploration in the fifteenth through seventeenth centuries, when seafarers and colonizing powers circled the globe, placed claims on undeveloped lands, and worked out rules for ownership of the lands and seas. But now the new territory is the electronic frontier or "cyberspace," and numerous factions, from individual computer whizzes to big companies and the government are trying to lay claim to this space and work out laws and policies, including about protecting personal privacy.

The Major Battles

Besides the many battles already described over using the new data technologies for medical information, criminal justice files, and consumer marketing, the major privacy battles involving the new information technologies are over the phones, including Caller ID and wiretapping; encryption and the Clipper Chip; computer bulletin boards and data bases.

The End of the "Private" Line

At one time phones were considered very private. Even the 1967 *Katz* decision that prevented the FBI from listening in on a bookie's conversation in a phone booth reaffirmed the private nature of a phone conversation. Though one could secretly tape or listen in on a private conversation if one was present, one couldn't listen in on the phone. Even the government needed to get a warrant by showing a judge there was probable cause to believe a crime was being committed using the phone in order to tap it.

But the new technologies have made the old techniques and laws based on phones with wires passé, because the new cordless and cellular phones don't generally have the same expectation of privacy, nor do messages sent over phone lines by E-mail or fax. Cellular phones, E-mail, and fax are supposed to be protected under existing federal law from eavesdropping; and the Digital Telephony bill which passed in 1994 has extended these protections to cordless phones.[1] Still, in practice it may be hard to tell who is listening in or passing by when such a call or message comes in.

Cordless and Cellular Phones

Cordless and cellular phones don't have the traditional expectation of privacy because they operate like miniradio stations sending signals by radio waves, which can be picked up with radio scanners. The cordless phones have a range of up to about a quarter of a mile, sometimes up to two miles; cellular phones, about five to twelve miles. With very powerful scanners, the pickup range might be even further.[2] And if you talk to anyone over a walkie-talkie, home intercom system, or baby monitor, these also give off radio signals that can be picked up by nearby receivers.

In theory, federal law makes it a crime to intercept private communications. But in practice, just about anyone can listen in on these wireless phone conversations. And should someone tune in with a radio scanner, there's no way to even know they have listened in, unless the eavesdropper talks about what he or she has heard. Still, California has tighter privacy laws than most states, making it illegal to intentionally and maliciously intercept or record phone conversations, including calls on cordless and cellular phones.[3]

The Phone Biz

Besides the problems of invasive telemarketing discussed in Chapter 14, another problem is the potential for the greater collection and misuse of phone data with the new technologies. Although many basic policies have been worked out for dealing with telemarketers (such as asking them not to call again and having one's name put on a drop list), consider some of these latest technological developments. They create even more ways your phone number can be used by marketers to sell to you or sell your phone number to others, making it even more difficult to stop the process, should you want to do that.

For example, say you call an 800 or 900 number to request information or learn about some subject of interest (including making what you think is a private call to an erotic phone service). Some companies with these numbers are now using an Automatic Number Identification (ANI) service, which has been approved by the Federal Communications Commission (FCC), to add your number to their customer data base. However, not only are companies not required to tell you they have this ANI service, but they can use your phone number to get more information about you (such as your address, income level, and recent purchases). They can also give your number to other telemarketers who will make pitches to you. As a result, unwitting consumers who think they are making a free call or getting a convenient service by phone may find they are giving away much more information about themselves than they think.

Still, just as you can limit the use of this personal information about you with marketing companies generally, so you can with the 800 and 900 number. You simply advise whoever answers or leaves a message on a recording that you do not want your number, name, or address kept in company records or sold to other companies. You can even request that the company not use your number to solicit future business from you.[4] This way, you can ask the company to treat your call as a one-shot request for information or to order a product or service. Then they are supposed to honor your request according to the Telephone Consumer Protection Act of 1991.

The Caller ID Fight

Meanwhile, the battle over Caller ID is on, with different policies emerging in different states, and at least one case in court. A central issue is whose privacy should be given the most protection—the person making the call or the one receiving it, since Caller ID displays the number of the person making the call, so the recipient knows who is calling. Then, the recipient can decide whether to receive that call or not—or later, can use the ID to learn where the call came from (say in the case of an obscene or harassing call).

There are some good arguments on both sides. Those supporting Caller ID feel it is valuable as a crime deterrent or investigative tool, since it might discourage obscene or harassing calls or help the police to track down a criminal caller. Also, they argue that the person making the call already knows the number or name of the party he is calling; why shouldn't the receiver have similar advance information to decide whether to take the call.[5]

Conversely, those opposed to Caller ID point to the many privacy problems that might occur for the caller in revealing his own number. Say she calls a company for information, like an 800 number, her phone number could be recorded, then used to access information in data bases linked to phone numbers, perhaps to create a marketing profile for a direct sales company. Or all of this information could be put to fraudulent use—an increasing risk as the phone number is used as an identifier that unlocks much other information about a person. Also, opponents argue that the protection of Caller ID is illusory, since a person using a phone to commit a crime could easily use a phone booth, phone forwarding service, or a credit card or operator-assisted call which don't transmit the number of the caller, thereby defeating the purpose of Caller ID. They also argue that without Caller ID, an individual can still track down abusive callers, using a service offered by the phone company, such as a call trace service, in which an individual lets the phone company know he or she has just had an objectionable call which the company can then automatically trace, and advise the police if necessary. This way, though the individual can't find out who called, the phone company can learn this, as can the police, and they can take the appropriate action, if any, which both protects the privacy of the caller, but allows a remedy if necessary for abusive or criminal callers.

So whose privacy should be protected? According to Michael A. Hamilton, that issue is so heated today because the new technology is changing the priority of whose privacy we want to protect. Initially, when the automated phone switch replaced the telephone operator, our priority was on protecting the privacy of the calling party. But now the new Caller ID technology changes the old balance by displaying the calling party's number.[6]

The problem is we don't seem to be quite sure how to balance out these priorities. As a result, due to all this uncertainty and controversy, Caller ID has been turned down in some states (such as Pennsylvania), allowed in others without restriction (such as New Jersey, Virginia, and West Virginia, among the early states to permit Caller ID), and been subject to controls in many others, notably through call-blocking arrangements in which the person making a call can block his number from being seen on a per-call or per-line basis, depending on prevailing state laws.[7] Overall, though, the trend had been for the states to approve per-line or per-call blocking, and probably there will be some federal regulation to work out the details on what happens when someone from one state calls another.

Meanwhile, as their way of creating privacy, many individuals have developed their own personalized Caller ID, such as using an answering machine to screen calls. Then, as the caller announces him- or herself, the receiver can decide whether to talk to the caller or not. If the caller doesn't speak up, the receiver doesn't pick up the phone. And should someone leave a harassing message, perhaps that could be evidence for any future civil or criminal action.

Recording, Listening In, Wiretapping, and Encryption

Another big battle is over recording, listening in, and wiretapping, due to changing technologies as phones and computers are increasingly merged together and communication goes digital. Though there is a variation from state to state, the general rule throughout the United States is that individuals can't secretly tap or record other people's conversations on the phone, even for evidence, and secret taping is a crime, so it cannot be used in court, and the person doing so can find him- or herself being prosecuted. The federal law affecting interstate calls is that one party to a conversation must agree for any taping to occur, while some states (like California which requires all parties to agree) are even stricter. Still, despite only individual restrictions, law enforcement can still tap or record with a court order.

One police officer in Suisin City, California, Officer Welch, discovered firsthand that he couldn't use such evidence from private taping in the case of *People v. Murtha,* decided in April 1993, when he tried to use a tape cassette that an informant had given him. On the tape, two men discussed robbing a house in the informant's neighborhood. In one conversation they spoke about the planned job, noting there were guns and money at the victim's house, and in a second conversation, they talked about being ready and agreed to meet by a fence. But while Welch got a search warrant and found evidence of the burglary, when one burglar, John Francis Murtha, appealed his conviction, the judge said Welch couldn't use the tape, since the conversation was illegally intercepted and taped by a private citizen. So potentially, Welch might have found the whole case thrown out due to the illegal taping, although fortunately, Welch had gotten enough information through other means from the informant's tip, so the case was saved and Murtha stayed in jail.[8]

In a civil case, real estate broker Michael Friddle of Livermore, California, wasn't so lucky. Instead, he was fined $3000 because he secretly taped a conversation to support his claim against two clients who didn't pay him his full commission, in the case of *Friddle v. Epstein,* decided in July 1993. Friddle had sold a large parcel of land for two clients, Robert Epstein and Richard Chi, and after he heard reports leading him to question Epstein's trustworthiness, he secretly taped their discussion of the purchase agreement. But it couldn't be used and cost him money. While the California Appeals Court agreed that Friddle could keep the part of the commission he was already paid but Epstein and Chi wanted back, he couldn't get anymore. Also, because the court felt the tape was an invasion of the California Privacy Act, it awarded Epstein and Chi the $3000, regardless of any actual damages they suffered.[9]

Meanwhile, a heated battle is shaping up over what government and law enforcement can do in monitoring the use of these new technologies, because as more people turn to digital and radio-transmitted data instead of hard-wired phones, individuals and companies are increasingly turning to encryption—scrambling or encoding data. This way they can make what they say or transmit over the phones and computer lines secure, in that only the recipient can unscramble or decode the message, using a secret key.

However, the FBI and other law enforcement officials want to maintain their traditional ability to tap into these conversations and messages if necessary, just as they have been able, under warrant, to tap the old-fashioned hard-wired phones, say by finding and putting an alligator clip on the appropriate phone line.[10] Similarly, they want to be able to obtain a decryption key, if necessary, for law enforcement purposes, so that they can decrypt data that has been encrypted with a particular chip dubbed the Clipper Chip. This is a chip that can encrypt or decrypt data using a special mathematical formula called the "SKIPJACK" algorithm. The way this arrangement works is that each chip has its own unique key, which is split and stored with two key escrow agents for safe keeping. Then, after gaining approval to unlock the encrypted communication (presumably through the usual legal procedures), law enforcement must acquire the key to decrypt the communications encrypted with a particular chip.[11]

After the National Security Agency (NSA) designed this chip, the FBI contributed to the controversy in the fall of 1992 by urging that the chip be adopted and that standards be established for its use. According to David Banisar, policy analyst for the Electronic Privacy Information Center, the FBI initially approached AT&T about this policy and, thereafter, it became an active advocate to gain government support. Dorothy Denning, however, asks for a source for this statement. Then, in 1993, the Clinton Administration backed the chip. Now at this writing, these proposals are still the subject of heated debate, since many businesses, organizations, and privacy advocates feel the chip would be a serious incursion on personal privacy, as well as stifling the ability of businesses to compete if the chip is included on U.S. communication devices. Although the government is currently urging the voluntary use of the chip, opponents still feel that a voluntary agreement would turn into a de facto requirement that all manufacturers would need to follow to compete.

The Digital Phone Debate. A related and equally intense battle occurred over the digital telephony legislation, which was backed by the government, Department of Justice, and FBI, and finally passed in 1994. This legislation now requires all common carriers of electronic communications to use a system that enables the government to intercept these communications through electronic surveilance (also known as wiretapping), and it requires manufacturers of this equipment to design or redesign their system so that the government can do this. However, the government must still get a court order allowing it to monitor calls from a particular number (which is equivalent to getting a warrant to tap a line). Then, the provider has to transfer the signals to a remote government monitoring facility, without the caller or recipient knowing this, so enforcement officers can listen in.[12]

During the heated debate, supporters stressed the need for law enforcement to continue to be able to tap the calls of criminals. For example, Dorothy E. Denning, a professor of computer science at Georgetown University and the author of *Cryptography and Data Security,* pointed out that many serious crimes can only be solved or prevented by wiretapping. That's because, she noted, in the past, the FBI found phone surveillance "essential in preventing serious and often violent criminal activities including organized crime, drug trafficking, extortion, terrorism, kidnapping and murder." As an example, from 1985 to 1991, the FBI, which did about one-third of the court-ordered intercepts, netted about 7300 convictions, about $1 billion in fines, recoveries, restitution, and forfeitures, and $2 billion in prevented economic loss. As a result, Denning felt legislation to permit court-ordered electronic surveillance necessary to avoid these systems becoming "sanctuaries for criminality wherein Organized Crime leaders, drug dealers, terrorists, and other criminals could conspire and act with community."[13]

By contrast, privacy advocates argued against this act as a massive and costly expansion of government powers into uncharted territory, not just a simple matter of upgrading law enforcement's powers to collect phone data. David Banisar states the statistical arguments used by the FBI do not take into account the other investigative techniques used that contribute to catching and convicting criminals. Thus, these added powers are not necessary, given the threat they pose to privacy. Such new threats are described by Steven Levy, the author of *Hackers,* who, prior to the act's passage, warned in a *Wired* magazine feature on the new threats to privacy that: "Digital Telephony, if passed, would grant law-enforcement access not only to phone conversations, but a whole range of personal information previously stored in hard copy but ripe for plucking in the digital age. And if law enforcement can get at it, so can others—either government agents over-stepping their legal authority, or crooks."[14]

His warning may not prove true, since Denning observes that the bill actually increases privacy protection for transactional records, apart from its assistance to law enforcement in getting court-ordered taps.[15] But, in any case, digital telephony will be a closely watched arena as the newly passed legislation is put into practice beginning in 1995, and privacy advocates try to prevent this by mounting a campaign to stop funding for the bill in the new Republican congress.[16,17]

The Clipper Chip Controversy. But more than the digital telephony battle, the Clipper Chip controversy has stirred the most heat. It raises the question of whether the U.S. government should be able to get a key to unlock a secret encrypted message sent by one party to another. The government/law enforcement position is that it needs this key as a necessary trump card it can play at times with the appropriate safeguards of a warrant and probable cause to believe a crime has or is about to be committed. But many others don't trust the government to use this key appropriately, citing various dangers. For instance, the government could use this key against unpopular individuals and causes; go on unwarranted fishing expeditions for information; or perhaps, due to incompetence or malfeasance by a government official or employee, fail to safeguard the key, compromising privacy. Also, they feel there is a competitive trade disadvantage, since if U.S. manufacturers are pressured to install the chip in their products, U.S. industry will be hurt in the marketplace, since buyers in other countries will not want U.S. software and high-tech products with encryption keys held by the U.S. government. So U.S. companies will be less competitive with companies in other countries without a similar encryption requirement. Although the requirement to install the chip is voluntary, as noted, many manufacturers and others opposing the chip feel it will become a de facto standard.

Given these strong antichip feelings, one reaction to the Clipper Chip proposal has been a kind of grass roots rebellion to create popular forms of encryption. For example, concerned about the government crackdown on cryptography, software engineer Phil Zimmerman created and released for free his own encryption software, Pretty Good Privacy, in June 1991, based on the public/private key principle. What this means is that there is a public key like a public bulletin board name which everyone knows. But then, there is a private key known only to the person sending or receiving the message, like a secret password. To spread this tool for privacy protection, Zimmerman posted PGP on computer bulletin boards, and a friend put a copy out on the Internet. So within hours the program was spread to thousands of users, including many outside the U.S., and since then the government has been investigating the legality of allowing PGP to get out on the Internet outside of the U.S. and whether it might violate U.S. export laws.[18] In fact, at this writing, Zimmerman has recently been subject to a grand jury investigation by the U.S. Customs Office based in San Jose over the international distribution of PGP over the Internet, and is currently mounting a legal defense against possible criminal charges.

Meanwhile, the battle against government control of encryption has stimulated letter-writing campaigns, petitions, comments in electronic newsgroups and bulletin boards, and other actions by hundreds of groups and individuals who don't want the government to have the ultimate decoding key. For example, in one petition drive, the Computer Professionals for Social Responsibility gathered over 45,000 names of those opposing the Clipper Chip to send to the White House, using the computer bulletin boards and Internet to help it gain signatures.[19]

Also, some legislators have tried to pass legislation that could affect the use of the chip, such as Congresswoman Maria Cantwell, who in November 1993 introduced a law to amend the Export Administration Act to relax export controls on various products, including those with data encryption. This would allow U.S. companies to export software with strong encryption capabilities. In support of her bill, Cantwell argued that the worldwide demand for cryptographic software and computer systems employing such software is growing rapidly, and American companies must be allowed to meet that demand or lose critical international markets to foreign competitors, with few export restrictions.[20] But as of this writing, after much legislative infighting, the bill was killed by the Intelligence Committee at the urging of the NSA and it did not pass in the 1993–1994 session. Moreover, its sponsor, Maria Cantwell, did not get reelected, so the future of a bill to relax export controls in the new Congress is uncertain, although industry has been pleading for these controls to be relaxed for some time.

Meanwhile, at the Fourth Conference on Computers, Freedom, and Privacy, held in Chicago in March 1994, the Clipper Chip controversy was one of the major panels of interest. At it, privacy advocates, including Phil Zimmerman, PGP developer, and David Banisar, a lawyer and computer scientist with the Computer Professionals for Social Responsibility, Washington Office (now the Electronic Privacy Information Center) which sponsored the anti-Clipper Chip petition, reaffirmed their support for fighting the chip, while one lone voice, Stewart Baker, general counsel of the NSA, which originally developed the chip, gave the usual government arguments about its need for the chip to effectively patrol the information highway and cyberspace and protect society.[21]

At this writing, this debate has been going on for about two years, and the administration is still backing some kind of voluntary and exportable standard and seeking the support of industry, though many privacy advocates, business people, and others are still fighting against it. For a time one computer scientist, Dr. Matthew Blaze of AT&T Bell Labs, triggered some concerns about the effectiveness of the chip, when he announced his discovery of a potential vulnerability which allowed someone to evade lawful government decryption. But since then, NSA claims to have fixed the problem. In addition, the vulnerability didn't affect real-time phone communications using the chip.[22]

In any case, after all of this debate and lobbying, it seems that the Clipper Chip in some form will be used, as a final agreement for its use is worked out.

The Battle for the Bulletin Boards

Bulletin boards and the Internet have become another major battlefront. At one time, these bulletin board and Internet sites were like the Old West frontier, primarily inhabited by the new computer/cyberspace explorers, computer buffs, cyberpunks, academics, subject to little regulation. Instead, bulletin board operators (commonly called "sysops," for systems operators) and site moderators (sometimes dubbed "list" servers) worked out their own rules, customs, and etiquette, including ideas about privacy. For example, on many boards it was fine to use special "handles" or unique names as identifiers, as in the earlier CB days; and sometimes, one could even create a special digital persona, different from one's "real" self, under cover of anonymity. But there were understandings that one shouldn't take advantage of others, by using this anonymity to induce those met in cyberspace into fraudulent schemes. Also, there was a general objection to using the net for posting commercial messages.

However, with no way to formally police this electronic frontier, the BB users also adopted a kind of buyer beware outlook of "check it out." Then, if someone encountered a problem on-line, they could always report it to the sysop, who could, if the problem was serious enough, drop that problem person off the bulletin board (say for being especially insulting or abusive). But otherwise, sysops generally sought to protect the privacy of those on-line and their freedom to say what they wanted, supporting a kind of cyberspace "land of the free" ethos.

But in the late 1980s and early 1990s, things began to change as more and more people began going on-line. Commercial services like CompuServe, Prodigy, GEnie, and America Online started up or expanded rapidly; and by 1994 perhaps 10 million or more people were on-line as commercial subscribers, with many millions more having access to local bulletin boards and the Internet generally. As a result, some commercial services began to do their own policing of bulletin board posts, rejecting messages that were overly offensive or commercial, as well as anything that might violate current copyright laws. Still, E-mail was considered private, so the private companies didn't interfere with that.

Meanwhile, around 1993, as cyberspace became more populated, the government and law enforcement became interested, and now there's a battle over what kind of legal controls there will be over bulletin board posts and E-mail messages. Also, this battle is over who is responsible for what goes over the wires, when there is possible evidence of a crime being committed or of copyright violations. Is the sysop responsible? The online service provider? The person doing the posting? The creator of the objectionable material? And what law should apply? The law in the community where the material was downloaded or viewed? Where the material was posted? Or should there be some national or global standard to affect what is really an international medium. Currently, these questions of responsibility for what is posted and downloaded, and what law enforcement can do to investigate are still being debated and worked out in the media, legislature, and the courts.

The Hacker Crackdown

The first legal crackdown was against the hackers beginning in 1990, described in *The Hacker Crackdown* by science fiction writer Bruce Sterling. In brief, what started this crackdown is that some hackers, primarily teenagers and college kids, seemed to be getting into the phone system, and although one phone system, BellSouth, did crash for other technical reasons, AT&T and Bell South's concerns triggered a serious investigation. The result was the discovery of an underground subculture of hackers, who were proudly sharing information of their feats of cyberspace exploration on-line and through a growing number of hacker magazines, like *Phrack*. Though most of these hackers were not doing any physical damage, since they were just exploring by discovering secret passwords and seeing what was in different systems, and they weren't changing or destroying data, their growing presence sent a chill through the government and corporate America. Despite the benign intentions of most, just their growing presence in an increasingly important communications system meant the potential for undermining the security of the system, particularly since some could be criminally inclined and do real damage, including planting viruses.

As a result, the Secret Service and the U.S. Attorney's Office in Chicago launched its first major case against *Phrack* magazine and publisher Craig Neidorf because the publication allegedly printed a secret document on the 911 system which had been obtained illegally. However, the case was quietly dropped after three days of trial when it was discovered that the information in the 911 document could be bought by anyone for $13.00 from the different phone companies.[23]

The next major law enforcement thrust in 1990 was conducted by the U.S. Attorney's Office in Chicago, and this not only resulted in the arrests of key hackers and the seizure of their equipment, but billboard operator Steve Jackson of Steve Jackson Games in Austin, Texas got pulled into the web, too.[24] Though Jackson himself wasn't involved in any hacking, he ran a small computer bulletin board, the Illuminati BBS, on the side, and one of his employees was believed to be a member of a hackers' group, the Legion of Doom, which Secret Service agents believed was involved in breaking into the BellSouth's computer system.[25] Thus, in the ensuing raids by the U.S. Secret Service and state and local law enforcement, Jackson's company was stripped of its several computers, software, hundreds of floppy disks, modems, a laser printer, and other equipment, which completely disrupted Jackson's regular business. He was literally out of operation for awhile, since he lost electronically stored contracts, address directories, mailing lists, personnel files, business correspondence, and the drafts of forthcoming games and books. In the end, Jackson was never arrested, nor were any of his employees, and no charges were ever filed. But the material taken was kept as "evidence" of a crime[26] for several years before finally being returned.

Meanwhile, the incident became something of a watershed case in the bulletin boards and E-mail battle, since its outcome is helping to determine what rights and responsibilities billboards and E-mail system operators have, and to what extent the material posted on-line is private. The incident has had this influence, because in May 1991, Steve Jackson filed suit against the U.S. Secret Service in U.S. District Court in Austin, claiming that the government overstepped its limits in conducting the raid, since the First Amendment protects electronic information and the Privacy Protection Act of 1980 and the Electronic Communications Privacy Act of 1986 protect the privacy of E-mail users. Then, in March 1993, Jackson helped to chart out some basic protections for innocent sysops when he won his motion for summary judgment, in which the District Court agreed that the Secret Service had violated the Privacy Protection Act in removing all of these items from his business. As a result, it ordered the government to pay Steve Jackson Games about $50,000 in expenses and compensatory damages and to return all seized material, suggesting that the government should have just asked Jackson to cooperate with the investigation, as Jackson had originally offered to do.[27]

In short, the outcome of the Jackson case suggests that sysops and bulletin board operators should have some protection when they're not involved in criminal activity themselves, although when it comes to giving users access to child pornography and copyrighted materials, that's a different story, and the sysops have been losing these cases.

The Crackdown on Sex and Crime in Cyberspace

This change to hold the sysops more responsible for some things has occurred as the crackdown on the bulletin boards has shifted from smoking out computer hackers to cracking down on pornography, pedophiles, and other sexual activity on-line. And again, not only those accused of crimes but the BB operators have been sucked into these investigations and their equipment confiscated.

The approach of the computer community seems mixed. Many feel that the sysops should make their own decisions about what is appropriate or not, leaving private self-censorship up to them. Then, if they wish to include any raunchy or offensive material, they can post this in a separate area for those who want access to it. Or they choose not to have such material on their own BB. But in either case, the matter should be up to them; outside authorities shouldn't have a right to interfere.

For example, in one issue of *Computer Privacy Digest,* correspondent Donald Burr made the case for self-policing thus:

> I do not believe that external authorities (i.e., the FBI, FCC, etc.) should censor BBS's, because this would be in violation of freedom of speech. HOWEVER, I do believe that the individual SYSOPS of each BBS should decide which is appropriate and which is not . . .
>
> There are some BBS's where profanity, etc. is inappropriate—for example, in the nationwide nets . . . which are accessed mainly by "family-oriented" systems. You don't want your kids to be exposed to that profane kind of stuff. Also many adults find it distasteful or profane, and we should not condemn them because of the way they were raised (traditional family values, etc.), nor should we force them to be exposed to this kind of stuff. . . .
>
> I believe there is a "right" way to handle this. . . . Many of the local BBS's have "adult-only" areas, where you are required to

> send in some sort of proof of age. . . . This is a good thing, IMHO, because the information ITSELF is not censored—it is just not made available to people of an inappropriate age.[28]

But while that seems to be a common view of many BB sysops and users, many others feel that sysops must take responsibility for what is there, particularly when it comes to posting copyrighted material and pirated software—and they shouldn't do this. Also, the growing government/law enforcement view seems to be to regard the BBs, E-mail, and Internet generally as an increasingly expanding and lawless place that requires increased policing, because it is increasingly being used by "cybercriminals," using cyberspace to engage in criminal acts, from pedophilia to terrorism and software piracy. Accordingly, they believe that the BB operators have to take responsibility for what goes on their BBs to help protect society from this increase in cybercrime.

Meanwhile, the media has contributed to the growing awareness and concern about sex and violence on the net, with stories like *Newsweek*'s March 1994 feature: "Sex on the Info Highway."[29] Similarly, a growing number of TV specials and news show segments have highlighted the growing danger of cybercrimes, such as several stories on shows like *Hard Copy* and *Inside Edition* about how pedophiles are meeting unsuspecting kids on the BBs, and then setting up meetings to molest the kids.

But while the computer community may not support the criminals using the BBs to engage in crime, the concern is about the BB owners and sysops, who may not know what is going on. But should they know? Can they realistically check the hundreds of files crossing cyberspace each day on their BBs? How can they invade the privacy of their own users by monitoring their conversations to check for possible criminal activity? How private can or should the BBs and E-mail exchanges be? These questions are increasingly being raised as the law enforcement crackdown and battle over the privacy rights of those on the BBs goes on.

The Crackdown on Porn on the Bulletin Boards

In general, law enforcement seems to be winning in these porn crackdowns, despite growing free speech and privacy concerns about their actions by privacy advocates and members of the computer/BB community. A key reason for this concern is that the busts are occurring in more conservative communities, particularly in the South, while the BBs are used by people all over the United States, as well as globally.

For example, one such bust occurred in Oklahoma in July 1993, when four Oklahoma City Police officers swooped down on the offices of a small ten-line bulletin board, the Oklahoma Information Exchange BB run by Tony Davis. They claimed that his BB and publishing company, Mid-America Digital Publishing, was selling and distributing pornographic CD-ROMS, and they took about fifty of his CD-ROM disks and about $75,000 worth of BB equipment, including two computers, disk drives, modems, and software. The case began when an undercover agent contacted Davis's publishing company and purchased two CD-ROM disks with adult material. Davis's happened to mention to the investigator that people could dial in and access the same type of disks. So the search was expanded to confiscate the BBs, although it wasn't mentioned in the warrant authorizing the police to seek evidence related to selling the allegedly pornographic disks.[30]

But should the police have been able to take the whole BB? As in the Jackson case, privacy advocate and members of the computer/BB community view the police action as part of a growing "legal assault on bulletin boards" generally, in which the more restrictive laws in one state or community, like Oklahoma, are used to clamp down on the freedom and privacy rights of people throughout the country, if not the world, accessing the bulletin boards. Moreover, the police don't even seem to be aware of these privacy concerns, according to one commentator on the Davis case in the *Computer Underground Digest,* Lance Rose. That's because, as Rose notes, when the police raided Davis's offices with their warrant, they did not appear to know about the Electronic Communications Privacy Act, for when Davis advised them that he handled the electronic mail for about 2,000 BB users on the system and carried over one 1,000 FidoNet conferences and Usenet Newsgroups, the officers took everything anyway, even though the search warrant didn't include the BB system and the alleged pornographic materials sent over it might be just a very small part of the system.[31]

Another case involving a postal sting initiated in Memphis, Tennessee, resulted in a conviction in July 1994. Robert and Carleen Thomas operated the Amateur Action Bulletin Board, with sexually explicit materials, in Milpitas, California, some alleged to be child pornography, although these charges were later dismissed. They were each convicted of eleven counts of transmitting obscenity through interstate phone lines via their members-only computer bulletin board, with each count carrying up to five years in prison and a $250,000 fine. They eventually were each sentenced to about three years in jail, but are now planning to appeal, arguing a series of procedure errors.[32] In support, a number of public interest groups are planning to file amicus briefs based on the question of which jurisdiction's laws should govern in cyberspace—the laws of the local jurisdiction or of the cyberspace community. This issue has become of major concern to privacy advocates because, though the materials on the BB may have been legal in California, a U.S. postal inspector in Memphis, Tennessee ordered and downloaded them, and that's where the Thomases were charged with violating state laws in January 1994.[33]

The case began after a computer hacker in western Tennessee contacted the U.S. Postal Inspectors in Memphis, claiming that he had come across the Amateur Action Bulletin Board which offered photos and videos of nude children. So armed with this information, the Memphis Postal Inspectors set up a sting beginning in July 1993. Using a fake name, Lance White, Dirmeyer sent Thomas a computer message indicating his interest, and in August, after becoming a subscriber, he obtained lists of videos and GIF photo files of some extremely explicit materials.[34] These included everything from nude closeups to heavy S&M videos and photos. In some cases, the ad copy highlighted the raunchy, outrageous, taboo quality of these materials with copy like: "The nastiest video in the world! A young slut gets humiliated by a kinky guy! He slaps her face and makes her lick his boots!" or "This is a very kinky and nasty hard bondage and torture video!" Some of the descriptions of particular scenes were even more graphic, promising even raunchier materials.[35]

Perhaps all of this might have been considered legal in California, since the Thomases' billboard was previously raided by local law enforcement, but no charges were filed, and their equipment was returned. But in western Tennessee, this was all a bit much. So Dirmeyer continued ordering, obtaining even more steamy photos and videos, and at one point, he offered to send Thomas some "hardcore sex magazines featuring young girls having sex with adults and other children," so Thomas could borrow these magazines to scan and create GIF files. Finally, convinced he had enough evidence, Dirmeyer went to Milpitas, California himself, and filed his request to seize the Thomases' whole computer system, so he could carefully search all the hard and floppy disks for evidence, without the Thomases having a chance to destroy them.[36]

Then, after the search warrant was approved, Dirmeyer sent the Thomases a package of child pornography on 10 January, and within minutes of their receiving it, Dirmeyer appeared with his search warrant, and took the computer and bulletin board system. Though the Thomases' attorney, Richard Williams tried to get the case overturned on the grounds the police officer violated his clients' due process rights through its deception in getting the warrant,[37] this didn't work, and the case was tried, leading to the Thomases' conviction.

Since then, however, the privacy advocates and BB community has mobilized to protest these convictions as an invasion of privacy and an attack on free speech. For example, in a report on this reaction, Prodigy's news service reported that "the Internet flashed with protests . . . after a California couple was convicted of federal obscenity charges for sending images of bestiality and sexual fetishes to a members-only computer bulletin board," noting some of the comments in reaction. For example, one privacy advocate, lawyer Mike Godwin of the Electronic Frontier Foundation commented: "This case . . . has one community attempting to dictate standards for the whole country." And Stephen Bates, a senior fellow with the Annenberg Washington Program, a communications think tank, expressed his concern that: "If the 1973 Supreme Court standard [for obscenity] is applied to cyberspace, juries in the most conservative parts of the country could decide what images and words get onto computer networks," noting that this was the first time prosecutors in an obscenity case went after a bulletin board operator in the locale where the material was received, rather than where it originated.[38]

It may be just the beginning, given the increasing commercialization of the BBs and Internet and the concern about porn, pedophiles, and criminal predators using the information highway.

The Privacy/Free Speech versus Crimes and Porn Battle

These cases and the growing media attack on sex and crime on the BBs and Internet raise particular concerns because of the many privacy and free speech questions they raise. What can people freely say on-line? How privately can they choose what to order and view? How secure are they in supposedly "private" BB areas? What is the responsibility of the BBs' owner or sysop to know what is going on on the BBs he or she managed? Given the difficulty of monitoring the thousands of postings and messages that cross the board in a day, can the BBs operator become criminally or civilly liable, even if he or she isn't aware of what is going on? And what about the providers who maintain web sites (like library file areas) on the Internet? Can they, and should they, know everything in their files?

Even members of the BBs and Internet community are split over these issues. While some favor the notion of total privacy and free speech, appreciating the freedom and anarchy of an unregulated net, others fear that the "glue of social cohesion and human civility" holding it together are being corroded by violations of that trust. They feel some people have been taking advantage of the relative lack of law to distribute pornography, engage in black marketeering, and participate in other criminal activities, creating a kind of "cyberspatial hell," despite the free speech, free market dogma that has glorified anarchy and individualism. It's a "ticking time bomb and a recipe for an apocalypse," comments one computer poster, L. Detweiler, who fears total disorder, of what he calls "Anarchy Gone Awry."[39]

In any event, now that there are millions of users of bulletin boards, E-mail networks, and Internet web sites, this raging battle has gone mainstream, reflected in the recent law enforcement crackdown and media attention to the uses and misuses of cyberspace. These issues are far from settled, and they are now being hotly debated, as one more arena where individual rights to privacy, as well as to free choice and free expression are being weighed with concerns about protecting the rights of others from those using privacy as a cover for antisocial behavior and crime.

But then, what is antisocial behavior? What is crime? And who has a right to define it?

It is as if the new world of cyberspace has created a new frontier where traditional ideas about the border between what should be private and public have become unclear, so we have to redefine them. And that's what's happening now in public debates, in the media, in the legislatures, and in administration-sponsored discussions about the new information highway. The Davis and Thomas cases are but the tip of the iceberg in the swirling debate over law and order on the net and who is in control of the information passing over it. Should these messages be viewed more like private letters, or are the bulletin boards, E-mail, and Internet sites, more like publications, in which the sysops and site managers as editors become responsible for what goes out on the net? Or would an open marketplace, like a field where vendors set up tables and no one is really in charge, be more appropriate?

Right now, no one is sure, and the current debate is helping to shape new laws and codes of personal behavior to suit the new technology. Over the next few years, the outcome of the battle going on now will determine the rules of the road—and the rules about privacy—in this new infohighway across cyberspace.

Notes

1. The existing federal law is Title 18, Section 2511. The Digital Telephony bills which passed were S.2375 and H.R.4922.
2. "Cordless and Cellular Phones: Is Everybody Listening," *Privacy Rights Clearinghouse,* Fact Sheet No. 2, October 1992, 1.
3. Ibid., 2.
4. "800 and 900 Telephone Numbers," *Consumer Advisory* Flyer from the California Public Utilities Commission, March 1993.
5. Michael A. Hamilton, "Caller ID and the Great Privacy Debate: Whose Phone Call Is It, Anyway?" *Dickinson Law Review* (Winter 1993): 357–82.
6. Ibid., 366.
7. Ibid., 366.
8. *People v. Murtha,* 18 Cal. Rptr.2d 324 (Cal. App. 1 Dist. 1993), 324–25.
9. *Friddle v. Epstein,* 21 Cal. Rptr.2d 85 (Cal. App. 1 Dist. 1993), 86–88.
10. Editor's Introduction. "To Tap or Not to Tap," *Communications of the ACM,* 36 (March 1993): 25.
11. Letter from Dorothy E. Denning, Professor, Computer Science Department, Georgetown University, Washington, DC, 20 September 1994.
12. Dorothy E. Denning, "To Tap or Not to Tap," *Communications of the ACM,* 36 (March 1993).
13. Steven Levy, "Crypto Rebels," *Wired* (May/June 1993): 53–61; 60.
14. Ibid., 61.
15. Letter from David Banisar, Policy Analyst of the Electronic Privacy Information Center, 17 January 1995.
16. Denning, 20 September 1994, letter.
17. Interview with David Banisar, 13 February 1995.

18. Levy, 57, 59.
19. CPRSR/PDX, Vol. 7, #02, March 1994.
20. Press release from Maria Cantwell, 23 November 1993, posted on *Computer Privacy Digest* (29 November 1993).
21. Transcript of "Data Encryption: Who Holds the Key?" Panel at the Fourth Conference on Computers, Freedom and Privacy, Chicago, Illinois, 24 March 1994, reported in *Computer Underground Digest,* 5 (6 April 1994).
22. Denning, 20 September 1994, letter, 3.
23. Letter from David Banisar, Policy Analyst of the Electronic Privacy Information Center, 26 September 1994, 1.
24. Bruce Sterling, *The Hacker Crackdown* (New York: Bantam Books, 1992), 138–40.
25. "Court Says Search, Seizure Violated Federal Privacy Law," *The News Media & The Law* (Spring 1993).
26. Sterling, 140–41.
27. "Court Says Search, Seizure Violated Federal Privacy Laws."
28. Donald Burr, "Re: Computer Bulletin Boards Should NOT Be Censored," *Computer Privacy Digest* 3 (18 November 1992).
29. Barbara Kantrowitz, "Sex on the Info Highway," *Newsweek,* March 14, 1994.
30. Lance Rose," "BBS Burnings," in the "Legally Online" column, *Boardwatch Magazine,* September 1993, 62; cited in *CU Digest,* (1 September 1994).
31. Ibid., 62.
32. "Two Convicted of Hi-Tech Porn Peddling," *San Francisco Chronicle,* 29 July 1994, A-5.
33. Interview with David Banisar, 13 February 1995.
34. "Search Warrant Affidavit in Amateur Action BBS Case," H.K. Hensen, in *CU Digest,* 6, (4 April 1994).
35. Ibid.
36. Ibid.
37. "Defense Motion Filed in Amateur Action BBS Case," File 2 in *CU Digest,* 6, 36 (April 24, 1994).
38. "Computer Porn Verdict Brings Howls," Prodigy Services Corporation news release from AP, 29 July 1994.
39. L. Detweiler, "Anarchy Gone Awry," *CU Digest,* File 1, 5 (5 December 1993).

Conclusion

In conclusion, the battle for personal privacy has gone on in all arenas of life, and as we have developed new technologies and social institutions, these have triggered new struggles for personal privacy. The creation of the mass media at the end of the nineteenth century initiated the first struggles as the new press and advertising industries found new ways to pry into people's personal lives. Then, new battle lines emerged over the next decades, resulting in new policies and agreements about how to balance personal privacy and individual rights against the public's right to know and be protected.

For example, the development of new phone technologies and wiretapping capabilities led to new laws about privacy on the phones in the 1920s. Later, the rise of big government and surveillance due to the Red Scare in the 1940s and 1950s led to more privacy laws. More recently, more new technologies, like the computerization of data and DNA typing, and new institutions, like the rise of a huge medical bureaucracy and the insurance industry, have resulted in new privacy concerns and policies to regulate personal information.

At each stage in the process, there have been lawsuits, legislative battles, and media and grass roots debates over what those new policies should be. Then, general agreements, understandings, and laws have emerged from this process.

So it is today. Once again, we are in the midst of a new technological revolution creating the information highway, as well as further computerizing and digitizing records already in data bases. As a result, much of the current battle has turned to this arena. Meanwhile in other arenas, battles between individuals, institutions, and the government continue, because the conflict between individual privacy rights and the rights and protection of society is so fundamental. There will always be points of dissension, even when general policies and agreements are in place, since different people have different ways of interpreting what's appropriate, what's legal, and what's not.

Yet what is different about today's battle over the information highway and the new computer and telecommunications technologies is that everything appears to be in flux and up for grabs. That's because numerous interest groups and individuals are trying to work out the basic laws of the land, like creating the laws for a new country—in this case in cyberspace. That's why the administration has many task forces and committees working on setting up systems and establishing policies, and these groups have been holding hearings and seeking input throughout the country. At the same time, privacy intersects with so many other issues, such as immigration, crime prevention, and health care, that privacy considerations are being reviewed carefully, too. As an example, to take one recent hot button topic: what number to use to provide health services or check on immigration status, to streamline a system and avoid fraud, yet make sure this personal information can't be inappropriately accessed or misused.

In the process, increasing consideration is being given to the more comprehensive privacy policies developed in other countries. I have barely touched on these policies here, because the United States has largely gone it alone in these privacy battles. Until recently, there has been relatively little interest in the more comprehensive planning approaches developed in other countries to protect privacy, particularly in keeping massive centralized records. But now, as the U.S. government is getting more involved in establishing policies that involve privacy, and as modern technology itself creates global links through instant worldwide communication, global solutions are necessary to develop privacy policies. So increasingly, privacy regulations in other countries are being studied.

However, the outcome is far from clear. Over the next few years, the legislative process, media, law enforcement crackdowns, court cases, conferences, and ideas of what works from other countries will all contribute to the process—to be described in a future book.

Appendix

Selected List of Companies with Privacy Products and Services; Books and Catalogs; Privacy Organizations; Magazines, Journals, and Newsletters; and Resources for Getting off Mailing and Phone Lists

Some companies whose catalogs I used in referring to privacy products and services include the following:

Baker Systems, 535 N. 87th Street, Omaha, NE 68114. (800) 841-2024; (402) 391-6023. Psychological tests, drug testing programs, personal profile reports.

Baxall, AB Security Products, Inc., 57 West Timonium Road, Suite 210, P.O. Box 5005, Lutherville, MD 21093. (301) 561-2333, FAX: (301) 561-2412. Infrared and zoom cameras.

Canon Company, 1 Canon Plaza, Lake Success, NY 11042. (516) 488-6700. Optical card systems for storing data.

CBI/Equifax, 1600 Peachtree Street, NW, Atlanta, GA 30309. Psychological tests, drug testing programs, personal profile reports.

The Computer Security Institute, 500 Howard Street, San Francisco, CA 94105. (415) 267-7651. Training on computer security.

Covert Operations International, 5000 Brush Hollow Road, Westbury, NY 11590. (516) 876-2116. Infrared and zoom cameras.

Cubicle Cues, Inc., 714 Germantown Parkway, Suite 5, Cordona, TN 38018. "Cubicle Cue" office privacy signs.

Equifax Pre-Employment Services, Suite 210, 2635 Century Parkway, Atlanta, GA 30345. (404) 320-8613. Psychological tests, drug testing programs, personal profile reports.

Equifax Security and Research Management Services Catalog, 1600 Peachtree Street, NW, Atlanta, GA 30309. Psychological tests, drug testing programs, personal profile reports.

Eyedentify, Inc., P.O. Box 3827, Portland, OR 97208. (503) 645-6666. Unique eye identifiers.

Executive Protection Products, Inc., 1325 Imola Avenue, 504C, Napa, CA 94559. (707) 253-7142. Audio listening and data recording devices; Caller ID devices.

InterGram, 3465 North Desert Drive, Atlanta, GA 30344. (800) 227-TRUE. Psychological tests, drug testing programs, personal profile reports.

London House, 1550 Northwest Highway, Park Ridge, IL 60068. (708) 298-7311; (800) 221-8378. Psychological tests, drug testing programs, personal profile reports.

Motorola, P.O. Box 1417, 8201 East McDowell Road, Scottsdale, AZ 852. (602) 441-4300. Untappable phones.

Organization of Protective Agents and Consultants, 1605 116th Avenue, NE, Suite 210, Bellevue, WA 98004. (206) 451-1920. Celebrity and executive protection.

Professional Security Consultants, 6464 Sunset Blvd., Suite 710, Hollywood, CA 90028. (213) 465-2460. Celebrity and executive protection.

Recognition Systems, Inc., 1589 Provincetown Drive, San Jose, CA 95129. (408) 257-2477. Hand reading identifier.

Security Tag Systems, P.O. Box 23000, St. Petersburg, FL 33742. (813) 576-6399; (800) 451-6610. Personal monitoring equipment.

Stanton, 6100 Fairview Road, Suite 900, Charlotte, NC 28210. (704) 552-1119. (800) 528-5745. Psychological tests, drug testing programs, personal profile reports.

Team Building Systems, 363 North Belt, Suite 990, Houston, TX 77060. (800) 422-8326; (713) 591-8326.

Visual Methods, Inc., 35 Charles Street, Westwood, NJ 07675. (201) 666-3950. Supersensitive cameras, including one in the handle of a garbage can.

Some security and investigative books and catalogs are:

Butterworth-Heinemann, 80 Montvale Avenue, Stoneham, MA 02180. 1-800-366-BOOK.

Executive Protection Products, Inc., 1325 Imola Avenue, West #504NL, Napa, CA 94559.

Life Force Technologies Ltd., 45 Duroux Lane, P.O. Box 755, Basalt, Colorado 81612.

Loompanics Unlimited, P.O. Box 1197, Pt. Townsend, WA 983. Send $5 for the current catalog.

P.I. Catalog, Thomas Publications and the National Association of Investigative Specialists, P.O. Box 33244, Austin, TX 78764.

Some organizations, training programs, magazines, newsletters, and journals are:

American Civil Liberties Union, 322 Eighth Avenue, New York, NY 10001. Executive Director: Ira Glasser.

American Society for Industrial Security, 1655 North Fort Myer Drive, Suite 1200, Arlington, VA 22209. (703) 522-5800.

Asisnet, the ASIS Electronic Network, 1725 K Street, N.W., Washington, DC 20006. (202) 429-8730.

Computer Professionals for Social Responsibility, P.O. Box 717, Palo Alto, CA 94301. Managing Director: Kathleen Kells. (415) 322-3778.

Electronic Frontier Foundation, 1667 K Street NW, Suite 801, Washington, DC 20006-1605. Director: Andrew Taubman. (202) 861-7700; FAX: 861-1258.

Electronic Privacy Information Center (EPIC), 666 Pennsylvania Avenue, Suite 301, Washington, DC 20003. (202) 544-9240; FAX: (202) 547-5482. Director: Marc Rotenberg. E-mail: info@epic.org.

The Financial Privacy Report, P.O. Box 1277, Burnsville, MN 55337. (612) 895-8757, FAX: (612) 895-5526. Subscription: $156 a year, $15 single issue.

Full Disclosure, Box 734, Antioch, IL 60002. Editor: Glen Roberts. (708) 395-6200. Subscription: $29.95/year.

The Information Society, RAND Corporation, 1700 Main Street, P.O. Box 2138, Santa Monica, CA 90407-2138; Editor in Chief, Robert H. Anderson. Subscription Information: Taylor & Francisco Inc., 1900 Frost Road, Suite 101, Bristol, PA 19007-1598. (800) 821-8312.

International Privacy Bulletin, 666 Pennsylvania Avenue, Suite #301, Washington, DC 20003. Editor: David Banisar. (202) 544-9240. Subscription: $50/year individuals, $200/year organizations.

Internet Society, 12020 Sunrise Valley Drive, Suite 270, Reston, VA 22091. Executive Director: Anthony Rutkowski. (703) 648-9888.

Library Hi Tech News, P.O. Box 1808, Ann Arbor, Michigan 48106. (313) 434-5530.

Low Profile, P.O. Box 84910, Phoenix, AZ 85701. Editor: Mark Nestman. (702) 333-5942. Subscription: $149/year.

National Computer Security Association, Suite 309, 4401-A Connecticut Avenue, NW, Washington, DC 20008. (202) 364-8252.

Privacy and American Business, 2 University Plaza, Suite 414, Hackensack, NJ 07601. Editor: Bob Belair. (201) 996-1154. Bi-monthly. $395/year.

Privacy and Security 2001, 504 Shaw Road, Suite 222, Sterling, VA 20166. Editor: Jim Ross. (703) 318-8600. Subscription: 10/year; $35/year.

Privacy Journal, P.O. Box 28577, Providence, RI 02908. Editor: Robert Ellis Smith. (410) 274-7861. Subscription: $109 per year; special discounts for students and members of the press.

Privacy International, Washington Office, c/o EPIC, 666 Pennsylvania Avenue, Suite 301, Washington, DC 20003. Director General: Simon Davies. (202) 544-9240.

Privacy Rights Clearinghouse, Center for Public Interest Law, University of San Diego, 5998 Alcala Park, San Diego, CA 92110-2492. Director: Beth Givens. (619) 260-4806.

Privacy Times, P.O. Box 21501, Washington, DC 20009. (202) 829-3660. Editor: Evan Hendricks. Subscription: $250 a year.

Security Insider Report, 11567 Grove Street North, Seminole, FL 34642. (813) 393-6600.

Security Law Newsletter, 1603 Thomas Jefferson Street, N.W., Washington, DC 20007. (202) 237-2700.

Security Management, 1655 North Fort Myer Drive, Suite 1200, Arlington, VA 22209. (703) 522-5800.

Security: The Magazine for Security Decision Makers, 275 Washington Street, Newton, MA 02158-1630.

U.S. Privacy Council, P.O. Box 15060, Washington, DC 20093. Chair: Evan Hendricks. (202) 829-3660.

Some electronic publications and newsgroups on privacy:

The Computer Privacy Digest. Moderator: Len Levine. Newsgroup is: comp.society.privacy. To subscribe: Send message to: comp-privacy-request@uwm.edu with the first line: subscribe; or send message to: comp-privacy@uwm.edu.

Computer Underground Digest. Moderator: Jim Thomas. Newsgroup: comp.society.cu-digest. To subscribe: E-mail listserv@vmd.cso,uiuc,edu with the first line: sub cudigest <your name>.

Computer Privacy Forum. Moderator: Lauren Weinstein. To subscribe: send message: help to privacy-request@vortex.com.

EPIC Alert. Biweekly of the Electronic Privacy Information Center. To subscribe: E-mail listserv@cpsr.org with the 1st line: subscribe cpsr-announce.

The Privacy Forum Digest. To subscribe: Send message to: privacy@vortex.com.

Some organizations to contact to remove your name from mailing and phone lists:

Private Citizen, P.O. Box 233, Naperville, IL 60566. (708) 393-1555.

The Stop Junk Mail Association, 3020 Bridgeway, Suite 150, Sausalito, CA 94965. (800) 827-5549.

To contact the Direct Marketing Association to remove your name from lists:

To get off direct mail lists, write: Mail Preference Service, Direct Marketing Association, P.O. Box 9008, Farmingdale, New York 11735. Tell the DMA you don't want to receive any sales materials through the mail, and the DMA will put your name into their "delete" file which is sent to the members of the DMA four times a year.

To get off of telemarketing lists, write: Telephone Preference Service, Direct Marketing Association, P.O. Box 9014, Farmingdale, NY 11735. Ask to be on their "don't call" list and send your name, address, and phone number, including area code.

To get your name removed by the major companies that sell mailing lists, write:

Database America, Comp. Dept., 100 Paragon Drive, Montvale, NJ 07645-0419;

Donnelley Marketing, Inc., Data Base Operations, 1235 "N" Avenue, Nevada, IA 50202-1419;

Dun & Bradstreet, Customer Service, 899 Eaton Avenue, Bethlehem, PA 18025;

Metromail Corporation, List Maintenance, 901 West Bond, Lincoln, NE 68521;

R.L. Polk & Company, List Compilation & Development, 6400 Monroe Blvd., Taylor, MI 48180-1814.

To get your name out of future street address directories, write:

Haines & Company, Inc., Criss-Cross Directory, 2382 East Walnut Avenue, Fullerton, CA 92631;

R.L. Polk & Company, List Compilation & Development, 6400 Monroe Blvd., Taylor, MI 48180-1814;

Reuben H. Donnelley Corp., 287 Bowman Avenue, Purchase, NY 10577.

For workshops, seminars, and speaking:

Finally, if you are interested in workshops, seminars, or speaking on privacy, management, organizational development, conflict resolution, ethics in business, and related topics, you can contact Gini Graham Scott at Changemakers, 5091 Dublin Avenue, Oakland, CA 94602. (510) 530-3460; FAX: (510) 530-3461. E-mail: AOL: GiniS; CompuServe: 76122,2330; Prodigy: MBMV32A.

Index

About the Author

Gini Graham Scott, Ph.D. is a nationally known writer, consultant, speaker, and seminar/workshop leader, specializing in business and work relationships and professional and personal development. She is the founder of Changemakers and has published over 50 books on diverse subjects. Recent books include *Disagreements, Disputes, and All-Out War, 30 Days to a More Powerful Memory, A Survival Guide for Working with Bad Bosses* and *A Survival Guide for Working with Humans*, all from AMACOM, and *The Talk Show Revolution, You the Jury, Fantasy Worlds, The Creative Traveler, Mind Power, The Empowered Mind*, and *The Truth About Lying*. Scott has received national media exposure for her books, including appearances on Good Morning America, Oprah, Montel Williams, and CNN. Her Website is www.ginigrahamscott.com.

Printed in Dunstable, United Kingdom

91219944R00228